A Fluid Frontier

GREAT LAKES BOOKS

Editor
Charles K. Hyde, *Wayne State University*

Advisory Editors
Jeffrey Abt, *Wayne State University*

Fredric C. Bohm, *Michigan State University*

Sandra Sageser Clark, *Michigan Historical Center*

Brian Leigh Dunnigan, *Clements Library*

De Witt Dykes, *Oakland University*

Joe Grimm, *Michigan State University*

Richard H. Harms, *Calvin College*

Laurie Harris, *Pleasant Ridge, Michigan*

Thomas Klug, *Marygrove College*

Susan Higman Larsen, *Detroit Institute of Arts*

Philip P. Mason, *Prescott, Arizona and Eagle Harbor, Michigan*

Dennis Moore, *Consulate General of Canada*

Erik C. Nordberg, *Michigan Humanities Council*

Deborah Smith Pollard, *University of Michigan–Dearborn*

Michael O. Smith, *Wayne State University*

Joseph M. Turrini, *Wayne State University*

Arthur M. Woodford, *Harsens Island, Michigan*

A complete listing of the books in this series can be found online at wsupress.wayne.edu

A FLUID FRONTIER

SLAVERY, RESISTANCE,
AND THE
UNDERGROUND RAILROAD
IN THE
DETROIT RIVER BORDERLAND

Edited by KAROLYN SMARDZ FROST
and VETA SMITH TUCKER
With a foreword by DAVID W. BLIGHT

Wayne State University Press
Detroit

© 2016 by Wayne State University Press, Detroit, Michigan 48201.
All rights reserved. No part of this book may be reproduced without formal permission.
Manufactured in the United States of America.

20 19 18 17 16   5 4 3 2 1

Library of Congress Control Number: 2015946924

ISBN 978-0-8143-3959-6 (paperback)
ISBN 978-0-8143-3960-2 (ebook)

Published with support from the Arthur L. Johnson Fund for African American Studies.

Designed and typeset by Bryce Schimanski
Composed in Adobe Caslon Pro

"If I have seen further it is by standing on the shoulders of giants."
Sir Isaac Newton

We dedicate *A Fluid Frontier* to two giants, one American the other Canadian. Their insights on the Detroit River region influenced our thinking and motivated us to finish this project. To the late Dr. Norman McRae Jr. (1925–2010), historian, author, and educator, whose scholarship and dedication to truth continue to have a profound influence on both academic and popular perceptions of African American history in Detroit, Michigan, and to Dr. Daniel G. Hill, historian, sociologist, civil rights activist, and Chairman of the Ontario Human Rights Commission, whose research in the study of the African Canadian past will inspire scholars and students alike for generations to come.

CONTENTS

Acknowledgments vii
Foreword by David W. Blight ix

Introduction 1
KAROLYN SMARDZ FROST AND VETA SMITH TUCKER

PART I: CROSSING BOUNDARIES 25

1. Uncertain Freedom in Frontier Detroit 27
   VETA SMITH TUCKER

2. Forging Transnational Networks for Freedom: From the War of 1812 to the Blackburn Riots of 1833 43
   KAROLYN SMARDZ FROST

3. The Illusion of Safety: Attempts to Extradite Fugitive Slaves from Canada 67
   BRYAN PRINCE

PART II: COMMUNAL VOICES 81

4. Canadian Black Settlements in the Detroit River Region 83
   IRENE MOORE DAVIS

5. Worship Way Stations in Detroit 103
   BARBARA HUGHES SMITH

6. Extending the Right Hand of Fellowship: Sandwich Baptist Church, Amherstburg First Baptist, and the Amherstburg Baptist Association 120
   ADRIENNE SHADD

PART III: INSPIRED TRANSNATIONALISTS 133

7. The *Voice of the Fugitive:* A Transnational Abolitionist Organ 135
   AFUA COOPER

8. A Community Militant and Organized: The Colored Vigilant Committee of Detroit 154
   ROY FINKENBINE

9. "I Am Going Straight to Canada": Women Underground Railroad Activists in the Detroit River Border Zone 165
   MARGARET WASHINGTON

PART IV: RESILIENT FAMILIES 185

10. Bridging Rivers: Caroline Quarlls's Remarkable Journey 187
    KIMBERLY SIMMONS AND LARRY MCCLELLAN

11. One More River to Cross: The Crosswhites' Escapes from Slavery 199
    DEBIAN MARTY

12. The McCoys: Charting Freedom from Both Sides of the River 215
    CAROL E. MULL

PART V: THE TRUMPET SOUNDS 227

13. The Useful Frontier: John Brown's Detroit River Preface to the Harper's Ferry Raid 229
    LOUIS A. DECARO JR.

    Sources and Resources 247
    KAROLYN SMARDZ FROST AND VETA SMITH TUCKER

    Contributors 273
    Index 277

ACKNOWLEDGMENTS

For their unconditional love and support while we labored to complete *A Fluid Frontier*, we are grateful to Norm Frost, and all our family members and close friends; for their diligent research and excellent writing, we thank the twelve authors whose chapters give this volume life; and for her insightful editorial review, we thank Dr. Alisea McLeod. For kind and competent assistance from every librarian and archivist we consulted throughout the Midwest and Canada, we thank all of you.

For their remarkable generosity in sharing with us the findings of their ongoing research in African Canadian history, we thank Hilary Dawson, Natasha Henry, and Guylaine Petrin. For taking stunning photographs exclusively for this volume, we thank Elizabeth Clark of Detroit; and for their assiduous editorial support and encouragement, we thank the editor-in-chief of Wayne State University Press, Kathryn Wildfong, and her dedicated staff.

Finally, to those who supported us with and without our knowledge, whose names may not be listed here, it is also because of you that we were able to complete this book.

FOREWORD

I grew up in Flint, Michigan, an easy drive northwest of Detroit, in the 1950s and 1960s. I was fortunate to be taught by two excellent high school history teachers, one in "Western Civilization" and the other in "U. S. History." But I never learned anything about this epic, harrowing, and inspiring story of the Underground Railroad in the Detroit River region. I am grateful for two degrees in history from Michigan State University, where in the late 1960s I took the first course ever offered there in black history, taught by the late Leslie Rout. To say the least, I came to love history. I taught American history in the Flint Public Schools for seven years in the 1970s, and have practiced the craft as a scholar now for more than three decades. Countless times I traveled to the Motor City for all manner of events—sports, culture, road races on Belle Isle in the middle of the Detroit River.

But I never learned about the many thousands gone who had by so many paths over long journeys crossed over from the docks of Detroit to the shores of Windsor or Amherstburg. No one or no thing in particular is to blame for my lack of knowledge in these formative years. Great shifts and revolutions in historical knowledge take time and events to force them to the fore. But what a remarkable history and cultural memory was there in my youth hiding in plain sight. And that rich, profound history—a living history—is brought to life in this collection of essays about the people, the communities, the personalities, the places, and the institutions forged from the late eighteenth century through the Civil War. The Detroit River borderland was for decades a teeming, thriving landscape and waterscape by which thousands of African Americans became African Canadians or both. That story is now poignantly memorialized in monuments on both sides of the river.

In a recent important book, Eric Foner has shown how the "Metropolitan Corridor," the region connecting the Vigilance Committees of Philadelphia and New York City, and funneling fugitives slaves particularly out of Maryland and Delaware to New York and beyond, operated with great energy, both open and covert, in the 1850s.[1] Karolyn Smardz Frost and Veta Smith Tucker have assembled here in *A Fluid Frontier: Slavery, Resistance, and the Underground Railroad in the Detroit River Borderland* the story of how the Detroit River–Canadian border region was every bit as large and important as a place and a system through which African American former slaves found degrees of freedom. This book's research and scope, the poignant new stories it tells, and especially its international, borderlands approach ought to advance any effort to achieve a World Heritage designation for the Detroit River region. The Underground Railroad along this international border functioned both overtly and covertly as well as outside or in resistance to the law. Its leaders, like Henry and Mary Bibb and so many others, were full-throated revolutionaries; the people they assisted have millions of descendants today of all human colors and backgrounds in Canada, the United States, and other countries.

I witnessed the beauty and character of that diaspora several years ago as a very fortunate invited speaker at a conference on the Underground Railroad in Canada on the eve of the annual Buxton Homecoming, an event that those of us in the United States have to see to believe. Each year on Labour Day weekend, for four days, descendants and extended families from far-flung places come to the small town of Buxton, Ontario, a mere hour's drive east of Detroit. They camp out all over the agricultural landscape and commune with their own illusive but suddenly real past at the North Buxton Community Church and graveyard, as well as at the extraordinary Buxton National Historic Site and Museum. They come to learn about and celebrate the original fugitive slaves who settled in that community and built its great farming traditions. They also conduct spirited family baseball and softball tournaments. But I can attest that, as a historian of this subject, I have had few experiences as moving and special as the hayride and food fest hosted and led by Bryan and Shannon Prince. Bryan is himself a distinguished historian, direct descendant of Buxton founders, and a successful local farmer. The annual Buxton Homecoming, the ninetieth annual of which was held in 2013 and drew more than three thousand people, is a living legacy of the difficult but inspiring story represented by this book.[2]

As *A Fluid Frontier* demonstrates, the Detroit River corridor was the most active entry point along the United States–Canada border for fugitive slaves. They came from all over the American South, many with considerable stops in the Northern states as well. In 1856, the Massachusetts abolitionist Benjamin Drew, in the book *A North-Side View of Slavery*, recorded a remarkable oral history with approximately 116 former fugitives slaves living in Canada. He conducted his interviews, the first such oral histories ever done with living former slaves, in fourteen Canadian towns, cities, or agricultural settlements. They ranged from Windsor, Sandwich, and Amherstburg along the Detroit River all the way to Toronto and St. Catherines (another major entry point near Niagara Falls). In between, he conducted many interviews in places that became special enclaves of African American émigrés, such as Chatham and Buxton, only short distances east of Detroit.[3]

The stories Drew recorded show that fugitive slaves among the estimated thirty thousand blacks in Canada in the 1850s had escaped from all parts of the South, many from Virginia and Kentucky, but many also from as far as Savannah, Georgia, or New Orleans, Louisiana. They told stunning and unforgettable tales of treatment by their former masters, of "chains," "handcuffs," "iron rings," "bucking paddles," "whips," and all manner of other restraints and forms of psychological oppression practiced in the peculiar institution. Many also told of being "sold,"

FOREWORD

North Buxton Community Schoolhouse, now restored, at the former Elgin Association fugitive slave settlement in Raleigh Township, Canada West. (Courtesy of the Buxton Museum and National Historic Site)

often multiple times, of families and marriages severed by such commerce in the domestic slave trade across the continent into the Cotton Kingdom. But they also told of their own perseverance, courage, and good fortune. Some had only arrived days before being interviewed and many had already lived in Canada for a decade or two. Canada had not been hospitable in many cases; making a life, getting land, finding schools for children, feeling economically or personally secure were forever challenging. But as one immigrant, a sixty-year-old Methodist minister named Alexander Hemsley, put it, "I . . . made up my mind that salt and potatoes in Canada, were better than pound-cake and chickens in a state of suspense and anxiety in the United States." In Maryland, Hemsley said, he came to know "how tyranny operates on the mind of slaves"; he had felt like "poor Joseph in Egypt." In Canada he now lived in "a state of liberty for the mind" and "freedom of thought."[4]

Wherever they settled, and by whatever clandestine travail they made it to northern Ohio or southeast Michigan, for so many former fugitives, it was common to say, as Mrs. Isaac Riley of Buxton did, that "we crossed over at Windsor."[5] The slow wave of fugitives, by day and by night, as individuals but especially in groups aided by Detroit churches as well as the city's Vigilant Committee, and assisted in the Windsor area by the Refugee Home Society as well as networks of former slaves and other black and white allies, made the Canadian side of the

Detroit River and its extended hinterland for a hundred miles and more the final frontier of this astonishing North American exodus story.

And like the original Exodus, these American fugitive slaves sought and found, through great hardship and struggle, their own humanity and integrity; they found safety, a stake in the land, and a future. They did not have a single Moses, and their Red Sea—the Detroit River—never parted for them to rush through, killing Pharaoh's army in its wake. But they surely came to understand themselves as living in a great exodus story. They had known the depths of generations of bondage; they had experienced many trials in the wildernesses of Mississippi, Kentucky, Ohio, or Michigan. They had crossed many rivers, and they were looking for a Promised Land. As Michael Walzer writes in *Exodus and Revolution*, the great power in the Exodus story, and no story has had greater weight in African American history, "lies in its end, the divine promise." It promises that "Egyptian bondage" can be survived and that a "Canaan" can be found. "The Exodus is not a lucky escape from misfortune," writes Walzer. "Egypt is not just left behind; it is rejected; it is judged and condemned."[6] Today, on the farms around Buxton, in many Canadian and American cities, we can see that the experiences explored in this book about the Detroit River corridor of the Underground Railroad are still being lived, rejected, judged, and transcended.

David W. Blight
Professor of History and Director of The Gilder Lehrman Center for
the Study of Slavery, Resistance, and Abolition, Yale University

Author of numerous books, including the forthcoming *Frederick Douglass: A Life*; editor of *Passages to Freedom: The Underground Railroad in History and Memory* (2004); and winner of the 2002 Bancroft Prize, the Abraham Lincoln Prize and the Frederick Douglass Prize for *Race and Reunion: The Civil War in American Memory* (2001).

NOTES

1. Eric Foner, *Gateway to Freedom: The Hidden History of the Underground Railroad* (New York: Norton, 2015), 151–89.
2. See Bryan Prince, *A Shadow on the Household: One Enslaved Family's Incredible Struggle for Freedom* (Toronto: Emblem, imprint of McClelland & Stewart, 2010), *One More River to Cross* (Toronto: Dundurn, 2012), and *My Brother's Keeper: African Canadians in the American Civil War* (Toronto: Dundurn, 2015).
3. Drew's interviews were all conducted in 1855. The book was originally published as Benjamin Drew, *A The North-Side View of Slavery. The Refugee; or, The Narratives of Fugitive Slaves in Canada. Related by Themselves, with an Account of the History and Condition of the Colored Population of Upper Canada* (Boston: John P. Jewett, 1856).
4. Drew, *A The North-Side View of Slavery*, 2, 32–33, 38–39, 54–55, 69, 203.
5. Drew, *A The North-Side View of Slavery*, 300.
6. Michael Walzer, *Exodus and Revolution* (New York: Basic Books, 1985), 21; and see Eddie S. Glaude Jr., "A Sacred Drama: 'Exodus' and the Underground Railroad in African American Life," in *Passages to Freedom: The Underground Railroad in History and Memory*, ed. David W. Blight (Washington, DC: Smithsonian Books, 2004), 291–304.

Underground Railroad Routes to Canada. (Drawn from original by Timothy Walker)

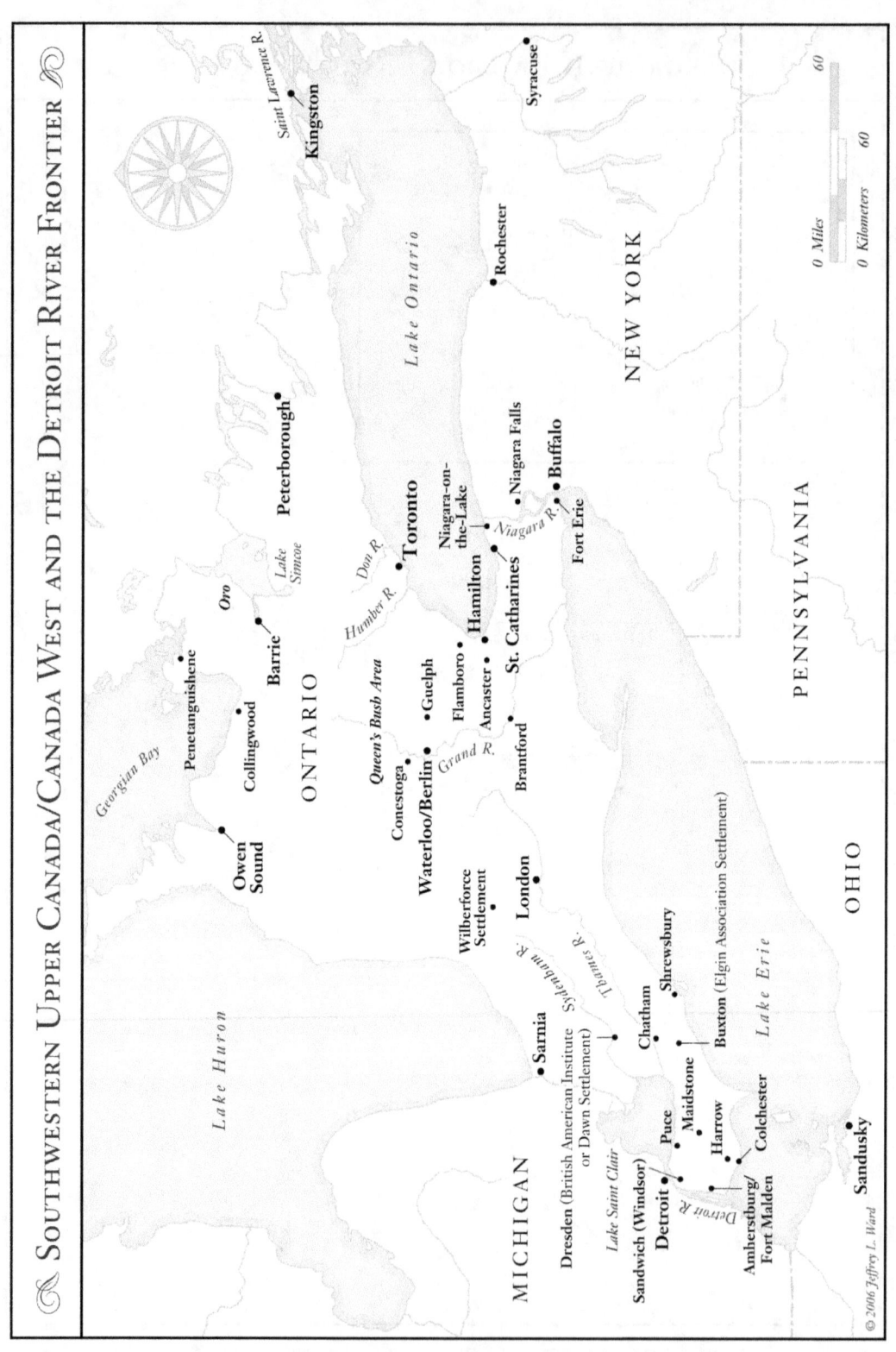

Southwestern Upper Canada/Canada West and the Detroit River Frontier.

A Fluid Frontier

INTRODUCTION

KAROLYN SMARDZ FROST
AND VETA SMITH TUCKER

On the facing shores of the Detroit River at Windsor, Ontario, and Detroit, Michigan, stand magnificent twin monuments created by African American sculptor Ed Dwight. The statues were erected in 2001 to celebrate the three hundredth anniversary of Detroit's founding and to honor the thousands of freedom-seekers who traversed this heritage waterway during the Underground Railroad era. Each half of the International Underground Railroad Memorial is composed of human figures cast in bronze and set on a granite base. The people depicted in the sculptures gesture toward one another across the wide expanse of water, reflecting the cooperative efforts of communities of rescuers along both sides of the Detroit River.

The Detroit sculpture at Hart Plaza is titled *Gateway to Freedom* and is bracketed by two soaring pillars crowned in flames. Its nine bronze figures represent weary yet hopeful freedom-seekers, together with the Underground Railroad operator who points their way to the Canadian shore. The base of the installation is inscribed with places, people, and events important to the Detroit branch of this mass social justice movement that assisted more than thirty thousand refugees to escape from bondage and reach free soil in the years before the Civil War.

On the opposite bank of the Detroit River, in downtown Windsor, Ontario, the twenty-foot-tall *Tower of Freedom* evokes the image of a burning candle, rendered in bronze. At its foot stands a newly arrived family, also in bronze. The man raises his arms heavenward in celebration while his wife, holding their baby, is welcomed by a female abolitionist to their new Canadian home. On the pillar are inscribed the words, "Keeping the Flame of Freedom Alive."[1]

These monuments honor the collaborative resistance that took place on both sides of the Detroit River when slavery was a fact of daily life. For most Americans, the Underground Railroad holds a paradoxical place in public memory. The very need for its existence profoundly contradicts the image of the United States as "the land of the free and the home of the brave." Indeed, the idea of desperate refugees fleeing *from* the United States with slavecatchers

International Underground Railroad Memorial, Hart Plaza, Detroit. Ed Dwight's sculpture at the Detroit River shows George DeBaptiste directing freedom-seekers to their final destination on the Canadian shore. (Courtesy of photographer Elizabeth Clark)

at their heels is a deeply troubling one for many Americans. Perhaps this is part of the reason why legends of the Underground Railroad, with secret codes in quilt squares, hidden tunnels, and such, are so popular. Does aggrandizing the part played by whites in helping black freedom-seekers somehow mitigate the fact that the number of abolitionists willing to stand up and take action on behalf of the South's 4 *million* slaves was so embarrassingly small, relative to the population of 27 million white Americans at the time the Civil War began in 1861?[2]

For their part, Canadians hold fast to the image of their homeland as the place where, as a popular contemporary song put it, "colored men are free."[3] However, while the degree of prejudice varied only slightly from South to North, Underground Railroad "passengers" who reached British North America also found themselves living within a deeply racist and discriminatory environment, despite the supposedly color-blind laws under which the colonies were governed. Formerly enslaved African Americans and free black immigrants, in fact, comprised a separate and often despised underclass in towns and cities along the Detroit River borderland, as they did elsewhere in Upper Canada/Canada West and later, after the land between the Detroit River and the Quebec border was renamed.* School doors were often locked against their children; churches, hotels, places of employment, and polling stations were closed to them; and local politicians even took up petitions to prevent black settlement in some areas. A small cadre of philanthropists concerned with the welfare of African American refugees in Canada, some based in Detroit, helped such immigrants to establish enclaves where they could live and work together, in part to lessen the effects of white prejudice. This certainly flies in the face of Canada's admirable contemporary image as a haven for refugees of all ethnicities. The portrayal of British North America as an all-embracing "Canaan Land" is much more palatable to modern tastes, and so the legends of the Underground Railroad comfort people on the Canadian side of the Detroit River border, just as they console their counterparts in the United States.

Amid the often withering prejudice on the Canadian side and legal slavery on the American side, the Detroit River borderland has been both a boundary and a passageway for people of African ancestry for more than three centuries. Along with the Niagara River and the rest of the Great Lakes Basin, this historic waterway served as the major gateway into British North America for thousands of passengers on the fabled Underground Railroad. Theoretically, since the time of the American Revolution, and in reality following the final transfer of Detroit to U.S. control after Jay's Treaty went into effect in 1796, an invisible line has run down the middle of the Detroit River. From the moment the boundary was legally established until the end of the

---

* It is important to note that the terminology referring to what today is Ontario, Canada, has changed over time. The westernmost British colony in Canada before the American Revolution was known as the province of Quebec. After the Revolutionary War, British North America was reorganized into Upper and Lower Canada, referencing their relative positions on the St. Lawrence River. Upper Canada encompassed much of modern Ontario, and Lower Canada today's province of Quebec. With the British North America Act, passed in 1840 and proclaimed in 1841, the two colonies were blended into a single governing district known as Canada, or "the Canadas": Canada West and Canada East. Canada West was renamed Ontario after Canada West, Canada East, New Brunswick, and Nova Scotia came together in "confederation" in 1867. This was the beginning of Canada as a nation. Thus, first Quebec, then Upper Canada, and after that Canada West and finally Ontario are names for more or less the same part of Canada, at different periods of its history.

Ed Dwight's matching sculpture on the Canadian side of the river shows freedom-seekers rejoicing at the end of their journey. (Courtesy of photographer Elizabeth Clark)

American Civil War, whether people of African descent could be subjected to enslavement or reenslavement, or whether they were living in a place where freedom and opportunity beckoned, depended on which side of that fluid boundary line they stood.

Despite the acknowledged importance of the Detroit River, there has never been a major scholarly analysis of the interconnected antebellum African American and African Canadian experience in this transnational region. It is this lacuna in the historical record that *A Fluid Frontier: Slavery, Resistance, and the Underground Railroad in the Detroit River Borderland* seeks to fill. More, in the absence of, and frequently in spite of, solid scholarship detailing the operations of this highly illegal clandestine system, a much-romanticized mythology regarding the Underground Railroad has flourished. The essays contained in this volume provide solid evidence for the ways in which individuals and communities along the Detroit River aided freedom-seekers on their way, while debunking some of the more egregious popular yarns about the Underground Railroad. The black communities that grew up on either side of the Detroit riverfront were linked by ties of family and faith and by their profound commitment to personal liberty. For Africans brought to the Americas, freedom was the original condition they had enjoyed before the horrific disruptions of the Atlantic slave trade. African people's experience of freedom predated their arrival in the West, fueled their discontent with slavery, and motivated the inexorable migrations that became the Underground Railroad. The underlying principles of this volume are informed by African peoples' historic and enduring commitment to freedom.

A Fluid Frontier charts the experiences of freedom-seekers and those who assisted them against the backdrop of geopolitical forces that shaped the meaning of race and the management of slavery on both sides of the Detroit River. The book is intended to examine expressions of early transnational abolitionist thought and activism in the Detroit River region, and it explores the lives of individuals, black and white, whose courage and ingenuity kept alive the flame of liberty along that contested boundary. *A Fluid Frontier* seeks to make visible the social formations—legal, political, social, religious, and economic—that conditioned the experience of African Americans and African Canadians, for whom the Detroit River borders represented a boundary between slavery and freedom.

The inspiration for *A Fluid Frontier* was a series of meetings that culminated in the formation of an international committee to support the Detroit River Project.[4] This joint American-Canadian initiative seeks to have the Detroit River designated a UNESCO World Heritage Site in recognition of its importance to African American/Canadian antislavery-related transnational activism. First envisioned as a rather slim volume that would encapsulate the history and rationale supporting the UNESCO designation, both the purpose and the content of this volume have very much "grown in the telling," as Bilbo said in the opening sentence of his foreword to *The Hobbit*.[5] Yet we see this volume as a beginning. During the process of its production it became apparent how few topics a single anthology such as ours could hope to cover. Indeed, in respect to the American side of the river, our project's purview does not extend far beyond the boundaries of Detroit itself. We hope that other editors and authors will take *A Fluid Frontier* as their inspiration and continue to elaborate this vital border region's history.

For the purposes of this volume, we have employed the term *Underground Railroad* in its broadest possible interpretation. Our use of the phrase refers to the out-migration of African Americans in search of freedom from slavery and racial oppression, whether they were assisted or not.⁶ Our title reprises the work of Afua Cooper, now the James R. Johnston Chair in Black Canadian Studies at Dalhousie University in Halifax, Nova Scotia, and author of chapter 7 in this volume. Cooper employs the term *fluid frontier* to denote the highly transnational nature of black life along the Detroit River border, and its use here pays homage to her pioneering scholarship. Cooper contends that a simplistic view of Canada as the "Promised Land" to which African Americans aspired in their search for freedom "fails to interrogate sufficiently the movement and migration of Blacks across the Canada/United States border."⁷ Cooper's insightful study *The Hanging of Angelique: The Untold Story of Canadian Slavery and the Burning of Old Montreal* (2006) troubles the myth of Canada as a permanent site of black freedom and initiates new understandings of the meaning and importance of the border to people of African descent in the Detroit River region while it was still part of eighteenth-century New France.⁸ Informed both by Cooper's scholarship on colonial Quebec and by her extensive studies of nineteenth-century black abolitionists Mary and Henry Bibb, who resided at various times on either side of the Detroit River, *A Fluid Frontier* offers nuanced readings of the Detroit River borderland and of the Blacks who navigated it, either temporarily or permanently, in order to pursue their dreams.

The thirteen chapters contained in these pages demonstrate the bravery and resourcefulness of black Americans and black Canadians in the face of harsh adversity. They illuminate the commonality of the lived experience of thousands of people of African descent who before the Civil War either settled in or passed through the two shores of this crucial river boundary. Isolated from their white neighbors because of prejudice and racial discrimination, the black communities on each side of the border developed their own cultural, political, and social identities in ways that often meant they had more in common with their counterparts across the river than they had with their own countrymen. As the following chapters so clearly show, relationships between the African American and African Canadian communities in the Detroit River borderlands were reinforced by their commitment to resisting both slavery and racial oppression. Black resistance can be traced, as our authors have done, through the early nineteenth-century development of religious, political, educational, and self-help organizations. It is also evident in the long struggle for equal access to education, public services, and public spaces, and in the battle to secure civil rights, all of which began with the first arrival of people of African ancestry in the Americas and which, of course, continues to this day.

A Fluid Frontier is a synthesis on a number of levels, and deliberately so. The two editors are, respectively and intentionally, one Canadian and one American specialist in Underground Railroad studies. The two came to their scholarly focus and strong community orientation from widely divergent fields: Veta Smith Tucker began this work as a professor at Grand Valley State University in Allendale, Michigan, teaching African American and American literature and African American Studies with a research concentration on the lives of nineteenth-century African American women. After she had published several articles on enslaved and free black women in literature and on nineteenth- and twentieth-century African American women writers, Tucker's literary focus expanded to the Underground Railroad when she was enlisted to write the history of an unsuccessful attempt by Kentucky slaveholders to capture and reenslave Blacks who were settled in Cass County, Michigan, in 1847.⁹ Tucker is a former chairperson of Michigan's (Underground Railroad) Freedom Trail Commission, and she speaks frequently on her literary and historical scholarship on African American women and on women's involvement in the Underground Railroad and abolitionist movements.

Karolyn Smardz Frost started out as an archaeologist with an ingrained commitment to public education and a profound curiosity about the lives of the so-called ordinary people whose names and narratives are all too often lost to history. Delving beneath the pavement of a downtown Toronto schoolyard in 1985, her team discovered the remnants of a home once occupied by fugitive slaves Thornton and Lucie Blackburn; the find made history as the first Underground Railroad site excavated in Canada. More than three thousand schoolchildren and members of the public took part in the Blackburn dig. This profoundly altered the direction of her professional career, a trajectory that included earning a doctorate in the History of Race, Slavery, and Imperialism from the University of Waterloo. Because the Blackburns' 1833 escape by way of the Detroit River had sparked the region's first racial riot, it also introduced Frost to the complex and fascinating study of black life along the Detroit River. Her landmark biography of the couple, *I've Got a Home in Glory Land: A Lost Tale of the Underground Railroad* (2007), was the first book on African Canadian history to win Canada's prestigious Governor General's Literary Award. It tells an explicitly transnational story, a considerable part of which took place on the two Detroit River shores during a single watershed summer in 1833. Now Senior Research Fellow for York University's Harriet Tubman Institute at Toronto and an adjunct professor at Acadia University in Nova Scotia, Frost continues to focus on issues of slavery and freedom, with particular interest in the lives of women, and she speaks and publishes on black transnationalism and resistance across North America and internationally.

The authors and their subjects for each chapter of *A Fluid Frontier* were carefully chosen. Our contributors are nearly evenly divided between specialists in Canadian history and those in American history to ensure a truly binational perspective. With very few exceptions, earlier studies of the black experience along the Detroit River have been written from the viewpoint of one or the other of the two nation-states that border the waterway. Yet Blacks along the two opposing shores had, in addition to multiple family ties, geographic, economic, political, and cultural affinities. This was a true borderland. Indeed, on both sides of the line, the ever-present pernicious fact of racism impacted black life even more than American or Canadian nationality did.

Authors are as equally split between community and academic historians. Several are university-based scholars whose work is significant in the study of the Underground Railroad in both Michigan and Ontario. However, long before contemporary academics turned their attention to Underground Railroad studies, community historians kept this rich history alive. Often descendants of freedom-seekers themselves, they preserved oral traditions, carefully protected artifacts, and maintained historic places evocative of this rich, elusive history. They thoughtfully collected documents, photographs, and newspaper accounts that supported memories of place, time, and experience circulating in local communities throughout North America to this day. Academic historians have benefited from community historians' preservation of oral histories and personal narratives and from their special insights into the meaning of these micro-histories.[10] *A Fluid Frontier* honors the tireless work of community historians and underscores the importance of their narratives, which are foundational to the continuing comparative and analytical research on the Underground Railroad era that engages many academic historians today.

From a scholarly perspective, *A Fluid Frontier: Slavery, Resistance, and the Underground Railroad in the Detroit River Borderland* is indebted to two main areas of study. First, and by far the most salient to the content, is the now-vast historiography of the Underground Railroad. The second is the study of borderlands. Some of the best of the recent African Disapora scholarship on the Detroit River which takes into account the activism that occurred in this liminal space is influenced by borderlands research. This is a very promising interdisciplinary field encompassing history, biography, archaeology, ethnography, historical geography, and a host of other fields, specifically as these are illuminated by authors who take a transnationalist approach.

For this volume, we borrowed liberally from Thomas M. Wilson and Hastings Donnan's discussions of borders in *Border Identities* (1998) and *Borders* (1999),[11] applying their theoretical analyses, along with concepts drawn from other borderland studies, retrospectively to the nineteenth-century activities and discourse of black and white Underground Railroad activists in the Detroit River region. During the late eighteenth to mid-nineteenth centuries, Blacks and their supporters enjoyed a period of relatively unregulated transnational movement across the Detroit River. According to Wilson and Donnan, such a condition set the stage for the development of unique communal and individual identities informed by experiences and policies that come to the foreground in borderland spaces. The recent work of scholars such as Gregory Wigmore and Sean Kelley also shows the rich potential the complex interdisciplinary borderlands approach offers to the study of black transnationalism in border regions in the Great Lakes Basin, particularly the Detroit and Niagara River boundaries.[12]

Border zones are places of conflict and change where alterations in such factors as trade, political treaties, population migration, or government, which might be relatively slow to affect people living in the interior, are more immediately and intensely felt. The African descendant population along the Detroit riverfront in the eighteenth and early to mid-nineteenth centuries had to respond to geographical shifts and political conflicts, including wars, as the chapters in the first section in this volume, "Crossing Boundaries," make clear. Adjusting to these changes forced Blacks in this borderland to become even more resourceful than they already were. They early on developed strategies to deal with the vicissitudes of borderland life. Most of those strategies called for joint action between the African American and African Canadian communities on opposite shores, and often between Blacks and white supporters. These joint actions and institutional formations, and the sensibilities that undergird them, are foregrounded in *A Fluid Frontier*. Many such collaborations are elucidated in this volume, but there was undoubtedly a great deal more such cooperative activism than has been documented.

Clearly, approaching nineteenth-century resistance to slavery and racial exclusion in the Detroit River borderland through the field of borderland studies contributes to scholarly understanding of the Detroit River region and its development in the nineteenth century. However, borderland studies in the North American context have generally concentrated on America's southern border. Important scholarship has also shone a spotlight on the experiences of American refugees from slavery at borderlands within the United States, mainly borders shared with Spanish Florida, Texas, and Mexico.[13]

Similarly, the international borderland at the Detroit River was not the singular focus of American abolitionists. Prior to the Civil War, advocates of African American emigration explored destinations in both Mexico and Canada. Solomon Northup in his iconic autobiography, now a multiple-award-winning film, *Twelve Years a Slave,* references slave lynchings in Louisiana following a collective attempt to run for the Mexican border.[14] Abolitionist publisher Benjamin Lundy visited both Mexico and Canada in the 1830s with African American colonization in mind. However, British Canada's liberal naturalization policies guaranteed legal immigration status to Blacks, an advantage not readily available to those who sought safe haven in Mexico. Furthermore, Canada's geographic proximity to free states and the presence of Underground Railroad networks in the U.S.-Canadian border zone made furtive journeys to Canada less onerous, while journeys to freedom from Texas into Mexico always involved traveling through slaveholding terrain. Nevertheless, significant numbers of Blacks fled to Mexico, exploiting geopolitical shifts in that region as Mexico slowly evolved from a slaveholding to a nonslaveholding nation and taking advantage of Mexico's instability as borders shifted between Mexico and Texas and between Mexico and the United States.[15]

Prominent black abolitionist leaders also championed international immigration beyond U.S. borders. Martin Delany and Mary Ann Shadd were among those who emigrated to Chatham, Canada West.[16] There they joined so substantial and sophisticated a community of African American expatriates that Chatham was dubbed "the colored man's Paris."[17] Dr. Delany had also recommended Mexico as well as the West Indies and Central and South America as potential destinations for African American emigration.[18] And from the mid-1850s to the end of his life, Delany advocated emigration to West Africa. Before the Civil War, he traveled to Nigeria's Niger Valley to explore that region as a destination for black American colonization.[19]

Considering the increasing focus on borderlands scholarship and the Detroit River's central importance to Underground Railroad operations along the U.S.-Canadian border, there are surprisingly few studies of the region. In the bibliographical essay that concludes *A Fluid Frontier,* we further discuss the relevance of borderland studies to the growing field of scholarship focused on the Canada-U.S. boundary, particularly those relevant to the dynamics of black transnationalism in the Underground Railroad era.

Along with Native Americans and European settlers who inhabited the Detroit River borderland over successive centuries, people of African ancestry also had to negotiate and navigate the literal and figurative terrain of this fluid frontier. Successively enslaved by Native, French, and British powers, people of African descent living in the Detroit River borderland tested the strength of the racially discriminatory legal, political, economic, and social strictures under which they lived. They achieved what liberties they could, often by crossing the Detroit River. Some who remained on the American side, however, dedicated themselves to improving conditions for themselves and their children and to establishing progressively sophisticated means to assist others who chose—or were forced by circumstances—to cross the river into British North America.

Ever since British colonial authorities moved to prohibit further importation of slaves into the province in 1793, Upper Canada had been a place where slavery existed but where, paradoxically, anti-importation laws meant that incoming bondspeople from the U.S. side of the river immediately achieved free status. For a time, Blacks enslaved in America crossed the Detroit River to gain freedom in British North America while enslaved Canadians traversed that same waterway in the opposite direction to gain liberty in the Northwest Territory, taking advantage of antislavery stipulations in the 1787 Northwest Ordinance passed by the U.S. Congress that prohibited "slavery or involuntary servitude" in the region north of the Ohio River. Indeed, such contradictions and ambiguities in law helped bring into focus possibilities that Blacks and their supporters in the Detroit River region exploited. As a consequence of territorial conflicts between the developing nation-state of the United States and the British imperial authorities who governed still-colonial Upper Canada, the Detroit River finally emerged as an international boundary and became a one-way conduit for freedom-seekers: from U.S. soil to the British colony.

The term *transnationalism* appears frequently throughout *A Fluid Frontier*. The Detroit River borderland merits a transnational designation because it was a highly permeable boundary long before the more formalized organization of the clandestine system of escape known as the Underground Railroad came into being. In the precolonial and colonial eras, Native peoples inhabited and extracted resources from the entire region and, in the colonial era, people of African descent traversed the river in both directions in search of freedom and opportunity. However, it is only today, in retrospect, that scholars have labeled the movement of African Americans and African Canadians across the international divide that the river represented "transnationalism." Yet the cultural dynamics operating in the Detroit River borderlands and the negotiation that took place in this important region during the Underground Railroad era typify what transnationalism means.

Nora Faires, in her groundbreaking studies of black transnationalism in the Great Lakes Basin, called Detroit the "metropolis of the Great Lakes." She pointed out that the repeated crossing and recrossing of the Detroit River border by people of African descent was an "uncelebrated migration that problematizes the national histories of both Canada and the United States."[20] Historian Graham Russell Gao Hodges contends that black cultural events, such as August 1st commemoration of the passage of the 1833 British Emancipation Act, often jointly celebrated by communities on both sides of the Detroit River border, should be placed in the wider context of antislavery struggles in the black Atlantic World.[21] Likewise, German scholar Heike Paul considers the antislavery activism of black Americans and Canadians in the Detroit River borderlands integral to international abolitionism.[22] During the Underground Railroad era, African Americans and African Canadians were well aware of the implications of local events on the world stage. When freedom-seeker Nelson Hackett was taken back across the river in 1842 for rendition to his Arkansas owner, the Detroit Vigilant Committee wrote directly to the British Colonial Office in England to register its protest.[23]

Due to the relative ease of crossing the river, the Detroit borderlands were a place that fostered unique social conditions and opportunities, which are catalogued in the scholarship mentioned above and explicitly described in *A Fluid Frontier*. Jeffrey R. Kerr-Ritchie, in a recent and compelling article, demonstrates how "territorial conflict between rival powers and states provided a *gateway* to freedom for fugitives" and explains that freedom-seekers in such circumstances "did not balk at the chance to repeatedly exploit these tensions ... the primary inducement [being] *less* official state policies than the prospect of permanent freedom during a time of shifting national and free-unfree borders."²⁴ Likewise, historians Pekka Hämäläinen and Samuel A. Truett, in an article devoted to the study of borders and borderlands, assert that such scholarship opens the door to new understandings of "spatial mobility, situational identity, local contingency, and the ambiguities of power." They assert, "If frontiers were the places where we once told our master American narratives, then borderlands are the places where those narratives come unraveled. They are ambiguous and often-unstable realms where boundaries are also crossroads, peripheries are also central places, homelands are also passing-through places, and the end points of empire are also forks in the road. If frontiers are spaces of narrative closure, then borderlands are places where stories take unpredictable turns and rarely end as expected."²⁵

During the era of the Underground Railroad, a unique transnational African American/Canadian society evolved in the Detroit River borderlands. We and our authors are interested in the early history, politics, and culture of the Detroit River as a passageway through a complex and often conflicted borderland, an often amorphous district where the peoples on either side of the divide shared common cultural traits and political aspirations, but also a tangible, concrete border that, when traversed by people of African descent in search of freedom, offered a more than reasonable chance that they would achieve their goal. This volume, therefore, attends to dimensions of the complete cultural framework within which fugitive slave assistance systems operated. More, it bears witness to some of the people, places, and events instrumental in or illustrative of the African American quest for liberty in the Detroit River borderlands. True to the transnational nature of this resistance movement, systems of assistance came into being independently in Michigan and Upper Canada, yet also in direct and intimate cooperation with one another, the common goal being to succor refugees on their way to what people hoped would be a life of freedom and opportunity.

All of the people depicted in the two halves of the International Underground Railroad Memorial that face one another across the Detroit River are anonymous except for one; he is the storied abolitionist activist, civil rights champion, and pillar of Detroit's black community, George DeBaptiste. DeBaptiste is mentioned frequently in the pages of *A Fluid Frontier*, for his lifework exemplifies the meaning of transnational antislavery activism in the region. Freeborn in Fredericksburg, Virginia, in 1815, he had been a dominant force in Underground Railroad and abolitionist networks in borderland cities of Cincinnati, Ohio, and Madison, Indiana, before moving to Detroit. Apparently conditioned by his experiences in multiple borderlands, DeBaptiste was a radical abolitionist in the tradition of Henry Highland Garnet and David Ruggles,²⁶ but a thorough examination of DeBaptiste's life has yet to be written.

In Detroit, DeBaptiste collaborated with William Lambert, who is remembered as the local "President of the Underground Railroad."²⁷ While Lambert took charge of fugitive travel to and through Detroit by land, DeBaptiste managed freedom-seekers' transportation to Canada by water. Because of his frequent visits across the Detroit River, DeBaptiste was well known in black settlements in Canada West, and he became an active member of the Refugee Home Society, founded by Kentucky-born freedom-seeker and newspaper publisher Henry Bibb with support from a largely Detroit-based group of philanthropists for the purpose of providing land for the resettlement of Blacks arriving in Canada West.²⁸ When self-emancipated African Americans living in Canada were in danger of being extradited back to the United

States, DeBaptiste and black residents of Detroit met to voice their concerns and sent written declarations of protest to the Boston-based abolitionist newspaper the *Liberator* and also directly to the British government.[29] The *T. Whitney*, the steamer that DeBaptiste purchased, transported fugitives to Canada and served as a space for African Americans/Canadians to commune together. On August 1st, 1854, while cruising the Detroit River celebrating the 1833 passage of the British Imperial Act that abolished slavery throughout the Empire, DeBaptiste and others from both sides of the river learned the sad news of their comrade Henry Bibb's death, and turned their Emancipation Day excursion into a waterborne memorial service.[30]

The work of George DeBaptist and his contemporaries on either shore also demonstrates the centrality of the role played by people of African descent in Underground Railroad operations. While images of benevolent white "conductors" hiding fugitive slaves beneath the seats of carriages and comforting terrified runaways at clandestine Underground Railroad stations still maintain their hold on the public imagination, black agency in facilitating freedom-seekers' escape and resettlement has long been acknowledged and celebrated by both academic and community historians. Indeed, scholars now realize that the majority of freedom-seekers found their way to the borders of British North America without any assistance at all. The older, Eurocentric vision of the Underground Railroad that still unfortunately dominates popular culture flows from the work of nineteenth-century historian Wilbur H. Siebert, whose volume *The Underground Railroad From Slavery to Freedom* (1898) set the tone for decades of focus on white abolitionists as the "heroes" of the Underground Railroad. However, over the course of the past half century, scholarship has built upon and substantially expanded the revisionist thinking of Larry Gara, who exploded the traditional Eurocentric conception of this unique period in North American history in his 1961 volume, *The Liberty Line: The Legend of the Underground Railroad*.[31] But despite Gara's work and that of historians who came after him, the courage, ingenuity, and initiative of people of African descent continue to be either omitted entirely or marginalized in the much-mythologized portrayals of African American/Canadian abolitionism in the media, school curricula, and public discourse. Such accounts ignore the evolution of increasingly sophisticated black-led institutions and organizations operating in the Detroit River borderland, although they were the hallmark of Underground Railroad–era communal operations everywhere. The U.S. Park Service's Network to Freedom Program; the National Underground Railroad Freedom Center at Cincinnati; the heroic efforts of museums in Michigan, such as Detroit's Charles H. Wright Museum of African American History and the Detroit Historical Museum, and of museums in Southwestern Ontario, including those at Buxton, Dresden, and Amherstburg; and a host of local and governmental organizations as well as the Ontario Black History Society, the Ontario Heritage Trust, and the Michigan Freedom Trail Commission have sought to correct this false Eurocentric focus in materials used to teach students and the public about the Underground Railroad, but the battle is not yet won.

Furthermore, the importance of political activism by antislavery advocates, black and white, on both sides of this critical boundary remains relatively unknown to all but the most specialized academic historians. *A Fluid Frontier* therefore explicitly seeks to foreground the agency of Blacks living along this riverfront and their central role in determining the work that would be undertaken there in the cause of freedom. Communities on either side of this artificial line joined in a cooperative and highly organized effort to assist freedom-seekers on their way to Canada and to help them find employment, housing, fellowship, and *home* once they reached the other shore.

Mythology aside, there was in fact a real and heavily traveled Underground Railroad. The name was commonly used in contemporary literature and newspaper accounts. Indeed, it was so openly discussed by some of its proponents that Frederick Douglass disapprovingly suggested it ought to be called the "upper-ground railroad."[32] People of all ethnic and religious backgrounds joined ranks to help the intrepid refugees on their way and eventually devised clandestine systems to facilitate their safe passage. By the 1830s, freedom-seekers and those who supported them had borrowed the language of the latest technological marvel of the day—the steam-powered trains that were linking the continent. However, the seduction of railroading language for too long suppressed scholarly investigation into other dimensions of freedom-seekers' escapes. Gradually detaching from railroading metaphors, historians have recently investigated waterways as a heavily used means of escape, and this scholarship is yielding significant insights about Underground Railroad networks, especially in border zones near waterways.

Although the Great Lakes Basin presented formidable obstacles to freedom-seekers' movement, waterways offered a fast alternative to travel overland. The prominence of rivers and streams in the American landscape made travel by water a necessity for almost all freedom-seekers at some point in their journey out of the South. Migrating Blacks often established their rural settlements near waterways, and many urban centers with efficient Underground Railroad networks were, like Detroit, port cities.[33] Quick water access to Canada from Detroit made the city a well-known destination. According to the mid-twentieth-century journalist, novelist, and historian Henrietta Buckmaster, Detroit earned a unique code name, "Midnight," meaning the last stop before freedom dawned.[34]

Southerners were so alarmed at the prospect of escapes on northbound vessels that laws were passed to prohibit boat captains and crewmen from assisting fugitives. In addition, free black seamen were so highly suspect that they were strictly monitored and regularly incarcerated while in Southern ports.[35] These measures affected the Detroit River border, too. As slave hunters trying to seize human "bounty" searched the docks for runaways, a number of memorable rescues took place at the Detroit River. (See details of Ben and Daniel's and Thornton and Lucie Blackburn's rescues in chapter 2, Caroline Quarlls's narrow escape at Detroit in chapter 10, the Crosswhite family's flight to the river in chapter 11, and a group of twelve freedom-seekers escorted to the Detroit River by John Brown in chapter 13.) The new, defensive laws necessitated exceptional cunning and ingenuity on the part of fugitives traveling by water and the mariners who transported them, but the ever-present specter of exposure was a constant fear for every fugitive freedom-seeker who boarded a watercraft.

Perhaps the most famous fugitive of the period, Frederick Douglass, found ways to book passage on trains, a ferry, and a steamer in his escape from slavery; outfitted in a sailor's suit and carrying with him a borrowed sailor's certificate, which served the same purpose as free papers, he made his way to New York.[36] For his part, Henry Bibb recalled that the empty trunk he shouldered enabled him to walk unnoticed up a steamboat ramp without a ticket. Once on board, Bibb "insinuated" himself into the company of a group of Irish passengers who were drinking in the vessel's saloon and enlisted one of them to purchase a ticket for him.

> I placed myself in a little crowd of them, and invited them all up to the bar with me, stating that it was my treat. This was responded to, and they walked up and drank and I footed the bill. This, of course, brought us into a kind of a union. We sat together and laughed and talked freely. Within ten or fifteen minutes I remarked that I was getting dry again, and invited them up and treated again. By this time I was thought to be one of the most liberal and gentlemanly men on board, by these deck passengers; they were ready to do any thing for me—they got to singing songs, and telling long yarns in which I took quite an active part, but it was all for effect.[37]

Having attempted several previous escapes, Bibb apparently knew some routines of riverboat travel that helped facilitate his successful deception. The stratagems that Douglass and Bibb and many others employed were so clever, they seem almost fictional. To escape by water, deception was essential and, it seems from fugitives' accounts documented in this volume and elsewhere, quite commonplace. Josiah Henson's life provides another perfect example of water travel negotiation and transnational black agency in the borderlands. Henson, who, arguably, may have served as the prototype of Harriet Beecher Stowe's fictional character Uncle Tom, credited no organized network of abolitionists and safe houses for his family's successful escape from Kentucky slavery in 1831. He describes how an anonymous slave boatman ferried them across the Ohio River, a curious and kindly band of Native people hosted them on their way northwards, and a ship captain and his black crewmen on the shores of Lake Erie aided them in crossing over to Canada. Henson's two trips back to the South to rescue others and bring them safely to Upper Canada illuminate another phenomenon unique to Underground Railroad networks in borderlands: freedom-seekers who became Underground Railroad agents themselves and traveled their Underground Railroad journeys in reverse in order to rescue loved ones and others from slavery.[38]

In exploring the experiences of these and multiple other freedom-seekers in the Detroit River borderland, *A Fluid Frontier* documents the construction and articulation of unique sensibilities in the communities that grew up along the Detroit River, sensibilities in which ethnicity, common experiences of oppression and of potential, and as-yet-unrealized, political aspirations are salient. This cultural experience helped to form transnational individual and communal identities and informed transnational individual and communal actions. It is evident that the concept of "nationality" was, at least for some of the African-descended peoples who lived along this borderland, *less* important than the commonality of their shared experience and aspirations. While their personal security and legal status were starkly and concretely different from one side of the river to the other, their adherence to the concept of the nation-state was clearly secondary to ties of family and faith, cultural homogeneity, community institutions and organizations, political activism, and the various vehicles they created to secure the continuity of all these social structures. In "Transnationalism in California and Mexico at the End of Empire," Michael Kearney fittingly explains: "Members of transnational communities escape the power of the nation-state to shape and inform their sense of collective identity," thus enabling the creation of "forms of organization not constrained by national boundaries."[39] Kearney's point, meant to explain developments in the Mexico/California borderland, also characterizes, precisely, corresponding developments in African American/Canadian communities along the Detroit River during the Underground Railroad era.

In truth, it was not slavery alone that concerned Blacks in this liminal region. Among the issues that confronted communities and individuals of African ancestry living on both sides of the Detroit River throughout the nineteenth century was the struggle to gain and fully exercise civil and political rights. Free African Americans faced segregated public spaces, and while African Canadians, once naturalized, were technically entitled to full and equal rights as British subjects, both African Americans and African Canadians had to endure their children's exclusion from the Common Schools. Black men in Michigan did not achieve suffrage until 1870 with the passage of the Fifteenth Amendment to the American Constitution. More subtle were the daily insidious effects of racial discrimination on black American and black Canadian lives. Although Canada may have been a haven for refugees from American slavery, it was no heaven. The self-emancipated Reverend Samuel Ringgold Ward, writing to the *Voice of the Fugitive*, maintained that what he called "Canadian Negro hate" was even worse than the American phenomenon because it was so *polite*.[40] The first black politician elected in Canada West became a township reeve in 1859, but it was not until 1968 that Lincoln Alexander was elected to the federal House of Commons, while the first black woman, the Honourable Jean Augustine, finally entered the Parliament of Canada in 1993.

A Fluid Frontier: Slavery, Resistance, and the Underground Railroad in the Detroit River Borderland is divided into five parts: "Crossing Boundaries," "Communal Voices," "Inspired Transnationalists," "Resilient Families," and "The Trumpet Sounds," reflecting the thematic, geographic, and loosely chronological arrangement of this volume. Chapters contributed by experts in the field collectively tell the story of nineteenth-century African American freedom-seekers and those who helped them achieve and retain their liberty in this region.

PART I: CROSSING BOUNDARIES

In chapter 1, Veta Smith Tucker charts late eighteenth-century geopolitical shifts in the Detroit River region. She chronicles a legal challenge by young Elizabeth Denison and her brothers against Catherine Tucker, the widow who claimed ownership of them. The actions of the Denisons, who were determined to cross the line from slavery to freedom, illuminate transnational Underground Railroad activism in the frontier era and make visible personal and political identity transformations activated by the prospect of freedom on both sides of the Detroit River. Karolyn Smardz Frost in chapter 2 begins with an understudied perspective: the impact of the War of 1812 on the growth of the Underground Railroad in the region. As U.S. authorities attempted to curtail the swelling tide of freedom flight after the war, Upper Canada was forced to decide where to draw the line for the purpose of extradition. Frost details early fugitive slave cases that inspired joint resistance from black communities on both sides of the river, telling the story of Thornton and Lucie Blackburn, whose recapture and subsequent rescue in the Blackburn Riots of 1833 resulted in changes to law and custom on both sides of the U.S./Canadian border in ways that resonate to this day. In chapter 3, Bryan Prince traces permutations of Upper Canada's legal response to freedom-seekers' transnational flights and discusses the diplomatic dilemma presented by the refugees themselves, some of whom violated laws before crossing the line into the British colony. Each escape fanned the outrage of slavery's adherents, spurring slaveholders and their supporters to ever-more-sophisticated attempts to have fugitives extradited from Canada. These were matched by equally complex legal responses on the part of the British colonial government of the Canadas. Such cases stirred abolitionist optimism in Detroit, Canada, and Great Britain.

PART II: COMMUNAL VOICES

In chapter 4, Irene Moore Davis deftly charts the original African Canadian settlements in the Detroit River border zone founded during the long Underground Railroad era. Most settlements were established by U.S. fugitives, but also included numbers of free Blacks seeking relief from oppressive laws and discriminatory customs in the United States. All African American settlers in Canada faced challenges gaining an economic foothold, educating their children, and carving out a dignified and respected place for themselves in Canadian society. Many African Canadians today trace their ancestry back to these pioneers, whose determined voices can still be seen and heard in the community heritage they left behind. In chapter 5, Barbara Hughes Smith gathers, for the first time in one place, evidence of the origins of African American churches in Detroit. Smith also outlines the strong bonds of community solidarity these institutions forged. The founders of Detroit's African American churches were true transnationalists who secured help for fugitives on both sides of the river and participated in services and celebrations alongside their African Canadian friends and neighbors. Adrienne Shadd in chapter 6 explores parallel religious developments on the Canadian side of the river, illuminating the history and importance of transnational institutions that African Canadian immigrants built on faith. Early African Canadian churches, sometimes cofounded by black and white Americans, joined forces with African American religious denominations, transcended national boundaries to provide community leadership as well as fellowship, and established enduring institutions, several of which still exist today.

PART III: INSPIRED TRANSNATIONALISTS

In chapter 7, Afua Cooper honors the activism of one of the era's and the region's exceptional freedom fighters, Henry Bibb, whose impact on the abolitionist and Underground Railroad movements has not yet been fully appreciated. With his wife, Mary, Bibb established the first successful black newspaper enterprise in British North America. From its humble beginnings in Sandwich, Bibb's *Voice of the Fugitive* served as a megaphone through which the needs and longings of African Canadian and African American communities were broadcast throughout North America and across the Atlantic. Roy Finkenbine in chapter 8 demonstrates the formidable leadership and organizational efficiency of Detroit's black Underground Railroad community. Birthed in Second Baptist church, the Detroit Vigilant Committee worked with Detroit's white abolitionists and Blacks in Canada West, not only to shield free Blacks from kidnapping and to ease freedom-seekers' resettlement in the region but also to advocate for better schooling for black children and full political rights for Blacks in Michigan, long before these issues appeared on national agendas. In chapter 9, Margaret Washington narrates a new development in American politics engendered by the abolitionist and Underground Railroad movements: American women's visible and vocal presence in the political arena which, prior to the antislavery movement, had been bluntly discouraged. The three Michigan-based women whose work Washington traces embodied the spirit of transnational abolitionism and women's rights.

PART IV: RESILIENT FAMILIES

Kimberly Simmons and Larry McClellan trace in chapter 10 the escape of sixteen-year-old Caroline Quarlls, who was the property of her own aunt and uncle. Pursued by slavecatchers from St. Louis, Caroline's perilous journey in 1843 through Wisconsin, Illinois, Indiana, and Michigan covered more than six hundred miles. Years later, having transformed herself into a free literate woman with a family of her own in Canada West, Quarlls Watkins wrote letters to the abolitionist who had traveled with her from Wisconsin to the Detroit River. Her voice resounds more than a century later for her descendants, who today reside in the United States and Canada.

Debian Marty in chapter 11 examines the case of Adam and Sarah Crosswhite. Discovered in Marshall, Michigan, by slavecatchers, the Crosswhites resisted recapture, and members of the Marshall community among whom they were living joined them in frustrating their pursuers. The Crosswhite family finally found a safe haven in Canada West after crossing one more river to freedom, but their Marshall rescuers suffered the legal consequences of assisting the escape. Carol E. Mull details the lives of another unique family of freedom-seekers in chapter 12. After the formerly enslaved parents of famous inventor Elijah ("the real") McCoy reached freedom in Canada West, they made a reverse migration that foreshadowed the journey many self-emancipated Blacks would take in the late antebellum and post–Civil War years. The McCoys' return to American soil, after passage of the draconian 1850 Fugitive Slave Law, epitomized the fluidity of the liquid boundary between Detroit and Canada West.

PART V: THE TRUMPET SOUNDS

Louis A. DeCaro Jr. concludes this volume with a sympathetic portrait of iconic white abolitionist John Brown. DeCaro portrays Brown as a benevolent patriarch and impassioned idealist who sought to enlist black leadership in the Detroit River borderland to help him organize an international force to carry out his insurrectionary antislavery campaign at Harper's Ferry. Brown's transnational vision of liberation was finally vindicated when black Canadian and American men enlisted in the Union Army and Navy to fight and die for freedom.

John Brown's famous raid took place less than three decades after slavery had been abolished in the British Empire, including Canada West. But it is important to remember that Canada had its own history of slavery, and that this pertained along the Detroit River frontier well into the period of British hegemony there. The historical invisibility of slavery in Canada's national narrative is evident in the official record. A good example can be seen at Amherstburg, a place that white abolitionist Levi Coffin called "[t]he Main Terminus of the Underground Railroad" on the Canadian side of the river.[41] In the Amhurstburg Freedom Museum there, constructed around the log cabin of a mid-nineteenth-century freedom-seeker, is an artifact that evokes a much less celebratory perception of African Canadian history in the Detroit River region. It is an iron ring, still attached to a foot-long fragment of ironwood. This is all that remains of the huge tree that once stood in the yard of the Pennsylvanian-turned-British Canadian Loyalist Matthew Elliott's commodious estate. It was to this whipping post that Elliott used to attach one or another of his more than sixty slaves before administering brutal corporal punishment. Given Canada's positive reputation regarding refugee reception, it is of some note that no such grisly artifact of slavery survives on the Detroit River's American shore.

The provincial heritage plaque that commemorates the former site of the Matthew Elliott homestead—a plantation in the truest sense of the term—mentions only his meritorious service to the Crown in the Revolutionary War and as Superintendent of Indian Affairs, including not one word about the dozens of Blacks who were forced to work his fields. Nowhere are the contributions made by those enslaved African-descended people—clearing and planting the land, raising the children, draining marshes, building boats and wharves, and the myriad other tasks undertaken in the development of farms, towns, and cities of this shore—commemorated in ways tangible and visible, either to people visiting the Detroit River region for the first time or to those whose ancestors have lived here for generations.

A Fluid Frontier seeks to set this record straight. The book's purpose is to paint a fuller picture of the protracted struggle against state power and the cooperative antislavery activism that characterized the black American and black Canadian communities in the Detroit River borderlands. As noted borderlands scholar Victor Konrad shows, the study of such liminal cultures helps "illuminate the interplay of imagination, identity and affinity along the borderlines and in the borderlands between Canada and the United States."

> Borderlands culture may be conceptualized as "the way we live in, write about, talk about, and construct policies about the border, and the way in which we have constructed landscapes of bi-national regulation and exchange."... Today, an international border is at once a barrier, a conduit and a transition zone. Furthermore, the territorial ambiguity of borderlands signifies at once the transnational and transitional nature of these constructions.... [A]lthough borders may be the locus of attention, it is the changing, socially-constructed and re-constructed spatial dimension and cultural content of the borderlands that deserves scrutiny and analysis.... [N]on-statist cultural identification is operating to construct and re-construct borders, and ... this cultural imperative now prevails globally.... This cultural identification operates vigorously in borderlands where residents may choose and change identities.[42]

In *A Fluid Frontier* we recognize that the unique character of this borderland encompasses the two shores of the river and that the experience of the people living within it differs in significant ways from that of their compatriots living further from the boundary. Since our focus here is on black transnationalism and on the evolution and character of African American/Canadian resistance to slavery and racial discrimination within this borderland, we have concluded this volume with an essay citing the most significant publications from both Canadian and American historiography that have helped shape our thinking and that of our contributing authors.

INTRODUCTION

The Detroit River is the first waterway in North America recognized for its international heritage significance, so designated by both Canada (2001) and the United States (1998). Today, despite the pervasive security measures imposed by Homeland Security in the wake of 9/11, the border between Canada and the United States remains the longest undefended border in the world. People live in Windsor and work in Detroit and vice versa. Many families shop at favorite stores on either side of the river; others cross over to attend sporting and cultural events and to share in religious services. Festivals and family reunions still unite borderland residents. African Canadian and African Americans living on either side of the border continue to nurture ties forged in the desperate years when the river was the boundary between slavery and freedom. And the Detroit River region remains, indeed, a fluid frontier.

NOTES

1. Ed Dwight, "International Underground Railroad Memorial, Detroit, MI & Windsor, Canada," www.eddwight.com/memorial-public-art/international-underground-railroad-memorial-detroit-mi-windsor-canada (accessed December 30, 2012).
2. J.C.G. Kennedy, *Population of the United States in 1860; Compiled from the Original Returns of the Eighth Census under the Direction of the Secretary of the Interior* (Washington, DC: Government Printing Office, 1864), archive.org/details/populationofusinookennrich (accessed March 2, 2014).
3. This was the refrain of the popular 1860s tune "Away to Canada," which purportedly told the story of a fugitive slave fleeing Tennessee for the safety of Canada. Written by African American poet Joshua McCarter Simpson of Zanesville, Ohio, in 1848, it was sung to the tune of "Oh, Susannah" and the words were widely published in the antislavery press. See Van Goss, "'As a Nation, the English Are Our Friends': The Emergence of African American Politics in the British Atlantic World, 1772–1861," *American Historical Review* 113, no. 4 (2008): 1003–28, quoted on page 1022.
4. These meetings were held at the invitation of Detroit native Kimberly Simmons. A descendant of famous fugitive Caroline Quarlls, Simmons maintains an exhausting schedule as president/executive director of the Detroit River Heritage Initiative, Chair of the Detroit Historical Society's Black Historic Sites Committee, Vice President of the Essex County Black Historic Research Society (Ontario), founder of the Quarlls-Watkins Heritage Project, and former appointee of the Michigan Freedom Trail Commission.
5. "Foreword," J.R.R. Tolkein, *The Hobbit, Or There and Back Again,* 2nd ed. (London: George Allen & Unwin, 1951). This appears in the foreword to the second edition, not the first.
6. Our usage overlaps with the U.S. National Network to Freedom's official definition: "resistance to enslavement through escape and flight." National Park Service: Network to Freedom, www.nps.gov/subjects/ugrr/discover_history/index.htm (accessed January 24, 2014).
7. Afua Cooper, "The Fluid Frontier: Blacks and the Detroit River Region," *Canadian Review of American Studies* 3, no. 2 (2000): 129–49. There is little in the way of earlier studies of slavery in New France except for the seminal volume by the late Laval University scholar Marcel Trudel, *L'esclavage au Canada francais: histoire et conditions de l'esclavage* (Quebec: Presses Universitaires Laval, 1960), only now available in English translation by George

Tombs: *Canada's Forgotten Slaves: Two Centuries of Bondage* (Montreal: Véhicule, 2013). The legal history of slavery is provided in the antiquated but still excellent articles in the *Journal of Negro History* by Judge William Renwick Riddell, including "Notes on Slavery in Canada," 4 (January 1919): 396–408; "The Slave in Upper Canada," 4 (October 1919): 372–95; "The Slave in Canada," 5 (1920): 261–375. See also his "Some References to Negroes in Upper Canada," *Ontario Historical Society Papers and Records* 19 (1922): 144–46.

8. Afua Cooper, *The Hanging of Angelique: The Untold Story of Canadian Slavery and the Burning of Old Montreal* (Toronto: HarperCollins, 2006).

9. Veta Smith Tucker, *A Twenty-First Century History of the 1847 Kentucky Raid in Cass County, Michigan* (Kalamazoo, MI: Fortitude, 2010).

10. The importance of community narratives is highlighted most recently in Cheryl Janifer LaRoche, *The Geography of Resistance: Free Black Communities and the Underground Railroad* (Urbana: University of Illinois, 2014), 83. Archaeologist-historian LaRoche articulates that her effort to reclaim black settlements now erased from the landscape benefited greatly from "the oral record [that] yielded information equal to, if not more compelling, than the written record."

11. Thomas M. Wilson and Hastings Donnan, eds., *Border Identities: Nation and State at International Frontiers* (New York: Cambridge University Press, 1998), 123–31; Thomas M. Wilson and Hastings Donnan, *Borders: Frontiers of Identity, Nation and State* (Oxford: Oxford University Press, 1999).

12. Gregory Wigmore, "Before the Railroad: From Slavery to Freedom in the Canadian-American Borderland," *Journal of American History* 98, no. 2 (2011): 437–54; Sean Kelley, "'Mexico in His Head': Slavery and the Texas-Mexico Border, 1810–1860," *Journal of Social History* 37 (Spring 2004): 709–23. See also Karen Marrero, "On the Edge of the West: The Roots and Routes of Detroit's Urban Eighteenth Century," in *Frontier Cities: Encounters at the Crossroads of Empire*, ed. Jay Gitlin, Barbara Berglund, and Adam Arenson (Philadelphia: University of Pennsylvania Press, 2013), 66–86; and Lisa Philips Valentine and Allan K. McDougall, "Imposing the Border: The Detroit River from 1786 to 1807," *Journal of Borderland Studies* 19, no. 1 (2004): 13–22.

13. The term *borderlands* was first coined in respect to its modern usage by historians, historical geographers, and other specialists by Herbert Eugene Bolton in his landmark *The Spanish Borderlands: A Chronicle of Old Florida and the Southwest* (New Haven, CT: Yale University Press, 1921). More recent work on Underground Railroad–era activities in the area include Ronnie C. Tyler, "Fugitive Slaves in Mexico," *Journal of Negro History* 57 (January 1972): 1–12; Kelley, "'Mexico in His Head'" 709–23; Rosalie Schwartz, *Across the Rio to Freedom: U.S. Negroes in Mexico* (El Paso: University of Western Texas Press, 1975); Sarah B. Cornell, "Citizens of Nowhere: Fugitive Slaves and Free African Americans in Mexico, 1833–1857," *Journal of American History* 100, no. 2 (2013): 351–74.

14. Solomon Northup, *Twelve Years a Slave*, ed. Sue Eakin and Joseph Logsdon (1968; repr., Baton Rouge: Louisiana State University Press, 2014), 188, cited in Cornell, "Citizens of Nowhere," 351.

15. Kelley provides ample evidence that enslaved Texans appropriated the rhetoric of Mexican independence and reinterpreted it to construct Mexico as a site of liberation from the time

that Texas was a province of Mexico through Texas's independence and its annexation to the United States. "'Mexico in His Head,'" 713, 717–19.

16. Mary Ann Shadd was her maiden name; after her 1856 marriage to Toronto barber and activist Thomas F. Cary she became, as she is more commonly known, Mary Ann Shadd Cary. For Delany, see Mark Roth, "Martin Delany: Father of Black Nationalism," *Pittsburg Post-Gazette*, February 6, 2011, www.blackpast.org/aah/delany-major-martin-robison-1812-1885#sthash.Lfja02C1.dpuf (accessed May 23, 2014).

17. Reverend Richard Disney, "Chatham was not a mecca only. In a broader and truer sense it was the colored man's Paris," African Methodist Church, *Church Review*, II (1895), 5.

18. Martin R. Delany, *The Condition, Elevation, Emigration and Destiny of the Colored People of the United States, Politically Considered* (Philadelphia: privately published, 1852), 159–90.

19. Nell Irvin Painter, *Creating Black Americans African-American History and Its Meanings, 1619 to the Present* (New York: Oxford University Press, 2006), 8; Robert G. Weisbord, *Ebony Kinship: Africa, Africans and the Afro-American* (Westport, CT: Greenwood, 1973), 24.

20. Nora Faires, "Going Across the River: Black Canadians and Detroit Before the Great Migration," *Citizenship Studies* 10, no. 1 (2006): 117–34, 129.

21. Graham Russell Gao Hodges, *David Ruggles: A Radical Black Abolitionist and the Underground Railroad in New York*, John Hope Franklin Series in African American History and Culture (Chapel Hill: University of North Carolina Press, 2010).

22. Heike Paul, "Out of Chatham: Abolitionism on the Canadian Frontier," *Atlantic Studies* 8, no. 2 (2011): 165–88.

23. David Murray, *Colonial Justice: Justice, Morality, and Crime in the Niagara District, 1791–1849*, Osgoode Society for Canadian Legal History (Toronto: University of Toronto Press, 2002), 197–216; Robin W. Winks, *The Blacks in Canada: A History*, 2nd ed. (Montreal: McGill-Queen's University Press, 1997), 174–75; Roman J. Zorn, "An Arkansas Fugitive Slave Incident and Its International Repercussions," *American Historical Quarterly* 16 (Summer 1957): 139–49. While the term used for such groups is more often "Vigilance" Committee, the Detroit organization chose the name Detroit Vigilant Committee and used it consistently.

24. Jeffrey R. Kerr-Ritchie, "Fugitive Slaves across North America," in *Workers across the Americas: The Transnational Turn in Labor History* (New York: Oxford University Press, 2011), 363–83, 368.

25. Pekka Hämäläinen and Samuel A. Truett, "On Borderlands," *Journal of American History* 98 (September 2011), 338, 339.

26. "Death of George DeBaptiste," *Detroit Daily Post*, February 23, 1875; "George DeBaptiste—His Death Yesterday," *Detroit Advertiser and Tribune*, February 23, 1875; Hodges, *David Ruggles*, 69; Earl Ofari Hutchinson, *Let Your Motto Be Resistance: The Life and Thought of Henry Highland Garnet* (Boston: Beacon, 1972); Stanley Harrold, *The Rise of Aggressive Abolitionism: Addresses to the Slaves* (Lexington: University Press of Kentucky, 2004).

27. "Successful Working of the Underground Railroad," *Detroit Daily Post*, February 7, 1870; Katherine DuPre Lumpkin, "'The General Plan was Freedom': A Negro Secret Order on the Underground Railroad," *Phylon* 28 (1st quarter 1967): 63–77.

28. Peter Carlesimo, "The Refugee Home Society: Its Origin, Operation and Results, 1851–1876" (MA thesis, University of Windsor, 1973), 63, 82, 95.
29. *The North Star*, December 29, 1848. Others present at the meeting to protest Nelson Hackett's extradition included Henry Bibb and William Lambert. See "Annual Report of the Colored Vigilant Committee of Detroit, Delivered at Detroit City Hall," Detroit, Michigan, January 10, 1843, in C. Peter Ripley et al., eds., *The Black Abolitionist Papers, 1830–1865*, vol. 3, *United States* (Chapel Hill: University of North Carolina Press, 1986), 397–402.
30. Ronald D. Palmer, "George DeBaptiste: One of the Underground Railroad Heroes," unpublished manuscript, n.d. (Moorland-Spingarn Library, Howard University: Washington, DC); Afua Cooper, "'Doing Battle in Freedom's Cause': Henry Bibb, Abolistionism, Race Uplift, and Black Manhood, 1842–1854" (PhD diss., University of Toronto, 2000), 476–78.
31. Larry Gara, *The Liberty Line: The Legend of the Underground Railroad* (1961; repr., Lexington: University Press of Kentucky, 1996). The contrasting influence of Siebert and Gara is discussed at length in the bibliographical essay that completes this volume.
32. Frederick Douglass, *Narrative of the Life of Frederick Douglass, an American Slave: Written by Himself* (Boston: Anti-Slavery Office, 1845), 101.
33. LaRoche, *The Geography of Resistance*, 94.
34. Henrietta Buckmaster, *Let My People Go: The Story of the Underground Railroad and the Growth of the Abolitionist Movement* (1941; repr., Columbia: University of South Carolina Press, 1992), 249. There is some question about this, as modern scholars suggest the term originated with Buckmaster herself.
35. W. Jeffrey Bolster details the "stringent legislation restricting black seamens' freedom and livelihoods" that was passed in the wake of the foiled Denmark Vesey insurrection that had been planned at Charleston, South Carolina, in 1822. (For a detailed analysis of the insurrection, as well as its aftermath, see Tracy Keith Flemming, "Denmark Vesey: An Atlantic Perspective," *Journal of Pan African Studies* 7, no. 4 (2014): 7–114, www.jpanafrican.com/docs/vol7no4/7.4-3-Flemming-NovDenmark%20Vesey.pdf, and Douglas R. Egerton, *He Shall Go out Free: The Lives of Denmark Vesey*, 2nd ed (Lanham, MD: Rowman & Littlefield, 2004.) Passage of these laws began in 1822 and extended through the 1850s in South Carolina, Georgia, North Carolina, and the Gulf states of Florida, Louisiana, and Alabama. *Black Jacks: African American Seamen in the Age of Sail* (Cambridge, MA: Harvard University Press, 1997), 194–200. See also Stephanie M. H. Camp, *Closer to Freedom: Enslaved Women and Everyday Resistance in the Plantation South* (Chapel Hill: University of North Carolina Press, 2004), 16, 98, 105.
36. Frederick Douglass, *The Life and Times of Frederick Douglass, Written by Himself* (Boston: DeWolf & Fiske, 1892), 245–50.
37. Henry Bibb, *Narrative of the Life and Adventures of Henry Bibb, an American Slave, Written by Himself* (New York: Macdonald & Lee, 1849), 167–69.
38. Josiah Henson, *The Life of Josiah Henson, Formerly a Slave, Now an Inhabitant of Canada, as Narrated by Himself* (Boston: Arthur D. Phelps, 1849). Stowe herself lent credence to her dependency on Henson's autobiography, which remains questionable for a number of reasons, by writing the Preface to Henson's revised version, *Truth Stranger Than Fiction: Father Henson's Story of His Own Life* (Boston: John P. Jewett, 1858). Henson's final revised edition

was published in 1879 in London, England, by John Lobb, and titled *Uncle Tom's Story of His Life: An Autobiography of the Rev. Josiah Henson (Mrs. Harriet Beecher Stowe's "Uncle Tom"), from 1789 to 1876*, with a Preface by Mrs. Harriet Beecher Stowe, and an Introductory Note by George Sturge, and S. Morley, Esq., M.P.

39. Michael Kearney, "Transnationalism in California and Mexico at the End of Empire," in Wilson and Donnan, *Border Identities*, 117–41.

40. See, for example, Samuel Ringgold Ward, "Canadian Negro Hate," *Voice of the Fugitive*, October 12, 1852.

41. Fred Landon, "Amherstburg: Terminus of the Underground Railroad," *Journal of Negro History* 10 (January 1925): 1–9, reprinted in Karolyn Smardz Frost, Bryan Walls, Hilary Bates Neary, and Frederick H. Armstrong, *Ontario's African-Canadian Heritage: Collected Writings by Fred Landon, 1918–1967* (Toronto: Natural Heritage, 2009), 66–74.

42. Victor Konrad, "Imagination, Identity, Affinity, and the Social Construction of Borderlands Culture," paper presented at the American Folklife Center, Library of Congress, Washington, DC, June 15, 2010, 2. The quotations come from Victor Konrad and Heather Nicol, *Beyond Walls: Reinventing the Canada–United States Borderlands* (Aldershot, UK: Ashgate, 2008), 287, 292. Another version of the paper is published in Victor Konrad, "Conflating Imagination, Identity, and Affinity in the Social Construction of Borderlands Culture between Canada and the United States," *American Review of Canadian Studies* 42, no. 4 (2012): 530–48. Quoted with the kind permission of the author.

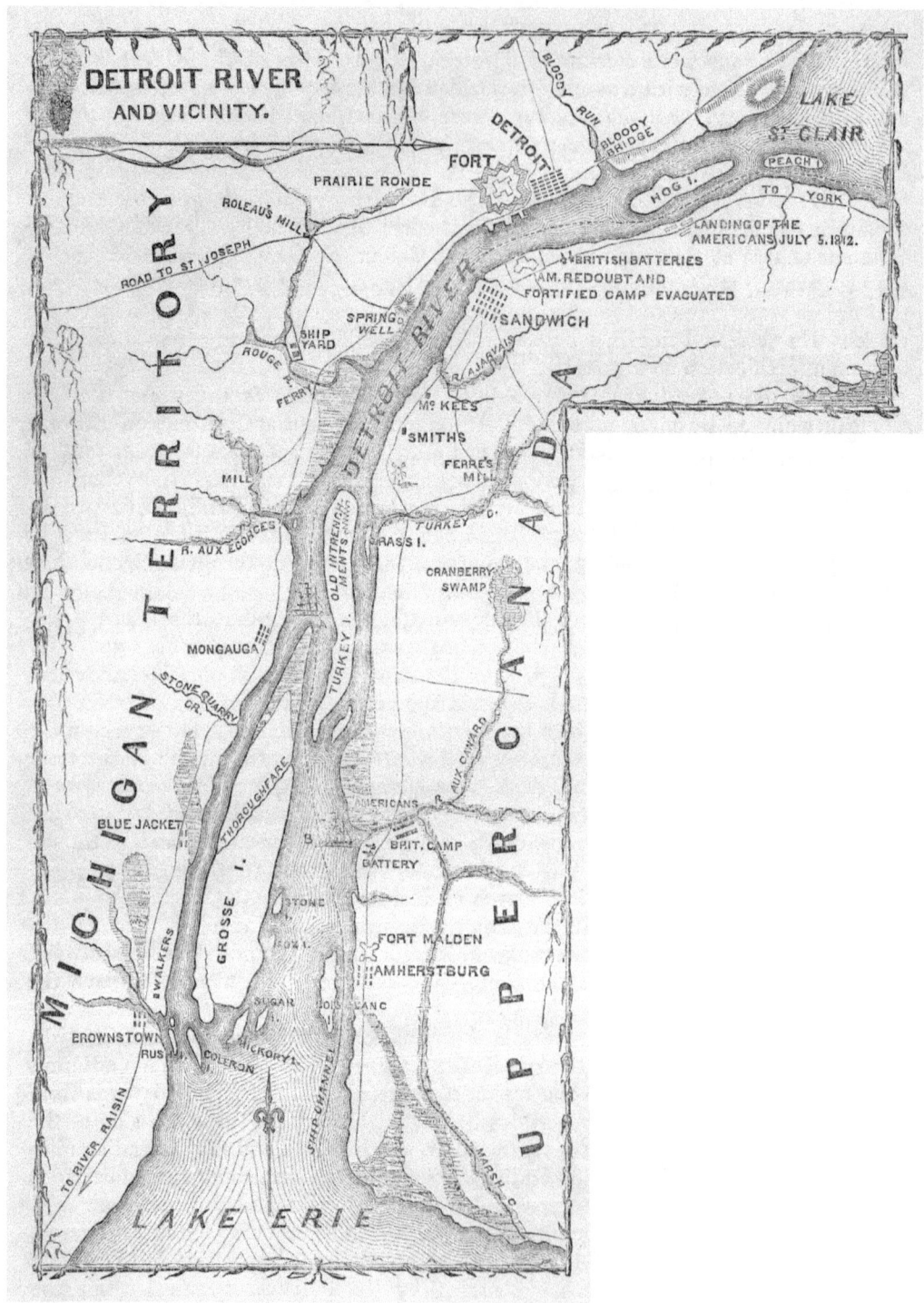

"Map of Detroit River and Vicinity, 1812," in Benson John Lossing, *The Pictorial Field-book of the War of 1812* (New York: Harper & Brothers, 1869), 266. (Courtesy of the Toronto Public Library)

PART I

CROSSING BOUNDARIES

People of African descent brought to or born in North America were constrained by socially and legally constructed boundaries that classified them as property. Keenly aware that the boundaries rendered them ineligible to receive the social benefits and political rights that whites enjoyed, they engaged in a protracted struggle for inclusion, although restrictions, both legal and psychological, formed unyielding barriers around their humanity. In the Detroit River region, the boundary to cross to gain social and political personhood was physical and visible: the river itself.

African people had enjoyed freedom in their native lands, and many lived within reach of it in the Americas; therefore, no boundary denying them freedom was too formidable or too onerous for thousands to attempt to cross. Yearning for lost liberty and political personhood, African-descended people were determined to break through the barriers of exclusion. Their collective aspirations and individual desires converged into an irrepressible moral and political surge. Their inexorable migrations in search of freedom coalesced into what came to be called the Underground Railroad. Awakening the conscience of nations, the Underground Railroad symbolized the insistent longing of African people in North America to cross over and cross out every unjust boundary erected to restrict their lives, hopes, and dreams.

ONE

UNCERTAIN FREEDOM IN FRONTIER DETROIT

VETA SMITH TUCKER

In 1807, when Elizabeth Denison and her brothers challenged Catherine Tucker's right to retain them in perpetual slavery, Detroit had not yet outgrown its frontier beginnings. At the riverfront, vanes of French windmills paddled the breeze, the steeples of St. Anne's Catholic Church graced the sky, and wolves in forests surrounding the town howled through the night. Native people and Métis *voyageurs* canoed the river and inland waterways,[1] British colonists and American settlers plied lakes and rivers in sailboats, and farmers from the Canadian side of the river carried their produce to Detroit markets in a horse-powered ferry. Enslaved U.S. Blacks also navigated the river, seeking freedom in colonial Canada, while Blacks held in bondage in the British colony crossed from the opposite shore seeking freedom in frontier Detroit. Elizabeth Denison's father, like all black Americans who had earned their freedom, also had to negotiate the international boundary and his political identity and national loyalty, just as had Native peoples, French and British settlers, and enslaved African Canadians in this frontier borderland. A thorough analysis of the Denison family's trials and those of others enslaved in the Detroit River border region provides ample evidence that what became the legendary Underground Railroad manifested itself very early in the American/British Canadian border zone along the Detroit River.

After its military defeat by the British in 1760, France ceded some of its North American territory, including its Detroit River settlement, to Britain. Under the British regime, slavery expanded in the newly acquired province of Quebec, which included much of what became

Ontario, as it had in previous decades in Britain's colonies along the Atlantic Seaboard. Settlers migrating from eastern seaboard colonies to the newly acquired province brought enslaved Blacks with them. The British preference for African slaves rather than *panis* (Native) ones gradually transformed the demographic of North American slavery. Quebec's first British governor, General James Murray, made an urgent plea for black workers: "[W]ithout servants nothing can be done, had I the intention to employ soldiers ... they would disappoint me, and Canadians will work for nobody but themselves. Black slaves are certainly the only people to be depended upon."[2]

Two decades later, Britain suffered a military defeat in the American Revolutionary War and had to shed some of its territory in North America. The issue over the border between the United States and the remaining portion of British North America was settled in 1783 and involved establishing a boundary line down the middle of the Detroit River. Agreement on a firm political border between the United States and British colonial Canada, however, proved more difficult to achieve. In spite of the geographical boundary, the Detroit River frontier remained a contested borderland. In the wake of their defeat in the American Revolutionary War, the British refused to withdraw from the Detroit garrison, alleging that some former U.S. colonies refused "payment of debts to British creditors" for property seized during the war. British officials also claimed that British settlers who had remained loyal to the Crown (termed United Empire Loyalists in Canada) had not received compensation for their losses, and the British contended that the area north of the Ohio River and west of the Detroit River had been Indian Territory during the war and therefore was not included in the original Thirteen Colonies.[3] Part of the disputed territory included Detroit, which the British continued to occupy. Additional complications came as a result of the Canadian Constitutional Act of 1791, which divided the province of Quebec into Upper and Lower Canada, and included Detroit in the newly created province of Upper Canada.[4] These competing claims to the Detroit River border zone would produce unsettling complications for many living there, including enslaved Blacks and Native people.

For a decade after the American Revolutionary War, Detroit was simultaneously "free" American territory and "slave" British territory. The Northwest Ordinance of 1787 mandated that the newly acquired territory on the American side of the Detroit River be free of slavery; therefore, no more enslaved individuals were to be imported. However, the Northwest Ordinance conflicted with the Canadian Constitutional Act of 1791 and with Jay's Treaty of 1794, which affirmed that British settlers who remained in the Detroit River settlement after the British exit "shall continue to enjoy, unmolested, all their property of any kind."[5] Exploiting this legal ambiguity, enslaved Canadian and American Blacks fled to freedom in opposite directions across the Detroit River, and several "British Detroiters" held office in the government of Upper Canada.[6]

This ambiguity was partially addressed in 1793 when Upper Canada's Lieutenant Governor, John Graves Simcoe, proposed legislation similar to the Northwest Ordinance to prohibit the introduction of new slaves into Upper Canada.[7] Slaveholders in Parliament who opposed Simcoe's new law succeeded in modifying it to affirm slaveholders' right to retain slaves already in their possession. Thus, the final legislation did not actually free anyone enslaved in Upper Canada at the time. Nevertheless, the act slowed the growth of slavery in the province and helped to establish a solid political boundary between the two nations. The 1793 act also stipulated that any child born after 1793 of an enslaved mother had to be emancipated at age twenty-five and that the child of a mother serving the mandated twenty-five-year term of bondage would be born free.[8] As a result of this legislation, Upper Canada became an enticing destination to U.S. Blacks seeking freedom. However, enslaved Canadian Blacks born prior to 1793 were destined for lifelong enslavement, and therefore continued to flee from Upper Canada to freedom in "American" Detroit. In 1795, for instance, Canadian Alexander McKee complained, "[A] Negro man of mine whom I left in charge of my House . . . has been seduced away to General Wayne's camp."[9] McKee's attempt to recover the runaway from General Wayne's military encampment in Indiana Territory proved futile.

Jay's Treaty, ratified in 1794, finally resolved the simultaneous British and American claims to Detroit, although the British did not physically withdraw from the garrison until 1796. After the British withdrawal, however, the Detroit region remained unstable. Blacks continued to seek freedom on opposite shores of the river, and Native people, having been deserted by their British allies, resisted the American takeover.[10] Severed from British protection, Native tribes lost the leverage with which they had extracted political concessions and secured material necessities from both British and American officials. First Nations peoples in the region also no longer possessed the ability to obstruct American expansion into Native land. The accelerating American encroachment into traditional Native residential and hunting land led to warfare.[11]

In 1795, a confederacy of Native tribes battled American forces near Toledo, Ohio.[12] Their ultimate defeat resulted in the tribes surrendering most of their land in the Ohio Valley.[13] With their extensive land loss, Native tribes forfeited the foundation of their sovereignty. They were effectively "stateless,"[14] that is, neither American nor British Canadian, prohibited from extracting resources from the land as they had previously and ineligible to claim political rights in either the United States or British Canada.

From the time of Detroit's founding by the French in 1701 through its transfer to the United States in 1796, enslaved U.S. and Canadian Blacks had exploited geopolitical shifts in the Detroit River borderland and contrived self-propelled, self-planned escapes heading in both directions across the Detroit River. These early Detroit River crossings can be theorized as some of the earliest manifestations of what would later be known as the Underground Railroad. The dramatic upheavals that had taken place in the region since the eighteenth century set the stage for the nineteenth-century confrontation between newly freed citizen Peter Denison and Catherine Tucker, the widow who inherited Denison and his family. The conflict soon to trouble the Denisons and Tucker also reflected borderland contests that had embroiled French, British, and Native people in the waning moments of the frontier era.

Peter Denison's destiny on the Detroit frontier was tied to that of his former owner, William Tucker. In the late 1750s, William Tucker had begun serving the British command at the Detroit garrison as an Indian trader and language interpreter.[15] In 1773, Tucker left his affairs at the garrison and traveled to his boyhood home near Stoverstown, Virginia. He returned to Detroit with a bride, Catherine Hezel, and resumed his garrison post. He was valued at the garrison because of his command of Native languages. Tucker had learned the Chippewa/Ottawa language from intimate experience. At age eleven, William and his brother were captured during an Indian raid on their father's Virginia farm. Their captors brought the brothers to the Detroit area and they were adopted into a Chippewa family, in which William remained through age eighteen.[16] (William's brother did not survive captivity.)

Near the end of the American Revolutionary War, Chippewa chiefs bequeathed to Tucker a large tract of land west of Detroit in an area that would become Macomb County. He took possession of the land and added farming to his occupations of trader and interpreter.[17] Tucker acquired the additional labor he needed to develop his land by purchasing a "Negro" woman and man—Hannah in 1780 and Peter Denison in 1784.[18] Tucker's life at the frontier farmstead proved productive and profitable. He and his wife had ten children.[19] Peter Denison and Hannah became a couple and had four. Native youth frequented the farm. The Tuckers' son Edward later recalled that he played "many a day with the Indian boys."[20] The Denisons' only daughter, Elizabeth, also learned to converse in the language of the Native youth who visited the farm.[21]

The prosperity Tucker enjoyed is apparent in his 1805 will, signed with his mark. The multipage inventory lists property valued at $4,447, no meager amount for a farmer in 1805. Included were the farmhouse, outbuildings, horses, oxen, cows, sheep, cattle, hogs, farm utensils, carpenter's tools, household furniture, silver set, linens, clothing, and his "Negroe man and Woman Peter and Hannah & their daughter and their sons." (The statement indicates that at the signing of the will, there was only one Denison daughter.) In the will the value of Tucker's human property is calculated to be $600. Upon his death all Tucker's possessions were to go to his wife, Catherine, and upon her death, Tucker's sons would receive land, livestock, and "an equal share of the Negroe children." In an addendum to his will, Tucker gave to his "Black man and Black woman . . . Peter and Hannah . . . their freedom after the decease of . . . Catherine Tucker."[22]

Peter and Hannah must have served Tucker admirably to be granted their freedom; however, Tucker's gratitude did not extend to the Denison children. Perhaps due to Peter and Hannah's age, Catherine released them from her service after her husband's death. The two were indentured for one year to the Attorney General of Michigan Territory Elijah Brush and then gained full freedom. Brush must have been impressed with Peter Denison, for it was likely he who recommended Denison to Michigan's Governor William Hull. Later that year, when Hull organized a black militia to defend Detroit from "marauding Indians," he made Denison commander of the unit.[23]

In 1806, tension still prevailed in the Detroit River region. Neither the Michigan Territorial government nor the colonial government of Upper Canada could curtail the two-way stream of runaways from slavery. Moreover, Detroiters residing outside the garrison constantly feared Native attacks. According to Friend Palmer, "It was perilous at that time for people living so far from the fort as the Indians were none too friendly. Children were admonished to keep indoors after dark for fear of being carried off by redskins."[24] Having lost land and bargaining power, Native peoples in the area were restive. Northwest Fur Company merchants depended on good relations with tribes in the Detroit area and the Upper Great Lakes to move furs bound for markets in Montreal down the Detroit River into Lake Erie as well as to ship supplies and commodities back to traders for tribes in the Upper Lakes. Along the route American settlers harassed Canadian traders; they blamed Canadians for Native resistance to American expansion into the Territory and held Canadians responsible for providing weapons

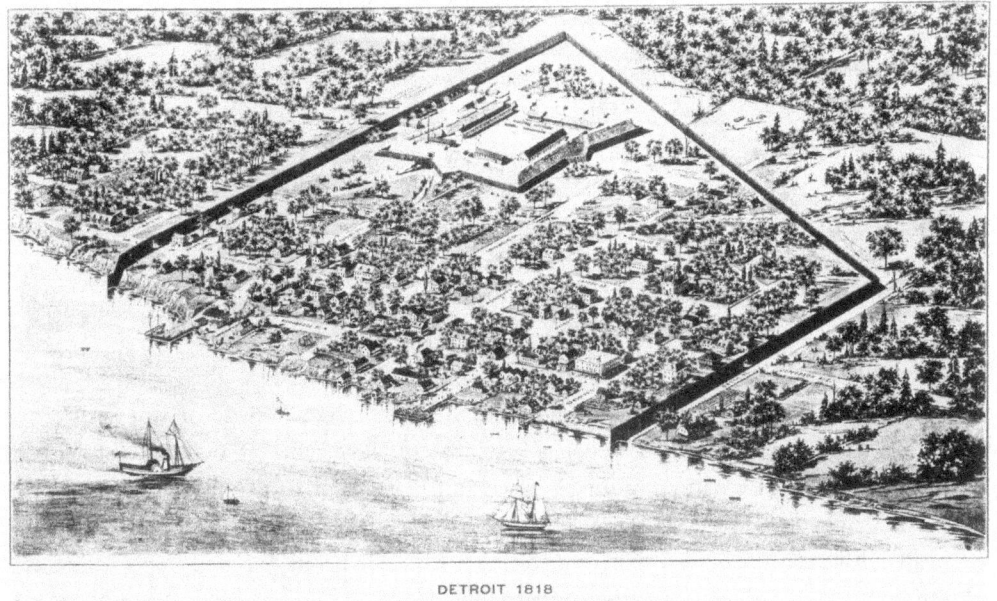

DETROIT 1818
HISTORICALLY CORRECT IN EVERY POINT OF DETAIL

As a garrisoned town, Detroit was patrolled by the black militia unit that Peter Denison commanded. (Courtesy of the Burton Historical Collection, Detroit Public Library)

and supplies that facilitated Native attacks.[25] Indeed, in spite of the United States finally taking full possession of Detroit in 1796, in the first decade of the nineteenth century the Detroit River region continued to be an unruly border zone.

The presence of Governor Hull's black militia in Detroit also heightened anxiety on both sides of the border. Residents on the Canadian side of the river contended that the ranks of the Detroit militia included runaways from Upper Canadian slavery. Prominent fur trader, United Empire Loyalist, and slaveholder John Askin, who had relocated from Detroit to Sandwich, the capital of the Western District of Upper Canada directly across the river from Detroit, complained in a September 1807 letter to his son that "our runaway negroes have had arms given them and mount guard" in the town of Detroit.[26] The enlistment of Upper Canadian runaways in the Detroit militia also disturbed Augustus B. Woodward, Michigan Territorial Supreme Court justice. He complained to the Michigan legislature's Sundry Committee that reports circulating throughout the territory "respecting an invasion . . . by a savage force" were unfounded and "excited for sinister and speculative purposes." Woodward's stated objections to the black militia, however, revealed more than skepticism about Governor Hull's motives. In addition to his discomfort about runaways in the unit, Woodward also expressed his reservations about having a black man in command of the men. Woodward wrote: "[T]he embodying of slaves belonging to the subjects of his Britannic Majesty residing in the province of Upper Canada into a militia company, and the issuing of commissions, or other authority, to such persons or other slaves, or black persons, to be officers in such militia company, has a tendency to be injurious to the proprietors of slaves, both in his Britannic Majesty's province of Upper Canada, adjacent to this Territory, and in this Territory."[27]

It is highly unlikely that Peter Denison had any idea what Justice Woodward's sentiments were concerning either his own commission or the status of the recruits under his command. However, hearing Canadian runaways share their experiences in slavery might well have troubled Denison, whose own children remained enslaved on the Tucker farm. While still in command of his unit, perhaps counting on assistance from his former employer, Attorney General Brush, and trusting his record of service to Governor Hull, Denison initiated a bold stratagem. He enlisted Brush to file a legal complaint on behalf of the Denison children against their owner, Catherine Tucker, pleading for their release from slavery.

The arguments presented by attorneys for Tucker and Denison foreground issues of shifting political allegiance and pliable political identities characteristic of frontier/borderland culture. Opposing claims in *Denison et al. v. Tucker* (1807) reflected dynamics endemic to borderland conflicts that had embroiled France and Britain, British Canada and the United States, Native peoples, and enslaved Blacks in the Great Lakes region since the beginning of European settlement.[28] Elijah Brush, as attorney for the Denisons, pleaded that the Denison children ought to have been considered free under U.S. law, specifically the 1787 Northwest Ordinance, Article VI. Brush argued further that the term *property* in Jay's Treaty did not include the "human species." Brush could have been alluding to arguments from the precedent-setting British case *Somerset v. Stewart* (1772), in which Lord Mansfield's ruling effectively manumitted James Somerset, an enslaved man brought to England temporarily by his master. The enslaved man fled. Captured, he was imprisoned in a ship on the Thames to be transported to Jamaica for sale, but abolitionist Granville Sharp defended his right to freedom in British courts. The Lord Chief Justice of England, Lord Mansfield, ruled that Somerset was entitled to liberty since there was no "positive law" specifying the conditions and legality of enslavement on British soil.[29] Lord Mansfield's ruling applied to Somerset only; however, some British and American observers anticipated a wider application and concluded, erroneously, that slavery in England had ended with Lord Mansfield's decision.[30]

In Detroit, Harris Hickman, counsel for the defense in the Denison case, built Catherine Tucker's defense on Jay's Treaty, primarily its stipulation that protected "property of any kind" for "settlers and traders within the precincts of the [Detroit] post."[31] Hickman further contended that provisions in the 1793 Upper Canadian Act to Prevent the Further Introduction of Slaves also supported Mrs. Tucker's claim. Although she had become a U.S. resident when British Detroit was officially transferred into U.S. possession, Hickman argued that the rights given British subjects at the moment of territorial transition applied to Catherine Tucker in this case (even though her case commenced a decade after the territorial transfer).

U.S. Statute 309, enacted by Congress in 1805, was also relevant to the Denison case. In addition to creating Michigan Territory out of Indiana Territory, the statute stipulated that a government be formed in Michigan Territory "in all respects" similar to that provided for by the Northwest Ordinance. That would have entailed a local prohibition against slavery, according to legal scholar W. James Ellison; the "property of any kind" mentioned in Jay's Treaty was congressionally modified by Statute 309 to *exclude* property in the human species.[32]

Judge Augustus Woodward had arrived in Detroit in 1805, the very first Justice of the Michigan Territorial Supreme Court, appointed to the bench by President Thomas Jefferson. Woodward must have known about U.S. Statute 309 since it created the territory to which he had been appointed. Therefore, he could have invoked it in the Denison case and decided that former British and French Canadians who continued to reside in Michigan Territory after the United States took possession would be governed by the laws enacted by Congress. Ellison contends that based on both Statute 309 and the Northwest Ordinance, Tucker and those in her class, having chosen to remain in Michigan Territory after British evacuation, would have had to accept the benefits and restrictions of these laws.[33]

Clearly, other considerations weighed more heavily than U.S. Statute 309 and the Northwest Ordinance on Justice Woodward's deliberation in the Denison case. In his September 27, 1807, ruling, Justice Woodward acknowledged that, until 1796, Michigan had been part of Upper Canada, thus affirming Tucker's claim to have been a British settler subject to the terms of Jay's Treaty. Woodward also carefully denounced slavery: "The existence at this day of an absolute & unqualified Slavery of the human Species in the United States of America is universally and justly considered their deepest reproach." The prohibition of slavery in the Northwest Ordinance, Woodward continued, "ought to be considered as imposing a most serious and sacred duty."[34]

Then, paradoxically, Chief Justice Woodward declared that the "greater duty" was to uphold the compact made with Great Britain in 1794 to protect the rights of British settlers and their property.[35] Woodward concluded that the term *property* as used in Jay's Treaty included slaves, as slaves were recognized as property by both of the countries that signed the treaty.[36] Woodward, in effect setting aside both the antislavery clause of the Northwest Ordinance and congressional Statute 309, affirmed Catherine Tucker's defense, which was that she be granted the same property rights as British settlers who had remained in Michigan Territory after British evacuation.

Since Justice Woodward upheld Jay's Treaty in *Denison v. Tucker,* the 1793 Upper Canadian Act to Prevent the Further Introduction of Slaves could also be enforced. That act, along with its prohibition against the importation of slaves into Upper Canada, also provided that from 1793 forward, children born of a slave mother would become free at age twenty-five (though anyone born in slavery before 1793 would remain enslaved for life). Application of the act in this case resulted in the three eldest Denison children, Elizabeth, Scipio, and James, all born before 1793, being returned to slavery for the remainder of their lives, while Peter Jr., born after 1793, would be granted his freedom after serving twenty-five years in slavery. The overall effect of Woodward's decision was to return all the Denison children to Tucker. Yet in addition to cementing permanent enslavement for three of the Denison children, Judge Woodward's ruling effectively rendered all of them ineligible for political rights or citizenship; the older children would henceforth be permanently "stateless," a status similar to that of Native people at the moment the United States consolidated its control of the Detroit frontier.

In response to the permanent liminality the ruling imposed on his children, that is to say, their legal classification as perpetual human property in the United States, Peter Denison pursued the only advantageous course available to him: Denison imagined new political identities as British Canadians for himself and his children. Denison set aside his patriotic allegiance

Elizabeth Denison Forth, daughter of Peter and Hannah Denison and lead plaintiff in Denison et al. v. Tucker (1807). (Courtesy of St. James Episcopal Church, Grosse Ile, Michigan)

to the United States as militia commander. He also made himself ineligible for any benefits resulting from his militia service, such as a land grant, which some black soldiers in the Detroit area later received.[37] Instead, he resolved to forfeit his newly acquired U.S. nationality and pursue a British Canadian nationality for himself and his children.

In the next few months, under a cloak of secrecy, Denison removed his entire family from U.S. authority by crossing the Detroit River to live in Upper Canada. There Simcoe's 1793 Act to Prevent the Further Introduction of Slaves granted the Denison children perpetual freedom—the exact opposite of the effect the law had on them while they remained on U.S. soil, as a result of Woodward's verdict. Peter Denison, therefore, cleverly exploited geopolitical contradictions in the law and joined what would eventually become a tidal wave of Blacks fleeing the United States seeking freedom and political rights through settlement in Upper Canada.

Defense attorney Elijah Brush probably assisted the Denisons' escape to Canada. Brush was the son-in-law of former Detroiter, wealthy fur trader, and, ironically, slaveholder John Askin. Indeed, scholars have concluded that it was most likely Askin who received the Denisons when they crossed the border into Upper Canada.[38] An early Macomb County history states that a conspiracy of "prominent citizens of Detroit enticed the negroes from Mr. Tucker's farm."[39] Perhaps the belief that the conspirators were among Detroit's elite discouraged Tucker from attempting to recover her "property." Though she had legal right to the Denison children and their labor for the remainder of her life, as set forth in her husband's will, Catherine Tucker never made any attempt to recapture her human inheritance. She lived another forty years, until 1848.

During their time in Upper Canada, the Denisons attended St. John's Anglican Church in Sandwich, where church records written by the Reverend Richard Pollard document them, described as "people of color" and as "Negro's," in attendance at weddings, baptisms, and funerals. John Askin was a member of St. John's, as was Angus Mackintosh, another wealthy fur trader with Detroit ties.[40] All the Denisons are believed to have found employment in the homes of Askin, Mackintosh, and others. Peter was listed as Angus Mackintosh's "Negro servant" at the time of his death.[41]

The Detroit-Sandwich circle of elites who assisted the Denisons can be understood as an early formation of the Underground Railroad in the frontier era—a transnational network of freedom-seekers and accomplices operating on one or both sides of the river. The conspiracy that spirited the Denisons across the Detroit River illuminates a moment in the evolution of this clandestine network that can be traced back to the days of the French regime, when the Railroad was largely self-propelled and mostly, but not entirely, executed by freedom-seekers alone, fleeing *from* the Canadian shore to freedom in frontier Detroit.[42] Additionally, the experiences of the Denisons and other early freedom-seekers both to and from Upper Canada, such as William Kenny, the runaway mentioned above who escaped from Alexander McKee in 1795; Jane and Joseph, who fled from Amherstburg owner Matthew Elliott to Detroit in 1807; Ben and Daniel, who were rescued from a vessel anchored in the Detroit River by a group of Detroit and Upper Canadian Blacks in 1828, as discussed in chapter 2 of this volume,[43] and others suggest that early freedom-seekers could indeed rely on conspiratorial assistance from others.

Much contemporary discourse defines such assistance as an essential component of Underground Railroad activity. However, twentieth-century scholars, lacking knowledge of the identities of these anonymous co-conspirators in early escapes, missed their very presence. As a result, many eighteenth- and early nineteenth-century escapes have been excluded from twentieth-century conceptions of the Underground Railroad. Historian Keith Griffler contends that the traditional understanding of the Underground Railroad, focusing on "conductors, the routes they staffed and the numbers of fugitives they . . . aided," is a flawed approach that has yet to be overcome within the scholarly literature on the subject. Griffler insists there is a need for new "explanatory frameworks that differentiate the Underground Railroad into its parts and that thoroughly investigate the context in which the Underground Railroad existed."[44] Griffler also contends that the interpretation of the Underground Railroad changes if it is approached chronologically.

In his landmark 1961 study of the Underground Railroad, now more than half a century old, Larry Gara cautioned against the imprecise "time-setting" that places the Underground Railroad in a pre–Civil War setting without regard for the actual years involved.[45] In their volume *Runaway Slaves: Rebels on the Plantation* (1999), John Hope Franklin and Loren Schweninger approached their research on runaways chronologically. They compared runaway ads from an early period (1790–1816) and a late period (1838–60). Using their chronological heuristic, Franklin and Schweninger found several contrasting institutional features of slavery and of runaways between the two periods. One major contrast relevant to this discussion involved runaways' destinations. Contrary to conventional ideas about the Underground Railroad's northern terminus, Franklin and Schweninger found that most slaveholders in the early period—January 1812 to December 1816—"believed their slaves were moving south." The authors concluded: "It is clear that the so-called Promised Land to the north held only limited attraction for runaways whose owners advertised in the *Nashville Whig* during these early years. Indeed slaves were more likely to head for the Missouri Territory, Mississippi Territory or the Indian Nations than Ohio. In the early period, about one out of four runaways advertised in the *Whig* were thought to be going to another southern state; in the later period this dropped to one out of ten."[46] Escapes from slavery in the Detroit River borderland during the frontier era also contradict contemporary notions of Underground Railroad flights as one-way, one-directional journeys heading north.

To heed Griffler's caution to differentiate the Underground Railroad into its parts and thoroughly examine the historical context in which it existed, the chronology of Detroit River escapes must be systematically charted, and legal and jurisdictional shifts pertaining to the Detroit River region should be factored in as context. Griffler's approach applied to the Denisons' flight and other frontier-era Detroit escapes mentioned briefly here (and elaborated in chapter 2) makes a case for an earlier horizon than the antebellum decades for the Underground Railroad's emergence.

Review and systematic study of the earliest known escapes may also reveal new insights about the agency, forethought, and conspiracy that enabled Blacks to flee from bondage in the Detroit River borderland. Placed within the analytical framework that Griffler proposes, the case of Sandwich attorney James Woods and his freedom-bound servants discloses new insights. In a letter to Detroit attorney Solomon Sibley written May 14, 1807, Woods sought legal advice on how to recover his servants, a woman and her four-year-old son. "The woman," Woods wrote, "deserted from my house in the night of the 13th inst., taking with her the child who is aged about four years together with her trunks, etc, & has gone to Detroit."[47]

Most early fugitive cases such as Woods's enter the historical record as a legal petition, a personal letter, or a newspaper ad written by the slaveholder. In these early documents, slaveholders represented themselves as betrayed victims and represented runaways as naïve recruits. For example, although the Denisons' intentions were clear from their pleadings in court, one early history insisted that the Denisons were "enticed" from the Tucker farm.[48] Focusing more intentionally on each runaway's actions both during and prior to escape, however briefly mentioned in these early accounts, might enable scholars to notice freedom-seekers' forethought and agency and to recognize the presence of anonymous co-conspirators.

In the Woods case, for example, James Woods's question to Solomon Sibley in Detroit indicates Woods's certainty that his servant had accomplices: "Would trespass . . . lie against the mother, & *others who assisted her* in carrying off the boy against my will? Or would Trespass . . . lie against the mother and *those who assisted her*, for carrying off her trunk with property therein belonging to me?"[49] Woods's knowledge of the capacities of mother and son must have assured him that his servant could not have trudged to the riverbank in the dark of night managing a four-year-old, a trunk, and a boat by herself.

The virtual presence of anonymous accomplices in documents describing early escapes to and from Detroit should modify our understanding of these escapes and initiate their classification as Underground Railroad conspiracies. Careful study of evidence from such early cases, including the Denison case, could compel the establishment of an earlier horizon for the emergence of the Underground Railroad throughout the nation, and particularly in the Detroit River region. Within this analytic frame, it is impossible to miss Griffler's most substantial point: "The Underground Railroad did not organize the flight from slavery, but was organized by it."[50]

Neither Peter Denison nor his wife or children could read or write, so what is known about their petition for and pursuit of freedom comes from what others recorded about them. Yet placed within the context of contradictory borderland law and international disputes between border nations and among border zone residents, the Denisons' escape to Upper Canada strongly implies advance planning between themselves and co-conspirators on both sides of the river. The Denisons' actions also reveal their agency and their political aspirations as derived from a profound understanding of geopolitics in the Detroit River border zone.

At St. John's Anglican Church in Sandwich, the Reverend Richard Pollard recorded the names of Denisons who sponsored religious rites for family members from 1808 through 1817. St. John's Registry documents that "Peter and Hannah Donnison Adults, free Negroes" were baptized at St. John's on October 9, 1808, one year after their disappearance from Detroit. On August 28, 1812, Reverend Pollard entered the following in the registry: "Peter Dennison, a Negro servant of Angus Mackintosh, Esq. departed this life August 27, 1812 and was buried by me the day following."[51] Peter Denison's parentage and place and date of birth are unknown, so it is possible that he was an elderly man in 1807 when he renounced his newly acquired American citizenship and crossed the river to secure his children's freedom. Five years after his daring gambit, he was laid to rest in Upper Canada, his adopted land.

The Denison children remained in Upper Canada for at least a decade after their flight from Detroit, as St. John's Church Registry documents.[52] Their favorable political status as British subjects enabled them to live productive lives, as did thousands of American Blacks who exchanged subaltern status in America for freedom and full civil rights in colonial Canada. One of the Denison siblings, Elizabeth, known as "Lisette," left an indelible footprint in history. Over her lifetime she accumulated a small fortune, which she shared with her family and community.

Lisette's most enduring legacy was a chapel erected on the Detroit River island of Grosse Ile, built with assets left in her estate for that purpose.[53] Upper Canadian residency, with its grant of civil rights supporting a respected social identity, must have fostered Lisette's independence and prosperity—her entrepreneurial aspirations, her intercultural curiosity, her noble philanthropy, and her extraordinary dignity. Many Blacks living in frontier America achieved similar legacies. Frontier borderlands held a liberating potential for most people, and for Blacks especially. Many took advantage of opportunities available in frontier life, which enabled them to escape the legal chains of slavery and evade the psychic and social injuries resulting from denied political and human rights, as these denials were more strictly enforced in emerging cities and towns.[54]

The voices of Blacks who sought freedom in Canada came to prominence in the antebellum period. Both popular and scholarly discourse on the Underground Railroad have drawn heavily on those voices as well as on reminiscences from the post–Civil War period.[55] However, these latter-day voices must be juxtaposed with accounts of early escapes written by "victimized" slave owners. In addition, studied attention to Underground Railroad chronology and legal-political context may yield new insights about freedom-seekers' agency, the presence of co-conspirators, and the nature of their assistance—in sum, the structure of Underground Railroad activity in its infancy.

Repeated successful attempts by enslaved black Canadians to gain freedom in the United States and, inversely, by enslaved U.S. Blacks to gain freedom in Canada provide ample evidence that transnational Underground Railroad activity enacted by men and women on both sides of the Detroit River predates the antebellum decades. It was this insistent flow of Blacks seeking freedom and political recognition that launched what by the 1830s would come to be called the "Underground Railroad."

Many unnamed and understudied freedom-seekers and anonymous co-conspirators initiated a formidable line of resistance to U.S. laws that permanently assigned Blacks the subaltern status of "stateless" noncitizen slaves. From Griffler's perspective and the perspective of this volume, it was the extraordinary efforts of these freedom-seekers, from both sides of the Detroit River and from periods not typically associated with what is now considered the Underground Railroad era, that compel popular and scholarly revision and reinterpretation.[56] The Underground Railroad that freedom-seekers devised for themselves well before the antebellum period is finally becoming visible. Very early treks, many of which *began* rather than ended in Canada, provided essential inspiration and impetus for what ultimately became a transnational Underground Railroad migration along the Detroit River, a movement that continues to capture our imagination.

NOTES

1. Persons of indigenous Native and European ancestry were called Métis from the French construct of *métissage*, meaning French-Native marriage and French adaptation to and adoption of Native culture. Jeremy Adelman and Stephen Aron, "From Borderlands to Borders: Empires, Nation-States, and the Peoples in between in North American History," *American Historical Review* 104, no. 3 (1999), 819; John J. Bukowczyk, "Trade, War, Migration and Empire in the Great Lakes Basin, 1650–1850," in John J. Bukowczyk, Nora Faires, David

R. Smith, and Randy W. Widdis, *Permeable Border: The Great Lakes Region as Transnational Border, 1650–1990* (Calgary, AB: University of Calgary Press, 2005), 18.
2. Daniel G. Hill, *The Freedom-Seekers: Blacks in Early Canada* (1982; repr., Toronto: Stoddard, 1992), 7.
3. William Renwick Riddell, "Slavery in Michigan in the Early Part of the Nineteenth Century as Shown in Court Records," *Michigan Law Review* 1 (1935), 33; H. Palmer Westgate, *St. John's Church Sandwich, Windsor, Ontario: The Beginnings of the Anglican Church in the Western District, 1802–1952; A Goodly Heritage,* 2nd ed. (Windsor, ON: privately published, 1952), 8.
4. The Clergy Endowments (Canada) Act, 1791 (31 Geo. III, c. 31) is usually referred to as the Constitutional Act of 1791.
5. William W. Blume, *Transactions of the Supreme Court of the Territory of Michigan, 1805–1814* (Ann Arbor: University of Michigan Press, 1935), 1:135.
6. When Upper Canada's Lieutenant Governor Peter Hunter died in 1805, Alexander Grant was appointed to replace him temporarily. During his entire time as acting lieutenant governor, Grant resided at his home in Detroit in what is today Grosse Pointe Farms. See R. Alan Douglas, *Uppermost Canada: The Western District and the Detroit Frontier, 1800–1850* (Detroit: Wayne State University Press, 2001), 21, 66; Blume, *Transactions of the Supreme Court of the Territory of Michigan,* 390; Hill, *The Freedom-Seekers,* 13.
7. An Act to Prevent the Further Introduction of Slaves and to Limit the Term of Contracts for Servitude within This Province, 33 Geo. III, c. 7 (Upper Canada), passed July 9, 1793.
8. An Act to Prevent the Further Introduction of Slaves and to Limit the Term of Contracts for Servitude within This Province, 33 Geo. III, c. 7 (Upper Canada), passed July 9, 1793.
9. William Renwick Riddell, "Upper Canada, Early Period," *Journal of Negro History* 5, no. 3 (1920), 324.
10. Colin G. Calloway, *The Scratch of a Pen: 1763 and the Transformation of North America* (New York: Oxford University Press, 2006).
11. Calloway, *The Scratch of a Pen,* 100, 169.
12. The Western Confederacy of tribes defeated at Fallen Timbers included representatives of the Wyandot, Delaware, Shawnee, Ottawa, Chippewa, Pottawatomi, Miami, Wea, Kickapoo, and Kaskaskia tribes. Douglas, *Uppermost Canada,* 62.
13. The Western Confederacy of Indians ceded land in a large swath of Ohio Territory, which included most of Ohio and parts of Michigan, Indiana, and Illinois, including the future site of Chicago. Douglas, *Uppermost Canada,* 62.
14. A term referring to Native people's political status after U.S.–British Canada border enforcement used by Bukowczyk in "Trade, War, Migration and Empire in the Great Lakes Basin," 27.
15. "Through Pontiac's War [and the Revolutionary War], William Tucker was employed as interpreter by English officers in their intercourse with the Indians. His ability to speak the language of the various tribes made his services of importance.... Tucker had chiefly engaged in trading expeditions among the Indians, at times simply acting as interpreter for other traders." *The History of Macomb County, Michigan* (Chicago: M. A. Leeson, 1882), 232–34.
16. Robert F. Eldredge, *Past and Present of Macomb County, Michigan Together with Biographical Sketches of Many of Its Leading and Prominent Citizens and Illustrious Dead* (Chicago: S. J. Clark, 1905), 625–27; *The History of Macomb County, Michigan,* 232–36.

17. "At the close of the War, Mr. Tucker settled upon the north bank of the Huron River on this land deeded to him by the Indians and built a large double house of hewn logs, one and one-half stories high, and at once commenced the clearing up and cultivation of the farm." Eldredge, *Past and Present of Macomb County*, 627.
18. Norman McRae, "Blacks in Detroit, 1736–1833: The Search for Freedom and Community and Its Implications for Educators" (PhD diss., University of Michigan, 1982), 66; W. James Ellison, "*Denison et al v Tucker:* Judicial Abolition of Slavery in the Territory of Michigan" (unpublished MS, University of Michigan Law School, May 1976), 28.
19. "Tucker Family History" (unpublished genealogy notes, n.d.), Local History File on William Tucker, Mt. Clemens, Michigan, Public Library.
20. Edward Tucker, "Account Given by Edward Tucker at His Own House in 1852," *Michigan Pioneer Collections* 6 (1884), 361.
21. Elizabeth's biographer wrote, "As a child Lisette learned to speak the Indian language and is said to have acted as an interpreter occasionally." Isabella Swan, *Lisette* (Grosse Ile, MI: I. E. Swan, 1965), 5.
22. Manuscript will of William Tucker, March 2, 1805, Wayne County Probate File 50, Local History File on William Tucker, Mt. Clemens, Michigan, Public Library.
23. Reginald Larrie, *Makin' Free: African Americans in the Northwest Territory* (Detroit: Blaine Ethridge, 1981), 6–8; Ellison, "*Denison et al v Tucker,*" 15.
24. Friend Palmer, *Early Days in Detroit: Papers Written by General Friend Palmer of Detroit, Being his Personal Reminiscences of Important Events and Descriptions of the City for over Eighty Years* (Detroit: Hunt & June, 1906), 26.
25. Douglas, *Uppermost Canada*, 18, 28.
26. Milo M. Quaife, *John Askin Papers*, vol. 2, *1796–1820* (Detroit: Detroit Library Commission, 1931), johnaskin.umdl.umich.edu/AAY8775.0002.001 (accessed June–July 2005).
27. Augustus B. Woodward, "Report and Resolutions to the Sundry Committee of the Michigan Territorial Legislature," *Michigan Historical Collections* 12 (1888), 462–63.
28. 1807 WL 1109 (Mich. Terr.), (1 Blume Sup. Ct. Trans. 319).
29. Ellison, "*Denison et al v Tucker,*" 25; Jerome Nadelhaft, "The Somersett Case and Slavery: Myth, Reality, and Repercussions," *Journal of Negro History* 51, no. 3 (1966): 193–208.
30. Nadelhaft, "The Somersett Case and Slavery," 194–96.
31. Ellison, "*Denison et al v Tucker,*" 22.
32. Ellison, "*Denison et al v Tucker,*" 22.
33. Ellison, "*Denison et al v Tucker,*" 37–39.
34. "Opinions of Judge Woodward Relative to the Subject of Slavery," *Michigan Historical Collections* 12 (1888): 511–19.
35. Frank B. Woodford, *Mr. Jefferson's Disciple: A Life of Justice Woodward* (East Lansing: Michigan State University, 1953), 87.
36. 1807 WL 1109 (Mich. Terr.), (1 Blume Sup. Ct. Trans. 319).
37. David Katzman, "Black Slavery in Michigan," *American Midcontinent Studies Journal* 11, no. 2 (1970): 56–66.
38. Swan, *Lisette*, 8; Blume, *Transactions of the Supreme Court of the Territory of Michigan*, 87.

39. Warren Parker, "Early History of Macomb County," *Michigan Historical Collections* 18 (1892), 489.
40. Rev. Richard Pollard to John Askin, August 6, 1807, in Westgate, *St. John's Church*, 12; Rev. Richard Pollard to John Askin, August 10, 1807, in Quaife, *John Askin Papers*, 564–64; Vestry Minutes, St. John's Anglican Church, March 23, 1807, in Westgate, *St. John's Church*, 30.
41. Register of St. John's Anglican Church, University of Windsor Archives, 30.
42. Afua Cooper, *The Hanging of Angelique: The Untold Story of Canadian Slavery and the Burning of Old Montreal* (Toronto: HarperCollins, 2006), 70.
43. David G. Chardavoyne, "Michigan and the Fugitive Slave Acts," *The Court Legacy* (Historical Society for the United States District Court for the Eastern District of Michigan newsletter) 12, no. 3 (2004): 1–11, 3; Karolyn Smardz Frost, *I've Got a Home in Glory Land: A Lost Tale of the Underground Railroad* (New York: Farrar, Straus & Giroux, 2007; Toronto: Thomas Allen, 2007), 157–58.
44. Keith P. Griffler, *Front Line of Freedom: African Americans and the Forging of the Underground Railroad in the Ohio Valley* (Lexington: University of Kentucky Press, 2004), xii.
45. Larry Gara, *The Liberty Line: The Legend of the Underground Railroad* (Lexington: University of Kentucky Press, 1961), 8–9.
46. John Hope Franklin and Loren Schweninger, *Runaway Slaves: Rebels on the Plantation* (New York: Oxford University Press, 1999), 120–22.
47. James Woods to Solomon Sibley, May 14, 1807, Solomon Sibley Papers, Burton Historical Collection, Detroit Public Library.
48. Parker, "Early History of Macomb County," 489.
49. Woods to Sibley, May 14, 1807; my emphasis.
50. Griffler, *Front Line of Freedom*, 79.
51. Register of St. John's Anglican Church, 15, 30.
52. St. John's registry records the Denison children, including Lisette, as witnesses and sponsors of family religious ceremonies through 1817.
53. The fourth item in Lisette's 1860 will states: "Having long felt the inadequacy of the provisions made for the poor in our houses of worship, and knowing from sad experience that many devout believers, and humble followers of the lowly Jesus, are excluded from those courts, where the rich and the poor should meet together, shut out from those holy services by the mammon of unrighteousness, from that very church which declares the widow's mite to be more acceptable in the sight of the Lord than the careless offerings of those who give of their 'abundance' and wishing to do all in my power as far as God has given me the means to offer the poor man and the stranger 'wine and milk without price and without cost'; I therefore now give and bequeath to William S. Biddle ... the rest of my estate ... to be used in the erection of a Fine Chapel for the use of the Protestant Episcopal Church." (Swan, *Lisette*, 52).
54. Max L. Grivno, "'Black Frenchmen' and 'White Settlers': Race, Slavery and the Creation of African–American Identities along the Northwest Frontier, 1790–1840," *Slavery & Abolition* 21, no. 3 (2000): 75–93; Margaret Washington, "African American History and the Frontier Thesis," *Journal of the Early Republic* 13, no. 2 (1993): 230–41; Juliet E. K. Walker, *Free Frank: A Black Pioneer on the Antebellum Frontier* (Lexington: University of Kentucky Press, 1983).

55. Wilbur H. Seibert, *The Underground Railroad From Slavery to Freedom* (New York: Macmillan, 1898); Griffler discusses the romantic, self-promoting, and frequently partial narratives Seibert compiled about Underground Railroad activity from oral accounts given by activists in their old age and from their descendants. *Front Line of Freedom,* 2–4, 8–9.

56. In a recent *Journal of American History* article, Gregory Wigmore documents several cases of runaways from British Canada to Detroit during the frontier period. As Wigmore's title, "Before the Railroad," asserts, he does not include these escapes as Underground Railroad events. (Gregory Wigmore, "Before the Railroad: From Slavery to Freedom in the Canadian-American Borderland," *Journal of American History* 98, no. 2 [2011]: 437–54.) Wigmore thus reinscribes popular conceptions of the Underground Railroad first provided by Wilbur Siebert in 1898. Siebert constructed a popular image of the Underground Railroad based on the railroad industry's use of "stations," "station keepers," "conductors," "tunnels," "lines," "maps," "passengers," etc. In such popular conceptions, according to Keith Griffler, "[T]he ["Underground"] part of the name [Underground Railroad] is all but ignored. And yet it is solely this part that remains true to the nature of the institution described, perhaps the closest to an underground resistance movement that ever took root in American soil" (to which Canadian soil must also be added). *Front Line of Freedom,* 4–5.

TWO

FORGING TRANSNATIONAL NETWORKS FOR FREEDOM

From the War of 1812 to the Blackburn Riots of 1833

KAROLYN SMARDZ FROST

Dr. Norman McRae Jr., the late eminent historian of the city of Detroit, published an article titled "Crossing the Detroit River to Find Freedom" in the spring 1983 issue of *Michigan History*.[1] It detailed events surrounding the Blackburn Riots of 1833. The violent rescue of freedom-seekers Thornton and Lucie Blackburn* from Kentucky slavecatchers threw into high relief the promise of liberty that traversing the Detroit River into Canada held for African Americans at the dawn of the antebellum period. The quest for freedom in the colonial and Revolutionary War eras had sometimes directed the waterborne trajectories of Blacks living in Upper Canada toward, rather than away from, the Michigan shore, as Veta Tucker's work in chapter 1 of this volume shows.[2] The watershed in this two-way traffic was the War of 1812; after that conflict, cross-border migration generally moved in the direction of Upper Canada, as black Americans took the opportunity to cross over the Detroit River "to find freedom" in what remained of British North America.

This chapter traces the joint history of African Americans and African Canadians in the Detroit River borderlands from the end of the eighteenth century through the 1830s. It

---

* Mrs. Blackburn's name in slavery was "Ruthie" or "Rutha." However, she took the name Lucie after she found freedom, and never used her slave name again. Hence it is by her chosen name that she is identified here.

includes the evolution of the very different legislation pertaining to slavery that applied in Michigan Territory and Upper Canada, and seeks to explain the post–War of 1812 increase in escaped bondspeople trying to traverse the Detroit River boundary. This study then explores early black networks in the borderland region, outlining two incidents in which Blacks on both sides of the Detroit River cooperated to prevent freedom-seekers captured in Michigan being returned to slavery. Forged of blood, friendship, faith, and common cause, these links would be maintained for generations, greatly facilitating the establishment of formal Underground Railroad networks. By the mid-1830s, the Detroit River would be the busiest transit point for freedom-seekers along the entire Canada-U.S. border.

SLAVERY AND FREEDOM IN THE DETROIT RIVER BORDERLAND

At the turn of the nineteenth century, most black people living in this liminal region were enslaved. They came from diverse backgrounds and had vastly different experiences. A tiny minority were free, including Black Loyalists who had been rewarded with their liberty, and a few of those with land grants, by British officials in return for military service in the Revolutionary War. It is estimated that by 1800 there were about 700 African-descended men, women, and children, enslaved and free, in Upper Canada. North American census figures are notoriously inaccurate for people of African origin but suggest that there were 139 Blacks in all of Michigan in the same year.[3] Three decades later, however, only a tiny proportion of Michigan and Upper Canada's black populations remained enslaved. By 1830 the nucleus of a small free African American community had been established in Detroit. This was composed of longtime black residents and increasing numbers of newcomers. Black immigration was facilitated by the introduction of steamboat service on Lake Erie in 1818 and, after 1825, by the completion of the Erie Canal, which eased travel from the eastern United States to the Detroit River region.

There were clear ties between the nascent Detroit black community and settlements of free people on the Canadian side of the border. Some residents of this borderland region had once been enslaved by First Nations, French, or British owners, and others by United Empire Loyalists after the Revolutionary War. The latter had been permitted by the Imperial Act of 1790 (30 Geo. III, c. 27) to import their movable property into the British colonies, including their African American and *panis* (Native American) "servants." A number of enslaved people had also been carried across the river into Upper Canada by their Loyalist owners when Detroit was finally handed over to the United States in 1796 in accordance with Jay's Treaty (1794).[4] These new Upper Canadians settled along the Detroit River shore at Sandwich, capital of the Western District of Upper Canada; Amherstburg, which grew up around the British fort near the southern end of the river;[5] and also further inland.[6] In fact, so many people chose to cross over into Upper Canada at this time that Detroit's population plummeted to an all-time low of five hundred persons. Among those who left were some of Detroit's wealthiest and most prominent merchant families. Often of mixed Native, French, and sometimes British ancestry, they maintained strong business connections with Michigan even after moving to Upper Canada, continuing to trade in furs and other commodities within the Detroit River borderlands and beyond. These families were much intermarried, and their enslaved servants were equally linked to relatives, friends, and former neighbors at Detroit and all along that American shore.[7]

The significance of the Detroit River boundary in respect to black transnationalism in this period rested on two very different pieces of legislation, both passed in 1793, one in the United States and the other in Upper Canada. Since 1787, the Northwest Ordinance had prohibited American slavery north of the Ohio River. However, most slaveholders had interpreted this to mean that, although no further enslaved individuals could be imported, they could retain their existing human "property."[8] Then in 1793 the U.S. Congress passed the Fugitive Slave Law. This empowered slaveholders and their agents to seek out "fugitives from labor" anywhere in the United States and its territories. Should the accused be unable to provide iron-clad legal proof of free status, "it shall be the duty of such Judge or magistrate to give a certificate thereof to such claimant, his agent, or attorney, which shall be sufficient warrant for removing the said fugitive from labor to the State or Territory from which he or she fled."[9] The law also set the penalty for assisting a freedom-seeker or for knowingly impeding his or her arrest at the extremely large fine of $500, plus up to a year in prison. This opened the door for slavecatchers—bounty hunters specializing in slave recapture—to pursue their highly lucrative calling. They stationed themselves first along the Ohio River, the boundary between slave soil and free in the western districts of the United States, and were regularly seen in the Great Lakes Basin and at crossing points along the Detroit and Niagara rivers. Some even had the temerity to kidnap former American slaves from the British provinces.[10]

In Upper Canada, Lieutenant Governor John Graves Simcoe's landmark legislation of 1793 established Upper Canada as a place where African American freedom-seekers might go. A veteran officer of the British forces in the American Revolution who had fought alongside Black Loyalist troops, Simcoe was determined to abolish slavery in the new province. However, he was unable to secure enough votes since several members of his Executive Council owned slaves. Then two Revolutionary War veterans, Black Loyalist Peter Martin and his white associate William Grisley, witnessed a slave woman named Chloe Cooley being dragged, bound and gagged, to a small boat at Queenston. She struggled fiercely as her owner, one Adam Vrooman, carried her across the Niagara River to be sold into upstate New York. The resistance of Chloe Cooley turned the tide, for when Martin and Grisley reported the affair to Simcoe in the presence of Chief Justice William Osgoode, Attorney General John White was instructed to draft a new abolition law.[11]

The law, the Act to Prevent the Further Introduction of Slaves and to Limit the Term of Contracts for Servitude within This Province, prohibited further slave importation but, famously, freed not a single Upper Canadian slave. It was, however, cleverly framed: children of enslaved mothers were to be freed at age twenty-five, and offspring of mothers serving twenty-five-year terms were thereafter considered born free. Owners of enslaved mothers were required to maintain the women's children with "proper nourishment and cloathing" to the age of twenty-five, and their grandchildren as well until the third generation reached the age of twenty-five.[12] This made holding slaves in Upper Canada quite expensive, while the long cold winters limited people's productivity. It also meant that African American refugees from bondage were henceforth considered free as soon as they reached Upper Canadian soil.

Sadly, the new law did not prevent slaveholders from selling their human property to other jurisdictions. An unknown number were transported across the border into the United States and sold away. Still, coupled with the marked disapproval of a series of Crown-appointed lieutenant governors who followed Simcoe in the office and who were sensitive to mounting antislavery feeling in the British Isles, the act meant that the institution's days were numbered in Upper Canada. The brave service of many African Canadians during the War of 1812 effectively ended slavery in the province. There were, however, an unfortunate few who remained in forced servitude until the British government abolished the institution throughout the Empire in 1833, effective August 1st, 1834. Still, slavery was such a small part of the economy that Upper Canadian slaveholders were not accorded compensation in the 20 million–pound fund set aside for slave owners in the West Indies.[13]

THE WAR OF 1812 AND THE UNDERGROUND RAILROAD

The War of 1812 publicized the fact that enslaved African Americans might gain their freedom simply by crossing the border into British North America. When U.S. President James Madison declared war on Great Britain in June 1812, black Canadians, many of them born in the United States, were afraid that an American conquest of Canada would mean the reintroduction of slavery. Led by a sixty-eight-year-old African-born Black Loyalist named Richard Pierpoint, Niagara Blacks petitioned to participate in the defense of Upper Canada. Initially they were rebuffed. However, the British army was tied up in Europe fighting the Napoleonic Wars and there were no more than twelve hundred regular troops in Upper Canada. In the first month of the war General William Hull, who commanded at Detroit, traversed the river and occupied Sandwich, Upper Canada. Hull soon withdrew his troops when they came under withering fire as they advanced toward Fort Amherstburg and the Americans returned to fortified Detroit. The brilliant combined strategies of General Sir Isaac Brock and Britain's ally the Shawnee Chief Tecumseh then tricked General Hull into surrendering to a much smaller force. Detroit would remain in British hands for the next year. But more soldiers were desperately needed as all of Upper Canada prepared for war, from Canada's Maritime provinces to the Detroit River. It would be up to the few companies of regulars stationed in the Canadian provinces bolstered by the loyal militia to defend British North America. The government reconsidered its position on enlisting Blacks.

The famous Colored Corps was therefore formed at Niagara. Its ranks were filled out with African Canadian volunteers transferred from the York (Toronto) militia. Black soldiers fought bravely at Queenston Heights on the Niagara River, where General Brock was killed. Black troops also supported the offensive at Stoney Creek, defended Fort George at Newark (the modern Niagara-on-the-Lake) and, transformed into a corps of "artificers" (military engineers), constructed Fort Mississauga at the mouth of the Niagara River. Other African Canadians enlisted alongside their white neighbors in the Glengarry Fencibles, and at least one man, a regimental drummer, took part in an epic winter march from New Brunswick to Upper Canada with the 104th Regiment of Foot. Some British regiments employed black men as "Ethiopian musicians" who dressed in exotic clothing and played for military events; however, they were also regularly trained soldiers who fought in battle alongside their white comrades.[14] At sea and on the Great Lakes, at least 15 percent of the sailors in both the American

> ## *GLORIOUS NEWS!!!*
>
> *York, Auguſt 20, 1812.*
>
> Deſpatches have juſt now arrived from General Brock, dated Detroit Auguſt 17th 1812, ſtating that he took poſſeſſion of that important Poſt on the 16th without the ſacrifice of a drop of Britiſh blood.
>
> Every individual, together with their General, was animated with the moſt glorious ſpirit. Upwards of 2,500 Troops have ſurrendered priſoners of War, and about 25 pieces of Ordnance have been taken.
>
> Thus it hath pleaſed Providence to crown his Majeſty's Arms with an early and important Victory.

Broadside published at York (Toronto) announcing the surrender of Detroit to British forces on August 20, 1812. (Courtesy of the Toronto Public Library)

and British navies were black,[15] and African Canadians manned privateers out of Halifax and Liverpool harbors in Nova Scotia.[16]

During the War of 1812, the enslaved personal servants of Kentucky- and Virginia-born owners also participated in the invasion of Upper Canada. These men appear on the muster rolls of several companies, their slave status evident in the fact that they are designated only by their first names.[17] Invading militiamen and regulars were commanded by future American president, William Henry Harrison. They penetrated far into the province, surprised to discover black men fighting as soldiers in the combined British Canadian and First Nations forces arrayed against them.[18] Kentucky officers who traveled with their African American "servants" commanded American troops in a series of battles, including the Battle of the Thames, where the Shawnee ally of the British, Chief Tecumseh, was killed on October 5, 1813.[19]

Harrison's troops subsequently patrolled the southwestern part of the province, foraging for food and rooting out dissent. After the War of 1812, returning American soldiers described their encounters in Canada with uniformed black men, a factor that some historians have suggested accounted for the postwar influx of American fugitive slaves to Upper Canada. But it seems more likely that it was the American officers' enslaved servants who broadcast the fact that those in bondage had only to make their way to British North America in order to find freedom. It must be left to speculation how many of the same "servants" who had been brought to Upper Canada with the invading troops later found occasion to slip away and cross back over the border in their own quest for freedom. After all, they knew the way.

By whatever manner the news was spread, it was not long after the war ended that increasing numbers of American refugees arrived at the border on their way to Upper Canada. Most crossed into British North America by way of the Detroit and Niagara Rivers and on ships that plied the Great Lakes. By 1819, a substantial community had grown up on the Canadian side of the river at Amherstburg, LaSalle, and Sandwich as well as the Lake St. Clair and Lake Erie shores. In this recently contested borderland, black Americans and black Canadians worked in concert to help freedom-seekers, first to traverse the river in safety and then to establish themselves in their new British colonial homeland. As early as 1813, Detroit Blacks had already been accused of harboring fugitive Southern slaves, and a letter survives by one "L. Beckwith, of Belleview [plantation; no state given]" to this effect.[20] An early biography of abolitionist publisher and Liberty Party candidate James G. Birney, a Kentuckian and former slaveholder himself, maintained that "one group of abolition-minded Presbyterians in southern Ohio had aided over a thousand fugitive slaves to reach Canada before 1817."[21] By the 1830s, those who provided such assistance would borrow the terminology of the latest technological advance of the age—the steam train—as their coded language, calling themselves "conductors" helping "passengers" on an "Underground Railway."

The Detroit black community had been very small when the war broke out in 1812; the 1810 Census of the United States showed only 96 non-Europeans, 17 of whom were enslaved African Americans, in a total population of 1,650. Yet it was evidently substantial enough to attract missionary efforts. On March 2, 1811, Moravian missionaries at Fairfield in Upper Canada reported hosting a Baltimore-based Methodist minister who had been preaching to Blacks in Detroit for a period of some five months.[22] Another African American "exhorter" visited the city in 1816.[23]

American slaveholders were not at all sanguine about the fact that so much of their valuable "property" was absconding to the neighboring British colony. A long series of diplomatic incidents ensued, as Bryan Prince discusses in chapter 3. For the earliest freedom-seekers, their liberty was confirmed by a legal decision made in 1819 by Upper Canada's youthful Attorney General John Beverley Robinson.[24] When fugitives were discovered at Amherstburg in that year, the American Secretary of State requested permission for American slave owners to enter the province, presumably by way of Detroit, to retrieve them. Attorney General Robinson advised Lieutenant Governor Sir Peregrine Maitland that "whatever may have been the condition of... Negroes in the Country to which they formerly belonged, here they are free—For the enjoyment of all civil rights consequent to a mere residence in the country and among them the right to personal freedom as acknowledged and protected by the Laws of England."[25]

Attorney General Robinson was following Lord Mansfield's landmark decision of 1772 in the British case of *Somerset v. Stewart*. As discussed in chapter 1, a slave brought to Britain by his Virginian owner had fled; captured, he was imprisoned on a ship in the Thames River pending being taken to Jamaica for sale. When James Somerset's removal from Britain was challenged by abolitionist attorneys, Mansfield ruled that slavery was so "odious" that only positive law could support it: as British law did not actually have a formal piece of legislation spelling out the conditions of enslavement, Somerset's imprisonment was deemed illegal and he was freed.[26]

There were perhaps fourteen thousand enslaved Blacks in Great Britain when the case came to trial. Lord Mansfield's decision horrified Parliamentarians representing West Indian and British slave-trading interests. However, the ruling only prohibited the removal of slaves from Britain for sale and did not actually free British slaves, who continued to be bought and sold. It certainly did not apply to Britain's colonies (else it would have manifestly altered the situation in the sugar islands of the West Indies), but Upper Canada's Attorney General invoked it nevertheless. John Beverley Robinson had a warning for the Americans, too. He said that any attempt to infringe upon the personal liberty of a fugitive who had reached the soil of British North America would be harshly dealt with in Upper Canadian courts. Since Robinson was Attorney General and later Chief Justice of Upper Canada (and of Canada West, as the province was called after the Act of Union went into effect on February 10, 1841) for very nearly the entire period leading up to the American Civil War, his ruling was never challenged. The way was cleared for American fugitives from slavery to find a safe haven in Canada, and an estimated thirty thousand of them would do so before 1865.[27]

Kentucky was, by far, the state from or through which most fugitives came to Upper Canada. So it was the most vocal in its protest of the welcome afforded the fugitives by Upper Canadian officials. In January 1821, Kentucky politician Henry Clay made a direct petition to Congress regarding the issue. He demanded that the U.S. government open negotiations with the British to force Upper Canada to return runaway slaves to their "rightful" owners. The British summarily rebuffed the overture. In 1826 Clay, now President John Quincy Adams's Secretary of State, again broached the subject of fugitive extradition to the British government. The pretext was the need for a formal treaty between the United States and Great Britain for "the mutual delivery of criminals, the subjects or citizens of either party, taking refuge within the dominions of the other." But the real reason for Clay's insistence was clear: "[Slaves] escape, principally from Virginia and Kentucky to Upper Canada, whither they are pursued by those who are lawfully entitled to their labor; and, as there is no existing regulation by which they can be surrendered, the attempt to recapture them leads to disagreeable collisions."[28] As extradition agreements were formalized between British North America and the United States over the succeeding years, "disagreeable collisions" were inevitable. Fugitive slave cases were highly contentious, and each set a legal precedent. In a letter dated September 25, 1827, Henry Clay was informed that the British government would never "depart from the principle recognized by the British courts that every man is free who reaches British ground."[29]

In Territorial Michigan, there were local efforts to control African American mobility as well. In 1827 Assistant Marshall of the Michigan Territory Benjamin F. H. Witherell undertook a census of Detroit in which the free black population was enumerated at sixty-six people, of whom eighteen were children.[30] In that same year, a new *Code Noir*, or Black Code, was passed to discourage African American migration into Michigan from other states and territories. Yet it also provided for the prosecution of slavecatchers operating in Michigan Territory who kidnapped free African Americans for sale south. This suggests that, by 1827, slavecatchers were already entering the Territory in sufficient numbers to require some prohibition against their activities, for the new law detailed penalties. An Act to Regulate Blacks and Mulattos and to Punish the Kidnapping of Such Persons required that each incoming Black had to present a "certificate of freedom" and pay a $500 bond to ensure "good behavior." Anyone assisting fugitive slaves in evading their "rightful" owners or their agents, or who was convicted of obstructing their arrest, would incur heavy fines.[31] There is no evidence the law was regularly enforced, perhaps owing, as one author maintains, to its lack of general acceptance among the white populace.[32] However, a fugitive slave notice for an accomplished coachman named Hamlet from Baltimore, Maryland, was posted by his erstwhile owner in the *Detroit Gazette* as late as April 17, 1827.[33]

The occasion for Attorney General Henry Clay's 1821 query had been the discovery of African American freedom-seekers at Fort Malden and in the town of Amherstburg, located about fourteen miles south of Detroit.[34] The British fort had been constructed at the former location of the destroyed Fort Amherstburg. The adjacent town had gained a substantial population of Blacks in the decade immediately following the War of 1812, many of the families settling on lands given or sold them for a nominal fee by retired East India Company officer Captain Charles Stuart. Deeply antislavery in his convictions, Stuart transferred substantial amounts of his own thousand-acre land grant to incoming African American refugees.[35] Successful tobacco farmers, formerly enslaved men also worked in mining operations in nearby Anderdon Township and in harvesting whitefish commercially, a local industry that was just getting going at this period.[36]

Most slave escapes, of course, went undetected, or at least unprosecuted. The border was entirely porous as far as human passage over the river was concerned. The main concern of government officials was that customs duties be paid on incoming goods, a desire in which they were often frustrated. There was regular ferry service between Detroit and what today is Windsor, Ontario. Many trading families owned boats, so smuggling was rampant and indulged in by even the most respectable of local residents. Immigration restrictions on the passage of persons across the border were decades in the future, and travelers both black and white traversed the river at will.

By the 1820s an active black community had begun to coalesce in Detroit proper. Its members were engaged in a variety of entrepreneurial and service enterprises, including house painting, barbering, carting, and working on the docks and Detroit River boats. Women were engaged in household service, dressmaking, and taking in washing. It would not be until the early 1830s that there were sufficient numbers of black Detroiters to establish a church or to create the vigilant committees[37] and other organizations that would mount sustained political resistance to the dangers facing fugitive slaves.[38]

THE RESCUE OF BEN AND DANIEL, 1828–29

Regular intercourse between black settlements in Detroit and Upper Canada is suggested by later events, but these associations must have been established at a much earlier date than modern scholarship can reveal. Witness the apparently spontaneous rescue of a pair of runaways in 1828. Their plight drew the attention of Blacks from both sides of the river, suggesting that a nascent resistance movement to slavery and racial oppression had already taken shape in the Detroit River borderlands.

In mid-December 1828, a slave owner's agent named Ezekiel K. Hudnell discovered and attempted to remove four fugitive slaves from the Territory of Michigan, citing the federal Fugitive Slave Law of 1793.[39] His attempt was successful in the case of two of them, known only as Ben and Daniel (some sources call the latter David).[40] Hudnell petitioned for their apprehension and trial on behalf of their Harrison County, Kentucky, owners. This case was heard December 14, 1828. As Ben and Daniel were unable to prove any legal claim to freedom, a certificate in Hudnell's favor was issued by Justice John McDonnell, and the two young men were turned over to him. All that was lacking was the senior magistrate's signature on the certificate, something Magistrate James Witherell, a former Supreme Court judge in Michigan who had just been appointed Secretary of the Territory, was strangely slow to provide.[41]

Meanwhile, Blacks on both sides of the river expressed their dissatisfaction with Judge McDonnell's verdict. The atmosphere in Detroit turned threatening. Hudnell was wary that he would lose his prizes and thus his bounty for their return, so he imprisoned Ben and Daniel on a ship on the Detroit River opposite Grosse Ile, about fifteen miles downriver from the city wharf. The Territorial Papers for the United States contain Ezekiel K. Hudnell's testimony as to what happened after that:

> And after the trial before the Justice of the Peace as [aforesaid], The Said Slaves by a writ of Habeas Corpus were taken out the possession of this Affiant and Carried before the Judges of the Supreme Court before which the right of this Affiant to Said Slaves was again investigated & established & they restored to his possession. . . [when] he was advised by his Attorney Mr. Cole that it would be necessary to have the Certificate of the Magistrate Countersigned or authenticated by the Secretary Jas Witheril (The Governor being absent).[42]

But Judge Witherell put off signing the document for as long as possible. It was suspected that he did this in order to permit the rescue of Ben and Daniel by unnamed members of the Detroit black community.[43] Certainly Hudnell thought this was the case for, as he swore: "Next morning this Affiant Sent for the Certificate, and was informed that the Secretary had not Signed it, & probably would not—Nor would he redeliver the fee or certificate of the Magistrate. This Affiant then gave a written order for the Certificate, and being in danger of losing a passage down the lake Set off with the Slaves and in the night on the adjacent Island the Slaves made their escape, as this Affiant believes, in consequence of the delay occasioned by the neglect of the Secretary James Witherel to Sign the Certificate."[44]

Sheriff Thomas Sheldon later testified that both Michigan and Canadian Blacks had taken an active and decisive part in the rescue of Ben and Daniel: "[T]here existed great excitement in Detroit in consequence of the arrest of said slaves, which excitement extended itself to the Canada shore opposite, where great numbers of runaway slaves had collected & armed themselves for the purpose of boarding the vessel & rescuing the slaves.... [B]oth slaves made their escape from the possession of said Hudnell; whether through the inattention of said Hudnell or by the assistance of any person I have never been able to satisfy myself." Sheldon added: "[T]o my certain knowledge large rewards were offered to any person or persons who would set at liberty said slaves." On January 6, 1829, Hudnell went so far as to swear out a complaint, filed in the Harrison County Court of Kentucky, against Judge Witherell for his alleged role in the matter.[45]

Whether or not James Witherell was guilty of expediting Ben and Daniel's escape, it seems that President Andrew Jackson believed he was. In 1830, Witherell lost his position as [Territorial] Secretary to an old friend of Jackson's, John Thomson Mason. Mason ignored the antislavery clause in the Northwest Ordinance; when he and his family arrived in Detroit from Kentucky in the summer of 1831, they brought along their "servants." Mason would not long hold his new position, but his brilliant young son, Stevens Thomson Mason, would be appointed Acting Territorial Secretary at age nineteen, and acting governor at twenty-two. Fondly remembered as the "Boy Governor," the younger Mason would ably prosecute the Black Hawk War and see Michigan become a state in 1837.[46]

ORGANIZING RESISTANCE IN THE DETROIT RIVER BORDERLANDS

African Americans living along the Detroit River had many friends and relatives on the Canadian shore. Together they laid the groundwork for assisting refugees in crossing into their own "Promised Land." A leadership was emerging by the early 1830s, the same individuals appearing in membership lists of black churches, associations devoted to organized resistance and political protest, fraternal orders, and those that were focused on benevolent and charitable activities. These people included Virginia-born Madison J. Lightfoot and his wife, Tabitha; George French, born free in Kentucky, and his wife, Caroline; and Deborah and Benjamin Willoughby, the latter the most affluent of all early Detroit black families. Benjamin had been freed August 1, 1817, at the age of thirty-eight or so, by his owner, Charles Sterne, as was recorded in the Pendleton County, Kentucky, courthouse.[47] The Willoughbys' younger daughter was born free in Ohio, but by the early 1820s the family was living in Detroit, where Benjamin owned a successful lumberyard. He also loaned money at interest, a service of which both white and black Detroiters took advantage.[48]

In 1836, these same leading families would found Detroit's first and most enduring African American institution, Second Baptist Church, the subject of chapter 5 in this volume.[49] They would be joined by experienced Underground Railroad operator George DeBaptiste; noted Kentucky freedom-seeker, publisher, and antislavery lecturer Henry Bibb; and William Lambert. A free man who had been educated by Quakers at Trenton, New Jersey, Lambert married Benjamin Willoughby's daughter Julia and became so active in antislavery and community organizing that he was called the "President" of the Underground Railroad in the Detroit River borderland. (The Underground Railroad network that Lambert and DeBaptiste spearheaded is the subject of chapter 8 of this volume). At great peril to themselves and their families, Julia Lambert and other women welcomed freedom-seekers into their own homes, providing them with clothing, medicine, food, and comfort—but, as was often the case with women's contributions, the essential services they provided in the abolitionist cause generally went unrecorded. Together these civic-minded Detroiters formed the Detroit Vigilant Committee.[50] It was established to help prevent the kidnapping of free and formerly enslaved African Americans from Michigan soil.

Whites were active in the movement as well, including attorney Charles Stewart, who wrote the foreword for Henry Bibb's autobiography when it was published in 1849,[51] and innkeeper Seymour Finney, whose barn near the Detroit waterfront was a famous hideout for refugees waiting for safe passage across the river. Sympathetic ship captains, too, often landed freedom-seekers safely on the Upper Canadian shore. In the 1840s, a group of Detroit's white citizens would assist in providing financial backing for the fugitive slave resettlement venture called the Refugee Home Society. Located in Essex County, Canada West, it was the brainchild of Henry Bibb and his freeborn wife, Mary Miles Bibb, both featured in Afua Cooper's chapter 7 in this volume.[52]

THORNTON AND LUCIE BLACKBURN AND THE BLACKBURN RIOTS OF 1833

The next major fugitive slave rescue in the Detroit River region was that of Thornton and Lucie Blackburn, formerly of Louisville, Kentucky. In June 1831, Mrs. Blackburn was sold and was about to be transported from her Kentucky home to the slave markets at the mouth of the Mississippi, where with her beauty, grace, and accomplishments she was sure to fetch a much higher price as a "fancy girl" than she had as a house servant in Louisville. She and her enslaved husband staged a daring daylight escape. Equipped with tickets, ample funds, and forged freedom papers, on July 4, 1831, they brazenly boarded a steamboat out of Louisville harbor and arrived in Cincinnati. Despite pursuit by their respective owners, they escaped detection in the confusion occasioned by the Independence Day celebrations and continued north by stagecoach to Detroit, where they settled. The audacity of their flight, its intricate level of planning, and its smooth execution suggest that there was a coordinated effort by accomplices in Louisville—and perhaps in Detroit, since the couple did not immediately choose to cross the Detroit River to the more certain safety of Upper Canada. The Blackburns were befriended by the Lightfoots, Frenches, and Willoughbys, and joined the fledgling church congregation, as yet without a physical home, that would become Second Baptist Church.[53]

Two years later, in June 1833, Thornton and Lucie Blackburn were claimed as fugitive slaves by agents of their owners. Judge Henry Chipman of the Wayne County court was married to a Southern slaveholder's daughter but abolitionist in his convictions.[54] However, because of the Fugitive Slave Law of 1793, Chipman was forced to rule in favor of the slave owners' agents. Despite a spirited defense by the Scottish-born City Attorney Alexander Frazier, who later earned the sobriquet "Father of the Michigan Bar," Judge Chipman sentenced the Blackburns to return to Kentucky and lifelong bondage. But the black community of Detroit packed the courthouse balcony. Furious at the sentence, they threatened to set Detroit aflame. Dozens of people gathered about the courthouse when the Blackburns were incarcerated pending the departure of the steamboat that would return them to the South and to slavery. Again, African Canadians took the ferry across the Detroit River to join the protest, and Blacks from rural Michigan also filtered into the city. Sporting guns, clubs, knives, and swords, they milled about the Detroit Common for three days, while other protesters occupied the steamboat docks.[55]

On the very night after the trial, a secret meeting was held at the home of Benjamin Willoughby, where the conspirators hatched an elaborate rescue scheme. Principal among the organizers were the Willoughbys; George and Caroline French; the Lightfoots; and two prominent white men, Alexander Frazier and his friend Charles Cleland, the latter publisher of the *Detroit Courier* and also an attorney. Frazier was probably there to offer his legal opinion on the potential impact of Upper Canada's new Fugitive Offenders Act should the Blackburns be taken into custody once they crossed the Detroit River.[56] Upper Canada had just passed the first piece of legislation spelling out formal procedures for extradition from British North America to the United States.

The first step of the carefully orchestrated rescue was the most dangerous. Mrs. French and Mrs. Lightfoot visited the jail on June 16, 1833, a Sunday, and implored the sheriff to allow them to sit with Lucie Blackburn to offer her the solace of prayer. Two women remained until nightfall, then departed from the darkened jail, weeping into their handkerchiefs and covering their faces with veils to hide their tears. The ruse was successful. Caroline French remained behind in the cell, while Mrs. Blackburn, dressed in Mrs. French's clothes, was spirited across the river to Upper Canada. Her flight was not discovered until the next morning, and steps were taken to retain Caroline French and sell her into Kentucky slavery in Mrs. Blackburn's stead. Fortunately, her father's influence and a writ of *habeas corpus* provided by a sympathetic local judge were sufficient to free her from prison, and Caroline joined Lucie Blackburn in Amherstburg, on the Upper Canadian side of the border, to wait out the furor.[57]

Later that afternoon, Thornton Blackburn was brought to the door of the jail. Manacled and closely guarded, he was to be taken by cart down to the steamboat docks and securely placed on board a waiting steamer to begin his journey back to slavery. The jailer and Sheriff Wilson stood guard on their prisoner, along with one of the slavecatchers, and the men watched as a heavily armed band of men and women, young and old, white and black, and led by an elderly woman, marched up Gratiot Street and stopped before the jail. Fearing for their lives, both the jailor and the Kentuckian claiming Blackburn's labor retreated into the jailhouse, leaving Sheriff Wilson to face the crowd alone.[58] Someone tossed Blackburn a pistol and he fired in the air. The throng surged forward, and thus began the Blackburn Riots of 1833. At least one of the protesters was shot in the ensuing melee and Sheriff Wilson was badly beaten.

The prisoner, still in his chains, was placed in a cart and taken off on a wild ride through the woods near the waterfront. Hearing the pursuers' dogs barking in the distance, his rescuers pulled Blackburn out of the conveyance and broke his manacles with an ax, tying their bandanas around his ankles to silence the rattling chains. The cart and horse were sent off in a different direction to decoy the dogs while seven young men, all but one fugitive slaves themselves, fled on foot with Blackburn to a boat waiting at the riverfront. Lacking funds to pay the boatman, one man offered his father's prized gold pocket watch to pay their passage, and the boatman, satisfied, took the entire party across the river. At Sandwich, the capital of Upper Canada, they were all captured and thrown in jail. The mayor of Detroit had sent a letter across the river asking that the Blackburns be detained pending the preparation of a formal extradition request. Lucie Blackburn was arrested at the home of friends in Amherstburg and also brought to a cell in the Western District courthouse jail.[59]

In Detroit, the aftermath of the riot was dramatic. A special patrol of prominent white citizens was set up. Lewis Cass, Secretary of War in President Jackson's cabinet, happened to be visiting his Michigan home; he declared martial law and soldiers from Fort Gratiot were called up to patrol the streets.[60] Every black person suspected of involvement in the Blackburn Riots was detained, and some served hard time for their part in the events. African American homes were burnt to the ground. Such was people's fear that a substantial proportion of Detroit's black community moved across the river to Upper Canada. They settled in Sandwich, Amherstburg, and other Detroit River communities, many never to return to their Michigan homes. The population of Detroit did not again reach pre-riot figures until after laws protecting Blacks were put in place in 1837, when Michigan became a state.

But the Blackburns were not yet safe, even on the Upper Canadian side of the river. Their extradition and that of their rescuers was demanded by Acting Governor Stevens Thomson Mason of Michigan. Upper Canada's Lieutenant Governor John Colborne, Attorney General Robert Simpson Jameson, and the Executive Council of Upper Canada would deliberate over the case of Thornton and Lucie Blackburn for much of the summer. Jameson had earlier practiced law in the West Indies and was familiar with British legislation as it pertained to slavery. It was his job to provide the legal arguments for refuting Michigan's claim to the Blackburns.[61]

Until 1833, there had existed a fairly cozy arrangement between law officers and magistrates in Detroit and at Sandwich, where Upper Canada's Western District courts were located. It being in neither nation's best interest to retain actual criminals from the other country, fugitive offenders had long been traded back and forth between jurisdictions, with officials observing only the barest of formalities. However, continued pressure from the U.S. government to establish formal machinery for criminal extradition eventually had an effect. In February 1833, the Upper Canada Parliament passed An Act to Provide for the Apprehending of Fugitive Offenders from Foreign Countries, and Delivering Them Up to Justice.[62] This required that there be reasonable proof presented to the Lieutenant Governor of Upper Canada that the accused had actually committed a crime. Furthermore, it had to be a crime of a capital nature and so adjudged under British colonial law, not solely under the law of the country requesting the extradition. The final decision in each case was to be made "at the discretion" of the "Lieutenant Governor of the Province of Upper Canada." In other words, Colborne had the power to refuse to extradite the accused, whatever the evidence, if he deemed extradition "inexpedient."

The first case to be tried under the new law was that of Thornton and Lucie Blackburn. They were in fact accused of two capital crimes by Michigan's Acting Governor Mason: inciting the riot that had rescued Thornton and attempting to kill Sheriff Wilson. Craftily, the extradition documents did not demand the Blackburns' return on the grounds that they were slaves, since Michigan officials were well aware of Upper Canada's welcoming attitudes toward refugees from bondage. Attorney General Jameson in any case advised the Executive Council, which in turn told Lieutenant Governor Sir John Colborne, that escaping from slavery could not be considered a crime in Upper Canada, where slavery, to all intents and purposes, did not exist. Also, accused criminals who sought asylum in Canada could not be returned if the crimes they were supposed to have committed in the United States were not capital crimes—that is, if they were not punishable by death, whipping, the pillory, or incarceration at hard labor. Third, and crucially, Jameson gave the opinion that an accused criminal could not be returned to a foreign jurisdiction if the punishment for the crime would be more severe than the sentence the British colonial government of Upper Canada would impose for the same offense.

Meanwhile, Thornton Blackburn dictated his own petition to a local minister, who then passed it to a number of local elites. Signatories included former slaveholders as well as the Blackburns' Canadian jailer. The petition was then forwarded to Lieutenant Governor Sir John Colborne. This is the only document that survives in Blackburn's own words, albeit filtered through the High Church Anglican tones of the Reverend William Johnson of St. John's Church, Sandwich. Thornton himself could not read or write. Addressed to Colborne, the petition read:

> Your Excellency's Petitioner . . . humbly prays that you will take his case and that of his unfortunate wife under your Merciful consideration. Were Your Petitioner convinced that, should he be sent to the other side of the River, he would be put upon his trial for any crime that might be charged against him, he would unwillingly have put Your Excellency to the trouble of perusing this tedious statement. But Your Petitioner is convinced that the object of the Party is to have him and his wife carried back to Hopeless Slavery, where complaints can neither be heard, nor grievances redressed.[63]

As it turns out, Detroit's elite whites were not uniformly in favor of sending escaped slaves back to their Southern owners. They therefore sent their own petition to Upper Canada for presentation to the Western District courts. At their behest, both Charles Cleland and Detroit City Attorney Alexander Frazier crossed the river to offer legal and strategic advice to the Upper Canadian officials.[64] They wanted to prevent the Blackburns being sent back to Detroit for what everyone knew would be a sham trial. The Blackburns' wellwishers need not have worried; according to Attorney General Jameson, there was no place in British jurisprudence for enslaving someone as punishment for a crime. Knowing that whether they were judged guilty or innocent by an American court, enslavement would be the couple's ultimate fate, Jameson advised the Lieutenant Governor in Council that Thornton and Lucie Blackburn should not be extradited.[65] They were set free in early August 1833.

Like many refugees who crossed into Canada at the Detroit River, the Blackburns initially remained near the border, settling among their friends at Amherstburg. Most freedom-seekers were constrained by lack of finances from traveling into the interior of the province, while the existence of successful settled communities in the borderlands proved an attraction for people hungry to put down roots in their adopted homeland. After a year, however, Thornton and Lucie Blackburn made their way to the more distant safety of Toronto, where they began the city's first taxi business. Upper Canada's capital was sufficiently far from the border to reduce the threat of being seized by any slavecatchers who might stray across it. The Blackburns dedicated themselves to assisting other refugees from slavery, donating both funds and

The Thornton and Lucie Blackburn archaeological site in Toronto, 1985. (Courtesy of photographer Christopher Koch)

time to antislavery causes and constructing six small homes that they rented for nominal sums to successive families of fugitive slaves.

Incredibly, early in 1837, Thornton Blackburn secretly returned to the Detroit River border. Crossing over, he took the Underground Railroad in reverse, one might say. He traveled to Augusta, Kentucky, where he rescued his beloved mother, from whom he had been sold away at the age of three. Sibby Blackburn would die in freedom in Toronto, Canada West, in 1855 at the age of eighty, and be laid to rest in the Blackburn plot at the Toronto Necropolis Cemetery.[66]

The Blackburn Riots of 1833 engendered the first major extradition case between British North America and the United States over a fugitive slave, and the only one in which the freedom of a woman—Lucie Blackburn—was in dispute.[67] Its deliberation resulted in the core of public and legal policy regarding refugee reception that for more than 180 years has been foundational to Canadian extradition law. Canada still does not return accused criminals to jurisdictions where extreme punishments such as execution or torture will be their ultimate fate. The reception of the Blackburns in Upper Canada in 1833 set a precedent that still protects freedom-seekers to this day.

Thousands of African American refugees to Canada—no one will ever know how many—traversed the Detroit River boundary before the Civil War. African Canadians living in the Detroit River borderland worked in concert with a highly secretive band of Michigan-based black conspirators and a few white sympathizers to ensure that such refugees could indeed, as Dr. McRae wrote in 1983, "cross the Detroit River to find freedom."[68] Such organized conspiracies began in the period immediately following the War of 1812, but their foundations were laid in earlier decades. The embryonic resistance movement that in 1828 rescued Ben and Daniel from the clutches of a Kentucky slavecatcher evolved quickly; it was much more sophisticated five short years later when the highly choreographed rescue of the Blackburns took place. Both cases demonstrate the early flowering of the transnational African American–African Canadian antislavery resistance that forged networks of freedom along the Detroit River.

NOTES

1. Norman McRae, "Crossing the Detroit River to Find Freedom," *Michigan History* 67, no. 2 (1983): 35–39.
2. See, for instance, D. M. Erskin, British Minister at New York, to the Lieutenant Governor of Upper Canada, Sir Francis Gore, May 26, 1807, in William Renwick Riddell, "Additional Notes on Slavery," *Journal of Negro History* 17, no. 3 (1932), 369. The letter was copied to Matthew Elliott, a New York Loyalist and Superintendent of the Upper Canadian Indian Department, at the time living south of Amherstburg on a plantation worked by more than sixty enslaved men, women, and children. Elliott was believed to be the largest slaveholder in Upper Canada. "I regret equally with yourself the Inconvenience which His Majesty's subjects in Upper Canada experience from the Desertion of their slaves into the Territory of the United States . . . but I fear no Representation to the Government of the United States will at present avail in checking the evils complained of. . . . The answer that has been usually given, has been, 'That the Treaty between Great Britain & the United States which alone gave them the Power to surrender Deserters having expired, it was impossible for them to exercise such an authority without the Sanction of the Laws.'" See "An Ordinance for the Government of the Territory of the United States North-West of the River Ohio" passed July 13, 1787, in *Journals of the Continental Congress,* 32:334–43, Library of Congress.memory.loc.gov/ammem/collections/continental/index.html (accessed July 23, 2011).
3. U.S. Census Bureau, "Table 37: Michigan—Race and Hispanic Origin: 1800 to 1990," September 13, 2002, www.census.gov/population/www/documentation/.../tab37.pdf (accessed January 10, 2013).
4. Jay's Treaty was passed on November 19, 1794, and went into effect on February 29, 1796, although Detroit was not actually transferred from British to American rule until July 11, 1796, when American soldiers under Captain Moses Porter formally took over the garrison.
5. Confusingly, the fortification was called Fort Amherstburg in its earliest incarnation, but after it was burned in the War of 1812 and subsequently reconstructed by the Americans, it became Fort Malden. So it remains, Malden also the name of the surrounding township; while the village is Amherstburg.
6. This was not in fact "importation" as prohibited by Upper Canada's anti-importation law of 1793. Slaveholders from Detroit were regarded as British subjects who were simply moving to another British territory. For details of the transfer, a concise description is provided in R. Alan Douglas, *Uppermost Canada: The Western District and the Detroit Frontier, 1800–1850* (Detroit: Wayne State University Press, 2001), 8–9.

7. Ernest B. Laieuness, *The Windsor Border Region: Canada's Southernmost Frontier* (Toronto: Champlain Society, 1960), cxvii, 187 ("List of Persons Residing in Detroit in 1796 Who Elected to Remain British Subjects"). See also Roy E. Fleming, "Negro Slaves with the United Empire Loyalists in Upper Canada," *Ontario History* 43 (1953), 27–29.

8. An Act Respecting Fugitives from Justice, and Persons Escaping from the Service of Their Masters" stated that "no person held to service of labor in one state, under the laws thereof, escaping into another, shall, in consequence of any law or regulation therein, be discharged from such labor or service or labor, but shall be delivered up on claim of the party to whom such service or labor may be due." See *Statutes at Large*, c. 7, 302, February 12, 1793, c. 7, www.michigan.gov/dnr/0,4570,7-153-54463_18670_44390-160655—,00.html (accessed November 12, 2012).

9. The Act Respecting Fugitives from Justice, and Persons Escaping from the Service of Their Masters was signed into law by President George Washington on February 12, 1793. U.S. Congress, *Abridgment of the Debates of Congress, from 1789 to 1856: March 4, 1789–June 1, 1796*, ed. Thomas Hart Benton (New York: D. Appleton, 1857), 1:417.

10. See, for example, the 1828 petition from Blacks living at Ancaster, near Hamilton, to Lieutenant Governor Sir Peregrine Maitland requesting a large land grant where incoming families could live in close proximity. The purpose was not only so they could provide mutual assistance in the settlement process but also to allow them to protect one another from American slavecatchers operating in Upper Canada. William Renwick Riddell, ed., "A Petition," *Journal of Negro History* 15 (1930): 115–16.

11. The Honorable Peter Russell, a slaveholder himself who would succeed Simcoe as Administrator of the province, was also present. William Osgoode would go on to become Chief Justice of Quebec (Canada East after 1841), where slaveholding soon was rendered difficult, but through judicial rather than legislative means. See Robin W. Winks, *The Blacks in Canada*, 2nd ed. (Montreal: McGill-Queen's University Press, 1997), 99–102. I am indebted to my colleague Guylaine Pétrin for the correction to Vrooman's name, which in every secondary source appears as "William." Sergeant Adam Vrooman of Queenston, Upper Canada, addresses the issue of his ownership of Chloe Cooley in a petition to Lieutenant Governor Simcoe dated April 21, 1793. He respectfully defends his right to sell the "unruly" woman, whom he had lately purchased from Benjamin Hardiman of Niagara, there not being laws contrary to slave ownership in the province. See Upper Canada Land Petitions, U-V Bundle 1, 1792–1796, RG 1, L3, Vol. 541, Library and Archives Canada.

12. An Act to Prevent the Further Introduction of Slaves and to Limit the Term of Contracts for Servitude within this Province, in *Statutes of Upper Canada*, 3 Geo. III, c. 7 (1793), Archives of Ontario, Toronto. The report of Martin to Simcoe is detailed in William Renwick Riddell, "The Slave in Upper Canada," *Journal of Negro History* (October 1919), 372–86.

13. Winks, *The Blacks in Canada*, 111.

14. Peter Meyler and David Meyler, *A Stolen Life: Searching for Richard Pierpoint* (Toronto: Natural Heritage Books, 1999), esp. chap. 6. James Oliver Horton and Lois E. Horton, in *In Search of Liberty: Culture, Community and Protest among Northern Free Blacks, 1700–1860* (New York: Oxford University Press, 1997), 157–58, note that there were also black musicians in American regimental bands during the War of 1812. See, for instance, the pension application of an African American named George Washington, who served as a drummer

in the troops of Colonel Robert Rose, Virginia Militia: War of 1812 Pension Applications, Pension Record #SO 29898, reel M313, National Archives, Washington DC.

15. James Baker Farr, *Black Odyssey: The Seafaring Traditions of Afro-Americans* (New York: P. Lang, 1989), 109–14. Congress passed a law on March 3, 1813, stating that "persons of color, natives of the United States" were to be accepted into the U.S. Navy. According to Alexander S. Mackenzie, *Life of Commodore Oliver Hazard Perry* (New York: Harper & Bros., 1940), 1:165–66, and 186–87, when Oliver Hazzard Perry, the hero of the Great Lakes in the War of 1812, complained that Commodore Chauncey had sent him a motley crew of soldiers, boys, and Blacks to fill out his very thin ranks on Lake Erie, the admiral retorted: "[T]o my knowledge a part of them are not surpassed by any seamen we have on the fleet, and I have yet to learn that the Colour of the skin, or cut and trimmings of the coat, can effect a man's qualifications or usefulness. I have nearly 50 Blacks on board of this Ship [his own flagship, the *General Pike*], and many of them are amongst my best men." Following the success of the Battle for the Great Lakes on September 20, 1813, however, Perry praised the courage of his African American sailors to Chauncey: "They seemed to be absolutely insensible to danger." See also Gerald Altoff, *Amongst My Best Men: African Americans and the War of 1812* (Put-in-Bay, OH: Perry Group, 1996); Steven Ramold, *Slaves, Sailors, Citizens: African Americans in the Union Navy* (Dekalb: Northern Illinois University Press, 2002); Joseph T. Wilson, *The Black Phalanx: African American Soldiers in the War of Independence, the War of 1812, and the Civil War* (Hartford, CT: American Publishing, 1888), chap. 3.

16. Ernest Green, "Upper Canada's Black Defenders," *Ontario History* 27 (1931): 365–91; Gareth Newfield, "Upper Canada's Black Defenders? Reexamining the War of 1812 Coloured Corps," *Canadian Military History* 18, no. 3 (2009): 31–34. The Colored Corps served out the rest of the war building fortifications and barracks rather than as line troops. According to one British engineer, "When I visited the Niagara Frontier . . . I found that a corps of Free Men of Colour had been raised . . . but had been turned over to that of the Engineers, any necessity for this I never could learn, but it seems to have been the fashion in Canada to heap all kinds of duties upon the latter." Cited in Gareth Newfield, "The Coloured Corps: African Canadians in the War of 1812," Report for the Canadian War Museum, www.eighteentwelve.ca/?q=eng/Topic/25 (accessed February 2, 2013). For privateering, see Dan Conlin, "Privateer Entrepôt: Commercial Militarization in Liverpool, Nova Scotia, 1793–1805," *The Northern Mariner* 8, no. 2 (1998): 21–38. The black sailors on Canadian privateers were likely a mix of formerly enslaved men from both British and American sources. Some had been imported to Halifax in the early years of British colonial rule from New England and the West Indies, while others had fled to the British lines in the American Revolution. The latter were the Black Loyalists who accepted Lord Dunmore's offer of freedom in return for their service. Still others may have been former slaves of United Empire Loyalists, who were permitted to import their movable property to Canada after the Revolutionary War, including enslaved African Americans. See Harvey Amani Whitfield, "Slavery in English Nova Scotia," *Journal of the Royal Nova Scotia Historical Society* 13 (2010): 1–19; also "African and New World African Immigration to Mainland Nova Scotia, 1749–1816," *Journal of the Royal Nova Scotia Historical Society* 7 (2004): 102–11.

17. *Report of the Adjutant General of the State of Kentucky: Soldiers in the War of 1812* (Frankfort, KY: Capital Office, E. Polk Johnson, 1891). See, for instance, 189, 262, and 357 for muster

rolls listing "servants." The individuals with only a first name recorded are believed to have been enslaved African Americans. Enslaved individuals had last names, but their owners rarely used them, as a means of demeaning those they considered their property. For an extensive study on slave naming, see Herbert Gutman, *The Black Family in Slavery and Freedom, 1750–1925* (New York: Vintage Books, 1977), 230–56.

18. "The British forces consist of regulars, flankers, Militia, *Negroes*, and Indians. . . . I heard of two companies of *Negroes*, runaways from Kentucky and other states, who are commanded by white men," in "Winchester's Campaign." Elias Darnell, *A Journal, Containing an Accurate and Interesting Account of the Hardships, Sufferings, Battles, Defeat, and Captivity of Those Heroic Kentucky Volunteers and Regulars: Commanded by General Winchester, in the Years 1812–13; Also, Two Narratives by Men That Were Wounded in the Battles on the River Raisin and Taken Captive by the Indians* (Philadelphia: Lippincott, Grambo, 1854), 78. See Lisa Philips Valentine and Allan K. McDougall, "Imposing the Border: The Detroit River from 1786 to 1807," in "The Canadian-American Border: Toward a Transparent Border?" special issue, *Journal of Borderlands Studies* 19, no. 1 (2004): 13–22; and Douglass, *Uppermost Canada*, chap. 1.

19. Sixty-four-year-old Kentucky pioneer William Whiteley (1749–1813) had been a companion of Daniel Boone. He enlisted as a private in the War of 1812 and died in that conflict. According to contemporary accounts, Whiteley was carried off the field by the two enslaved black men who had accompanied him throughout the campaign. He was wrapped in a blanket and buried near where he fell. His rifle, powder horn, and belt eventually were returned to his family, possibly by the same two servants. See "An Old Indian Killer: Interesting Events in the History of an Ancient Rifle," *Fort Wayne (IN) Daily Sentinel*, November 27, 1874, reprinted from the *Louisville Courier Journal* of unknown date. Popular Canadian journalist and author Pierre Berton also mentions in his *Flames Across the Border* (Toronto: Little, Brown, 1981), 193, that Whiteley was accompanied in the Battle of the Thames by two "black servants."

20. Robert E. Hayden, "History of the Negro in Michigan" (1940), Michigan Historical Records Survey, Works Progress Administration, typewritten copy in the Michigan Historical Collections, Ann Arbor, and in the Bentley Historical Library, roll 52, microfilm, 107, University of Michigan, Ann Arbor; William Birney, *James G. Birney and His Times* (New York: D. Appleton, 1890), 435, cited in Arthur R. Kooker, "The Antislavery Movement in Michigan, 1798–1840: A Study in Humanitarianism on the American Frontier" (PhD diss., University of Michigan, 1941), 50. Kooker's papers are also at the Bentley Library.

21. Birney, *James G. Birney*, cited in Kooker, "The Antislavery Movement in Michigan," 50.

22. The unnamed missionary stayed at the Moravian community on his way home and talked about the Moravian "Brother Schlegel" whom he had known in Maryland. Linda Sabathy-Judd, ed., *Moravians in Upper Canada: The Diary of the Indian Mission of Fairfield on the Thames, 1792–1813* (Toronto: Champlain Society, 1999), 455.

23. Montieth Papers, Burton Historical Collection, Detroit Public Library, cited in Norman McRae, "Blacks in Detroit, 1736–1833: The Search for Freedom and Community and Its Implications for Educators" (PhD diss., University of Michigan, 1982), 122, 141n34.

24. Attorney General John Beverley Robinson was the son of Christopher Robinson, a Virginia-born Loyalist who unsuccessfully tried to reintroduce slave importation into Upper Canada immediately after Lieutenant Governor Simcoe's departure. William Renwick

Riddell, "The Slave in Upper Canada," *Journal of Negro History* 4 (October 1919), 384, 384n20. Christopher Robinson's bill was hotly contested by Solicitor General Robert Isaac Dey Grey, himself a Loyalist and a slaveholder, with the support of Richard Cartwright and Robert Hamilton. Both had originally opposed Simcoe's antislavery measure as they, too, owned slaves. Russell's measure initially passed, but was tabled for a period of three months after the second reading (three readings of a bill are required before it passes into law even today). This usually means that it is held over for the next parliamentary session and never revived, a process known as the "three month's hoist." See Government of Canada, "Parliamentary Procedure," www.parl.gc.ca/procedure-book-livre/Document.aspx (accessed November 16, 2012). The younger Robinson was himself a veteran of the Battle of Queenston Heights, in which the Colored Corps had played an important role.

25. William Renwick Riddell, "The Fugitive Slave in Upper Canada," *Journal of Negro History* 5 (June 1920), 343–45.

26. William M. Wiecek, "Somerset: Lord Mansfield and the Legitimacy of Slavery in the Anglo-American World," *University of Chicago Law Review* 42, no. 1 (1974): 86–146; Steven M. Wise, *Though Heavens May Fall: The Landmark Trial That Led to the End of Human Slavery* (Cambridge, MA: Da Capo, 2005), esp. 190–91. Despite the decision, British slave owners and those from the Caribbean colonies continued to advertise for fugitive slaves in the British papers, and there seems to have been no diminution in the number of slaves taken out of England for sale. For a detailed discussion of British attitudes toward slavery both before and after the Mansfield decision, see James Walvin, *Black and White: The Negro and English Society, 1555–1945* (London: Macmillan, 1982); and Jerome Nadelhaft, "The Somersett [sic] Case and Slavery: Myth, Reality, and Repercussions," *Journal of Negro History* 51, no. 3 (1966): 193–208.

27. William Renwick Riddell, "Notes on Slavery in Canada," *Journal of Negro History* 4 (January 1919), 397–98. Sir John Beverley Robinson (1791–1863) was knighted in 1854, awarding him the Baronetcy of Toronto.

28. These various attempts on the part of the United States to influence British policy regarding fugitive slaves are detailed in *State Journal*, 16th Cong., 1st sess., 319, 326; *Annals of Congress*, 618; *House Journal*, 17th Cong., 1st sess., 143; *Annals of Congress*, 553, 448, 710; *Annals of Congress*, 17th Cong., 1st sess., 1379, 1415, 1444, available online at memory.loc.gov/ammem/amlaw/lwhj-link.html (accessed June 1, 2015). See William R. Manning, ed., *Diplomatic Correspondence of the United States, Canadian Relations 1784–1860* (Washington, DC: Carnegie Endowment for International Peace, 1943), 2:109–11, 132, 181, 633–35, 771–72, and Wilbur H. Siebert, *The Underground Railroad From Slavery to Freedom* (New York: Macmillan, 1898), 22, 299–300.

29. Albert Gallatin to Henry Clay, September 25, 1827, *Nile's Weekly Register*, December 27, 1828. See Karolyn Smardz Frost, *I've Got a Home in Glory Land: A Lost Tale of the Underground Railroad* (New York: Farrar, Straus & Giroux, 2007; Toronto: Thomas Allen, 2007), 241–53, for an analysis of the precedents. See also Alexander Murray, "The Extradition of Fugitive Slaves from Canada: A Re-evaluation," *Canadian Historical Review* 43, no. 4 (1962): 298–314; David Murray, *Colonial Justice: Justice, Morality, and Crime in the Niagara District, 1791–1849*, Osgoode Society for Canadian Legal History (Toronto: University of Toronto Press, 2002), 197–216, and "Criminal Boundaries: The Frontier and the Contours of Upper Canadian Justice, 1792–1840," *Canadian Review of American Studies / American Review of Canadian Studies*

26, no. 3 (1996): 341–66; Roman J. Zorn, "Criminal Extradition Menaces the Canadian Haven for Fugitive Slaves," *Canadian Historical Review* 38 (December 1957): 284–94.

30. Arnett G. Lindsay, "Diplomatic Relations Between the United States and Great Britain Bearing on the Return of Negro Slaves," *Journal of Negro History* 5 (October 1920), 417–19; Secretary of State Henry Clay to James Barbour, U.S. ambassador to Great Britain, June 13, 1828, in *Diplomatic Correspondence of the United States, Canadian Relations*, ed. William R. Manning (Washington, DC: Carnegie Endowment for World Peace, 1940), 2:181; *Nile's Weekly Register*, December 27, 1828, 290.

31. *Laws of the Territory of Michigan, Condensed, Arranged, and Passed by the Fifth Legislative Council* (Detroit: S. McKnight, 1833), 470–72.

32. Hayden, "History of the Negro in Michigan," 13–14.

33. Paul Finkelman, Martin J. Hershock, and Clifford W. Taylor, *History of Michigan Law* (Athens: Ohio University Press, 2006), 87.

34. This was not the first diplomatic incident between Upper Canada and the United States over the return of fugitive slaves: interestingly, a similar request was rebuffed in 1807, when Lieutenant Governor Sir Francis Gore of Upper Canada demanded the return of Canadian slaves who had found refuge in New York State. His request was denied on the grounds that there was no current extradition treaty between Britain and the United States. See Erskin to Gore, May 26, 1807, Upper Canada Sundries, LAC.

35. Charles Stuart (1783–1865) left Upper Canada in 1822 to become the president of what would become the Oneida Institute in upstate New York, where he was converted by evangelist Charles Grandison Finney and became a close friend of future abolitionist leader Theodore Dwight Weld. Stuart was a very important figure who would support efforts of British abolitionists to end slavery throughout the British Empire. He authored literally hundreds of abolitionist tracts over his long career. He eventually returned to Upper Canada, where he helped to found the British-American Antislavery Society in the 1830s and the Canadian Anti-Slavery Society in 1851. Stuart died at Lora Bay, near Collingwood, Ontario, in 1865. Fred Landon, "Captain Charles Stuart, Abolitionist," *Western Ontario History Nuggets* (London, ON) 24 (1956): 1–19; Fred Landon, "Amherstburg, Terminus of the Underground Railway," *Journal of Negro History* 10 (January 1925): 1–9.

36. For a contemporary reference to the Amherstburg lands Stuart ceded to Blacks and the settlers' agricultural accomplishments, see John Jeremiah Bigsby, *The Shoe and Canoe; or, Pictures of Travel in the Canadas* (London: Chapman & Hall, 1850), 2:263–66.

37. The terms *Vigilant* and *Vigilance* were variously employed to describe committees formed to afford protection to fugitive slaves and to protect free Blacks from kidnapping, violence and oppression. The New York Committee of Vigilance had been founded in 1835, and the Vigilant Association of Philadelphia two years later. The Detroit group took the name Colored Vigilant Committee, as discussed by Roy Finkenbine in chapter 8 of this volume.

38. McRae, "Blacks in Detroit," 114–42.

39. Very little information has survived about this case. Ezekiel K. Hudnell appeared in the 1840 U.S. Census for Montgomery County, Kentucky. He had seven slaves: four little girls under ten, one man and one woman between the ages of twenty-four and thirty-six, and an elderly woman between the age of fifty-five and one hundred. The best secondary source

for this event is David G. Chardavoyne, "Michigan and the Fugitive Slave Acts," *The Court Legacy* (Historical Society for the United States District Court of the Eastern District of Michigan newsletter) 12, no. 3 (2004): 1–11.

40. The court documents do not seem to have survived, so there is no information as to why Hudnell was not awarded the other two refugees whom he claimed, nor are they named.

41. James B. Witherell (1759–1838) was born in Massachusetts, served honorably in the Revolutionary War, and then settled in Vermont. He was elected Congressman in 1807 but was appointed in 1808 to the position of Supreme Court Judge for Michigan. He commanded a regiment raised for the defense of Detroit in the War of 1812. Witherell resigned to become Territorial Secretary from 1828 to 1830. He was also the acting Governor of the Territory for January–March 1830. See *Early History of Michigan, with Biographies of State Officers, Members of the Congress, Judges and Legislators* (Lansing: Thorp & Godfrey, 1888), 708–9.

42. Clarence Edwin Carter, ed., *The Territorial Papers of the United States*, vol. 11, *The Territory of Michigan, 1820–1829* (Washington, DC: Government Printing Office, 1943), 1241–42, clarke.cmich.edu/resource_tab/information_and_exhibits/i_arrived_at_detroit/ezekiel_hudnall.html (accessed June 23, 2011).

43. A detailed description of the rescue of Ben and Daniel is contained in Carter, *The Territorial Papers*, 1241–42.

44. Carter, *The Territorial Papers*, 1241–42.

45. Cited in Chardavoyne, "Michigan and the Fugitive Slave Acts"; Carol E. Mull, *The Underground Railroad in Michigan* (Jefferson, NC: McFarland, 2010), 15.

46. Silas Farmer, *History of Detroit and Wayne County and Early Michigan*, 3rd ed. (Detroit: Silas Farmer, 1890), 3–4; Lawton T. Hemans, *Life and Times of Stevens Thomson Mason, the Boy Governor of Michigan*, 2nd ed. (Lansing: Michigan Historical Commission, 1930), 59–60. For the death of Granny Peg, a favorite family "servant," see Emily V. Mason, "Chapters from the Autobiography of an Octogenarian (Miss Emily V. Mason), 1830–1850," *Michigan Pioneer and Historical Collections* 35 (1907): 248–52, clarke.cmich.edu/resource_tab/information_and_exhibits/i_arrived_at_detroit/emily_mason.html (accessed June 25, 2011).

47. Manumission papers for "Willoughby," August 1, 1817, issued at the Pendleton County, Kentucky, courthouse, William Lambert Papers, Burton Historical Collection, Detroit Public Library.

48. Also in the William Lambert Papers is a series of promissory notes, some signed by Charles Cleland, publisher of the *Detroit Courier* and bon vivant. Cleland was prominent in the aftermath of the Blackburn Riots, advising Upper Canadian officials of ways in which they could circumvent American slave law so they could refuse to extradite the couple. See Smardz Frost, *I've Got a Home in Glory Land*, 169–74, 380n173.

49. Nathaniel Leach, *The Second Baptist Connection: Reaching Out to Freedom—History of Second Baptist Church in Detroit* (Detroit: Second Baptist Church, 1988), 14–15.

50. As in the case of churches, the terms *vigilant* and *vigilance* were both used to describe such organizations. In the Detroit instance, it was indeed the Detroit Vigilant Committee, although the name is often incorrectly transcribed in both popular and scholarly sources.

51. Henry Bibb, *Narrative of the Life and Adventures of Henry Bibb, an American Slave, Written by Himself* (New York: privately published, 1849).

52. Afua Cooper, "The Fluid Frontier: Blacks and the Detroit River Region; A Focus on Henry Bibb," *Canadian Review of American Studies* 30, no. 2 (2000): 129–49; Roy Finkenbine's contribution to this volume (chapter 8); Katherine DuPre Lumpkin, "'The General Plan was Freedom': A Negro Secret Order on the Underground Railroad," *Phylon* 28 (1st quarter 1967): 63–77; Mull, *The Underground Railroad in Michigan*, 84–91.
53. There were later ties between Baptist churchmen in Detroit and Louisville as well as between the Detroit River communities and certain of the more prominent Louisville black families, such as that of Washington Spradling, who is probably the free African American who provided the Blackburns with their forged manumission documents (J. Blaine Hudson, personal communication, 1999). Kentuckians regularly made their way to the riverfront in the succeeding years, suggesting a level of communication and organization between black communities in Louisville and Detroit riverfront towns and cities.
54. Judge Henry Chipman, who had arrived in Detroit in 1824, said he came to the Michigan frontier "seeking the education of my children beyond the influence of slavery." Cited in David M. Katzman, "Black Slavery in Michigan," *Midcontinent American Studies Journal* 11, no. 2 (1970): 56–67, 56.
55. *Democratic Free Press*, June 19, 1833; *Detroit Journal and Advertiser*, July 19, 1833; *Detroit Journal and Advertiser*, July 24, 1833; and Friend Palmer, *Early Days in Detroit: Papers Written by General Friend Palmer of Detroit, Being his Personal Reminiscences of Important Events and Descriptions of the City for over Eighty Years* (Detroit: Hunt & June, 1906), 78. See also "Our New Voters: Past History of the Colored People of Detroit with Exciting Scenes of the Riots in 1833, 1839, and 1850," *Detroit Daily Post*, February 7, 1870.
56. An Act to Provide for the Apprehending of Fugitive Offenders from Foreign Countries, and Delivering Them Up to Justice, February 13, 1833, Eleventh Parliament (3 Will. IV, c. 7), in Sir. John Colborne, K.C.B., Lieutenant Governor, *Statutes of His Majesty's Province of Upper Canada, Passed in the Third Session of the Eleventh Provincial Parliament of Upper Canada* (York: Robert Stanton, Printer to the King's Most Excellent Majesty, 1833), 37–38.
57. "Affidavit of Alexander McArthur, Deputy Sheriff of Wayne County, Taken before the Said Henry Chipman, Esq.," August 10, 1833, Jameson Papers, document 7, Archives of Ontario, Toronto. For details of the black community meetings and leadership, see Reginald Larrie, *Makin' Free: African Americans in the Northwest Territory* (Detroit: Blaine Ethridge, 1981), 104, 119; and Mrs. June Barber Woodson, "A Century with the Negroes of Detroit, 1830–1930," *A.M.E. Church Review* 68 (1953): 38–49. Caroline French's father was Cornelius Leonard Lenox, who had come to Detroit with General William Hull and owned a substantial farm. See Betty DeRamus, *Forbidden Fruit: Love Stories from the Underground Railroad* (New York: Atria Books, 2005), 67.
58. The jailor was Lemeul Goodell and the slave owner's agent was Clayton T. Oldham, son of John Pope Oldham, who administered the estate of which Thornton Blackburn formed a part. Blackburn's legal owner was Clayton Talbot Oldham's aunt and John Pope Oldham's sister-in-law, Susan Talbot Brown.
59. There are numerous contemporary accounts in newspapers and letters as well as in later speeches delivered by those who witnessed the events. Sheriff Wilson gave his own sworn statement for the purposes of the extradition case, which is puzzling since he had been so badly injured that

he was never able to recall the events leading up to Blackburn's rescue. "Deposition of John M. Wilson, Sheriff of Wayne County, Taken before the Said Henry Chipman, Esq.," Blackburn File, document 6, Michigan State Archives, Lansing; E. Backus to Judge B.F.H. Witherell, April 2, 1860, in Witherell, "Papers Relative to Insurrection of Negroes," Burton Historical Collection, Detroit Public Library, 593; Palmer, *Early Days in Detroit*, 707–8; Samuel Zug's Scrapbook, 1:20, Burton Historical Collection, Detroit Public Library. See also Kooker, "The Antislavery Movement in Michigan," 65; William Stocking, "Slavery and the Underground Railroad," in *The City of Detroit, Michigan, 1701–1922*, ed. Clarence Monroe Burton, William Stocking, and Gordon K. Miller (Detroit: S. J. Clark, 1922), 1:476–77.

60. Charles M. Bull to John Bull Jr., July 23, 1833, Witherell Papers, Burton Historical Collection, Detroit Public Library; Sidney Glazer, "In Old Detroit," *Michigan History Magazine* 26 (Spring 1942): 206–7; "Report of the Committee," *Detroit Journal and Advertiser*, July 19, 1833; *Detroit Courier*, July 24, 1833.

61. There are substantial primary collections detailing the Blackburn extradition case. Individual documents appear in the Executive Council Papers for Upper Canada, the Upper Canada Sundries, and the official correspondence of both Lieutenant Governor Sir John Colborne and his secretary, but the most complete set survives in the Robert Simpson Jameson Papers, 38, Papers of the Attorney General, Executive Council Papers for Upper Canada, RG1, Library and Archives Canada. For the Michigan side of the dispute, and multiple duplicates of the Upper Canadian documents, see the affidavits filed in the case as well as relevant correspondence in "Thornton Blackburn, Fugitive Slave, 1833," Papers of the Secretary of State, RG 56-26, box 198, folder 9, Michigan State Archives, Lansing. For discussion, see also McRae, "Blacks in Detroit," chaps. 5 and 6.

62. An Act to Provide for the Apprehending of Fugitive Offenders from Foreign Countries, and Delivering Them Up to Justice, February 13, 1833, Eleventh Parliament (3 Will. IV, c. 7).

63. "The Petition of Thornton Blackburn on Behalf of Himself, and His Wife Ruth Blackburn, Both People of Color, at Present Confined in the Gaol of Sandwich, Western District," June 22, 1833, Robert Simpson Jameson Papers, 90–93, Archives of Ontario, Toronto.

64. Alexander Frazier was not reappointed city attorney, although an early attempt to censure his behavior in the Blackburn affair was tabled at Detroit City Council and never reopened. The petition bearing the signatures of the Blackburns' white supporters, unfortunately, does not seem to have been preserved. However, the affidavits of both Cleland and Frazier sworn before Judge George Jacob in the Western District Court at Sandwich, Upper Canada, on June 25, 1833, are contained in the Robert Simpson Jameson Papers cited above, 78–79, 82–84.

65. His opinion can be found in Robert Simpson Jameson to Lieutenant Colonel Rowan, Secretary to His Excellency, the Lieutenant Governor, July 16, 1833, Correspondence of the Civil Secretary, Upper Canada Sundries, Vol. 130 (July 1833), RG 5A1, Library and Archives Canada.

66. Burial Ledger, Toronto Necropolis, Toronto Trust Cemeteries, Lot 100E, October 27, 1855.

67. It is interesting that Lucie Blackburn was the only female slave for whom extradition from Upper Canada was demanded by judicial and state authorities in the entire period before the Civil War.

68. McRae, "Crossing the Detroit River."

THREE

THE ILLUSION OF SAFETY

Attempts to Extradite Fugitive Slaves from Canada

BRYAN PRINCE

From the American Revolutionary War period through the antebellum era, the waters of the Great Lakes system that separate the United States and Canada offered a psychological—but not always physically insurmountable—barrier between slavery and freedom. The notion of the British colony as a safe haven had been prompted by the 1793 Act to Prevent the Further Introduction of Slaves and to Limit the Term of Contracts for Servitude within This Province, advanced by the 1807 British abolition of the transatlantic slave trade, and fortified by the 1833 Imperial Act for the Abolition of Slavery throughout the British Colonies, which went into effect on August 1st, 1834. However, that decades-old impression was constantly scrutinized and attacked. Formal extradition requests by U.S. authorities for the return of runaway slaves from Canada were common in the years following the American Revolution. Article VII of the 1783 Definitive Treaty of Peace between the United States of America and His Britannic Majesty that concluded the American Revolution stated that, after the British surrender, British forces were to leave the country quickly, "without causing any destruction, or carrying away any Negroes, or other property, of the American inhabitants."[1] The Americans, however, claimed that their defeated enemy repeatedly violated those terms. Thomas Jefferson believed that over three thousand slaves had been removed by the British; actually there were many more. The dismissive response from the unrepentant British was that "every slave like every horse, which escaped or strayed from within the American lines, and came into the possession of the British army, became by the laws and rights of war, British property."[2]

One of the earliest extradition disputes between the United States and British Canada had an unusual twist. When nine slaves belonging to Loyalists Matthew Elliott and Richard

Pattinson of Amherstburg, Upper Canada, escaped into Michigan Territory in 1807, the attorney general of the Territorial government commenced proceedings to return them to their Canadian owners. Elliott sent his overseer, James Heward, to Detroit to testify on his behalf and, hopefully, retrieve his property. The overseer, however, underestimated the anti-Canadian sentiment of some Detroiters and, after a few drinks, foolishly referred to the Americans in the tavern as "a damned rascally set of beggers." Several men responded by tarring and feathering Heward, who then prudently recrossed the Detroit River. Heward's departure did not delay the extradition hearing, however. Chief Justice Augustus Woodward of the Michigan Supreme Court heard the extradition petition and ruled that provisions in the 1787 Northwest Ordinance providing for the recapture of slaves applied only to states in the Union. Elliott and Pattinson had, therefore, forfeited those rights when they removed to British Canada after the Revolutionary War.[3]

As discussed in the previous chapter of this volume, in 1819, U.S. slave owners received no better comfort than their Canadian counterparts had when Attorney General John Beverley Robinson of Upper Canada responded to requests made by Secretary of State John Quincy Adams on behalf of Tennessee slave owners. The latter wanted to come to the province to retrieve their runaways. Robinson denied the request on the grounds that once the bondspeople reached the British province they were free.[4] Gibbs Antrobus, the British chargé d'affaires, confirmed Robinson's stance in his official reply to U.S. authorities: "The Negroes have by their residence in Canada, become free . . . and should [there be] any attempt to infringe upon this right of freedom, these Negroes would have it in their power to compel the interference of the courts of law for their protection."[5]

Dissatisfied with this response, Southern politicians doggedly—but unsuccessfully—continued the argument for years. In January 1821, Kentucky Congressman Henry Clay petitioned Congress to demand that the U.S. government commence negotiations with the British about Upper Canada's refusal to return runaways to their "rightful" owners: "An application was made a short time ago by Mr. Quincy Adams to the British Charge d'Affaires at Washington, to know if American slave owners could follow fugitive slaves into His Majesty's Provinces with a hope of recovering their property. Mr. Antrobus sent to Gr. [Lieutenant Governor] Peregrine Maitland who forwarded him in reply the opinion of the Attorney General for Upper Canada, which was decidedly negative to the proposition. This . . . was brought on by two or three slaves having been traced from the Michigan Territory to some of our most Western Settlements."[6]

After John Quincy Adams became president of the United States in 1825, he gave newly appointed Secretary of State Henry Clay the task of securing treaties with both Mexico and Britain to return runaways.[7] Clay tried to influence government officials in England by assuring them that runaways who sought asylum "are generally the most worthless of their class, and far, therefore, from being an acquisition which the British Government can be anxious to make. The sooner, we should think, they are gotten rid of, the better for Canada." Addressing the obvious question that his own words aroused, he continued: "It may be asked why, if they are so worthless, are we desirous of getting them back?" Clay responded, "The motive is to be found in the particular interest which those have who are entitled to their service, and the desire which is generally felt to prevent the example of the fugitives becoming contagious."[8] Clay's repeated requests, made from 1826 to 1828, were all refused. [9]

Home of Loyalist Matthew Elliott near Amherstburg. He was the local Indian Department supervisor and the largest slaveholder in Upper Canada. (Courtesy of the Fort Malden National Historic Site, Amherstburg, Ontario)

Such demands, however, eventually prompted a legal response in the Upper Canadian legislature. On February 13, 1833, Upper Canada passed An Act to Provide for the Apprehending of Fugitive Offenders from Foreign Countries, and Delivering Them Up to Justice. Under its terms, if a foreign government requested the extradition of anyone charged with "Murder, Forgery, Larceny or other crime," the accused was to be detained and, if evidence was compelling enough, transported to the foreign jurisdiction to stand trial.[10] The law was quickly tested when Lieutenant Governor John Colborne refused the request of Stevens Thomson Mason, Acting Governor of Michigan Territory, to extradite runaway slaves Thornton and Lucie Blackburn (for the full incident, see Karolyn Smardz Frost's chapter 2 in this volume). The Blackburns had been charged with inciting civil disobedience on the occasion of their tumultuous rescues from a Detroit jail and subsequent flights to Canada.[11] Colborne's decision was easy in Lucie's case—she had quietly slipped away from her cell after disguising herself by exchanging clothing with a female visitor. While Thornton's situation was more complex, Colborne and his officials exercised their option of relying on the clause in the Offenders Act that the accused need not be returned if the official "shall deem it inexpedient so to do."[12]

Following that refusal, the government of Upper Canada was faced with several requisitions, each somewhat similar in nature. In 1834, Stevens T. Mason, now governor of Michigan, sent a requisition to Upper Canadian authorities for Abraham Johnson, a Virginia runaway who had fled on his master's horse. Johnson was arrested at Sandwich but was eventually freed after the Executive Council, noting that escaping from slavery was not illegal under British law, ruled that Johnson's only crime had been the theft of the horse.[13] Since Johnson's motive for stealing the horse was only to facilitate his escape, his case did not meet the capital crime criterion for extradition.

Three years later, the governor of Kentucky made two nearly simultaneous requests for the return of runaways.[14] Solomon Moseby had fled on his master's horse to Buffalo, from whence he crossed the Niagara River into Canada. Moseby had then sold his master's horse and pocketed the money. Jesse Happy's flight four years earlier had differed in one significant detail. After Happy arrived in Buffalo, he wrote to his master informing him of where he could retrieve his horse. Moseby's owner, the wealthy Kentucky horse breeder David Castleman, arrived in Niagara in August 1837, laden with both formal requisitions and supporting documents. It was historian David Murray who first recognized that Castleman was the claimant for both Happy and Moseby, which points to how important the issue of fugitive slave rendition was to the Kentucky elite.[15]

After review, Canadian magistrates ordered that both Moseby and Happy be arrested. Solomon Moseby was placed in the Niagara jail and Happy was incarcerated in Hamilton. Both the Executive Council and the attorney general ignored a brief presented by Moseby's attorney, who had been hired by Blacks in the Niagara district to defend the fugitive. They agreed that there was sufficient proof to return Moseby on the grounds that he was a horse thief. Moseby's Niagara friends offered Castleman $1,000 to withdraw his suit, enough to cover the slaveholder's travel expenses and compensate him for the loss of his horse. Demonstrating that he was trying to prove a broader point, Castleman refused.[16]

Worried residents of the area then petitioned for Lieutenant Governor Sir Francis Bond Head to refer the issue to the British government, but Bond Head was convinced that Moseby's guilt was clear. He did, however, at the request of the Executive Council, ask for guidance from the British government on the Jesse Happy case because of a technicality—although Happy had fled four years earlier, the Kentucky indictment was only two years old, suggesting that the delay proved that there was no real intent to punish Happy for the theft of the horse, but rather the purpose of the indictment was to return him to slavery. The legal authorities consulted by the British government opined that in the case of horse theft, it was irrelevant whether the accused were enslaved or free, but ruled that any evidence regarding the crime had to be taken in Canada to allow for perjury charges in the case of false testimony. They concluded that they did not believe the evidence pointed to criminal behavior on Happy's part—only the temporary unauthorized use of the horse—and ordered that the accused be set free. Even before receiving the reply, however, the Executive Council of Upper Canada had found that there was insufficient proof of Happy's guilt and ordered his release on November 14, 1837.[17]

Moseby's case had a more dramatic ending. While he was incarcerated at Niagara, local Blacks camped around the jail for several days to prevent him being spirited away across the border. About one hundred African Canadians blocked the route when the deputy sheriff and four uniformed soldiers of the Royal Artillery brought the shackled Moseby out of jail with the intention of taking him across the river on the Niagara ferry and handing him over to U.S. authorities. The deputy ordered his men to open fire, killing two people and wounding another. In the confusion, Solomon Moseby slipped out of his handcuffs and fled, initially finding refuge in the Toronto home of Wilson Ruffin Abbott, a freeborn American Black who had left behind the overt discrimination and oppressive laws of the United States two years previously.[18] Moseby remained secreted with the Abbott family until sufficient funds were raised to send him to England. Sometime later he returned to Canada, where no attempt was apparently ever made to recapture him. However, the fact that officials were willing to hand him over terrified Canadian Blacks, a sentiment most passionately expressed by Sarah Carter, who had participated in the fray: "I thought we were safe here—I thought that nothing could touch us here, on your British ground, but it seems I was mistaken, and if so I won't stay here—I won't—I won't! I'll go and find some country where they cannot reach us! I'll go to the end of the world, I will!"[19]

As Britain's own involvement in the institution of slavery gradually faded from memory, its resolve to defend the rights of Blacks in its colonies strengthened. That position was tested in 1841 when many of the 135 slaves on board the U.S. slave ship *Creole* bound from Richmond, Virginia, for sale in New Orleans mutinied, seizing the ship and sailing to a British port in the Bahamas.[20] Enraged U.S. authorities sought the return of the human cargo, which included ringleader Madison Washington, a slave who had successfully fled to Canada but had returned to the South in the hopes of rescuing his enslaved wife. However, British authorities steadfastly refused the request to extradite the mutineers, despite the fact that many of their U.S. counterparts labeled them "pirates," thus igniting a firestorm of protest in the American South that was fanned further by members of the Senate and the House of Representatives.[21]

The next year, the specter of the "*Creole* Affair" weighed heavily on the minds of British Foreign Minister Lord Ashburton and U.S. Secretary of State Daniel Webster as they attempted to negotiate an agreement that addressed various contentious issues—including dealing with fugitive slaves. There had been considerable pressure on Ashburton to ensure that fugitive slaves residing in British North America were not endangered by the treaty. On August 9, 1842, an accord was reached, the Webster-Ashburton Treaty. In light of U.S. history, the agreement contained some curious terminology: "Whereas the traffic in slaves is irreconcilable with the principles of humanity and justice; and whereas both His Majesty and the United States are desirous of continuing their efforts to promote its entire abolition, it is hereby agreed that both the contracting parties shall use their best endeavors to accomplish so desirable an object."[22] While the *Creole* issue was not specifically addressed in the treaty, the tenth article alluded to it and future fugitive slave cases in a more general way: "It is agreed that the United States and Her Britannic Majesty shall, upon mutual requisitions by them, or their Ministers, officers, or authorities, respectively made, deliver up to justice all persons who, being charged with the crime of murder, or assault with intent to commit murder, or piracy, or arson, or robbery, or forgery, or the utterance of forged paper, committed within the jurisdiction of either, shall seek an asylum or shall be found within the territories of the other."

Before the new treaty had been ratified by both countries, its terms were tested. The previous year, Nelson Hackett, an Arkansas slave, took his master's beaver overcoat, saddle, and gold watch as well as items belonging to a neighboring slave owner and rode toward freedom on his master's valuable racehorse. He eventually crossed the Detroit River and reached what he supposed would be the safety of Canada. However, Hackett's owner followed the trail to Chatham, Canada West, and enlisted the aid of Canadian officials, who had Hackett arrested, beaten, and placed in the Sandwich jail. The owner then crossed back into Michigan and pled his case to the acting governor who, under the terms of Upper Canada's Fugitive Offenders Act, requested that Hackett be extradited. The request was refused because the requisition originated in Michigan rather than Arkansas, the original jurisdiction where the purported crime had taken place.[23]

The editors of Boston's *Emancipator and Republican* spoke for abolitionists on both sides of the border when they celebrated the fact that the governments of Canada and Great Britain would not bow to "tyrants." After learning that the British Cabinet was devoting time to discuss the case of "a poor fugitive slave," they were confident of the outcome: "We rejoice that this dark plot is to be investigated. Slave catchers may depend upon it that the vigilant eye of British liberty will keep their cursed feet off her free soil; false pleas, pretended crimes and devilish cunning, will not avail. Let the slave only reach Canada and he SHALL BE FREE."[24]

But the editors' jubilant refrain was premature. Rather than being released, Hackett remained incarcerated in Sandwich, allowing time for his master to return to Arkansas and initiate a grand jury hearing that indicted the runaway on a charge of larceny.[25] Now feeling that he was on solid legal footing, Arkansas Governor Archibald Yell requisitioned Canadian authorities to return Hackett to his state for trial. Believing that the stated grounds met the criterion that the charge would be considered a capital crime in Canada West as well as in Arkansas, Governor General Sir Charles Bagot acquiesced and—after five months of holding Hackett in custody—ordered that the prisoner be surrendered to Arkansas authorities.[26]

A wave of protest erupted on both sides of the Atlantic. Suspicions were raised that corrupt Canadian authorities had accepted bribes to detain Hackett until Arkansas officials had time to issue an indictment and had never intended to allow the fugitive to be tried in their own jurisdiction, before any decision had been made concerning the propriety of extradition.[27] Despite assurances that Queen Victoria herself was committed to protecting the rights and freedoms of African Americans who escaped to Canada, and that Hackett's case had been laid before the Imperial Parliament, it was too late for any British official to reverse the effect of the earlier action.[28] After a period of incarceration in the Detroit jail, Hackett had already been returned to slavery in Arkansas. There he was kept in chains, flogged on several occasions, then sold away from his family and friends to the interior of Texas.[29]

Both the Michigan State Anti-Slavery Society and the African American Detroit Vigilant Committee expressed disgust at the secrecy and deceit that surrounded the entire Hackett affair. The latter group was particularly disturbed. Members of the committee had crossed the Detroit River to attend Hackett's court hearing and had thereafter kept a nervous eye on the Sandwich jail, anxiously seeking news of developments on either side of the border. When they learned of the disappointing outcome, the Detroit Vigilant Committee officers called a general meeting to urge calm among the black citizens of Detroit. At that meeting they decided to publicize details of the case widely, hoping that this would stir public sentiment enough to prevent similar outcomes in the future. However, they philosophically joined with the state Anti-Slavery Society in refraining from aggressively defending Hackett, fearing that to do so for someone who had stolen a coat, a watch, and other valuables for his own benefit would only cloud the issue and weaken future attempts to save other refugees.[30] British Foreign Minister Lord Aberdeen agreed, believing that had Hackett only stolen a horse on which to escape, he would not have been extradited.[31]

Several fugitive slaves benefited from the furor resulting from Hackett's case. In August 1847, the Attorney General of Canada East, William Badgley, and Governor General Lord

THE FIRST BRICK COURT HOUSE AND JAIL.
Erected about the year 1800. During the Fenian troubles of 1866 and 1870 it was used part of the time for a barracks for the militia. The soldiers in the pacture are some of the Quebec Rifles, stationed at Sandwich at that time.

Old Sandwich Gaol, where Thornton and Lucie Blackburn (1833) and Nelson Hackett (1841) were incarcerated. (Courtesy of Windsor Community Museum)

Elgin refused the Governor of Maryland's extradition request for the return of Isaac Brown, despite a rather dubious grand jury indictment that accused the former slave of attempting to kill his master.[32] Disparate groups of Canadians demonstrated their support for the decision: a crowd in Montreal chased away the Maryland agents who sought to take Brown back, and some forty-six Blacks from Toronto posted a large advertisement in the *Toronto Globe* heaping praise on the Attorney General of Canada East for the humanitarian stance he had taken and scorning his counterpart from Canada West for not doing likewise.[33]

In January of that same year, slave hunters broke into the Marshall, Michigan, home of Adam and Sarah Crosswhite who, along with four of their children, had fled slavery in Kentucky some time before. A large crowd of both whites and Blacks came to the family's rescue and succeeded in sending the Crosswhites by train to Detroit and across the river into Canada. The enraged Kentuckians demanded redress through the courts and brought charges against several individuals who had prevented the Crosswhites' owner from regaining his property. While the Governor of Kentucky may not have made a formal request for extradition of the Crosswhite family, there is a fascinating document associated with the case: a letter witnessed by the Chief Justice of the U.S. Supreme Court and addressed to two Canadian Justices of the Peace. It begins:

CIRCUIT COURT OF THE UNITED STATES FOR THE DISTRICT OF MICHIGAN
THE PRESIDENT OF THE UNITED STATES OF AMERICA
TO ALEXANDER MCLEAN & BABY OF CHATHAM IN THE PROVINCE
OF CANADA WEST

Greeting ...

Know ye, that in confidence of your prudence and fidelity, the Circuit Court ... nominated and appointed you or either of you and give unto you or either of you full power and authority to examine upon oath (or affirmation) Adam Crosswhite and Sarah Crosswhite now of said Chatham in the Province of Canada West.[34]

As described in chapter 11 of this volume, the letter went on to "command" the justices to interrogate the Crosswhites, record their responses, and return same to the Michigan court that would try the case of the slave owner versus the abolitionists. Both Adam and Sarah complied and gave their statements. But Adam went a hazardous step further. When the actual trial began in Detroit, he crossed *back* over the Detroit River so he could appear in person to testify on behalf of those who had risked so much to protect him and his family. As a runaway, he could have easily been seized by the slaveholders or U.S. officials. Fortunately, the courtroom was so crowded with antislavery friends that no one molested him and Adam Crosswhite, after making his statement, was whisked back to safety in Canada West.[35] Ultimately, the court ruled that the claims of the owner and his grandson were legitimate, and the Crosswhites' rescuers were ordered to pay all legal costs plus the value of the slaves, amounting to nearly $4,800.[36]

Once again a mass meeting of the black citizens of Detroit—many of whom had been involved in the Blackburn and Hackett cases and had ties on both sides of the border—was called to protest what they felt was the trampling of their rights and the uncertainty of their protection under the law. Together they resolved that "we hold our liberty dearer than we do our lives, and we will organize and prepare ourselves with the determination, live or die, sink or swim, we will never be taken back into slavery." They further pledged: "[W]e will never voluntarily separate ourselves from the slave population in the country, for they are our fathers and mothers, and sisters and our brothers, their interest is our interest, their wrongs and their sufferings are ours, the injury inflicted on them are alike afflicted on us."[37]

The Crosswhite case galvanized abolitionists in Michigan but fomented outrage in Kentucky, which led to dramatic proposals in the U.S. Congress. Debian Marty explains the intricacies of the Crosswhites' lives, the significance of this incident, and the crises it created for the United States in chapter 11 of this volume.

Another seminal event occurred on the morning of September 11, 1851, when Edward Gorsuch, a Maryland slaveholder, along with a posse that included his son, two nephews, and a U.S. marshal, attempted to retrieve four runaways who had found refuge near the small village of Christiana in the free state of Pennsylvania. There the fugitives had been taken under the wing of a vigilance organization for mutual protection led by William Parker, himself a fugitive slave. In a scene reminiscent of the Crosswhite case but more violent, many neighbours responded to the call to resist the slavecatchers. In the ensuing battle, in which guns, clubs, and farm tools were used as weapons, Edward Gorsuch was killed and his son gravely injured. Anticipating the fierce retribution and the national furor that would inevitably follow, Parker and his two closest companions, Alexander Pinckney and Abraham Johnson, bid good-bye to their wives and children and began a circuitous route through Pennsylvania and New York toward Canada. Traveling on foot, by carriage, by stagecoach, and by train, occasionally aided by sympathetic abolitionists, including Frederick Douglass, then a Rochester, New York, resident, the trio eventually succeeded in boarding a steamship bound for Canada, thereby eluding would-be captors drawn to the pursuit of these men who had quickly become the subjects of international news because of what was labeled the "Christiana Riot."

After crossing Lake Ontario and docking in Kingston, the men traveled to Toronto. By then, word had reached them that the governor of Pennsylvania was demanding of the governor general of Canada that Parker be returned to the United States to face legal charges. According to William Parker's account, he boldly went to the government offices to plead his case and was assured by an official representative of the governor general that "you are as free a man as I am" and advised "to take no further trouble about it."[38] After being reunited with their wives and children, who had suffered their own nightmarish ordeal as they made their escape from Pennsylvania to Toronto, Parker and his associates boarded a vessel sailing to the Detroit River, stopping in both Windsor and Detroit before traveling to their enduring safe haven at the Buxton Settlement.

The final and certainly most complex extradition request took place on the eve of the American Civil War. Jack Burton, a Missouri slave, had fatally stabbed a white farmer named Seneca Diggs who attempted to capture him in the early stages of his escape. After crossing the Detroit River into Canada West in November 1853, Jack changed his name to John Anderson. In 1854, the governor of Missouri requested Anderson's extradition, but the fugitive could not be found. Over the next several years, Anderson took the precaution of occasionally changing his name and frequently moving his place of residence in the province. While living in Caledonia, he confided his secret to someone and was betrayed. Canadian officials ultimately arrested Anderson in March 1860. Although he was released on April 28, 1860, for lack of witnesses, word of the case reached a Detroit slave hunter named James Gunning, who contacted the Diggs family. Two days after Anderson's release, Gunning provided evidence of Anderson's crime, prompting a province-wide search for the elusive accused who had taken flight, before being arrested again in September. In December, the Canadian Court of Queen's Bench sitting at Toronto decided that, under the terms of the Webster-Ashburton Treaty, Anderson should be extradited, pending official orders from Governor General Edmund Walker Head of Canada. As had happened in Nelson Hackett's case, the Anderson decision prompted an international hue and cry. The Colonial Secretary ordered that John Anderson remain in Canada until the British government could make a ruling in his case. Confusion and contradictions abounded as Canadian officials differed from their British counterparts over who had final jurisdiction in this case. An executive member of the Anti-Slavery Society of Canada requested the assistance of the British and Foreign Anti-Slavery Society, which successfully appealed to British legal authorities to have Anderson set free. Finally, the Court of Common Pleas in Toronto ruled Anderson innocent of the extraditable charge of murder and ordered his release on February 16, 1861. With the first shots of the Civil War only weeks away, Anderson's case marked the final page of Canada's contentious chapter on extradition of American fugitive slaves.[39]

NOTES

1. Article VII of Definitive Treaty of Peace between the United States of America and His Britannic Majesty, September 3, 1783, memory.loc.gov/ (accessed November 27, 2012).
2. John Jay to Edmund Randolph, September 13, 1794, in *The Correspondence and Public Papers of John Jay*, vol. 4, *1794–1826*, ed. Henry P. Johnston (New York: G. P. Putnam's Sons, 1893), 61, oll.libertyfund.org/index.php?option=com_frontpage&Itemid=149 (accessed November 28, 2012). At least thirty-five hundred Black Loyalists were removed on British ships to Canada alone, with many more transported to Great Britain and the West Indies. Paradoxically, under the terms of the Imperial Act of 1790 (30 Geo. III, c. 27), white Loyalists also brought to Canada an uncounted number of enslaved African Americans. See James St. G. Walker, *The Black Loyalists: The Search for a Promised Land in Nova Scotia and Sierra Leone* (Toronto: University of Toronto Press, 1992), 32; Harvey Amani Whitfield, "The American Background of Loyalist Slaves," *Left History* 14, no. 1 (2009): 58–87. For a discussion of this topic, see Noah Webster, *Collection of Papers on Political, Literary and Moral Subjects* (New York: Webster & Clark, 1843), 183–86.
3. David G. Chardavoyne, "Michigan and the Fugitive Slave Acts," *The Court Legacy* (Historical Society for the United States District Court for the Eastern District of Michigan newsletter) 12, no. 3 (2004), www.mied.uscourts.gov/HistoricalSociety/pages/newsletters/200411.php (accessed April 2, 2011).
4. William Renwick Riddell, "Notes on Slavery in Canada," *Journal of Negro History* 4 (January 1919), 397, and "The Fugitive Slave in Upper Canada," *Journal of Negro History* 5 (June 1920), 333–34.
5. Harriet C. Frazier, *Runaway and Freed Missouri Slaves and Those Who Helped Them, 1763–1865* (Jefferson, NC: McFarland, 2004), 107–8.
6. John Quincy Adams to G. Crawford Antrobus, June 11, 1819, Upper Canada Sundries, Vol. 40, RG 5 A1, Library and Archives of Canada; Goulbourn to Major Hillier, October 24, 1819, "private," Colonial Office Papers, Library and Archives Canada.
7. Editor's note: It was Henry Clay who had insisted that John R. Poinsett, who represented American interests in Mexico, include a clause in a proposed 1825 treaty with that nation to provide for the mutual extradition of fugitive slaves, of which the vast majority were, of course, American in origin. Mexico refused and abolished slavery entirely in 1829. However, Clay also opposed the Mexican War, in which he lost a beloved son, partly because it would facilitate the extension of slavery into new territory. See Don E. Fehrenbacher, *The Slaveholding Republic: An Account of the United States Government's Relations to Slavery* (New York: Oxford University Press, 2001), 101; Ethan A. Nadelmann, *Cops across Borders: The Internationalization of U. S. Criminal Law Enforcement* (University Park: University of Pennsylvania Press, 1993), 142–44.
8. *The Anti-Slavery Reporter and Aborigines' Friend*, June 1899, 149.

9. These various attempts on the part of the United States to influence British policy regarding fugitive slaves are detailed in *State Journal,* 16th Cong., 1st sess., 319, 326; *Annals of Congress,* 618; *House Journal,* 17th Cong., 1st sess., 143; *Annals of Congress,* 553, 448, 710; *Annals of Congress,* 17th Cong., 1st sess., 1379, 1415, 1444, available online at memory.loc.gov/ammem/amlaw/lwhjlink.html (accessed June 1, 2015). See William R. Manning, ed., *Diplomatic Correspondence of the United States, Canadian Relations 1784–1860* (Washington, DC: Carnegie Endowment for International Peace, 1943), 2:109–11, 132, 181, 633–35, 771–72, and Wilbur H. Siebert, *The Underground Railroad From Slavery to Freedom* (New York: Macmillan, 1898), 22, 299–300.

10. An Act to Provide for the Apprehending of Fugitive Offenders from Foreign Countries, and Delivering Them Up to Justice, February 13, 1833, Eleventh Parliament (3 Will. IV, c. 7), in Sir. John Colborne, K.C.B., Lieutenant Governor, *Statutes of His Majesty's Province of Upper Canada, Passed in the Third Session of the Eleventh Provincial Parliament of Upper Canada* (York: Robert Stanton, Printer to the King's Most Excellent Majesty, 1833), 37–38, hereafter designated as Fugitive Offenders Act.

11. The Blackburn story is covered by Dr. Karolyn Smardz Frost in her award-winning book *I've Got a Home in Glory Land: A Lost Tale of the Underground Railroad* (New York: Farrar, Straus & Giroux, 2007; Toronto: Thomas Allen, 2007), 209–25.

12. Fugitive Offenders Act, 38.

13. Smardz Frost, *I've Got a Home in Glory Land,* 241–42; Alexander Murray, "The Extradition of Fugitive Slaves from Canada: A Re-evaluation," *Canadian Historical Review* 43, no. 4 (1962): 298–314.

14. These cases have been extensively covered by Riddell, "The Fugitive Slave in Upper Canada," 347–54; and David Murray, *Colonial Justice: Justice, Morality, and Crime in the Niagara District, 1791–1849,* Osgoode Society for Canadian Legal History (Toronto: University of Toronto Press, 2002), 196–216. Janet Carnochan interviewed some of the Blacks who lived in Niagara at the time of the Moseby affair and wrote a unique and important piece on the subject titled *A Slave Rescue in Niagara Sixty Years Ago,* Niagara Historical Society Publication No. 2, images.ourontario.ca/Partners/nhsm/NHSM0570271T.pdf (accessed September 21, 2011). Historians now believe the return of these particular slaves was not the point—the two were claimed by the same slaveholder, a prominent Kentuckian with family ties to John C. Breckinridge, former Vice President of the United States, to see if the Canadian position on the return of fugitive slaves to the United States could be forced. See Murray, *Colonial Justice,* 197–216; Smardz Frost, *I've Got a Home in Glory Land,* 242–43.

15. David Murray, "Criminal Boundaries: The Frontier and the Contours of Upper Canadian Justice, 1792–1840," *Canadian Review of American Studies/American Review of Canadian Studies* 26, no. 3 (1996): 341–66, and "Hands Across the Border: The Abortive Extradition of Solomon Moseby," *Canadian Review of American Studies* 30, no. 2 (2000): 187–209. Historian Adrienne Shadd provides additional fascinating details on Moseby and Happy in *The Journey from Tollgate to Parkway: African Canadians in Hamilton* (Toronto: Dundurn, 2010), 96–103.

16. For an early but still useful account, see J. Mackenzie Leaske, "Jesse Happy, A Fugitive Slave from Kentucky," *Ontario Historical Society Papers and Records* 54 (June 1962): 85–98;

see also Jason H. Silverman, "Kentucky, Canada, and Extradition: The Jesse Happy Case," *Filson Club History Quarterly* 54, no. 1 (1980): 50–60; Murray, *Colonial Justice*, 199.

17. Riddell, "The Fugitive Slave in Upper Canada," 353.
18. Anderson Ruffin Abbott Papers, Vol. 9, S. 90, Baldwin Room, Toronto Reference Library, Toronto.
19. Anna Jameson, *Winter Studies and Summer Rambles in Canada* (New York: Wiley & Putnam, 1839), 250.
20. A recent article on this topic is Walter Johnson, "White Lies: Human Property and Domestic Slavery Aboard the Slave Ship *Creole*," *Atlantic Studies* 5, no. 2 (2008): 237–63.
21. Edward D. Jervey and C. Harold Huber, "The Creole Affair," *Journal of Negro History* 65, no. 3 (1980): 196–211.
22. "Webster-Ashburton Treaty with Great Britain, 1842," in *American Historical Documents, 1000–1904*, ed. Charles W. Eliot, vol. 43, Harvard Classics (New York: P. F. Collier & Son, 1909–14), www.bartleby.com/43 (accessed November 28, 2012). The authoritative volume on the treaty is Howard Jones, *To the Webster-Ashburton Treaty: A Study in Anglo-American Relations, 1783–1843* (Chapel Hill: University of North Carolina Press, 1977).
23. Roman J. Zorn, "Arkansas Fugitive Slave Incident and Its International Repercussions," *Arkansas Historical Quarterly* 16 (Summer 1957): 139–44, and "Criminal Extradition Menaces the Canadian Haven for Fugitive Slaves," *Canadian Historical Review* 38 (December 1957): 284–94. Much more recently, Ontario's then-assistant attorney general, Ministry of the Attorney General analyzed the legal implication of these decisions in respect to the Webster-Ashburton Treaty and its effect on the John Anderson Case (discussed below). See Donald V. Macdougall, "Habeas Corpus, Extradition and a Fugitive Slave in Canada," *Slavery & Abolition* 7, no. 2 (1986): 118–28.
24. *Emancipator and Republican*, October 6, 1842, 91.
25. *Emancipator and Republican*, September 15, 1842, 77.
26. *Emancipator and Republican*, September 15, 1842, 77.
27. *Emancipator and Republican*, September 15, 1842, 77; *Liberator*, April 21, 1843, 62. The *British and Foreign Anti-Slavery Reporter*, January 11, 1843, 2, carried an insightful letter from Canadian-based missionary Hiram Wilson, who gave firsthand observations of the case.
28. *Boston Evening Transcript*, April 29, 1842, 2; *Philadelphia Inquirer*, April 2, 1842, 2; *New Bedford Register*, April 3, 1842, 2; *Vermont Gazette*, April 10, 1842, 2; *Augusta (GA) Chronicle*, August 3, 1842, 2; *Daily National Intelligencer* (Washington, DC), August 13, 1842, 2.
29. *The Anti-Slavery Reporter*, July 1, 1851, carries the story (reported by Hiram Wilson) of a runaway slave who was held on the same Arkansas plantation as Nelson Hackett. Also see *Emancipator and Republican*, January 19, 1843, 146.
30. *Emancipator and Republican*, September 15, 1842, 77, carried a letter from Michigan attorney Charles H. Stewart, who was also president of the Anti-Slavery Society of Michigan. See *Signal of Liberty*, March 9, 1842, and January 25, 1843.
31. *North American*, September 12, 1842, 1. The members of the committee were S. S. Jocelyn, Leonard Gibbs, La Roy Sunderland, and Lewis Tappan.
32. *New York Daily Tribune*, October 1, 1847 (reprint of an article from the Canadian newspaper *Galt Reporter*). See also *Boston Daily Courier*, September 27, 1847; *Trenton State Gazette*,

September 27, 1847; *Pennsylvania Freeman*, September 30, 1847, October 7, 1847; *Emancipator* (NY), October 6, 1847; Toronto *Banner*, September 17, 1847; *Boston Daily Transcript*, October 5, 1847; *Liberator*, October 1, 1847, October 15, 1847; *The North Star*, September 7, 1849.

33. Toronto *Globe*, December 11, 1847; interview with Thomas Smallwood, American Freedmen's Inquiry Commission, 1863, War Department, Letters Received by the Adjutant General, National Archives, Washington, DC; Hiram Wilson Papers, Oberlin College, Ohio.

34. Undated letter from October 1848, U.S. Circuit Court, Eastern District of Michigan, Southern Division at Detroit, RG 21, Law Records, Law Case Files, Case 1900, National Archives, Great Lakes Region, Chicago.

35. *Pennsylvania Freeman*, December 21, 1848; *The North Star*, December 15, 1848.

36. The exact figure is elusive. *The North Star*, April 7, 1849, reported that the judgment was for $1,926 plus expenses, which could amount to a figure as high as $6,000.

37. *The North Star*, December 29, 1848. Among those present were prominent Detroit activists George DeBaptiste, Madison J. Lightfoot, Henry Bibb, and William Lambert.

38. William Parker, "The Freedman's Story," *Atlantic Monthly*, March 1866, 291.

39. Macdougall, "Habeas Corpus, Extradition and a Fugitive Slave in Canada," 120–25. See also Patrick Brode, *The Odyssey of John Anderson* (Toronto: University of Toronto Press 1989), 291; and, for an account almost contemporary with the case, Harper Twelvetrees, *The Story of the Life of John Anderson, The Fugitive Slave* (London: William Tweedie, 1863).

STOCKHOLDERS
OF THE UNDERGROUND
R. R. COMPANY
Hold on to Your Stock!!

The market has an upward tendency. By the express train which arrived this morning at 3 o'clock, fifteen thousand dollars worth of human merchandise, consisting of twenty-nine able bodied men and women, fresh and sound, from the Carolina and Kentucky plantations, have arrived safe at the depot on the other side, where all our sympathising colonization friends may have an opportunity of expressing their sympathy by bringing forward donations of ploughs, &c., farming utensils, pick axes and hoes, and not old clothes; as these emigrants all can till the soil. N. B.—Stockholders don't forget, the meeting to-day at 2 o'clock at the ferry on the Canada side. All persons desiring to take stock in this prosperous company, be sure to be on hand. By Order of the

Detroit, April 19, 1853.   BOARD OF DIRECTORS.

Detroit broadside advising Underground Railroad sympathizers and operatives to support the cause and attend a meeting in Canada West. (Courtesy of the Burton Historical Collection, Detroit Public Library)

II

COMMUNAL VOICES

Scholars today are indebted to Wilbur Siebert, distinguished professor of history at Ohio State University, for his pioneering 1898 volume *The Underground Railroad From Slavery to Freedom*. However, scholarship has been restricted by Siebert's research. Siebert constructed an elaborate map of the Underground Railroad's human structure and variegated landscape. Largely as a consequence of Siebert's conception, railroad terminology—*stations, depots, conductors, passengers,* secret *cargo* and regular *schedules* and *routes*—dominates our understanding of the Underground Railroad. Although it captivates the imagination, the railroad metaphor undermines efforts to rethink alternative human and geographical dimensions of the mass migration of African Americans out of slavery. Recent research has uncovered new facets of this migration that indicate multicommunity, multiethnic, multinational, and multigenerational features—all of which evolved in unique ways over successive decades.

Additional voices that Seibert's informants rarely mentioned as well as unexamined locations and spaces of which Siebert's informants seemed unaware are today being recovered and mapped into contemporary conceptions of the Underground Railroad. Recent scholarship also emphasizes the voices of African Americans, both enslaved and free, whose intentional efforts to secure safety, security, community, and political agency have brought to light new episodes and established a much broader conceptual framework for the grand proportions of the Underground Railroad movement.

FOUR

CANADIAN BLACK SETTLEMENTS IN THE DETROIT RIVER REGION

IRENE MOORE DAVIS

It is a well-established fact that during the Underground Railroad–era, thousands of people of African descent made their way across the Detroit River to freedom into what we now know as Ontario. They included self-emancipated formerly enslaved people, propelled forward by their desire for freedom, as well as free people of color who were seeking relief from oppressive laws, racial harassment, and the constant threat of kidnapping and enslavement, or reenslavement for those who had earlier escaped to Northern states.

Many of these newcomers stayed briefly near the border in what is now Essex County, Ontario, before moving on to points at a greater distance from the British Canada–U.S. border. They traveled inland, perhaps to join other black pioneers who had already populated the interior of the province or to seek greater safety from the incursions of aggressive slavecatchers. However, many others chose to make the Detroit River region their home. The black population of Essex County was enumerated at 1,871, or 11.2 percent of the total population, in 1851, and 2,381, or 9.5 percent, by 1861, although these census figures were lower than contemporary unofficial estimates.[1] Often remaining close to the water, these black pioneers settled near the river in such places as Anderdon, Gosfield, Colchester, Harrow, New Canaan, Maidstone, Fort Malden, and Amherstburg.[2]

An individual's choice to remain in Essex County may have reflected his or her desire to be near friends and relatives there or to be easily found by those who had not yet emigrated from the United States. Some may have been attracted by the agricultural opportunities in the border region, facilitated by the relatively temperate climate and proximity to the Detroit marketplace. Black farmers in Essex County grew tobacco, wheat, corn, oats, potatoes, sweet potatoes, and a variety of other vegetables and fruits, and raised livestock and poultry—all of which they could transport with ease to the eager customers of Detroit.[3] Moreover, jobs were plentiful and laborers in demand.[4]

AMHERSTBURG

Amherstburg was founded in 1796, named after the original fort on the site. (After the fort was burnt in the War of 1812, the rebuilt fortification was called Fort Malden, taking the name of the surrounding township.) Located at one of the narrowest river crossings along the Detroit River, Amherstburg was both a logical place for nineteenth-century freedom-seekers to land and an appealing place for them to remain.[5] In the summer, it was possible (if not advisable) to reach Amherstburg by swimming across the river; in the winter, it was possible (albeit dangerous) to walk across on the ice. Most, however, crossed the river by raft or boat.[6]

There had been a black presence in Amherstburg from very early times. The first United Empire Loyalist settlers to arrive in Amherstburg at the end of the eighteenth century had included slaveholders, one of whom was Matthew Elliott, mentioned in the Introduction to this volume, who owned more than sixty slaves.[7] Other slave owners in the Amherstburg area included John Askin, Alexander Duff, James Donaldson, Simon Girty, and Richard Pattinson, considered among the most significant "founders" of Amherstburg.[8]

Thus almost since the founding of the Fort Malden and Amherstburg settlements, residents must have been accustomed to seeing black faces. However, not all of the early black residents were enslaved. Free Blacks such as William Lee and Thomas Fry had settled in the area as early as the 1790s. By 1820, there were five black families residing in the town of Amherstburg itself, and by 1828 there were one hundred Blacks living in Amherstburg and Malden Township.[9] The abolitionist Captain Charles Stuart estimated that about 150 refugees had come to Amherstburg when he resided there between 1817 and 1822, although it is not known how many stayed in the town. Stuart set up a colony for African American refugees on land he had been granted in Amherstburg for his military service.[10]

In December 1837, during the 1837–38 Mackenzie Rebellion, the Reverend Josiah Henson's company of black volunteers attached to the Essex Militia was part of the group that captured the rebel schooner *Anne* and made prisoners of its crew. Henson had fled Kentucky in 1830 with his wife and children when he was about to be sold away. Josiah Henson's unit defended Fort Malden from Christmas 1837 to May 1838, and another company of 123 black volunteers, Captain Caldwell's Coloured Corps, was subsequently stationed there for two months.[11] The black volunteers showed such bravery that Lieutenant Governor Sir Francis Bond Head commented on their service in his remarks to the legislature of Upper Canada in March 1838.[12] Even so, interracial relations in Amherstburg were not entirely rosy: in 1835, paranoid white residents petitioned the government of Upper Canada not to remove British troops from Fort Malden, fearing that they would be left defenseless against "the very numerous and troublesome black populations ... who are almost daily violating the laws."[13]

Nonetheless, black citizens of Amherstburg in the 1830s and 1840s contributed substantially to the prosperity of the town: they included an innkeeper, a tobacconist, a shoemaker, a miller, and the remarkable Levi Foster, who owned a plastering business, a tavern, and a livery stable. Foster had several homes and lots in Amherstburg as well as a farm in nearby Anderdon Township. By the 1850s, there were more black residents: mechanics, barbers, grocers, and teamsters. Laborers and sailors made up a large proportion of black inhabitants.[14] By 1856, Nasa McCurdy, one of three brothers to immigrate to Essex County from Pennsylvania, had settled in Amherstburg with his family, where after he practiced carpentry, became a member of the county constabulary, and served for many years as a trustee of the public school board.[15]

Americans interested in the slavery question were well aware of Amherstburg's significance. Resentment of Amherstburg's black population was reflected in the September 23, 1842, issue of the *Western Citizen* of Chicago, which stated that "there are over $400,000 worth of southern slaves in a town near Malden, Canada." American slave owners were nervous enough to propagate ominous myths about the district in order to discourage their slaves from seeking freedom. William Johnson, who escaped from slavery in Hopkins County, Virginia, reported having been told that the Detroit River was over three thousand miles wide, and that a ship starting out in the night would find itself in the morning "right whar she started from."[16] So populous was the black community in Amherstburg and so heavy the influx of refugees there that by 1848, Amherstburg was the regional headquarters for the American Missionary Society's operations in Canada.[17]

The census for Essex County, Canada West taken in 1850–51 indicated that there were 205 Blacks residing in Amherstburg.[18] Such figures were belied by the reports of the Amherstburg Regular Missionary Baptist Association, which noted in 1853 that there were about 600 black settlers in Amherstburg, and that, in 1859, there were 800.[19] By 1871, Blacks represented 15.5 percent of the total population in Amherstburg.[20] Contemporary estimates by (perhaps biased) abolitionist observers placed the black population in Amherstburg at 400–500 in 1855 and 800 by 1860.[21] When Samuel Gridley Howe of the Freedmen's Inquiry Commission visited Amherstburg in 1863, he reported that one in eleven Blacks was a taxpayer (and therefore owned property), as compared to one in three whites. Seventy-one of the five hundred taxpayers in the town were black. Howe found that the average tax paid by a white person was $9.52, compared to $5.12 paid by a Black. Contrary to the tales told by fund-raisers who claimed that the majority of African Canadians were destitute in order to garner support for refugees' basic needs, Howe found that there were numerous Blacks enjoying some prosperity in the town.[22] By 1867, Amherstburg had enough black residents to sustain a separate Masonic Lodge.[23]

In 1840 James Dougall, a Scottish immigrant, established an integrated school in Amherstburg, but it closed after six years due to financial difficulties.[24] Black children were prohibited from attending the Common School in Amherstburg in 1846. Despite the influence of Robert Peden, a superintendent of schools for Amherstburg and Malden who was somewhat sympathetic to education for black children, Blacks were forced to create their own separate school. The white missionary Isaac Rice, who had operated a school in the town since 1838, described the attitude of white Amherstburg residents: "Local trustees would cut their children's heads off and throw them across the roadside ditch before they would let them go to school with niggers."[25]

By 1851, a separate school for Blacks had been opened in a small log building on King Street under the Common Schools Act.[26] When American abolitionist Benjamin Drew visited the school, he reported dolefully: "The school house is a small, low building and contains neither blackboard nor chair. Long benches extend on the sides of the room, close to the walls, with desks of corresponding length in front of them. The whole interior is comfortless and repulsive. The teacher, a coloured lady, is much troubled by the frequent absences of the pupils, and the miserably tattered and worn-out condition of the books. Two inkstands were in use, which, on being nearly inverted, yielded a very little bad ink."[27]

In 1864, the King Street School was relocated from the rented log building to a frame building on the west side of King Street between Gore and Murray Streets. In 1875, a new limestone structure (which now houses Mount Beulah Church of God in Christ) was built to accommodate the sixty students there. By the late nineteenth century the schoolhouse was also serving as a multipurpose community center and meeting place for Amherstburg's black residents.[28] Beginning in about 1880 at the age of twenty-one, and for over thirty years, John H. Alexander ran the King Street School. Born in Anderdon to formerly enslaved black parents who had escaped from Kentucky, Alexander ultimately served on the Amherstburg Town Council and as Town Assessor.[29] The King Street School served the area's black students until 1912, when Amherstburg schools were finally integrated.

Connections between the black communities of Detroit and Essex County, particularly Amherstburg, were numerous, but perhaps one of the best examples of this early black transnationalism is evident in the formation of the Amherstburg Baptist Association. The black Baptists of Amherstburg are believed to have held undocumented meetings in the homes of the faithful as early as 1836, but by 1838, the congregation, known as First Baptist Church, Amherstburg, had been formally founded. An 1841 meeting called by the Reverend William C. Monroe of Detroit's Second Baptist Church and held in Amherstburg with members of his own congregation, along with those from the First Baptist Church of Amherstburg, and the Sandwich First Baptist Church resulted in the establishment of the Amherstburg Baptist Association. (More on this important group follows in chapter 6.) This organization still flourishes today as the Amherstburg Regular Missionary Baptist Association, a body to which the several black Baptist churches of Essex County, Ontario, continue to belong.[30] Under the Reverend Anthony Binga, land was purchased in 1845 on George Street in Amherstburg for the establishment of the current First Baptist Church building.[31]

Amherstburg's black Methodists began to meet in a log structure around 1840; and in 1848 the Nazrey African Methodist Episcopal church (AME) building was erected on King Street, where it now forms part of the Amherstburg Freedom Museum complex. Originally an AME Church, it became part of the British Methodist Episcopal Church (BME) conference for a time before reverting to the AME Church and being extensively remodeled in the 1880s.[32]

MALDEN

As early as 1828, according to the *Assessment of Malden Township with Amherstburg,* there were already one hundred Blacks living in Malden Township and Amherstburg.[33] By the 1850s, the talented McCurdys, a family of emigrants of partial African descent from Pennsylvania, had created their own prosperous settlement within the township of Malden.[34] At the time of the 1850–51 census, Malden was reported as having 279 black residents.[35] Reports from a New York conference of the AME Church in 1828 indicate that the congregation at Malden had eighty-five members by that time.³⁶ By 1853, the convention of the Amherstburg Regular Missionary Baptist Association reported that there were 900 black settlers in Malden Township.³⁷

Along with Colchester Township and to some degree Anderdon and Maidstone Townships, Malden Township was known for its tobacco production. While Blacks were not responsible for bringing tobacco to Essex County, as has sometimes been stated,³⁸ it has been correctly recorded that through their knowledge of tobacco cultivation, the black residents provided a very important stimulus to the tobacco industry in Essex County.³⁹

True Band Societies were early Canadian organizations designed for Blacks by Blacks to encourage self-help and mutual aid and to discourage the practice of begging from outsiders. The first True Band Society was organized at Malden in 1854 in reaction to the practices of fund-raising missionaries and clergy. The American Missionary Society representative at Amherstburg, Isaac Rice, was accused of painting a highly negative picture of the condition and progress of African Americans who had fled to British North America in order to enhance his fund-raising efforts. Within a few years there were fourteen True Band chapters across the province, with six hundred members at the mother chapter in Malden alone. Membership was open to both men and women, and the aims were to improve black schools, increase school attendance, counter incidents of racial prejudice, provide arbitration for disputes between people of African descent, offer assistance to new Underground Railroad arrivals, suppress begging by agents such as Isaac Rice on behalf of the African American immigrant population, and resolve religious disputes likely to result in the unnecessary division of church groups.⁴⁰

As in other parts of the province, African Canadian children were excluded from the Malden public schools. In 1857, black families petitioned trustees to let their children attend the white Common School in Malden Township's District 6. There were twenty-three black families in 1856–57, and forty-eight white families, and separate schools had been established for each group. The trustees rejected the black parents' petition.⁴¹

ANDERDON

When lands that had formerly been part of the Huron Reservation in Anderdon Township north of British Fort Malden were made available for settlement, numerous black families were among those who purchased them. The Census of the Canadas in 1850–51 reported that there were 349 black residents at Anderdon.⁴² Many self-emancipated, formerly enslaved black men obtained their first Canadian job at the limestone quarries there. As well, a white Anderdon resident opposed to slavery, Rowland Wingfield, established a settlement known as Marble Village along the Texas Road between the Front Road and the Second Concession in the 1850s and encouraged black refugees to settle there.⁴³ In 1856, Wingfield conveyed a one-acre lot on the west side of the Second Concession Road to the trustees of School Section No. 1. A Common School known as Quarry School or the Marble Village School was established on that lot. Later, a school attended solely by whites was established on Texas Road east of the Third Concession. Whites attempted to have that school made the official Common School for the district, which would have resulted in a loss of funding to the school attended by Blacks, but they were unsuccessful.

After the Civil War, the black population in Anderdon began to decrease. There were 450 black residents in Anderdon Township in 1861 but only 46 in 1921. The Marble Village School closed in 1917 and all of its students transferred to the new Public School Section 1.[44]

COLCHESTER, INCLUDING GILGAL, HARROW, AND NEW CANAAN

In Colchester Township on the northern shore of Lake Erie, east of Amherstburg, the black presence began with a few scattered slaves imported by white United Empire Loyalists who had fought for the British during the American Revolution and been rewarded with land and asylum in Upper Canada.[45] However, it is worthwhile to note that in 1787, Black Loyalists who had fought in the American Revolution on the side of the Crown, such as John Top, Prince Robinson, and James Fry, resettled as free Blacks in Upper Canada and were given land grants in the area.[46] From 1819 onward, a section of Colchester Township at the corner of Drummond and Third Concession roads populated by people of African descent became known as the Matthews Settlement.[47] Of course, subsequent Underground Railroad activity dramatically increased the black population of Colchester Township. By 1852, the Anti-Slavery Society of Canada estimated that there were between 1,200 and 1,500 Blacks residing in Colchester.[48] However, in keeping with a general pattern of underrepresentation of African Canadians in federal records, the 1850–51 census reported only 533 Blacks residing in Colchester.[49]

Many parcels of land in Colchester Township were cleared by hardworking black residents. Unfortunately, unscrupulous whites took advantage of the new immigrants. Visiting in the 1850s, American abolitionist Benjamin Drew was told by one farmer that Blacks had cut down two-thirds of the trees in Colchester, but that the land they had cleared had all too often been seized from them. Inexperienced in business affairs, they did not always understand the purchase agreements.[50] "Many Blacks [in Colchester Township] who could not read or write bought wild lands with ten-year mortgages, without understanding the terms. They cleared their land, made payments for 10 years, and then learned the payments covered only the interest, and that the whole principal came due after 10 years. Unable to pay the principal, they lost their farms to white mortgage holders."[51]

Early black residents of Colchester included the Reverend Josiah Henson, who after his escape to Canada with his family in 1830 stayed at Fort Erie for a time and then settled in Colchester, establishing a communal farm on rented land with other formerly enslaved people. Witnessing the mistreatment of naïve black residents by greedy white landowners, among other problems, he dreamed of creating a self-supporting black community along with an agricultural skills training program to help Blacks learn to own and manage their own farm operations. This was the inspiration for the Dawn Settlement, which Henson ultimately established at Dresden in 1842.[52]

Another early resident of African descent was Anthony Banks. He was born in 1840 in Colchester Township and became Canada's first black constable.[53] Then, too, there was William McCurdy, one of three McCurdy brothers to emigrate to Essex County from Pennsylvania in the 1850s. William purchased land in Colchester Township, became a school trustee, and ultimately was the first Black in Essex County, if not the province, to serve as a justice of the peace.⁵⁴ There was also Delos Rogest Davis, born in 1846 in Maryland and raised on property his formerly enslaved father bought near Gesto in Colchester Township. Like many African American migrants to the area, Davis worked as a deckhand and fireman on local Great Lakes ships until he was able to pay for a postsecondary education. He obtained a teaching certificate, taught school at the black settlement in Gilgal for four years, and studied to become a lawyer. Prejudice prevented him from articling with a lawyer, so after eleven years of trying to obtain a placement, Davis was given special permission to write the bar examination via a special act of the Ontario Legislature, An Act to Authorize the Supreme Court of Judicature for Ontario to Admit Delos Rogest Davis to Practice as a Solicitor (1884). Establishing law offices in Amherstburg and Windsor and serving as solicitor for the Town of Amherstburg and the Townships of Anderdon and Colchester North, Davis was such an outstanding lawyer, despite these unusual circumstances, that in 1910 he was the first black lawyer in the British Empire to be appointed a King's Counsel.⁵⁵

Another significant Colchester resident was the Reverend William Wilks, a middle-aged African who, after escaping from a Virginia slaveholder, made his way to Amherstburg in 1818. He had been kidnapped from the Congo at age ten. After residing near Fort Malden for approximately one year, he moved to the township of Colchester, where he purchased forty acres of land and built a log meetinghouse at the corner of his property in the early 1820s. A substantial congregation worshipped there even prior to his formal ordination. Wilks was eventually ordained through the intervention of two local white Baptist preachers as well as a minister from Detroit. He founded the First Africa Baptist Church, later known as the First Regular Baptist Church of Colchester.⁵⁶ By 1853 there was also an African Methodist Episcopal church in Colchester.⁵⁷ A British Methodist Episcopal Church and an African Methodist Episcopal Zion (AMEZ) Church soon followed. The latter denomination had been formally established in New York in 1821, but had actually begun in 1796 when black parishioners withdrew from St. John's Methodist Church after experiencing discrimination.⁵⁸

Unfortunately, as the number of Blacks increased in the Colchester area, white residents began to feel threatened by the competition for employment and resources. In 1849, when Blacks attempted to vote in the election of parish and township officers, they were prevented from doing so. Since this was a contravention of British colonial law, the result was that the chairman of the township meeting was prosecuted and fined. His heavy fines were paid by donations from sympathetic white residents. Friction between white and black residents remained well into the twentieth century, for the last segregated school in Ontario was closed in Colchester South Township amid controversy as recently as 1965.⁵⁹

At Harrow north of Colchester, there was an adequate population to establish a British Methodist Episcopal Church.⁶⁰ An abandoned black Methodist cemetery remains in the town from that period. The settlement once known as Gilgal, in Colchester South Township, is now part of the amalgamated Town of Harrow, Ontario. Here, black settlers established homes and farms along the western edge of a marsh at the Fifth Concession.⁶¹ An African Methodist Episcopal Church was established at Gilgal, later becoming a BME, and a black pioneer cemetery remains there, yielding much useful information about early residents. In 1852, the *Voice of the Fugitive* reported that the AME Church in Canada had established a total of five schools in which twenty-nine teachers were educating 250 students.⁶² One of these was at Gilgal, where Nasa McCurdy had donated land for the construction of a school and church building. Future attorney Delos Rogest Davis taught there for a time, and Elijah McCoy, inventor of the steam engine lubrication cup and many other products, was one of its early pupils before his family moved back across the Detroit River to Washtenaw County, Michigan.[63] The McCoy family's saga is detailed by Carol E. Mull in chapter 12 of this volume.

The settlement once known as New Canaan, nestled along Malden Road in Colchester North Township between Essex to the southeast and McGregor to the northwest, is now part of the amalgamated Town of Essex. The first settlers in New Canaan were transplanted African Americans who had escaped from slavery in the American South. Refugees could follow the Pike Road from Amherstburg east to the western end of Gesto Road, where New Canaan was established. The name given to the settlement in the 1820s speaks to an identity transformation from bondspeople to people guided by God to a new land of hope.[64] The Anti-Slavery Society of Canada reported that there were twenty families residing at New Canaan in 1852. The black population there was adequate to sustain its own Baptist church for a time.[65] There was also a British Methodist Episcopal church located there.[66] Abandoned tombstones are all that remain in place to tell the tale of this community today.

GOSFIELD

Gosfield Township sits on the north shore of Lake Erie, east of Colchester Township. One of the earliest records of a black presence in Gosfield Township relates to, of all things, a criminal case. After the American Revolutionary War, the United Empire Loyalist James Girty settled in Gosfield Township East, bringing with him his slaves.[67] These slaves, who are believed to have been captured during the war and "treated as personal booty rather than prisoners of war," included Jack York, who in 1800 was charged with burglary with intent to commit a felony (and was alleged to have raped a white female member of one of Essex County's oldest families, the Tofflemire family). York was convicted at Sandwich and sentenced to death, but he escaped.[68]

By the mid-nineteenth century, free persons of color and refugees from American slavery were beginning to make their way to the fertile land of Gosfield Township. There was a degree of prosperity there, and in the mid-1850s it was reported that of seventy-eight black settlers in Gosfield, the majority of the heads of households were property owners.[69] The population of Gosfield Township sustained a black Baptist church for a brief period.[70] An abandoned cemetery along Division Road near Kingsville remains a silent witness to a once-thriving Underground Railroad immigrant community.

THE SHORES OF LAKE ST. CLAIR: MAIDSTONE AND ROCHESTER TOWNSHIPS

By the last decade of the eighteenth century, there was already a black presence in Maidstone Township: the wealthy and powerful John Askin, formerly of Detroit and more usually associated after 1796 with Amherstburg and Sandwich, also had major landholdings in Maidstone Township and kept a number of black slaves there.[71] However, Underground Railroad activity dramatically increased the size of the population in the Maidstone area. For example, brothers Tom and Granville Lawson escaped slavery in Kentucky and settled in Maidstone Township in 1833. They acquired land by the Puce River and Pike's Creek, where they earned their living from the lumber business. Together they owned a single-masted schooner, which they used to transport lumber to Detroit.[72]

John Freeman Walls, a self-emancipated slave from North Carolina and his white wife, Jane, were important early settlers who made their way to Amherstburg before settling on Puce Road in Maidstone Township in about 1846. By 1848 the Walls family had a log cabin, two oxen, eight cows, three sheep, six horses, two dogs, and twenty-five acres of land. Within a few years, John Freeman Walls was raising 500 bushels of wheat, 150 bushels of potatoes, 75 bushels of peas, 100 bushels of oats, and 5 tons of hay.[73] The Walls family history is described in the book *The Road That Led to Somewhere* (1980) by Dr. Bryan Walls and is the main focus of the John Freeman Walls Historic Site and Museum in Lakeshore, Ontario.[74]

By the 1850s, there was already a substantial African Canadian community along the Base Line Road and south of it. This community was the primary source of hired help for the Scottish farmers in the Puce area.[75] In the early 1850s, the Refugee Home Society was formed to settle black refugees from American slavery along the Detroit River frontier in Canada West by selling them Canadian land. Founded in 1851 by Michigan abolitionists, the society merged in 1852 with the Windsor-based Fugitive Union Society. While the Puce River district was not the only part of Essex County in which the Refugee Home Society operated, it was one of the organization's major sites of interest. The society tended to purchase lands in regions where there was already some settlement, so the areas along Lake St. Clair settled by Refugee Home Society families included the Maidstone and Rochester Township settlements of Belle River, Little River, Spruce River, Pike's Creek, Pelee, Maidstone, and Puce.[76] While clearing their own farmland, the new landowners were able to work on other farms as day laborers, making a decent living due to the relative shortage of workers in the area. The settlement scheme erupted into controversy, chiefly due to the mismanagement of funds raised and accusations that agents were paying themselves exorbitant commissions, but ultimately 150 new black residents were added to the Puce River district.[77] By 1861, sixty families had settled on one hundred Refugee Home Society lots.[78]

Laura Haviland, a white Canadian-born Quaker and abolitionist who operated a school in the Puce River district in 1852–53, observed that while black Baptists had been meeting in a log structure since about 1846, there were Blacks of other denominations moving into the district, so she recommended the establishment of a Christian Union Church that would be accessible to all.[79] (Laura Haviland's Underground Railroad mission is discussed in detail in chapter 9 of this volume). This Union Church thrived for a time, ultimately becoming the First Baptist Church of Puce.[80] In 1874 the permanent structure, which stands today as the Puce Baptist Church, was completed.[81] The 1875 "Statistical Report" of British Methodist Episcopal Bishop R. R. Disney indicated that there was also a BME church at Puce River at that time.[82] The Refugee Home Society had deeded a half acre for a church and cemetery. The cemetery, which was ultimately abandoned, has recently been restored and commemorated with an Ontario Heritage Trust plaque. It is believed to be the resting place of up to one hundred black settlers. An African Methodist Episcopal Zion church was also located at the Puce River settlement, not far from the location of the BME Church.

Although descendants of these early African American migrants continue to live on or near their ancestors' properties today, some black settlers were dissatisfied with their experiences in this part of Canada West and longed for a place where they could fulfill their destinies without encountering constant prejudice. Black settlers from the Puce River district were among those who accompanied the African American abolitionist and Episcopal priest James Theodore Holly to resettle in Haiti in 1861 (although, in part due to the settlers' struggles with malaria and yellow fever in Haiti, this venture did not prove successful either).[83]

In other areas near Lake St. Clair, black populations remained small even at the peak of Underground Railroad immigration. These populations had largely dispersed by the turn of the twentieth century. After toiling amid the refugees in Windsor from 1854 to 1857, the American Missionary Association's emissary the Reverend David Hotchkiss, who had succeeded Isaac Rice in the role, was dispatched to Rochester Township, where by 1859 he was running not only a church and school but smaller missions in Little River, Pike's Creek, and Puce River.[84] For a brief period, there was also a black Baptist church located in Little River on the Third Concession in Sandwich East Township.[85] Rochester and Little River were depopulated of Blacks shortly after the conclusion of the Civil War.

WINDSOR

Although nearby Sandwich had been the capital of the Western District of Upper Canada since the 1790s, black residents had been present in Windsor (a village originally known as the Ferry) since at least the 1830s. Black volunteers were instrumental in the recapture of the Ferry on December 4, 1838, when it had been invaded briefly during the 1837–38 Rebellion aroused by William Lyon Mackenzie, an event better known to American historians as the Patriot War.[86]

Whereas for a few decades, Amherstburg had been the chief point of entry into Canada West for people of African descent, the pronounced increase in black immigration due to the developing industrial and commercial center of Windsor in the 1850s created the need for relief associations to begin assisting the refugees there.[87] In the early 1850s, abandoned military barracks on the present Windsor City Hall Square were used to house newly arrived refugees from American slavery, although most had to stay there only a short while before finding employment and better housing.[88] In 1863, the Anglican Church's Colonial Church and School Society dispatched the Reverend John Hurst, who had been working among black refugees in Amherstburg, to Windsor. He carried out his mission work in his new locale from All Saints' Church.[89]

Visiting in 1855, American abolitionist Benjamin Drew declared that 259 of Windsor's 1,400 residents were black.[90] By 1859, a year after Windsor became a town, the total population was between 2,500 and 3,000, and the Reverend William Mitchell estimated that 700 to 800 of those residents were of African ancestry.[91] There were over 600 Blacks in Windsor by 1867, according to tax assessment rolls.[92] African Canadians made up 20.6 percent of the total population in Windsor by 1871.[93] The black community established itself on what was then the eastern edge of the town, primarily along McDougall, Mercer, Assumption, Pitt, and Goyeau streets, still the core of Windsor's traditional black neighborhood.[94]

These barracks on the site of what is now Windsor's City Hall Square were used as a refugee reception center for Underground Railroad arrivals. (Courtesy of Windsor Community Museum)

Unless they arrived sick or injured, most black settlers were able to establish themselves quickly as laborers (or domestic servants and laundresses, in the case of females), and the arrival of the Great Western Railway in Windsor in 1854 created even more employment opportunities.[95] The *Voice of the Fugitive,* published between 1851 and 1853 by Henry and Mary Bibb in nearby Sandwich, as discussed in chapter 7, contained numerous job advertisements related to railway construction jobs; obviously the company perceived the town's black residents as a suitable labor pool.[96] By the 1850s, black preachers, barbers, coopers, and one drayman had also settled in the town. Thomas Jones, a former Kentucky slave, owned a plastering business said to be worth $3,000 to $4,000. By 1862, there were ninety-seven black families totaling nearly five hundred persons on the Windsor tax assessment rolls, including seventeen skilled tradespeople, five grocers and merchants, and eight sailors. There were twenty black skilled tradespeople and six businesspeople listed in 1867.[97]

In February 1860, "a meeting of the coloured citizens of Windsor at the town hall was honoured by the presence of Mayor James Dougall and of other prominent white citizens. They met to eulogize John Brown, who had been hanged at Charlestown, Virginia, December 2, 1859, for his raid at Harper's Ferry in October."[98] Clearly, the status of the black population of Windsor was such that the city fathers believed it necessary to participate in this day of mourning. Blacks in Detroit and Canada West played crucial roles before and during John Brown's raid. Louis A. DeCaro Jr. explores these connections in chapter 13.

First Baptist Church of Windsor was founded by the Reverend William Troy, a native of Virginia. Troy was stationed in Amherstburg in the early 1850s but in 1853 began to attend prayer meetings in Windsor. He relocated there in 1856, and in 1858 the First Baptist Church was established at McDougall and London Streets (the latter now University Avenue).[99] By 1865, the church boasted 147 members. Citing the need for expansion, the congregation moved to the present church building at Mercer and Tuscarora in 1915.[100]

An African Methodist Episcopal congregation was meeting in Windsor by 1853.[101] These worshippers were among those who decided to separate from the American body and form the British Methodist Episcopal Church. In April 1854, property was deeded to the BME congregation. Services were held in a small frame structure for two years until a substantial church was completed on McDougall Street in 1856. By 1865, the BME church in Windsor had 146 members, ten Sunday School teachers, eighty-four pupils, and a library of five hundred books. Mercer Street Baptist Church was built in 1877 and was bought by the AME Church in 1888. Both original structures were torn down in 1963 as part of the City of Windsor's downtown redevelopment strategy, but their respective members built new edifices elsewhere in the downtown area,[102] where the Ontario Chapel BME Church and Tanner-Price AME Church can be found today.

In Windsor Mary Ann Shadd opened the first school for Blacks in 1851 in the old barracks building, but the school was closed in 1853.[103] In 1854, in response to the Common Schools Act, the Windsor School Board promised to establish separate schools for the black, Catholic, and Protestant communities but did not actually provide a building for black students until 1858, when a rundown "coop" was rented for them.[104] Clayborn Harris of Windsor asked the Windsor School Board to let his son attend the Common School in 1859 instead of the dilapidated property used by black students, since the nearby white school was comfortable with room to spare. He hired a lawyer to press the issue but was unsuccessful.[105] In 1862 a proper building, St. George School, was erected for African Canadian pupils at the corner of McDougall and Assumption. Schools in Windsor remained segregated until 1888 despite multiple protests[106] and a high-profile lawsuit initiated by the prosperous black manufacturer James L. Dunn of Windsor.[107]

SANDWICH

Now a part of the City of Windsor, Sandwich, although it was the capital of Upper Canada's Western District, remained a village from 1796 until 1858, when it was incorporated as a town. It became part of the amalgamated City of Windsor in 1935. It was settled by white Americans who moved across the Detroit River in the wake of Jay's Treaty, as discussed by Veta Smith Tucker in chapter 1, a number of them bringing their slaves. Sandwich was the location of one of the homes of the wealthy and powerful John Askin, whose slave Joseph Cutten became the first person to die on the gallows in Upper Canada. Cutten's crime was stealing rum and furs from a Detroit merchant.[108]

In 1845 the African Methodist Episcopal Church set up a land colonization scheme for black refugees in Sandwich Township; by 1851 this project had been given the name the Colored Industrial Society. Tracts of land were bought on the Third Concession of the Township of Sandwich and divided into four-hectare lots. Unfortunately, the settlement never succeeded: only a handful of families settled there. A Reverend Willis disappeared with a substantial amount of money, and ultimately the settlement was dissolved.[109]

In the early 1850s, African American abolitionists Henry and Mary Bibb chose Sandwich as the site for their comprehensive antislavery operations, including the newspaper *Voice of the Fugitive.* From his vantage point at this busy Detroit River crossing, Bibb was able to comment regularly on the numbers of refugees crossing into Canada West at Sandwich, which ranged from fifteen per week to as many as sixty-five in one day.[110] He noted that while many who crossed were destitute and required assistance to meet their basic needs, this was not true of all. As a result of the passage by the U.S. Congress of the Fugitive Slave Law in 1850, "men of capital with good property, some of whom are worth thousands, are settling among us from the northern states," Bibb reported on October 22, 1851.[111] In 1852, the Anti-Slavery Society of Canada estimated that there were 300 Blacks residing in Sandwich.[112] Rather unusually, the census of 1850–51 actually reported a higher figure for the black population in Sandwich: 407 persons.[113] While the population decreased after the Civil War, some of the earliest black families of Sandwich, most notably the Watkins family, descendants of Caroline Quarlls Watkins, remain in the area today (see chapter 10 by Caroline Quarlls's descendant Kimberly Simmons and colleague Larry McClellan).

In 1851, Sandwich First Baptist Church was established on lot 22, West Peter Street.[114] Erected on the site of a former log cabin where founding members had been holding prayer meetings since 1841, the church was built by its members, many of whom were formerly enslaved Blacks, with handmade clay bricks. Madison J. Lightfoot, who was so instrumental in the Blackburn rescue of 1833 described in chapter 2, was the minister at the time. Today it is the oldest existing original black church building in Windsor.[115] By 1853, there was an AME Church in Sandwich as well.[116]

The black population of Sandwich was well known for Emancipation Day celebrations, which were held there on the first day of August each year commemorating the 1833 passage of the act to end slavery throughout the British Empire. These annual events drew as many as three thousand formerly enslaved and free black people residing in the surrounding districts of Canada West as well as in Michigan and were characterized by general goodwill, speeches, band concerts, picnics, river excursions, and balls.[117]

In the autumn of 1850 in Sandwich, Mary Miles Bibb, the African American educator and wife of Henry Bibb, started a school in her home, then eventually moved it to a shabby rented schoolroom. The school did not last long, although it was reopened after Henry Bibb's untimely death in 1854.[118] Again, black farmers and landowners in Sandwich attempted to send their children to the town's Common School but were rebuffed. Benjamin Drew reported of Sandwich:

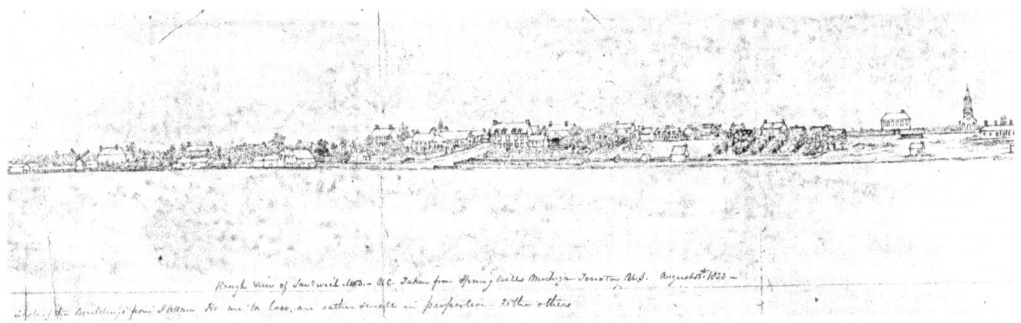

Dated August 13, 1833, this rough sketch of Sandwich, Upper Canada, as seen from Michigan Territory, represents the view that would have greeted many freedom-seekers as they prepared to cross the Detroit River. (Courtesy of Windsor Community Museum)

> The prejudice against the African race is here very strongly marked. It had not been customary to levy school taxes on the colored people. Some three or four years since, a trustee assessed a school tax on some of the wealthier citizens of that class. They sent their children at once to the public school. As these sat down, the white children near them deserted the benches: and in a day or two, the white children were wholly withdrawn, leaving the school-house to the teacher and his colored pupils. The matter was at last "compromised": a notice—"Select School"—was put up on the schoolhouse: the white children were selected in, and the black were selected out.[119]

In some of the Essex County communities where black settlements once existed, such as Little River, Rochester, New Canaan, and Gosfield Township, few signs of the black pioneers remain except for the almost indecipherable weather-worn grave markers that dot a few abandoned cemeteries. However, to this day descendants of the Underground Railroad immigrant communities remain in large numbers in Amherstburg (inclusive of Anderdon and Malden), Colchester (inclusive of Harrow), Puce, and Windsor (inclusive of Sandwich), many of them continuing to prosper in the Detroit River region as their hopeful, prayerful, determined ancestors once did.

NOTES

1. Rudolf A. Helling, *The Position of Negroes, Chinese and Italians in the Social Structure of Windsor, Ontario* (Windsor: University of Windsor, 1965), 4–5.
2. Daniel G. Hill, *The Freedom-Seekers: Blacks in Early Canada* (1982; repr., Toronto: Stoddard, 1992), 48. Evelyn Couch Walker, in *The Three Rs of Essex* (Windsor: self-published, 1979), 1, has pointed out that until the 1870s, "although Essex County was one of the first in Ontario to be settled, there was little settlement in the interior because of the swampy terrain."
3. Fred Landon, "Agriculture Among the Negro Refugees in Upper Canada," in *Ontario's African-Canadian Heritage: Collected Writings by Fred Landon, 1918–1967*, ed. Karolyn Smardz Frost, Bryan Walls, Hilary Bates Neary, and Frederick H. Armstrong (Toronto: Natural Heritage Books, 2009), 112–13.
4. Wilbur H. Siebert, *The Underground Railroad From Slavery to Freedom* (New York: Macmillan, 1898), 204.
5. Elise Harding-Davis, Eleanor Gignac, Doris Gaspar, and Enith Henderson, Amherstburg Bicentennial Book Committee, *Amherstburg, 1796–1996: The New Town on the Garrison Grounds* (Amherstburg, ON: Marsh Collection Society, 1996), 1:239.
6. Hill, *The Freedom-Seekers*, 48.
7. Gregory Wigmore, "Before the Railroad: From Slavery to Freedom in the Canadian-American Borderland," *Journal of American History* 98, no. 2 (2011), 442.
8. Harding-Davis et al., *Amherstburg*, 238; Francis Cleary, "Fort Malden or Amherstburg," *Ontario Historical Society Papers and Records* 9 (1910): 1–19; Wigmore, "Before the Railroad," 439. Some of these slaves had been taken in raids on Kentucky fortified "stations," or settlements, during the American Revolution. For instance, see Consul Wilshire Butterfield, *History of the Girtys* (1890; repr., Lodi, OH: Log Cabin Shop, 1995), 86–91.

9. Harding-Davis et al., *Amherstburg*, 239.
10. Stuart reported to the New England Anti-Slavery Society that the fugitive slave community had doubled in size when he visited again in 1826. William Lloyd Garrison, ed., "Immediate Emancipation, No. III," in *The Abolitionist; or, The Record of the New England Anti-Slavery Society* (Boston: Garrison & Knapp, 1833), 1:37. See also Fred Landon, "Abolitionist Interest in Upper Canada, 1830–65," in *Ontario's African-Canadian Heritage*, 205.
11. Josiah Henson, *"Uncle Tom's Story of His Life": An Autobiography of the Rev. Josiah Henson (Mrs. Harriet Beecher Stowe's "Uncle Tom"), from 1789 to 1876*, ed. John Lobb (London: Christian Age Offices, 1876), 173–74. The Rebellions of 1837–38 were armed uprisings in both Upper and Lower Canada (now Ontario and Quebec). The rebels' goals pertained to political reform, most notably responsible government. American readers may know this conflict (or some components thereof) as the "Patriot War" of 1837.
12. *Upper Canada Gazette*, March 6, 1838; Hill, *The Freedom-Seekers*, 121.
13. Robin W. Winks, *The Blacks in Canada: A History*, 2nd ed. (Montreal: McGill-Queen's University Press, 1997), 148.
14. Census of Canada, 1851, Essex County, Canada West; see also Hill, *The Freedom-Seekers*, 172; Harding-Davis et al., *Amherstburg*, 239.
15. "Nasa McCurdy," Alvin McCurdy Fonds, Archives of Ontario, Toronto; Harding-Davis et al., *Amherstburg*, 243–44.
16. Siebert, *The Underground Railroad*, 194.
17. Fred Landon, "The Work of the American Missionary Association," in *Ontario's African-Canadian Heritage*, 121.
18. Helling, *The Position of Negroes*, 4–5.
19. Hill, *The Freedom-Seekers*, 54. The discrepancy is no surprise. Census figures for people of African descent were notoriously underreported in both Canada and the United States. Fugitives from slavery in particular were reluctant to give their names to government officials for fear of recapture. Numerous scholars have noted regular undercounting of people of African descent in North American census documents. See, for instance, Michael Wayne, "The Black Population of Canada West on the Eve of the American Civil War: A Reassessment Based on the Manuscript Census of 1861," *Social History/Histoire Sociale* 28, no. 56 (1995): 465–85.
20. Colin McFarquhar, "The Black Occupational Structure in Late-Nineteenth-Century Ontario: Evidence from the Census," in *Racism, Eh? A Critical Inter-disciplinary Anthology of Race and Racism in Canada*, ed. Camille A. Nelson and Charmaine A. Nelson (Concord, ON: Captus, 2004), 53–54.
21. Fred Landon, "Amherstburg, Terminus of the Underground Railroad," in *Ontario's African-Canadian Heritage*, 66–67.
22. Landon, "Amherstburg," 72–73.
23. Harding-Davis et al., *Amherstburg*, 241.
24. Hill, *The Freedom-Seekers*, 149–50.
25. "Questions Arising under the New School Act of 1846—Report No. 10 by Isaac Rice," in *Documentary History of Education in Upper Canada: 1846*, ed. J. George Hodges (Toronto: Ontario Department of Education, 1846), 294. For Rice's school, see Levi Coffin,

Reminiscences, 2nd ed. (Cincinnati: Robert Clarke, 1880), 249–50; Carter G. Woodson, *The Education of the Negro Prior to 1861,* 2nd ed. (Washington, DC: Associated Publishers, 1919), 252, 252n2.

26. Amherstburg Bicentennial Book Committee, *Amherstburg, 1796–1996: The New Town on the Garrison Grounds* (Amherstburg, ON: Marsh Collection Society, 1996), 2:53; Hill, *The Freedom-Seekers,* 154.
27. Benjamin Drew, *The Refugee: Narratives of Fugitive Slaves in Canada* (1856; repr., Toronto: Dundurn, 2008), 314.
28. Harding-Davis et al., *Amherstburg,* 53.
29. John Henry Alexander (1857–1935) is buried in Rose Hill Cemetery, Amherstburg. *Toronto Daily Mail,* January 9, 1892; Harding-Davis et al., *Amherstburg,* 241; "J. H. Alexander and Class, King Street School, Amherstburg," Alvin McCurdy Fonds, reference Code: F 2076-16-7-4, No. I0027815, Archives of Ontario, Toronto. See www.archives.gov.on.ca/en/explore/online/black_history/big/big_35_students.aspx (accessed January 3, 2014).
30. Dorothy Shadd Shreve, *The AfriCanadian Church: A Stabilizer* (Jordan Station, ON: Paideia, 1983), 62–63; Harding-Davis et al., *Amherstburg,* 2, 7–8.
31. Shadd Shreve, *The AfriCanadian Church,* 47, 55, 60–63; Hill, *The Freedom-Seekers,* 140.
32. Daniel Alexander Payne, *History of the African Methodist Episcopal Church* (Nashville: AME Sunday School Union, 1891), 361–91; Shadd Shreve, *The AfriCanadian Church,* 80. The British Methodist Episcopal Church was founded in 1856 at the request of Canadian AME Churches. At issue was the requirement for clergy resident in Canada to attend church functions in the United States. This placed those who had escaped from slavery at considerable risk. Bishop Willis Nazrey formally resigned from the AME and became the BME's first bishop. The term *African* was replaced with *British* in the name of the denomination to honor the freedom found in British North America by refugee African Americans.
33. Harding-Davis et al., *Amherstburg,* 239.
34. Alvin McCurdy Papers, "Family Papers," F-2076, Archives of Ontario, Toronto; Landon, "Amherstburg," 72–73.
35. Census of the Canadas, 1851, Essex County, Canada West; Helling, *The Position of Negroes,* 4–5.
36. Shadd Shreve, *The AfriCanadian Church,* 78.
37. Hill, *The Freedom-Seekers,* 54.
38. "While the Blacks did not introduce the cultivation of tobacco to the area, as French settlers' records of the area give evidence of its cultivation as a sale crop as early as the beginning of the nineteenth century, they did bring from the Southern states their own unique method of curing it." Scott Burnside, Cathie Fenchak, Sandra Mulatti, and Mark Skursky, *Maidstone Township: An Historical Review* (Windsor: self-published, 1984), 48.
39. Neil F. Morrison, *Garden Gateway to Canada: One Hundred Years of Windsor and Essex County, 1854–1954* (Windsor: Herald, 1954), 29.
40. Siebert, *The Underground Railroad,* 230–31.
41. Hill, *The Freedom-Seekers,* 102; Robin Winks, "Negro School Segregation in Ontario and Nova Scotia," *Canadian Historical Review* 50, no. 2 (1969): 164–91.

42. Census of the Canadas, 1851, Essex County, Canada West; Helling, *The Position of Negroes*, 4–5.
43. Harding-Davis et al., *Amherstburg*, 239–40.
44. Amherstburg Bicentennial Book Committee, *Amherstburg*, 2:51.
45. Americans who remained loyal to the British Crown during the American Revolution were called United Empire Loyalists. They were permitted by the Imperial Act of 1790 (30 Geo. III, c. 27) to import into Upper Canada their household goods, livestock, and slaves.
46. Harrow Early Immigrant Research Society (HEIRS), *Harrow and Colchester South, 1792–1992* (Harrow, ON: Harrow History Book Committee, 1993), 11.
47. HEIRS, *Harrow and Colchester South*, 15.
48. Thomas Henning, *First Annual Report, Presented to the Anti-Slavery Society of Canada, By Its Executive Committee* (Toronto: Brown's, 1852), 17; Shadd Shreve, *The AfriCanadian Church*, 62–63.
49. Census of the Canadas, 1851, Essex County, Canada West; Helling, *The Position of Negroes*, 4–5.
50. Drew, *The Refugee*, 367.
51. HEIRS, *Harrow and Colchester South*, 15.
52. Josiah Henson, *The Life of Josiah Henson, Formerly a Slave, Now an Inhabitant of Canada, as Narrated by Himself* (Boston: Arthur D. Phelps, 1849), 67–72.
53. "Anthony Banks Named Constable," document B3-1, and "Anthony Banks (1840–1929): A Biographical Sketch of Banks by His Granddaughter, Cordella Anne MacRae," document B3-19, Amherstburg Freedom Museum, Amherstburg, Ontario; Harding-Davis et al., *Amherstburg*, 244.
54. Harding-Davis et al., *Amherstburg*, 243–44.
55. Owen Thomas, "Delos Rogest Davis," in *Dictionary of Canadian Biography Online*, www.biographi.ca/009004-119.01-e.php?&id_nbr=7322 (accessed January 10, 2012).
56. Shadd Shreve, *The AfriCanadian Church*, 42–43. The biography of Elder William Wilks was recorded at the beginning of the second volume of the Amherstburg Association Minutes, a handwritten ledger preserved in the Canadian Baptist Archives, McMaster University Divinity College, Hamilton, Ontario.
57. Shadd Shreve, *The AfriCanadian Church*, 80.
58. Carter G. Woodson, *The History of the Negro Church* (Washington, DC: Associated Publishers, 1921), 78–9.
59. HEIRS, *Harrow and Colchester South*, 15–16; Funke Aladejebi, "'I Didn't Want to Be Anything Special. I Just Wanted to Teach School': A Case Study of Black Female Educators in Colchester, Ontario, 1960," *Southern Journal of Canadian Studies* 5, nos. 1–2 (2012), 146.
60. Angela E. M. Files, *African Hope Renewed Along the Grand River* (Brantford, ON: Taylor Made, 2004), 124.
61. HEIRS, *Harrow and Colchester South*, 15.
62. *Voice of the Fugitive*, July 10, 1852, August 12, 1852.
63. Henning, *First Annual Report*, 17; Carol E. Mull, *The Underground Railroad in Michigan* (Jefferson, NC: McFarland, 2010), 83, 141–43; Shadd Shreve, *The AfriCanadian Church*, 90.
64. "A New Settlement," *Voice of the Fugitive*, February 12, 1851; HEIRS, *Harrow and Colchester South*, 15.

65. Shadd Shreve, *The AfriCanadian Church*, 62–63.
66. Files, *African Hope Renewed*, 124.
67. James Girty left at least a dozen slaves to his two children, and freed his personal servant, Paul, in his will. See "Last Will and Testament of Pioneer, Dated 1804, Proves Existence of Slavery in Essex," from an unidentified local newspaper dated March 22, 1916, "Black History" folder, 1, Fort Malden Collection, Windsor Community Museum.
68. Robert Lochiel Fraser III, "Jack York," in *Dictionary of Canadian Biography Online*, www.biographi.ca (accessed January 19, 2011); Hill, *The Freedom-Seekers*, 92–93.
69. *Report of the Committee on Emigration of the Amherstburg Convention Presented at the First Baptist Church, Amherstburg, Canada West, June 16–17, 1853* (Windsor: Bibb & Holly, 1852), 21, quoted in Siebert, *The Underground Railroad*, 227.
70. Shadd Shreve, *The AfriCanadian Church*, 62–63.
71. Burnside et al., *Maidstone Township*, 40.
72. Burnside et al., *Maidstone Township*, 42–43; Malcolm W. Wallace, "Pioneers of the Scotch Settlement on the Shore of Lake St. Clair," *Ontario History* 41, no. 4 (1949), 195, cited in Adrienne Shadd, "Historical Background: Puce River Black Community," *Ontario Heritage Trust*, August 2007, 2, www.heritagetrust.on.ca/CMSImages/34/3479a022-cc44-4415-99a0-a24365e1c9ce.pdf (accessed January 4, 2014).
73. Burnside et al., *Maidstone Township*, 46, 49.
74. Bryan E. Walls, *The Road That Led to Somewhere* (Windsor: Olive Books, 1980).
75. Wallace, "Pioneers of the Scotch Settlement," 195.
76. Hill, *The Freedom-Seekers*, 75; William H. Pease and Jane H. Pease, *Black Utopia: Negro Communal Experiments in America* (Madison: State Historical Society of Wisconsin, 1963), 112–22; Winks, *The Blacks in Canada*, 204–8.
77. Burnside et al., *Maidstone Township*, 47; Hill, *The Freedom-Seekers*, 75; C. Peter Ripley et al., eds., *The Black Abolitionist Papers, 1830–1865*, vol. 2, *Canada* (Chapel Hill: University of North Carolina Press, 1986), 147n.
78. "Eighth Annual Report of the Refugee Home Society," *Anti-Slavery Reporter and Aborigines' Friend*, January 1, 1861, 18–19, Hill, *The Freedom-Seekers,:* 76; Shadd, "Historical Background, 2–3.
79. Laura Haviland, *A Woman's Life-Work: Labors and Experiences of Laura S. Haviland* (Cincinnati: Walden & Stowe, 1882), 196.
80. Shadd Shreve, *The AfriCanadian Church*, 73–74.
81. Burnside et al., *Maidstone Township*, 51.
82. Bishop R. R. Disney, "Statistical Report of the British Methodist Episcopal Church (1875)," cited in Files, *African Hope Renewed*, 124; Winks, *The Blacks in Canada*, 243.
83. Burnside et al., *Maidstone Township*, 56.
84. Landon, "The Work of the American Missionary Association," 126–27; Ripley et al., *The Black Abolitionist Papers*, vol. 2, *Canada*, 117n.
85. Shadd Shreve, *The AfriCanadian Church*, 62–63.
86. Sir Francis Bond Head, *A Narrative* (London: J. Murray, 1839), 392; Fred Landon, "Canadian Negroes and the Rebellion of 1837," *Journal of Negro History* 7 (1922): 77–79; Ernest Green, "Upper Canada's Black Defenders," *Ontario History* 27 (1931): 365–91.

87. Morrison, *Garden Gateway to Canada*, 29; *Voice of the Fugitive*, February 12, 1851.
88. Hill, *The Freedom-Seekers*, 53; *Voice of the Fugitive*, February 12, 1851. See also Fred Landon, "The Negro Migration to Canada After the Passing of the Fugitive Slave Act," in *Ontario's African-Canadian Heritage*, 250.
89. Hill, *The Freedom-Seekers*, 131–32.
90. Drew, *The Refugee*, 321.
91. Reverend W. M. Mitchell, *The Under-Ground Railroad*, 2nd ed. (London: Tweedie, 1860), 142–43.
92. Hill, *The Freedom-Seekers*, 53.
93. McFarquhar, "The Black Occupational Structure," 53–54.
94. Carl Morgan, *Birth of a City* (Windsor: Border, 1991), 41.
95. Morgan, *Birth of a City*, 46.
96. Fred Landon, "Social Conditions Among the Negroes in Upper Canada Before 1865," in *Ontario's African-Canadian Heritage*, 190.
97. Hill, *The Freedom-Seekers*, 174.
98. Morrison, *Garden Gateway to Canada*, 50.
99. William Troy, *Hair-Breadth Escapes from Slavery to Freedom* (Manchester, UK: W. Bremner, 1861), 7–8; Morgan, *Birth of a City*, 45.
100. Hill, *The Freedom-Seekers*, 145; Morgan, *Birth of a City*, 45.
101. Shadd Shreve, *The AfriCanadian Church*, 80.
102. Hill, *The Freedom-Seekers*, 138; Morgan, *Birth of a City*, 45.
103. Jane Rhodes, *Mary Ann Shadd Cary: The Black Press and Protest in the Nineteenth Century* (Bloomington: University of Indiana Press, 1998), 36.
104. Hill, *The Freedom-Seekers*, 156.
105. Kristen McLaren, "'We had no desire to be set apart': Forced Segregation of Black Children in Canada Public Schools and Myths of British Egalitarianism," in *The History of Immigration and Racism in Canada: Essential Readings*, ed. Barrington Walker (Toronto: Canadian Scholars, 2008), 81n73, 81; Hill, *The Freedom-Seekers*, 101–2.
106. Hill, *The Freedom-Seekers*, 156; Morgan, *Birth of a City*, 41.
107. "Dunn v. Board of Education of the Town of Windsor," in *The Ontario Reports*, 4, High Court of Justice for Ontario, Chancery Division (Toronto: Bowsell & Hutchison, 1885), 125–28.
108. Hill, *The Freedom-Seekers*, 91–92.
109. "Colored Industrial Settlement," *Voice of the Fugitive*, January 29, 1851, Black Abolitionist Archive, University of Detroit Mercy, research.udmercy.edu/find/special_collections/digital/baa/item.php?record_id=234&collectionCode=baa (accessed January 5, 2014); Hill, *The Freedom-Seekers*, 74.
110. *Voice of the Fugitive*, April 22, 1852.
111. Landon, "Negro Migration to Canada," 245.
112. Henning, *First Annual Report*, 17.

113. Census of Canada, 1851, Essex County, Canada West; Helling, *The Position of Negroes*, 4–5.
114. Shadd Shreve, *The AfriCanadian Church*, 62–63.
115. Morgan, *Birth of a City*, 45; Karolyn Smardz Frost, "African American and African Canadian Transnationalism along Detroit River Borderland: The Example of Madison J. Lightfoot," *Journal of American Ethnic History* 32, no. 2 (2013): 78–88.
116. Shadd Shreve, *The AfriCanadian Church*, 80.
117. Natasha Henry, *Emancipation Day: Celebrating Freedom in Canada* (Toronto: Natural Heritage Books, 2010), chap. 3; Morrison, *Garden Gateway to Canada*, 74–75.
118. Hill, *The Freedom-Seekers*, 156; Afua Cooper, "Black Women and Work in Nineteenth-Century Canada West: Black Woman Teacher Mary Bibb," in *We're Rooted Here and They Can't Pull Us Up: Essays in African Canadian Women's History*, ed. Peggy Bristow et al. (1994; repr., Toronto: University of Toronto Press, 1999), 143–70, esp. 147–48.
119. Drew, *The Refugee*, 308.

FIVE

WORSHIP WAY STATIONS IN DETROIT

BARBARA HUGHES SMITH

Black churches were central to the lives of Underground Railroad settlers and served as a source of support and comfort to African Americans in both the North and South. Isolated as they were in a strange city, newcomers to Detroit sought the familiar comfort of God and their church. When others ignored, mocked, censured, or harassed Blacks, they could turn to the church, the nucleus of African American social life, for fellowship.

Under the French regime, enslaved African people living in the Detroit River region had been served by St. Anne's Roman Catholic Church in accordance with the 1724 ordinance of King Louis XV that required all slaves in New France to be baptized and educated in the faith.[1] After the British conquest in 1760 and the subsequent American settlement in the Detroit River borderlands, both enslaved and free people of African descent migrated into the area, most of them adhering to various Protestant denominations. According to historian David M. Katzman: "By 1846, the small Detroit black community had three churches, Second Baptist Church with roots back to 1836, Bethel African Methodist Episcopal Church, organized in 1839 and St. Matthew's Church, a protestant Episcopal mission founded in 1846."[2]

Detroit's Second Baptist Church, which still serves the downtown African American community, was founded in 1836 as a direct result of racial discrimination within the city's white-dominated First Baptist Church. On March 5, 1836, thirteen black protesters took a leap of faith by removing themselves from First Baptist Church, which stood at Fort and Griswold Streets. First Baptist confined its members of color to segregated gallery seating and excluded them from both fellowship and holding church offices. First Baptist also voted to remove members from the rolls of the church who were not in regular attendance, a fate that befell African American member William Butler in 1834.³

In 1837, Madison J. Lightfoot flatly refused to submit to the rules of First Baptist Church regarding gallery seating for Blacks. As anticipated, he was excluded from membership and all fellowship. Others who withdrew from First Baptist in the same year were Cornelius Mitchell and William Scott as well as Lightfoot's wife, Tabitha, Caroline and George W. French, and Deborah and Benjamin Willoughby and their daughters, Frances and Julia. These trailblazing families then set about creating independent black institutions that would be examples of courage and conviction for Blacks in Detroit. For a generation, their names headed the lists of officers of benevolent societies, civil rights groups, and vigilance committees.

The ringleaders of the riots, examined in chapter 2 of this volume, that freed Thornton and Lucie Blackburn in 1833 were thus among the founders of Detroit's first black institution, Second Baptist Church. Its first building was located on land donated by George and Caroline French. The fledgling congregation requested permission of the Territorial Legislature of Michigan to found its own church. The first Society of Second Baptist Church was organized at George French's house "on Fort Street, between Beaubien and St. Antoine Streets" in the spring of 1836. The trustees were George French, Jacob Brown, Richard Evans, Madison Lightfoot, Robert Allen, Daniel Buchanan, William Brown, William Nash, and Samuel Robinson. The Reverend William C. Monroe was its first regular minister, appointed in 1840.⁴ Many of the antislavery black leaders in Detroit belonged to Second Baptist Church, and the Detroit community sheltered numerous escapees who traveled one of many routes through Michigan, making the Detroit River district the most frequented passage into Canada for Underground Railroad travelers.⁵ Detroit was a center of abolitionist activity, much of it focused around Second Baptist Church where antislavery activism escalated throughout the antebellum years.⁶ As a result of the courage, ingenuity, and tenacity of its members, Second Baptist Church stresses that its members helped nearly five thousand fugitives escape to Canada.⁷

Realizing that African American refugees arriving in Canada needed personal and financial assistance as well as a spiritual home, the Reverend Monroe instructed Second Baptist's clerk, Madison J. Lightfoot, to send letters requesting an organizational meeting to be held in Amherstburg, just across the Detroit River in Canada West. It was to be hosted by the Reverend Anthony Binga Sr., founder of the First Baptist Church of Amherstburg. Church leaders on both sides of the border came together with insight and passion to collaborate for the cause of freedom.⁸

The Baptist Association for Colored People was organized on October 8, 1841, by forty-seven delegates from three churches: First Baptist of Amherstburg (nineteen), First Baptist Church, Sandwich (eleven), and Second Baptist Church, Detroit (seventeen). The transnational cooperation between congregations was instrumental in facilitating border crossings from the United States and the reception in Canada West of literally thousands of fugitive slaves during the antebellum years. In 1842, the Baptist Association for Colored People changed its name to the Amherstburg Baptist Association. Second Baptist withdrew in 1850 because of disagreements with the association's governing body, the American Baptist Free Mission Society. By 1854, Second Baptist Church was associated with another group, the Canadian Anti-Slavery Baptist Association.⁹ The objectives of the two associations were to meet the religious needs of Blacks neglected in white churches, promote unity among black Baptists, exchange ideas, and assist

Current site of Detroit's Second Baptist Church. At this location and earlier locations, from the church's founding in 1836 to the beginning of the Civil War, members of the congregation assisted more than five thousand fugitives from slavery on their journeys to freedom. (Courtesy of photographer Elizabeth Clark)

in organizing other Baptist churches. The second organization was also established primarily to aid escaping slaves and eradicate slavery. The groups reunited in 1857 and the association has continued in various forms to the present day.[10] (A detailed history of the Amherstburg Baptist Association's early days of operation in Canada West follows in chapter 6.)

In addition to the cross-border cooperation facilitated by the Amherstburg Baptist Association, there were several individuals associated specifically with Detroit's Second Baptist Church who emerged as notable Underground Railroad operatives, most prominently William Lambert, who would come to be called the "President" of the Michigan Underground Railroad. Born free in 1817 in Trenton, New Jersey, and educated in Quaker schools, Lambert visited Detroit as a cabin boy on a steamer in 1837 and then migrated to Detroit on January 1, 1840. He was listed in Detroit's First Baptist Church minutes, four years after the establishment of Second Baptist.[11] Lambert married Julia Willoughby, daughter of Benjamin Willoughby, who was a founder of Second Baptist Church and one of the ringleaders of the Blackburn Riots.[12] Reared in the Quaker philosophy, Lambert ardently campaigned for freedom, equality, and education. Lambert's closest associate was George DeBaptiste, who arrived in Detroit in 1846 and also became very active in Underground Railroad activities on the Detroit River frontier.[13] DeBaptiste's unwavering commitment to transnational antislavery efforts in the region is featured in the Introduction to this volume, and in chapter 8, Roy Finkenbine discusses Lambert and DeBaptiste's concerted Underground Railroad activities in Detroit.

George DeBaptiste was born about 1815 in Fredericksburg, Virginia, to influential freeborn parents. DeBaptiste apprenticed with a barber, and he worked as a steward on an Ohio River steamer at Cincinnati. He and his young wife moved to Madison, Indiana, in 1838, where he again worked on steamboats and opened a barbershop. He was involved in Underground Railroad activities in Madison until 1840, when he was employed by William Henry Harrison as his personal valet during the presidential campaign of 1840. DeBaptiste eventually became a steward in the White House when Harrison was elected ninth president of the United States in 1840. After Harrison's untimely death, DeBaptiste returned to Indiana and to Underground Railroad activity. Racial violence in Madison forced him to seek a new home for his family, and he migrated to Detroit in 1846. The DeBaptistes became members of Second Baptist Church, while George continued his work as a barber and clothing salesman; later he invested in a bakery.[14]

DeBaptiste was in Madison in 1843 when Adam and Sarah Crosswhite and their four children arrived from slavery in Carroll County, Kentucky. DeBaptiste conducted the Crosswhites again in 1847, this time across the Detroit River to safety in Canada West, their pursuers hot on their heels.[15] (The Crosswhites' escape to freedom is detailed in chapter 11 of this volume.)

In 1850, DeBaptiste purchased the *T. Whitney*, an excursion steamboat. However, as a black man he was not permitted to hold a license to operate a vessel, so he hired a white captain. The boat ran the Sandusky, Ohio, route to Chatham, Canada West, stopping in Canadian ports at Amherstburg and Wallaceburg. The *T. Whitney* transported fugitives as well as other cargo into Canada.[16] DeBaptiste later served as a Union Army sutler during the Civil War and subsequently opened a catering business in Detroit. From 1865 until his death in 1875, he continued his advocacy on behalf of civil rights, particularly the issue of gaining access for black children to attend Michigan's public schools. He was a faithful member of Second Baptist Church, then located on Croghan Street, and a major contributor to the church over the years.[17]

In addition to its clandestine Underground Railroad activities, Second Baptist Church sponsored many meetings to protest and organize against slavery. On March 12, 1859, one of its most famed guests, black abolitionist and orator Frederick Douglass, was invited to speak at Detroit City Hall. Reacting to Chief Justice Roger B. Taney's assault on Blacks' rights in the 1857 Dred Scott Decision, Frederick Douglass implied in his speech that the Declaration of Independence and Constitution were written for whites only.[18] Hours later, Douglass left the Second Baptist gathering to meet at the home of William Webb with Detroit's Underground Railroad leaders and John Brown, the fiery white abolitionist.[19] (Chapter 13 exposes the clash of ideas at this fateful Detroit meeting.) Attending the historic meeting were Detroiters Reverend William C. Monroe, William Lambert, John D. Richards, Joseph Ferguson, Willis Wilson, John Jackson, Elijah Willis, George DeBaptiste, Canadian Osborne Perry Anderson, and Henry Bibb, who, since the passage of the 1850 Fugitive Slave Law, had been residing in Canada.[20] During his stay in Detroit, Douglass was hosted by the Lamberts.[21]

Second Baptist Church appointed seven pastors between 1836 and 1874. Five served churches on both sides of the U.S.-Canadian border. Each member of the clergy moved the church forward in spite of the double burden of protecting fugitives and attending to the religious needs of their congregations in the midst of persistent racism and hostility, all of which tested the members' faith. The ministers of Second Baptist spearheaded transnational cooperation and institution-building, and each minister left a personal legacy. Second Baptist's first pastor, the Reverend William C. Monroe, for instance, operated one of the first schools for Blacks in Detroit, beginning in 1841, holding classes in Second Baptist Church.[22] Fugitive adults also attended the Reverend Monroe's classes. Monroe helped eleven former slaves organize First Baptist Church of Sandwich, Canada West, in 1840, aided by Madison J. Lightfoot of Detroit, who served as its first pastor. From 1842 to 1844, Monroe served as moderator of the Amherstburg Baptist Association, the organization he had been instrumental in establishing.

Later, however, the Reverend Monroe converted to the Episcopal faith, as did William Lambert. The two began organizing St. Matthew's Episcopal Church in 1846 (on September 6, in St. Paul's Church, Monroe was ordained a deacon by Bishop Samuel A. McCrosky) and left Second Baptist in 1847.[23] The Reverend Monroe migrated to Liberia in 1859 to conduct missionary work. He passed away several years later.[24]

After Monroe's exit in 1847, the Reverend William P. Newman, a former fugitive slave and graduate of Oberlin College, served as temporary pastor of Second Baptist. A transnationalist in every sense, the Reverend Newman had previously worked with Josiah Henson at the British American Institute at the Dawn Settlement in Dresden, Canada West. When Newman left Second Baptist he again pastored in Canada West churches: Dresden Baptist Church and First Baptist Church of Dawn. He also assisted with the management of the British American Institute, the manual labor institution founded by Josiah Henson at Dawn, until 1852 and was clerk and recording secretary of the Canadian Anti-Slavery Baptist Association. Newman then moved to Toronto and worked with Mary Ann Shadd as editor of the *Provincial Freeman* newspaper. Over the course of his long ministry, the Reverend Newman was active in a number of antislavery and vigilant organizations and helped support churches in the Canada West communities of Colchester, Toronto, Hamilton, St. Thomas, St. Catharines, Sandwich, and Amherstburg.[25]

In January 1848, following Newman's appointment, the Reverend Samuel H. Davis received advanced training in ministry and teaching and subsequently moved to Dresden to assist with the operation of the British American Institute and to teach in the Chatham schools. Success came his way; he added thirty new members to the church, which reached a total of 180 in 1851, in spite of the passage of the 1850 Fugitive Slave Law. In 1851, Detroit's Second Baptist was host to the annual meeting of the Amherstburg Baptist Association. It was the Reverend Davis who recommended that Second Baptist sever its membership and become active in the Anti-Slavery Baptist Association. He helped to relocate classes for black children to St. Matthew's Episcopal Church, where the Reverend Monroe was teaching. Soon after, Davis resigned from Second Baptist to continue his teaching in Chatham. During his career, he was the pastor of several Canadian Baptist churches, including Dresden, Chatham, Sandwich, and Buxton.[26]

In December 1851, D. G. Lett, the fourth pastor of Second Baptist Church, witnessed the April 12, 1852, dedication of Zion German Reformed Lutheran Church at 441 Croghan Street near Beaubien in Detroit. Two years later, after the burning of Second Baptist's Liberty Hall, which served as both church and school, the Reverend Lett recommended purchasing and renovating an old schoolhouse at Fort and Hastings as Second Baptist's second building. On September 5, 1856, Lett hosted the Sixth Annual Meeting of the Canadian Anti-Slavery Baptist Association in an attempt to heal the rift between the association and the Amherstburg Baptist Association. The Reverend Lett left in December 1856 to minister to congregations in Chicago and later in Lawrence, Kansas.[27]

Second Baptist's fifth minister, the Reverend William Troy, pastored two churches concurrently: First Baptist Church of Windsor, Canada West, which he organized, and Second Baptist Church of Detroit. Previously he had lived in Cincinnati, where he was a member of Zion Baptist Church and involved in its Underground Railroad activities. Troy first came to Windsor in 1853 and initiated prayer meetings in the home of Joseph Faulkner on McDougall Street. The twenty-six members of the congregation, realizing they needed a facility for worship, sent the Reverend Troy to England to raise funds for a church building and to request a charter.

While the Reverend Troy was in England, he wrote a book, *Hair-Breadth Escapes from Slavery to Freedom*.[28] Born free himself, Troy felt deep compassion for those who had been enslaved and was infuriated by the Dred Scott decision. At a special meeting he called to discuss implications of the Supreme Court's decision, Second Baptist members resolved to redouble their efforts to assist freedom-seekers. Reverend Troy also led his congregation at Second Baptist Church to purchase the German Zion Church building on Monroe Street, the third and final site for Second Baptist Church. After serving two churches in two countries separated by the Detroit River and located less than two miles apart, the Reverend Troy returned to his native Virginia to continue ministerial work.[29]

The final two pastors who led Second Baptist Church in Underground Railroad activities were the Reverend Duke William Anderson, a dedicated preacher, educator, and Underground Railroad operator formerly of Alton, Illinois, and Supply Chase, the latter a well-respected white minister whose career in Michigan spanned several decades. Appointed by the Freeman's Aid Society to the pulpit of Second Baptist in 1853, the Reverend Chase would remain through the Civil War, ending his tenure in 1866.[30]

The Methodist denomination also had an important role to play in Detroit's Underground Railroad activities. There were fewer than fifty black residences in Detroit when the first Colored Methodist Society was established.[31] Knowing it was the policy of the city government to encourage religious exercises, the group appealed to the city council for permission to use Military Hall, the building formerly employed as the council's meeting place.[32] Permission was granted on July 9, 1839, and thus the Bethel Church became the second black church in Detroit. Two weeks later the congregation relocated to a facility on Croghan Street near the northwest corner of Hastings Street, where the church remained for nearly two years. While in this location, on May 10, 1841, the society was reorganized under the control of the African Methodist Episcopal Church and assumed the name of Bethel AME Church of Detroit.[33] Later in 1841, Bethel moved its services to a building on Fort Street west of Beaubien Street. The church was housed there until a brick building south of Lafayette was completed, the lot having been purchased on June 5, 1845, for $300. The brick building, erected at a cost of $2,000, was dedicated September 19, 1847, by the Reverend Edward Heart. A publicly funded school for black children was located in the basement of this building. Incorporated on July 30, 1849, under the pastorate of the Reverend Peter Garner, Detroit Bethel had the largest congregation of any black church in Detroit throughout the nineteenth century.[34] Pastors during Bethel's early years were M. Hargraves, J. Thomas, Edward Davis, Edward Heart, Peter Gardner, Isaac Williams, John A. Warren, A. H. Turpin, A. R. Green, R. A. Johnson, H. J. Young, A. McIntosh, W. C. Lankford, W. R. Revels, G. C. Booth, A. T. Hall, A. A. Burleigh, Jessie Bass, and James Henderson.[35]

Unlike Second Baptist, not much is recorded about the early Underground Railroad activities of Bethel's Church leaders. Perhaps the church's clandestine Underground Railroad activity was not documented as a cautionary measure because of the infiltration of bounty hunters who rummaged the city to return fugitives to captivity. However, like Second Baptist, the proximity of Bethel to the Detroit River made it a natural connection for Underground Railroad involvement. Moreover, the Methodist doctrine was based on strong antislavery sentiment advocated by the denomination's founder, John Wesley.[36] Further, campaigns against the poverty and oppression of Blacks were prominently articulated and strategized by black national crusaders and supporters of the AME Church in America. These trailblazers passed along a strong legacy of church activism on which Detroit pastors could build and with which they could nurture their congregations.

The African Methodist Episcopal denomination had its origins in Philadelphia, where ordained Methodist minister Richard Allen, offended by the discriminatory practices of white Methodism, broke away from the established church just after the Revolutionary War. He and his friend Absalom Jones founded the Free African Society as a mutual-aid association for the city's black residents in 1787. Progressive dissatisfaction with their treatment at the hands of established churches caused the Reverend Jones and his followers to organize St. Thomas, the first African Episcopal Church (1794). Richard Allen, adhering to the Methodist doctrine, founded Mother Bethel African Methodist Episcopal Church in the same year. Allen was appointed the church's first minister in 1799. In 1816, he united the churches of Philadelphia, Delaware, Maryland, and Salem, New Jersey, into the AME denomination and was appointed bishop of the very first African American religious denomination. The AME Church took an activist stance, organizing and hosting a series of black conventions protesting slavery and racial discrimination. The Reverend Isaac Williams, one of Detroit Bethel's early ministers, was known to be an antislavery activist and Underground Railroad operative. "The AME Church relied heavily on traveling preachers to set up churches and return now and then to preach. Lay preachers and local ministers kept their congregations alive."[37]

After Bishop Richard Allen, Bishop William Paul Quinn, the fourth bishop of the AME Church, had the most significant role in establishing the denomination in Detroit. In 1832, Quinn migrated from New Jersey across the Allegheny Mountains and organized churches in Indiana, Illinois, Michigan, Kentucky, Missouri, and Iowa. Elected bishop in 1844, he continued extensive missionary and Underground Railroad work.[38] Since 1840, AME missionaries, who had first arrived in 1834, made the congregations of Canada West a regular part of their conference. However, the passage of the Fugitive Slave Law in 1850 made travel to American church conferences dangerous for formerly enslaved clergy residing in Canada. Further, it was inconvenient and confusing for Canadian black congregations to be subject to U.S. bishops. Therefore, a petition was carried to the General Conference of the AME Church from the Canadian Annual Conference, listing the disadvantages of being subjected to the U.S. conference and requesting to withdraw from the AME Church of the United States. On September 29, 1856, an independent church was established after a meeting of ministers and delegates in Chatham, Canada West. Bishop Willis Nazrey was elected the first bishop of the British Methodist Episcopal Church (BME) in Canada. His advancement did not come without fiery debate from the Canadian delegation, which included resolutions addressing the new governance connection between the AME and BME churches. Nevertheless, Nazrey was elected unanimously on October 3, 1856. Nazrey continued extensive missionary travel until August 1875. He ended his active life in Nova Scotia and was brought home to Chatham and buried by the BME Church.[39]

The Episcopalian faith also had a role to play, both in protest and in Underground Railroad operations in Detroit. When St. Matthew's Protestant Episcopal Mission was organized in 1846, it was considered the most influential black church in Detroit.[40] St. Matthew's founders were former members of Second Baptist, Detroit's oldest black congregation, who petitioned the Episcopal Bishop of Michigan, Samuel A. McCrosky, to establish St. Matthew's. Among them were the former pastor of Second Baptist Church, the Reverend William C. Monroe, and popular civic leader William Lambert. In the early years, only 10 percent of the black population of Detroit belonged to St. Matthew's, but almost all of the wealthiest Blacks in the city were members of the congregation.[41]

The first meetings of St. Matthew's Church were held in 1847 in an old building on Fort Street formerly used by the AME Zion Church. The congregation remained there until sufficient funds had been accumulated to build a church on the southeast corner of Congress and St. Antoine Streets. The building was completed in 1851 but, being encumbered by debt, the church was never consecrated. At this time, the dire effects of the 1850 Fugitive Slave Law had begun to decimate the ranks of the church. With Detroit being a key terminal of the Underground Railroad, hunts for fugitives and arrests became very frequent and a large number of terror-stricken African Americans took flight to Canada, leaving a burdened Reverend Monroe with just twenty worshippers to support the Episcopalian parish. As a result of mass emigration to Canada West, Monroe's work to meet the spiritual and literacy needs of his flock progressed slowly.[42]

However, the fading spirit of St. Matthew's Mission rallied under the generous support of members of Detroit's white elite. These included C. C. Trowbridge, the Honorable Henry C. Baldwin, the Honorable James V. Campbell, and the Honorable John Biddle; the mission began to revive in intelligent, spiritual, and orderly worship as it attracted new adherents to its ranks. On March 5, 1854, Reverend Monroe was advanced to the Episcopalian priesthood by Bishop McCrosky and undertook his labors in St. Matthew's.[43]

The Reverend Monroe had no difficulty standing his ground as an antislavery advocate. One of his last major activities in the fight against human bondage as a Detroiter was to help perfect the final plans for John Brown's raid on Harper's Ferry, an event further elaborated in chapter 13 of this volume. The "John Brown Convention," which included men of St. Matthews, met in Chatham, Canada West, in May 1858; Lambert was named treasurer and Monroe was elected chairman and presided over the convention until it closed.[44]

Another important church leader in Detroit was the Reverend James Theodore Holly, an abolitionist and the first African American bishop in the Episcopal Church. Holly was born in 1829 and raised by a family of Roman Catholic free persons of color. Trained as a shoemaker, he spent his early years in Washington, DC, and Brooklyn, New York, where he connected with Frederick Douglass and other black abolitionists. He was active in abolitionist activities and antislavery and emigration conventions in the free states and Canada. In Canada West, the Reverend Holly assisted formerly enslaved Kentuckian Henry Bibb in editing his newspaper, *Voice of the Fugitive*, and supported the Refugee Home Society that Bibb had founded with support from Detroit abolitionists and businessmen. Holly was a gifted speaker; his eloquence and proficiency with the language were considered masterful. See chapter 7 of this volume for further discussion of the relationship between the Bibbs and Holly in Canada West.

The Reverend Holly was ordained to the deaconate by the Reverend William C. Monroe of St. Matthew's and preached his first sermon there on June 17, 1855, at the age of twenty-seven. He was a strong advocate of emigration to Haiti, but it appeared that a majority of Blacks were not persuaded to take drastic relocation risks as the Civil War grew near. A relentless Holly dedicated a pamphlet of his writings and speeches promoting emigration and self-government in Haiti to Monroe, who had served as a missionary in Haiti. Holly moved to New Haven, Connecticut, in 1856 and pastored St. Luke's Church. In 1861, he finally realized his long-held dream, sailing from New York with his family and a group of 111 persons of color, including many from Canada West, to settle in Haiti, the Western Hemisphere's first black republic.[45]

After the passage of the 1850 Fugitive Slave Law, prominent religious and community leaders advocated for free and self-emancipated Blacks to join colonies abroad—in Haiti, Central America, and Nigeria's Niger Valley. But Canada and Liberia were the most popular destinations. The Reverend Monroe resigned from his assignment at St. Matthew's in about 1859 to begin missionary work in Liberia, where he served for several years.[46] At St. Matthew's, Monroe was succeeded by the Reverend King, who served for only a brief period and was followed by the Reverend Samuel Berry from 1860 to 1861, when he left to take up work in other fields. Without proper leadership, the mission declined, until finally the property was sold in 1864. All outstanding debts were paid and the remaining money was held in trust in the St. Matthew's Mission Fund to support mission work among Blacks in Detroit.[47]

Black houses of worship were not the only churches to provide shelter, comfort, and escape methods for African American refugees. At least two churches in Detroit's white community have documented written and oral histories of abolitionist activities; both must be added to the roster of churches that contributed to the physical, emotional, and social well-being of free Blacks and fugitives: St. John's German Lutheran Church, founded in 1833, and First Congregational Church, organized in 1844.

St. John's Church, the first German congregation in Detroit, was pastored by Friedrich Schmid, who had been sent by the Basel Missionary Society in Switzerland. En route to Ann Arbor, Michigan, Schmid spent a weekend in Detroit. German Protestants in Detroit asked him to preach on Sunday; his oratory must have been inspiring, since those who heard him decided to establish a church. In one of his earliest letters to Basel after arriving in Michigan, Schmid provides his thoughts regarding the spiritual level of the people he hoped to serve: "There is an immense unworked mission field here in which many souls can be led to the Lord in the power of his grace. Just so that souls are saved and led to the Lamb, be they white, black, or red pagans, it is all the same."[48] The first service took place on August 18, 1833, in a carpentry shop at Woodbridge and Bates streets, near the shores of the Detroit River. A month later, on September 22, the church was formally organized when the election of elders took place in a barn located on Jefferson and St. Antoine. For three years, Pastor Schmid walked every month from Ann Arbor to Detroit to preach the Gospel in German.[49]

St. John's first building was a wood frame edifice constructed in 1836 on the corner of Farmer and Monroe. In the same year, the Reverend J. Schwabe, also sent from Basel, became the first resident pastor of the church; he died after a short pastorate. Nine years later, under the Reverend M. Schaad, a school was built on the property. When the Reverend Schaad left in 1841, he was succeeded by the Reverend F. Herman, who served until 1852, when the Reverend C. Haas arrived. The increase in membership made a larger facility necessary. The frame building was sold and the congregation moved to a brick building that seated 850 at Gratiot and Farmer streets. It was dedicated January 9, 1853.[50]

St. John's Church engaged in a creative deceit to protect fugitives from slave hunters: staging mock funeral processions. "According to stories passed from one generation to the next, the church's original German speaking congregation sometimes staged fake funerals to aid escaping slaves. Runaways either hid in a leather casket or walked behind it with other make believe mourners from the church. The casket would roll along on its horse-drawn cart until the procession reached the Detroit River. The fugitive in their midst would then jump into a waiting boat and cross the river to Canada."[51] The casket that was used for hiding fugitives has been preserved by subsequent congregations and remains on display at St. John's Church. Such mock funerals, which baffled many pursuing slavecatchers, were a ruse used by the flamboyant white Underground Railroad conductor John Fairfield, who was well known for going into the South and personally escorting freedom-seekers to northern cities, particularly Detroit.[52] First Congregational Church also played an active role in Detroit's Underground Railroad. Congregationalism was brought to America in 1620 by the Pilgrims, called "Separatists" because of their lack of adherence to the Anglican Church. Their Covenant of Purpose, based on the desire for individual freedom of conscience and worship, began in Scrooby, England, in the sixteenth century. It grew under the leadership of Pastor John Robinson but met with widespread opposition that amounted to persecution, resulting in the migration to Holland of the more zealous Pilgrims. Continued hardships caused 102 of them to sail for the New World on the *Mayflower*, which landed at Plymouth in December 1620. Here they established the Massachusetts Bay Colony. Having experienced the consequences of persecution and man's inhumanity to man firsthand, it is no coincidence that many Congregational congregations have a rich history in the Underground Railroad. Many leaders in the antislavery movement nationally came from Congregational churches.[53]

By 1844, there were several Congregational churches in Michigan with a strong history of missionary and educational work, particularly among the Native peoples, but there was no church in Detroit. Charles G. Hammond, a prominent businessman of Detroit, with the assistance of the Reverend O. C. Thompson persuaded the former's brother, the Reverend Henry Hammond, to come to Detroit to discuss a possible assignment. On November 23, 1844, a preliminary meeting at the home of Charles Hammond was held to consider forming a church. One month later, thirteen Congregationalists organized the First Congregational Society of Detroit. Charles Hammond, Francis Raymond, Israel Coe, Elisha Taylor, and Lyman Baldwin were elected as the first trustees of the society.[54]

The First Congregational Society occupied two wooden churches near the riverfront before moving into the Old City Hall, a massive structure also housing the Circuit Court room, which was used for public gatherings.[55] The basement of this edifice, located at the corner of Fort and Wayne, was known as a safe house providing sanctuary for escaped slaves to sleep and eat as they approached the last leg of their journey. According to church lore, First Congregational members went further in their aid: they had boats waiting at the foot of Wayne Street to carry freedom-seekers across the Detroit River to Canada.[56]

When the Reverend Henry Hammond ended his ministry, various ministers and members provided services to the new church on the corner of Jefferson and Beaubien Streets until October 1848. At that time, the Reverend Harvey D. Kitchel of Thomaston, Connecticut, accepted the ministry. He was a man of winning personality and great ability. "His sermons were characterized by soundness of doctrine, fullness and ripeness of thought, with a purity of style and chasteness of diction that gave them a great charm and made them a power for good."[57] Within four years of Kitchel's coming to Detroit, the church had so increased in membership that the building proved to be entirely inadequate to hold the Sunday congregation. A new church was consecrated on September 21, 1854. The dedicatory service was officiated by the Reverend Dr. Leonard Bacon.[58]

Dr. Bacon was so involved with civil issues that he gave up his active pastorate. For several years, he was the editor of the *Christian Spectator* and was one of the founders of the *New Englander*, which was established primarily to combat slavery.[59] Bacon, although focused deeply on all matters concerning the well-being of his community, was particularly involved with the temperance and antislavery movements, taking an active role in the American Union for the Relief and Improvement of the Colored Race, founded in Boston in 1835. In most controversies, he took a moderate stand, however, condemning both the defenders of slavery and extremist abolitionists like William Lloyd Garrison.[60] His antislavery sentiments expressed in *Slavery Discussed in Occasional Essays from 1833 to 1846* (1846) exercised considerable influence on Abraham Lincoln. A sentence that appeared in Bacon's book was rephrased by Lincoln and has been widely quoted: "If that form of government, that system of social order is not

Established in 1844, First Congregational Church was an important stop on the Underground Railroad in Detroit. (Courtesy of photographer Elizabeth Clark)

wrong—if those laws of the Southern States, by virtue of which slavery exists there, and is what it is, are not wrong—nothing is wrong."[61]

The churches of the Detroit River region formed essential links in the chain that provided safe haven and assistance to refugees from bondage throughout the antebellum period. Church buildings and sometimes associated parish or community halls, often the only structures communally owned by African Americans, served not only as faith centers but also as lecture halls, schools, and a nexus for the development of self-help, fraternal, social, and political organizations. Connections between religious groups, and particularly the very active Amherstburg Baptist Association, which began as a means of church union between Detroit's landmark Second Baptist Church and congregations on the Canadian side of the border, facilitated the operations of fugitive slave assistance and protection on the American shore and reception on the Canadian shore. These churches' and church leaders' cross-border collaborations exemplify the essence of transnationalism. Active resistance to slavery and racial oppression on the part of white-led congregations such as St. John's Church, the first German congregation in Detroit, and First Congregational Church provided material and spiritual assistance to escaping refugees and also supported transnational efforts. St. John's, First Congregational, and the black churches in Detroit all demonstrated moral and ethical leadership with respect to antislavery. The central role played by churches along the Detroit River throughout the Underground Railroad era has only begun to be explored. It is hoped that this review will inspire further investigation of the documentary, oral, and material cultural history of Detroit's churches and their role in antislavery, antiracism, and fugitive slave assistance in the years before the Civil War.

NOTES

1. The Code Noir was established first in 1685 for the "Islands of French America," with Article II stating: "All slaves that shall be in our islands shall be baptized and instructed in the Roman, Catholic, and Apostolic Faith." This was expanded to include Louisiana in 1724. That it was also applied in French Canada, including the Detroit River region, is discussed by William Renwick Riddell, "The *Code Noir*," *Journal of Negro History* 10, no. 3 (1925): 321–29. For the text of the 1685 legislation, see *Édit du roi, touchant la police des isles de l'Amérique française* (Paris, 1687), 28–58, cited in chnm.gmu.edu/revolution/d/335/ (accessed February 12, 2013).
2. David M. Katzman, *Before the Ghetto: Black Detroit in the Nineteenth Century* (Urbana: University of Illinois Press, 1973), 18.
3. Nathaniel Leach, *The Second Baptist Connection: Reaching Out to Freedom—History of Second Baptist Church in Detroit* (Detroit: Second Baptist Church, 1988), 14.
4. J. William Cooper, V. A. Brisol, and R. L. Bradby, compl., *History of Second Baptist Church, Detroit* (Detroit: privately published, 1936), 1; Karolyn Smardz Frost, *I've Got a Home In Glory Land: A Lost Tale of the Underground Railroad* (New York: Farrar Straus, & Giroux, 2007; Toronto: Thomas Allen, 2007), 151–52.
5. "Second Baptist Celebrates 175 Years: Reaching Out to Freedom; The History of Second Baptist Church of Detroit and Historical Significance of Detroit," *Michigan Chronicle*, Community section, February 9–15, 2011, C-8.

6. Leach, *The Second Baptist Connection*, 20.
7. "Second Baptist Celebrates 175 Years."
8. Original ledgers containing the Minutes of the Amherstburg Baptist Association, for the first three decades in Madison J. Lightfoot's own hand, survive in the collections of the Canadian Baptist Archives at MacMaster Divinity College, McMaster University, Hamilton, Ontario.
9. *The Constitution, By-laws, Minutes . . . of the Canadian Anti-Slavery Baptist Association* (Windsor: Office of the *Voice of the Fugitive*, 1854); Linda Brown-Kubisch, *The Queen's Bush Settlement: Black Pioneers, 1839–1865* (Toronto: Natural Heritage Press, 2004), 15–16.
10. For a fuller discussion of the Amherstburg Baptist Association, see Dorothy Shadd Shreve, *The AfriCanadian Church: A Stabilizer* (Jordan Station, ON: Paideia, 1983); James K. Lewis, "Religious Nature of the Early Negro Migration to Canada and the Amherstburg Baptist Association," *Ontario History* 58 (June 1966): 117–32; James Melvin Washington, *Frustrated Fellowship: The Black Baptist Quest for Social Power* (Macon, GA: Mercer University Press, 2004), 36–38; Leach, *The Second Baptist Connection*, 21.
11. "Fifty Years a Detroiter: William Lambert, the Representative Negro of This Vicinity," *Detroit Free Press*, January 5, 1890. The article, published in the Sunday edition of the paper, reads, "Fifty years ago last Wednesday William Lambert, the veteran negro citizen of Detroit, reached this city to remain here permanently."
12. Smardz Frost, *I've Got a Home in Glory Land*, 154.
13. "Second Baptist Celebrates 175 Years"; "Took His Life: William Lambert, the Well-Known Colored Citizen, Commits Suicide; Sketch of the Life of the Deceased, Who Had Lived Here Fifty-Two Years," *Detroit Free Press*, April 29, 1890; William Lambert Papers, Historical Records Survey of Michigan, Michigan Historical Collections, Burton Historical Collection, Detroit Public Library.
14. "Death of George DeBaptiste," *Detroit Daily Post*, February 23, 1875.
15. "Death of George DeBaptiste"; "Our New Voters," *Detroit Daily Post*, February 7, 1870, newspaper clipping in William R. Stocking Papers, box B, Underground Railroad folder, Burton Historical Collection, Detroit Public Library.
16. "Death of George DeBaptiste."
17. "George DeBaptiste, His Death Yesterday—Sketch of His Active and Eventful Life . . . His Efforts to Rescue Negroes from Slavery," *Detroit Advertiser and Tribune*, February 23, 1875; Fergus Bordewich, *Bound for Canaan: The Epic Story of the Underground Railroad, America's First Civil Rights Movement* (New York: Amistad, 2005); Katherine DuPre Lumpkin, "'The General Plan was Freedom': A Negro Secret Order on the Underground Railroad," *Phylon* 28 (1st quarter 1967), 68–69; Carol E. Mull, *The Underground Railroad in Michigan* (Jefferson, NC: Farland, 2010), 30–31, 78, 88.
18. This was *Dred Scott v. John F. A. Sandford*, decided on March 6, 1857, when the Supreme Court of the United States voted 7-2 that African Americans could never be citizens of the United States and that the Missouri Compromise was unconstitutional.
19. Leach, *The Second Baptist Connection*, 23; Arthur M. Woodford, *This Is Detroit: 1701–2001* (Detroit: Wayne State University Press, 2001), 67.
20. Leach, *The Second Baptist Connection*, 28.
21. Smardz Frost, *I've Got a Home in Glory Land*, 154.

22. Katzman, *Before the Ghetto*, 23.
23. *St. Matthew's Episcopal Church Centennial Celebration, 1846–1946: 100 Years of Service to God and His People* (Detroit: privately published, ca. 1846), 1–3.
24. Leach, *The Second Baptist Connection*, 25; George F. Bragg, *History of the Afro-American Group of the Episcopal Church* (Baltimore, MD: Church Advocate, 1922), 117; *St. Matthew's Episcopal Church, Detroit Centennial Celebration, 1846–1946*, 3.
25. Leach, *The Second Baptist Connection*, 26; C. Peter Ripley et al., eds., *The Black Abolitionist Papers, 1830–1865*, vol. 2, *Canada* (Chapel Hill, NC: University of North Carolina Press, 1986), 302–3n.
26. William Richardson, "The Life and Times of Samuel H. Davis, Anti-Slavery Activist," *African Americans in New York Life and History* 33, no. 1 (2009); Leach, *The Second Baptist Connection*, 26; Ripley et al., *The Black Abolitionist Papers*, vol. 2, *Canada*, 494n54.
27. Alfred Theodore Andreas, *The History of Chicago* (Chicago: A. T. Andreas, 1884), 323; Leach, *The Second Baptist Connection*, 26.
28. William Troy, *Hair-Breadth Escapes from Slavery to Freedom* (Manchester, UK: W. Bremner, 1861).
29. Leach, *The Second Baptist Connection*, 26–27.
30. The biography of Duke William Anderson is detailed in George Washington Williams, *History of the Negro Race in America from 1619 to 1880: Negroes as Slaves, as Soldiers, and as Citizens* . . . (New York: G. P. Putnam's Sons, 1883), esp. 2:494–97 for his time at Second Baptist; "Obituary, Reverend Supply Chase," *Detroit Free Press*, June 3, 1887.
31. Arthur Randall, ed., *One Hundred Years at Bethel Detroit* (Detroit: Bethel Church, 1941), 3.
32. Katzman, *Before the Ghetto*, 20.
33. Ulysses W. Boykin, *A Handbook of the Detroit Negro* (Detroit: Minority Study Associates, 1943), 35.
34. Katzman, *Before the Ghetto*, 21–23.
35. Randall, *One Hundred Years at Bethel Detroit*, 4.
36. The white Methodist denomination split in 1844–45 over the issue of slaveholding, maintaining northern and southern branches for nearly a century.
37. Betty DeRamus, *Freedom by Any Means* (New York: Atria Books, 2009), 85; Richard S. Newman, *Freedom's Prophet: Bishop Richard Allen, the AME Church and the Black Founding Fathers* (New York: New York University Press, 2008), esp. chaps. 1 and 2.
38. James A. Handy, *Scraps of African Methodist Episcopal History* (Philadelphia: AME Book Concern, 1902), docsouth.unc.edu/church/handy/menu.html (accessed March 3, 2011). Bishop Quinn's Underground Railroad activism is well documented: "From Bethel AME Church in New Jersey through Pennsylvania, Maryland, and into Ohio, Indiana, and Illinois, the states of the Old Northwest, extending into Kentucky, Missouri, and farther west into Iowa and Kansas, and north into Canada, Bishop Quinn's name is consistently linked to escape from slavery and Underground Railroad churches." Cheryl Janifer LaRoche, *The Geography of Resistance: Free Black Communities and the Underground Railroad* (Urbana: University of Illinois, 2014), 140.
39. Handy, *Scraps of African Methodist Episcopal History*.
40. Katzman, *Before the Ghetto*, 21.

41. Katzman, *Before the Ghetto*, 136–37.
42. Boykin, *A Handbook of the Detroit Negro*, 36–37.
43. *St. Matthew's Episcopal Church, Detroit Centennial Celebration, 1846–1946*, 1–3.
44. "A Brief History of St. Matthew's Church," n.d., 19, St. Matthew's/St. Joseph's Collection, box 1, Michigan History Center, Lansing, MI.
45. Leon Denius Pamphile, *Haitians and African Americans: A Heritage of Tragedy and Hope* (Gainesville: University Press of Florida, 2001), 55; David M. Dean, *Defender of the Race: James Theodore Holly, Black Nationalist Bishop* (Boston: Lambeth, 1979); "James Theodore Holly," in Rev. George F. Bragg, *Men of Maryland* (Baltimore: Church Advocate, 1914), 79–85; Hollis Ralph Lynch, *James Theodore Holly: Ante-bellum Black Nationalist and Emigrationist* (Center for Afro-American Studies, University of California, 1977).
46. Bragg, *History of the Afro-American Group of the Episcopal Church*, 118.
47. *St. Matthew's Episcopal Church: A Brief History*; Bragg, *History of the Afro-American Group of the Episcopal Church*, 118. A new church was reorganized and consecrated in 1883.
48. Friedrich Schmid, *Michigan Memories: Selected Letters of Friedrich Schmid* (n.p.: Michigan District of the Evangelical Lutheran Synod, 1985), 33.
49. Silas Farmer, *History of Detroit and Wayne County and Early Michigan: Past and Present* (New York: Muncell, 1890), 40.
50. Farmer, *History of Detroit*.
51. DeRamus, *Freedom by Any Means*, 202.
52. Michigan Underground Railroad activist Laura Haviland wrote of John Fairfield's daring fugitive rescues and of the Canadian refugees who recognized Fairfield when he visited Canada West. Laura S. Haviland, *A Woman's Life-Work: Including Thirty Years of Service on the Underground Railroad and in the War* (Grand Rapids, MI: Tribune, 1881), 199; Henrietta Buckmaster, *Let My People Go: The Story of the Underground Railroad and the Growth of the Abolitionist Movement* (1941; repr., Columbia: University of South Carolina Press, 1992), 192–97.
53. Jon von Rohr, *The Shaping of American Congregationalism: 1620–1957* (Cleveland: Pilgrim, 1992).
54. *Minutes of the National Council of the Congregational Churches of the United States of America at the Third Session Held in Detroit Michigan, October 17–21, 1877* (Boston: Congregational Publishing Society, 1877), 247–49; *Fiftieth Anniversary of the Organization, 1894.* (1894; repr., London: Forgotten Books, 2013), 170–71.
55. Elizabeth L. Bishop, *The First Century: The First Congregational Church of Detroit, Michigan, 1844–1944* (Detroit: [The Church], 1945), 24.
56. "Underground Railroad Living Museum, 2004," www.friendsoffirst.com (accessed February 24, 2011).
57. Bishop, *The First Century*, 25.
58. Bishop, *The First Century*, 25.
59. *Leonard Bacon, Pastor of First Church in New Haven* (New Haven: Tuttle, Morehouse & Taylor, 1882), openlibrary.org/books/OL13515516M/Leonard_Bacon_pastor_of_the_First_Church_in_New_Haven (accessed December 26, 2012); Timothy J. Sehr, "Leonard Bacon and the Myth of the Good Slaveholder," *The New England Quarterly* 49, no. 2 (1976):

194–213; Hugh Davis, "Northern Colonizationists and Free Blacks, 1823-1837: A Case Study of Leonard Bacon," *Journal of the Early Republic* 17, no. 4 (1997): 651–75.

60. Bacon was a vocal proponent of gradualism and was a strong voice for the American Colonization Society, which sought to resettle freed American Blacks in the the West African colony of Liberia. See James R. Stirn, "Urgent Gradualism: The Case for the American Union for the Relief and Improvement of the Colored Race," *Civil War History* 25, no. 4 (1979): 309–28.

61. Leonard Bacon, *Slavery Discussed in Occasional Essays from 1833 to 1846* (1846; repr., New York: Amos, 1969), x.

SIX

EXTENDING THE RIGHT HAND OF FELLOWSHIP

Sandwich Baptist Church, Amherstburg First Baptist, and the Amherstburg Baptist Association

ADRIENNE SHADD

On Friday, October 8, 1841, Second Baptist Church of Detroit called a convention of Baptist churches at Amherstburg to discuss the formation of an association of black Baptists in Canada West. The minutes, penned by Detroit activist and community leader Madison J. Lightfoot, reveal not only the spirit of brotherhood and fellowship among these leading men of Detroit, Sandwich, and Amherstburg but also the sense of history and destiny shared by black Baptists on both sides of the Detroit River frontier:

> Resolved that we the Second Baptist Church of the City of Detroit believing that the time is now come that we should form ourselves into an association because we cannot enjoy the privileges we wish as Christians with the White Churches in Canada, that centuries have rolled along since our Fathers have gone down [to] the grave not enjoying their just privileges and rights in the Christian Churches among the Whites. We invite all the Christian Churches and orders to unite with us in the great Celestial Cause. Union is strength. United, we stand and divided we fall. Come up, brethren, from all parts of the provinces and let us see what we can do for ourselves and our children.[1]

The Amherstburg Baptist Association (ABA) minutes are a documentary legacy of the thoughts and aspirations of these early Baptists and provide a detailed history of the organization and its member churches. There is no better example of the cross-border exchange and cooperation between African Canadians and African Americans than that which developed among the Baptist churches along the Detroit River frontier that spawned the ABA. The phenomenon signals not just the permeable nature of the Detroit River border but also the transnational character of African Canadian/African American communities, their transcendence of national boundaries. It is also indicative of a broader Pan-African identity among people of African descent in North America.

As the seminal institution of the black communities in Canada and America, the black church represented far more than a sanctuary of worship and a place to practice one's faith. It was always the first piece of communally owned real estate. The church provided many of the leaders of the black communities. It was where leadership training took place. The church was the locus of community activism in general and antislavery activities, fugitive slave reception in particular. And it was through the churches that previously unschooled ex-slaves received the first inklings of literacy, because both children and adults attended and learned to read and write in Sabbath Schools.[2] In short, the church, in addition to the extended family, has been the cornerstone of African American and African Canadian socialization and support in adversity.

The vast majority of African Americans arriving in British Canada, whether they were fugitive slaves or free Blacks, had gravitated toward the Baptist and Methodist faiths. According to Dorothy Shadd Shreve, these denominations appealed to the soul and emotions of their congregants and "provided a natural outlet for feelings of frustration and despair."[3]

The first known black Baptist church established in Upper Canada was founded in the township of Colchester by Elder William Wilks, as is elaborated in chapter 4 of this volume. Born in the Congo (or "of the Conggo Tribe as Well as he Remembers"), Wilks was stolen from his homeland at the tender age of about ten years, brought to America, and enslaved. He lived in Virginia until he reached adulthood, and in about 1784, moved with his master John Vinison near Nashville, Tennessee. Ten years later, Wilks was converted to the Baptist faith and began to exhort and preach to the people.[4] In 1818, middle-aged by this time, Wilks escaped and made his way to Fort Malden (Amherstburg) in Upper Canada and remained there for a year before moving to the township of Colchester on the north shore of Lake Erie east of the Detroit River. There he bought forty acres in the wilderness and built a log meetinghouse on his land. Although unlettered and unordained, he began to preach the Gospel and baptize members of his congregation, the size of which continued to grow.[5]

Interestingly, two white Baptist ministers were approached by a white Baptist deacon, Francis F. Browning, from Detroit who had learned of Brother Wilks and his church. The ministers—Elder Comstock of Oakland County, Michigan, and Elder Stuart of the township of Gosfield, Upper Canada—paid a visit to the little log meetinghouse in Colchester in October 1821 and formed themselves into an Ecclesiastical Council. They ordained Wilks and also rebaptized all those whom Wilks had previously baptized before he had the authority to do so. The church, named First Africa Baptist Church of Colchester, Upper Canada, was organized with regular officers and Wilks as the regular pastor. This is an important early example not only of transnational exchange and cooperation but also of interracial fellowship and support. Elder Wilks led his church until his death in 1838. He left his property and his worldly belongings to the church he had founded.[6] It is fitting that First Africa Baptist Church, the very first

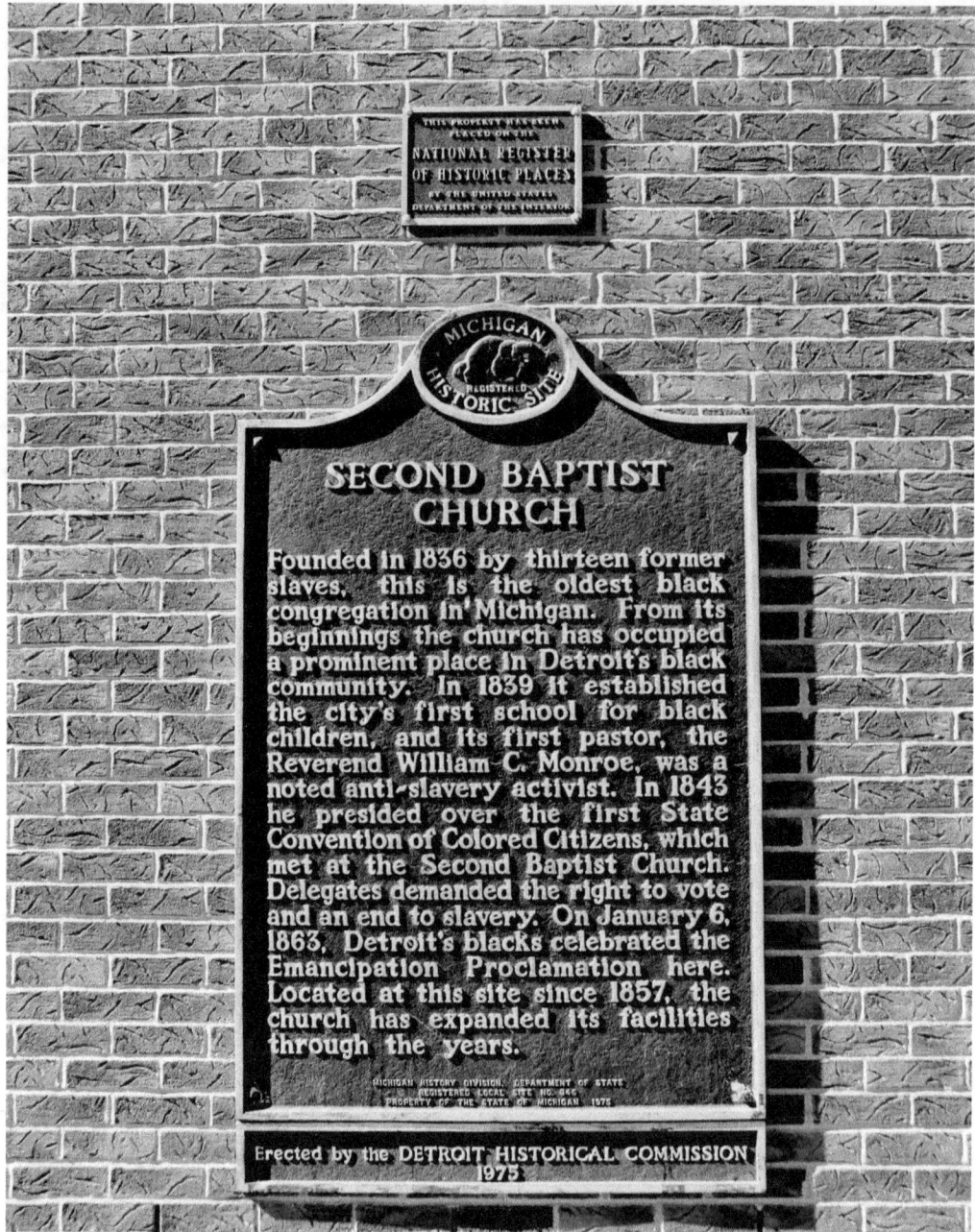

The oldest African American church in Michigan is Detroit's Second Baptist Church. (Courtesy of photographer Elizabeth Clark)

known black church in Upper Canada, was established by a man whose own life story spanned two continents and three separate polities.

As more and more African Americans trickled into Upper Canada, renamed Canada West in 1841, there was an increasing need to establish houses of worship for the incoming settlers. However, it was the members of the Second Baptist Church of Detroit, founded in 1836, who issued the call for an umbrella organization that would embrace the black Baptist churches of Canada West and unite them into a single body. Second Baptist, which continues to serve an inner-city congregation to this day, has had a long, illustrious history as a locus of antislavery and civil rights activism. Second Baptist of Detroit and the members of the Detroit Vigilant Committee are said to have safely hidden and spirited five thousand fugitive slaves across to Canada.[7] (Many of these would make up the communities and congregations of the Baptist churches of the Detroit border region that Detroit's Second Baptist soon organized into the Amherstburg Baptist Association).[8] The founding and leadership of Detroit's Second Baptist and other Detroit churches dedicated to antislavery are detailed in chapter 5 of this volume, and the Detroit Vigilant Committee's Underground Railroad work is the subject of chapter 8.

As already noted, at the convention in the village of Amherstburg on October 8, 1841, there were representatives of three participating churches: Second Baptist of Detroit (with seventeen members), Amherstburg Baptist (with nineteen members), and Sandwich Baptist (with eleven members). Deacon George French of Detroit was elected moderator of the convention, and Madison J. Lightfoot, also from Detroit, was elected clerk. A committee of four was appointed to prepare a constitution, rules of order, articles of faith, and a covenant, and to report on their work the following year. The committee comprised Deacon George French, N. Humphrey, Madison J. Lightfoot, and Jacob Branham.[9]

At the next annual session of the Amherstburg Baptist Association, Elder William C. Monroe, pastor of Detroit's Second Baptist, was elected moderator and Madison Lightfoot was again chosen as clerk. Daniel Binga Sr. was appointed treasurer, and Horace J. Hawkins was named traveling missionary. Hawkins was Binga's relative and a fugitive slave from Kentucky who fled to Canada with the Bingas and settled in Amherstburg.[10] It was Elder Hawkins's job to travel from one settlement to the next delivering sermons, baptizing and serving Communion. By the third year, two more churches were added to the association, Mount Pleasant and Chatham Baptist Church.

The first three meetings of the association were held at the First Baptist Church, Amherstburg, whence the association got its name. This church began as a mission to fugitive slaves as early as 1838, with services held in the homes of members. Because of its location at the narrows of the Detroit River across from Michigan, Amherstburg was naturally one of the first towns where incoming Blacks settled. By the 1840s, several thousand African Americans had put down roots in Amherstburg and surrounding communities in Essex County, and the need to assist and minister to recently escaped refugees was tremendous.[11] When the members of the church decided to erect a building, it was the Reverend Anthony Binga, Elder Daniel Binga's son, who raised the funds as an itinerant preacher, traveling on foot and on horseback across what today is Southwestern Ontario. First Baptist is variously reported to have been built in either 1845 or 1849.[12]

At these early meetings, the principles of temperance were upheld. Both the establishment of Sunday Schools and Bible classes and setting aside the collection plate offering on the first Sunday of each month for missionary work were encouraged. The association members did not forget about their people still enslaved. They recommended that monthly prayer concerts for the oppressed be held the first Monday of every month. The association also made it abundantly clear that its churches would have nothing to do with slaveholding Baptist churches or ministers, nor be permitted to partake of the Lord's Supper with them: "Resolved, that we recommend to the churches of this Association that no slaveholding ministers or Brethren holding slaves or trafficking in human blood shall have any fellowship with this Association believing that slavery is an open crying sin against the doctrine of the New Testament and heinous in the sight of a civilized world."[13]

In 1844, the fourth annual meeting of the association was held in a different location for the first time, namely, Sandwich. The Sandwich Baptist Church had been established in 1840 at the foot of Huron Line Road, but when the delegates of the 1844 convention met, it was in the Methodist meetinghouse. Eventually, in 1847, a rudimentary log cabin was constructed for the black Baptists of Sandwich. However, with the passage of the Fugitive Slave Act of 1850, thousands of those still legally enslaved, many of whom had been living as free people in the United States for years, poured into the province and swelled the ranks of black communities of Canada West, particularly the border communities. Free Blacks also came, their liberty, too, jeopardized by the new law. The congregation needed a larger church. The government granted a one-acre lot on West Peter Street for a church and cemetery, and a brick church was dedicated in August 1851, which ministers to a congregation to this day. None other than Madison J. Lightfoot of Detroit, a licentiate at the time, became the first pastor of the new edifice at First Baptist Church, Sandwich.[14]

Over time, and as more and more churches were added to the roster, the Amherstburg Association became increasingly influential among black Baptists in Canada West and Michigan. However, the organization understood that much of its work, such as the considerable exertions of the traveling missionaries on foot and horseback, required money that struggling congregations found difficult to muster. In 1849, the minutes reported a total of $2.50 in the treasury. It was probably no coincidence that that same year, the association resolved to become an auxiliary to the American Baptist Free Mission Society (ABFMS). Founded in 1843, the ABFMS was a predominantly white antislavery Baptist organization that had opened a coeducational and interracial institution called the New York Central College in 1849.[15] This college boasted the first African American professor at a predominantly white college as well as two female instructors—truly revolutionary steps for that time. The ABA had already made contact with the ABFMS because it had "recommended" this organization "to the confidence of its churches" in 1848, but the ABA had more grandiose plans in mind. That same year, George French, a founding member of Detroit's Second Baptist Church, made a call for a convention of "colored Baptist churches and ministers" to look into the establishment of an "institution of education" in which young licentiates could prepare for the ministry. This convention was to take place on the Thursday before the start of the 1850 annual meeting in Sandwich. The plan obviously required a substantial endowment, and the association leaders no doubt viewed a large, well-funded organization such as the Free Mission Society as a likely financial sponsor for these plans.[16]

The following year, the minutes reflected the association's "indebtedness" and gratitude to the ABFMS not only for its work on behalf of the "brethren in bonds" but also for its "effort now to establish an institution of learning among us."[17] It so happened that the American Baptist Free Mission Society had been brought in by the Reverend William P. Newman to revive the British American Institute at Dawn. An escaped slave from Richmond, Virginia, who had studied at Oberlin College (1842–43) and become an ordained minister, Newman had been an agent of the Free Mission Society in 1845 when he came to take over the British American

Now a Canadian National Historic Site, Amherstburg First Baptist Church was established in 1836 by the Reverend Anthony Binga, a freedom-seeker from Kentucky. (Courtesy of photographer Jennifer Cousineau)

Institute (BAI), which had been founded by Josiah Henson and the Reverend Hiram Wilson three years earlier. Newman quit the following year, according to his own account, because of a lack of financial accountability at Dawn. He returned to the Union Baptist Church in Cincinnati, where he had been pastor to a large congregation.[18] (The Reverend Newman's religious and abolitionist activities are also mentioned in chapter 5 of this volume.) It was Newman's idea to revive the BAI at Dawn by bringing the ABFMS on board to run the institute in 1850. It may well have been that the ministerial college envisioned by the association was to be set up at Dawn as part of the British American Institute once the Free Mission board took over. Once it did assume control, the Reverend Samuel H. Davis, current pastor of Second Baptist Church in Detroit, was hired as headmaster, and the BAI seemed to be on a sure footing.[19] Two years later, John Scoble from the British and Foreign Anti-Slavery Society gained control of the BAI and ended the brief reign of the Free Mission Society.

Sometime during 1850–51, a deep schism in the association took place related to the Free Mission Society. Second Baptist Detroit severed its connection with the ABA, as did Mount Pleasant and Colchester. What was the burning issue that caused this drastic schism? The ABA minutes for 1851 are vague, to say the least: "Resolved, That this Association do most deeply regret the course taken by the Free Mission Agent and Missionary among our churches, not only in this country but we are sorry to add, belonging to this Association, and believing such a course fraught with the most serious evils, that it should be discountenanced by all regular Baptist churches."[20] The circular letter for that session, composed by the Reverends Isaac Rice and Horace H. Hawkins, was not much clearer. Rice was a white missionary at Sandwich who had left his Presbyterian church in Ohio to minister to Blacks along the Detroit River border. Rice and Hawkins accused the ABFMS of trying to assert authority over the association and dictate to the various churches: "Fear not the assaults of covert foreign bodies, who secretly pull the wires, and hire men to scatter division and discord, amid your churches. Maintain firmly your manhood. As attaching yourselves as auxiliaries, has brought division, and set an all-devouring fire in your midst, learn henceforth to be independent."[21]

Reading between the lines, it appears that another bone of contention was the fact that the Free Mission Society did not regard the ABA as sufficiently antislavery, perhaps because its constitution was devoid of any mention of slavery.[22] In any case, the dissension split the churches into two camps, one comprised of churches that remained loyal to the association and a new body named the Canadian Anti-Slavery Baptist Association. The latter remained an auxiliary of the American Baptist Free Mission Society. Amherstburg, Chatham, Sandwich, Colchester, and two churches from Michigan, Marshall and Battle Creek, remained in the ABA. Hamilton opted out, primarily for reasons of distance, located as it was at the head of Lake Ontario. Churches in the Canadian Anti-Slavery Baptist Association were Detroit's Second Baptist Church and Chatham, Mount Pleasant, Colchester, Macedonia Church, Elgin (that is, Buxton), London, and Dawn, located at the British American Institute. (In Colchester and Chatham, there were now two Baptist churches, one under the umbrella of the ABA and the other a member of the Canadian Anti-Slavery Baptist Association.)[23]

This division held for several years, with both bodies presiding over their own churches and holding separate annual meetings. The ABA continued to expand, however, and the right hand of fellowship was given to First Baptist Church of Buxton, Little River, New Canaan, and Windsor churches, while Hamilton, which had previously withdrawn, came back into the fold.[24] In 1855, the ABA resolved to send a letter and delegate to the Anti-Slavery Baptist Association, which was meeting in Detroit the following year, and in 1856, the latter body in turn sent a letter to the ABA stating its desire to reunite with the Amherstburg Association. In 1857, the two entities reunited under the name of the Amherstburg Anti-Slavery Regular Baptist Association. Shrewsbury, a little settlement on the north shore of Lake Erie about eighteen miles southeast of Chatham, requested admittance for the first time, and the new body voted to add the word *antislavery* to its constitution.[25]

Second Baptist Church, Detroit regained admittance and was given the right hand of fellowship in 1858. Second Baptist's new, much larger house of worship had been constructed in 1857 at a cost of well over $1,400. There were now 212 church members.[26] After the passage of the Fugitive Slave Act of 1850, Second Baptist no doubt had stepped up its role of hiding and funneling fugitives from slavery across to Windsor, Amherstburg, and points beyond.[27]

Meanwhile, on the Canadian side, the churches in the border region were actively receiving escaped slaves and tending to their welfare. Sandwich Baptist Church, for example, only three blocks from the river in one of the most heavily traveled crossings on the entire Detroit riverfront, was certainly heavily engaged in receiving formerly enslaved refugees. Although only oral history of the church's activities in the Underground Railroad era survive, there is a persistent tradition that there was a series of secret tunnels leading from the waterfront to the cellar of the church.

Elder Wilson Carter and the eccentric Reverend Rice fell afoul of the Canada Colored Baptist Missionary Society, in which First Baptist Amherstburg and the Chatham Baptist Church were involved. Rice, after losing his support from the American Missionary Association, began to send "begging" agents out to raise money from the public, as Irene Moore Davis elaborates in chapter 4. He was soon accused of misrepresenting Canadian Blacks as "poor, starving, destitute fugitives" in order to increase revenues.[28] Two years later, more controversy erupted over Rice's mission and its begging practices. A meeting of the community was called in which it was established that little if any of the money or old clothing acquired was ever received by these "fugitives," and people had long since lost faith in Isaac Rice and his mission.[29]

The result was the creation of the True Band Society, a self-help organization of black men and women who paid monthly dues into a fund to help those truly in need, especially those who had recently arrived from slavery and needed assistance to get on their feet. This group met at First Baptist Church, Amherstburg, and some of its officers were leaders of the church.[30] The first president of the True Band Society of Amherstburg, for example, was Major Stevens, a deacon who had served as church clerk from 1848 to 1851 and later in the 1860s. Vice President Fountain Bush was a member of First Baptist who became an ordained minister and the regular preacher at the church by 1858. Corresponding secretary of the organization Nelson W. Brown took over as church clerk from 1852 to 1854, and recording secretary L. G. Spears was church clerk from 1855 to 1858. John Hatfield, on the True Band board of managers, was a delegate of the church at the ABA annual meeting in 1855. All of these men had also assumed important roles at ABA meetings over the years.[31] The True Band was a society with several hundred members who, above all, sought intellectual and moral elevation: "[W]e want food for our *souls* and clothing for our minds, and suitable *houses* for the work of God's praise." The physical necessities of their people, they maintained, they would take care of themselves.[32] The True Band movement was so popular that it spread to thirteen other centers of black settlement in the province.[33]

The year 1861 saw membership in the Amherstburg Baptist Association reach its highest point: 1,060 members and fourteen churches. In 1866, there were seventeen Baptist churches under the umbrella of the association: Amherstburg, Ann Arbor, Michigan, First Baptist of Buxton, Second Baptist of Buxton, Chatham, Colchester, Dresden, Gosfield, Hamilton, Little River, London, Mount Pleasant, Puce, Sandwich, Shrewsbury, Windsor, and Ypsilanti, Michigan.[34]

With the outbreak of the Civil War, however, many of the young men of the association's churches left to fight on the Union side, revealing once again the porous nature of the border between Canada West and its southern neighbor. In 1864, the association passed a resolution on the conflict to be published in the *Detroit Advertiser and Tribune* that read, in part: "[W]e are heart and hand with the present administration, and are willing to pledge ourselves, by all means in our power, not inconsistent with British subjects, to aid the Union, until the old flag floats over every state from the Atlantic to Pacific."[35] The following year, a collection was taken up for the Reverend Samuel H. Davis, pastor of the church in Dresden and recognized repeatedly in the minutes as one of the ablest ministers of the association, to assist him on a mission to the freedmen of the South.[36] This was at a time when many of the shining lights of the African Canadian community went to the American South to teach and minister to their newly freed African American brothers and sisters.

With the Emancipation Proclamation of 1863, the passage of the Thirteenth Amendment, and the end of the Civil War in 1865, all slaves were freed. Now the educated elite and many of the black war veterans who had once lived in Canada could reside in the United States. While some soldiers returned to Canada West and some African Americans migrated to Canada West to be with relatives, many families who had found refuge on Canadian soil returned to the South after the war, with the result that membership in the association had dwindled to 368 by 1887.[37]

The history of the Amherstburg Baptist Association, later renamed Amherstburg Regular Missionary Baptist Association, reveals the very fluid nature of black communities and churches in Canada and the United States—and elsewhere, for that matter. Begun by a call of Second Baptist Church of Detroit, the Amherstburg Baptist Association—its churches, pastors, and members—repeatedly crisscrossed national boundaries in an effort to extend the influence and activities of black Baptists in both countries. People not only moved across the Detroit River and other Canadian borders to attend meetings and events, they also lived for periods of time in both countries. Thus, it is clearly indicated that, in the case of African North Americans, race, or a Pan-African identity, trumped the authority of national political identities, and that international borders such as the Detroit River were indeed highly porous spaces.

NOTES

1. Amherstburg Baptist Association Minutes, book 1, 2–3, Canadian Baptist Archives, McMaster Divinity School, McMaster University, Hamilton, ON (hereafter ABA Minutes).
2. See, for example, Karolyn Smardz Frost, "Communities of Resistance: African Canadians and African Americans in Antebellum Toronto," *Ontario History* 99, no. 1 (2007), 52.
3. Dorothy Shadd Shreve, *The AfriCanadian Church: A Stabilizer* (Jordan Station, ON: Paideia, 1983), 42.
4. ABA Minutes, frontispiece.
5. ABA Minutes, frontispiece.
6. ABA Minutes, frontispiece; Estate of William Wilks, RG 22-311 Essex County Surrogate Court Estate Files #494 1838, Archives of Ontario. Microfilm GS 1 reel 720.
7. "FREEDOM'S RAILWAY: Reminiscences of the Brave Old Days of the Famous Underground Line Historic Scenes Recalled Detroit the Center of Operations That Freed Thousands of Slaves," *Detroit Tribune*, January 17, 1886; *Provincial Freeman*, May 31, 1856; Reverend W. M. Mitchell, The *Under-Ground Railroad*, 2nd ed. (London: Tweedie, 1860), 113.
8. See the Second Baptist Church, Detroit website, www.secondbaptistdetroit.org (accessed September 30, 2011).
9. ABA Minutes, book 1, 3. For the membership numbers of these three churches upon entry into the association, see Dorothy Shadd Shreve et al., *Pathfinders of Liberty and Truth: A Century with the Amherstburg Regular Missionary Baptist Association* (Jordan Station, ON: Paideia, 1940), 23; Shadd Shreve, *The AfriCanadian Church*, 42–43.
10. Carol E. Mull, *The Underground Railroad in Michigan* (Jefferson, NC: McFarland, 2010), 34.
11. The Reverend Isaac Rice, a white Presbyterian minister, left Trumbull County, Ohio, to minister among the black population in the Amherstburg area in 1838 and frequently wrote letters to the antislavery press as well as to the corresponding secretary of the American Missionary Association about the conditions of that community. He claimed that 3,000–4,000 Blacks were living in the area by the mid-1840s, and the number was increasing daily. See, for example, Isaac Rice to Hamilton Hill, March 12, 1845, *Oberlin Evangelist*, May 7, 1845; Isaac Rice to

Henry Cowles, December 25, 1846, *Oberlin Evangelist*, February 17, 1847; Rice's count was probably overestimated. See W. P. Newman, "The Colored People in Canada," *Oberlin Evangelist*, August 30, 1848. Newman conducted a survey of the black communities of Canada West and estimated the black population in Malden (Amherstburg) and vicinity to be 1,500. Michael Wayne's assessment of the 1861 census indicated a population of 373 in Amherstburg, 456 to its immediate north in Anderdon, and 937 to its immediate east in Colchester, with a total Essex County black population of 3,508. Michael Wayne, "The Black Population in Canada West on the Eve of the American Civil War: A Reassessment Based on the Manuscript Census of 1861," *Social History/Histoire Sociale* 28, no. 56 (1995), 465–85.

12. Shadd Shreve et al., *Pathfinders of Liberty and Truth*, 75; Jennifer A. Cousineau, Parks Canada, personal communication with author, October 4, 2011. Cousineau indicated that the official year of the completion of this church was 1849. See Jennifer A. Cousineau, Historical Services Branch, "Submission Report: First Baptist Church, Amherstburg, Historic Sites and Monuments Board of Canada" (April 2011).

13. ABA Minutes, book 1, 7; Shadd Shreve et al., *Pathfinders of Liberty and Truth*, 10.

14. Shadd Shreve et al., *Pathfinders of Liberty and Truth*, 91; James K. Lewis, *Religious Life of Fugitive Slaves and Rise of Coloured Baptist Churches, 1820–1865, in What Is Now Known as Ontario* (New York: Arno, 1980), 62–67. See also Sandwich First Baptist Church at "Windsor Mosaic," www.windsor-communities.com, under "African Canadian community, People" (accessed October 6, 2011). According to this source, the pastor at the time of the 1851 dedication was Robert H. Jackson. However, the ABA Minutes indicate that the Reverend M. J. Lightfoot was the minister of the Sandwich church as of September 1851.

15. C. Peter Ripley et al., eds. *The Black Abolitionist Papers, 1830–1865*, vol. 2, *Canada* (Chapel Hill: University of North Carolina Press, 1986), 319n. The organization was first founded under the name American and Foreign Baptist Mission Society.

16. ABA Minutes, book 1, 71, 84–85.

17. ABA Minutes, book 1, 99.

18. Ripley et al., *The Black Abolitionist Papers*, vol. 2, *Canada*, 302–3n; "No Account Yet of the $20,000 at Dawn," part 1 and conclusion, *The North Star*, March 2 and March 9, 1849.

19. *Anti-Slavery Missions. Review of the Operations of the American Baptist Free Mission Society for the Past Year* (Bristol, UK: Matthews Brothers, 1851), 7; Samuel J. May Anti-Slavery Collection, Rare Books and Manuscripts Division, Cornell University Library, Ithaca, NY, ebooks.library.cornell.edu/cgi/t/text/pageviewer-idx?c=mayantislavery;cc=mayantislavery;q1=anti-slavery%20missions;rgn=title;view=image;seq=1;idno=22876406;didno=22876406 (accessed September 30, 2011).

20. ABA Minutes, book 1, 117–18.

21. ABA Minutes, book 1, 123–24. The letter went on to state that the Mount Pleasant church had been excommunicated because it violated the constitution but had refused to receive or listen to the association's council that came to discuss the matter. "Your souls will mourn that brethren who seemed to love us, and respect the laws of this (we trust) heaven sanctioned and heaven constituted body should dare or wish to infringe its laws, especially since in doing so, they were obliged to treat unkindly some of our best brethren, sent as delegates to talk and reason with them. But refusing to hear council, or suffer as much as to *pray* or

speak in their churches, they drove us away. They say they are an abolition church and belong to the Free Mission Board" (124–25).

22. ABA Minutes, book 1, 123–24. Another example came toward the end of the circular. "Take no offence that your best ministers who have stood the long lasting storm, have been turned out of the few churches, which call themselves abolitionists, and had to preach in the streets."
23. ABA Minutes, book 1, 123–24. See the ABA Minutes for 1852, 140–43; *The Constitution, By-laws, Minutes, Circular Letter, Articles of Faith, and the Covenant, of the Canadian Anti-Slavery Baptist Association* (Windsor, ON: *Voice of the Fugitive* Office, 1854), 6–7.
24. ABA Minutes, book 1, 151–52, 188–97.
25. ABA Minutes, book 1, 169, 182–83, 188, 193, 194–95, 197.
26. ABA Minutes, book 1, 192, 202.
27. Fred Landon, "The Negro Migration to Canada After the Passing of the Fugitive Slave Act," in *Ontario's African-Canadian Heritage: Collected Writings by Fred Landon, 1918–1967*, ed. Karolyn Smardz Frost, Bryan Walls, Hilary Bates Neary, and Frederick H. Armstrong (Toronto: Dundurn, 2009), 241–46.
28. M. Stephens, E. Valentine, et al. to the editor, *Voice of the Fugitive*, February 26, 1852. In addition to Stephens (or Stevens, as the name is sometimes rendered) and Valentine, Amherstburg church deacons Daniel Binga Jr., David Medley, George M. Crawford, George Young, and J. Howard, and church members George S. Washington, J. Green, and P. Kidd as well as Chatham Baptist church secretary H. H. Hanks authored the letter.
29. This controversy about Rice and some of the black men with whom he worked touched the Amherstburg Baptist Association because Rice had been involved in the association for a number of years. In fact, at the 1854 annual meeting, he was elected clerk and traveling missionary for the upcoming year, placing the association in the awkward position of having to lend its unbridled support to him in the minutes: "Allusion was made to attacks on his character, accusing drunkenness etc. We declared to the world the utmost confidence in this brother, and defy the least proof for fourteen years. We have offered him some of us $10 and others $5 if he would prosecute slanderers but he said, no, I will bear this for my Savior's sake and let the Lord take care of me." At the 1855 meeting, part of the Amherstburg Baptist Church's report referring to I. J. Rice was canceled because church delegates "failed to report," and Rice was thereafter never mentioned in the ABA Minutes again—and was presumably no longer active in the organization. "Correspondence. Report of the True Band of Amherstburg to the Editor of the Provincial Freeman," *Provincial Freeman*, December 29, 1855; ABA Minutes, book 1, 155, 166.
30. "Report and Circular of the True Band Society of Amherstburg, C.W. to the Editor of the *Provincial Freeman*," March 13, 1855, *Provincial Freeman*, April 7, 1855; "An Appeal of the Fugitives in Canada to Their Friends in the U.S.," *Provincial Freeman*, June 30, 1855; Levi Foster to Editor, *Provincial Freeman*, June 30, 1855; "Correspondence: Report of the True Band of Amherstburg to the Editor of the *Provincial Freeman*."
31. ABA Minutes, book 1.
32. "Correspondence: Report of the True Band of Amherstburg to the Editor of the *Provincial Freeman*."

33. Benjamin Drew, *A North-Side View of Slavery. The Refugee; or, The Narratives of the Fugitive Slaves in Canada. Related by Themselves, with an Account of the History and Condition of the Colored Population of Upper Canada* (Boston: John P. Jewett, 1856), 165–66, 236–37.
34. Shadd Shreve et al., *Pathfinders of Liberty and Truth*, 19, 21.
35. ABA Minutes, book 1, 252–53; Shadd Shreve et al., *Pathfinders of Liberty and Truth*, 20.
36. ABA Minutes, book 1, 260–61; Shadd Shreve et al., *Pathfinders of Liberty and Truth*, 20.
37. Shadd Shreve et al., *Pathfinders of Liberty and Truth*, 21.

In 1852, Mary Ann Shadd Cary published *A Plea for Emigration; or, Notes of Canada West* to encourage enslaved and free African Americans to move to what is now Ontario. (Courtesy of the Toronto Public Library)

III

INSPIRED TRANSNATIONALISTS

Anguished as a result of generations of slavery and legalized racism in the United States, most Blacks, both free and enslaved, experienced a profound sense of disillusionment with the country of their birth. Many believed that political rights and social liberty could be achieved only by emigrating.

The American Colonization Society offered resettlement in Liberia for emancipated African Americans, but black leaders viewed the society's goals with suspicion. Slaveholders, among the organization's strongest supporters, openly promoted the need to "remove" free Blacks from proximity to the enslaved. Yet emigration remained an undercurrent in black consciousness, and black leaders throughout the nineteenth century and into the twentieth appealed to it as the best way to shed American racial oppression.

After passage of the 1850 Fugitive Slave Law and the unfavorable decision in the 1857 Dred Scott case, which denied black people any right of citizenship in American society, colonization debates intensified and Underground Railroad migration took on a new urgency.

Detroit Underground Railroad collaborators renewed their efforts to make life in Canada as satisfying as possible for the new settlers. Though they considered many destinations outside the United States that might be hospitable to black immigrants, Canada, where, reputedly, "men were not known by their color,"* was just across the river—so close they could join with the immigrants in common cause.

The courage that had pushed the freedom-seekers to the border did not abate when they crossed the river. Fully embracing their hard-won freedom and political status, the newest African Canadians built places of worship, cleared land to cultivate crops, started schools for themselves and their children, and challenged colonial officials to recognize the civil rights they were fully entitled to as British subjects.

---

* Harriet Martineau, "The Martyr Age in the United States," *London and Westminster Review* 32, no. 62 (1838), 2.

SEVEN

THE *VOICE OF THE FUGITIVE*

A Transnational Abolitionist Organ

AFUA COOPER

> [W]e need a printing press—for the press is the vehicle of thought—the ruler of opinions. We need a press, that we may be independent of those who have always oppressed us—we need a press that we may hang our banners on the outer wall, that all who pass by may read why we struggle, and what we struggle for.
>
> *Voice of the Fugitive,* January 1, 1851

Henry and Mary Bibb were abolition's poster couple par excellence. They worked together in various crucial antislavery endeavors in both the United States and Canada. Henry Bibb was a Kentucky runaway slave who escaped to freedom in Detroit, and later Sandwich, Canada West. He had tried repeatedly to rescue his wife, Malinda, and their daughter, but in the process had twice been reenslaved and twice escaped again. Finally, he had given up his struggle to rescue his wife and daughter and settled down to a new life of abolitionist activism on the American side of the Detroit River.

Mary Miles was a Quaker-raised, freeborn black schoolteacher from Rhode Island. She and Henry met at an antislavery convention in 1847, married in 1848, and in 1850, after the passage of the Fugitive Slave Law, migrated to Canada West where they became the de facto leaders of the burgeoning African Canadian community. Mary established a school, founded literary societies, and taught Sunday School. With abolitionist support from both sides of the Detroit River, Henry established the Refugee Home Society, a land settlement venture for fugitive Blacks. Bibb helped to found the Anti-Slavery Society of Canada and assisted

The Voice of the Fugitive *(1851–54) was published at Sandwich, Canada West, by Henry and Mary Bibb. (Courtesy of the Archives of Ontario, Toronto)*

runaways from slavery making their way to Canada on the Underground Railroad. Additionally, the Bibbs created several other organizations to contribute to the uplift of the black community in the Essex County region of the province. Essex was right on the Detroit River border, and Windsor and Sandwich were termini on the Underground Railroad—receiving stations for hundreds of fugitives. Mary and Henry helped runaways from American slavery who crossed the Detroit River into Canada find shelter, food, and clothing. They helped them find work, and even at times assisted them in locating scattered family members. Many freedom-seekers also stayed with the Bibbs. Several fugitives who achieved national and international fame (or infamy) passed through the Bibbs' home, such as John Anderson, who had accidentally killed a white slaveholder while escaping from Missouri, as discussed in chapter 3,[1] and William Parker, a fugitive from slavery remembered for his resistance to slavecatchers in what came to be called the Christiana Riot of 1851.[2]

But perhaps the most important undertaking with which the Bibbs were associated was the *Voice of the Fugitive*, the first successful black newspaper in Canada and a highly effective agent for change in the entire Detroit River border region.[3] In founding the African Canadian press, Henry and Mary Bibb contributed significantly to the print culture of black America and also established a tradition of cross-border publishing. The Bibbs, conceptually and literally, as this essay will show, used the *Voice* to create a black transnational antislavery awareness and culture, in respect not only to Canada and the United States but beyond. This essay focuses on the *Voice of the Fugitive*'s role in the Detroit River border region and the wider North American black community.

Henry Bibb had prior experience publishing in abolitionist and African American journals; he was a regular contributor to the *Signal of Liberty*, the *Emancipator*, the *Anti-Slavery Bugle, Frederick Douglass' Paper*, and the *National Anti-Slavery Standard* between 1846 and 1851.[4] He launched the *Voice of the Fugitive* as part of his community-building program, since there were no newspapers serving the African Canadian community, and he used it as a critical weapon in his struggle for freedom for people of African descent. Most of the white media in Canada West reported the news on Blacks in a pejorative manner, constructing a negative image of Blacks. Many newspapers published in what would become Ontario also opposed African American migration to the province. African Canadians did not have a newspaper to counter white malice, one that could be used as an effective tool in shaping and creating favorable images of themselves.[5] Bibb determined that the *Voice of the Fugitive* would help rectify the situation.

The *Voice of the Fugitive* originated at the Sandwich Colored Convention of November 1850, called and chaired by Henry Bibb. The delegates to this convention, led by Bibb, spoke passionately about the founding of a black press in Canada.[6] Their resolution indicates that they well understood the power of the press:

> *Whereas,* We as a people, have a great work to accomplish and we have no instrument that we can use with more effect than the public press—as we struggle against opinions, our warfare lies in the field of thought, embodying ourselves to field, we need a printing press—for the press is the vehicle of thought—the ruler of opinions. We need a press, that we may be independent of those who have always oppressed us—we need a press that we may hang our banners on the outer wall, that all who pass by may read why we struggle, and what we struggle for.
>
> *Resolved,* That we make immediate effort to have a newspaper established in our midst, which shall be the advocate of the colored people of Canada West.[7]

In this same month, Mary Bibb, "recognizing that black Canadians alone could not sustain the publication," began using her network of antislavery friends in the United States to gain subscribers for the paper.[8] Writing to wealthy American abolitionist Gerrit Smith in Peterboro, New York, she requested, "Will you aid us by sending as many subscribers as convenience will permit," because "there are hundreds of Slaves coming here daily."[9] She enclosed a copy of the paper's prospectus. (See the illustration of the prospectus in this volume's "Sources and Resources.")

The vision for the newspaper was expansive. The *Voice of the Fugitive* was not designed exclusively for a Detroit River region audience nor only for North American readers, but also for Europeans, with a long-term objective of evolving from a bimonthly to a weekly publication. It was to cost $1 a year. Calling on supporters to become subscribers, agents, and donors, Bibb advised U.S. writers to send their letters to a Detroit address, and those from Canada and England to send letters to Sandwich, Canada West. On January 1, 1851, the first issue rolled off the press, declaring the newspaper's objectives and grounding its journalistic platform on antislavery agitation and racial uplift in the free black communities:

> We expect, with the aid of good Providence, to advocate the cause of human liberty in the true meaning of that term. We shall advocate the immediate and unconditional abolition of chattel slavery everywhere, but especially on the American soil. We shall also persuade, as far as it may be practicable, every oppressed person of color in the United States to settle in Canada, where the laws make no distinction among men, based on complection, and upon whose soil "no slave can breathe." We shall advocate the claims of the American slave to the Bible, from whom it has ever been withheld. We shall advocate the cause of temperance and moral reform generally. The cause of education shall have a prominent space in our columns. We shall advocate the claims of agricultural pursuits among our people, as being the most certain road to independence and self-respect.[10]

The masthead named Henry Bibb editor. He brought to the *Voice of the Fugitive* his tremendous prestige as a prominent abolitionist orator and writer as well as the resources of his vast anti-slavery network in the United States and Canada. Mary Bibb also made major contributions to the project, although her name is not listed as coeditor or publisher. She wrote articles for the paper, called on her broad network of abolitionist contacts in the North, particularly the northeastern United States, to help her when necessary, and edited and published the paper when her husband was out of town. She was an educated teacher and accomplished literary woman—the elegant language of the paper, somewhat beyond the style of the self-taught Henry Bibb, suggests that she was more involved in its production than she has been given credit for.

The paper began life auspiciously. It listed twenty-eight agents, black and white, in different parts of the United States and Canada, reflecting its conscious outreach to the cross-border community. Agents included well-known activists in the black freedom struggle—Martin Delany in Pittsburgh; John T. Fisher in Toronto; Charles Langston of Columbus, Ohio; and, from New York City, the editor of Bibb's autobiography, Lucius Matlack. Bibb also had distributors in Britain in the persons of the Reverend Henry Highland Garnet, Josiah and Isaac Henson, and black abolitionist minister James W. C. Pennington. Lesser-known personalities who distributed the *Voice of the Fugitive* included James E. Grant, a Chatham, Canada West, schoolteacher, and John Miles, possibly a relative of Mary Bibb, of Albany, New York.[11]

Henry Bibb came into Canada West with a very clear aim of leading the black community. African American migration to Canada was rapidly increasing as people, free and enslaved, fled to the safety of British North America in response to the 1850 Fugitive Slave Law. Friends of Blacks were interested in knowing how they were doing in Canada, and a newspaper was the best way to disseminate such information. African Canadians and African Americans living along the Detroit River border also needed to know what was going on in the rest of the world, and both former slaves and people of freeborn origin now living in Canada West needed "uplift" guidance, or so black editors thought. Historian Frankie Hutton notes that black editors, given their strategic positioning as black leaders, consciously saw themselves as being in the best position to instruct their fellows in uplift.[12]

The founding of the *Voice of the Fugitive* also came in response to a very real need, given that Blacks were under attack from the white news media and other sectors. Even though the British government had offered Canada as a haven for fleeing fugitives, white public opinion generally opposed the increasing African American immigration. White Canadians, many of them recent emigrants from Britain, could tolerate the few thousand "indigenous" Blacks scattered across the Canadas and the Maritime colonies, but they found the idea of mass immigration of American Blacks into the country harder to accept. Governor General Elgin wrote to a colleague that, because of the Fugitive Slave Law, Canada would likely "be flooded with blackies."[13] Therefore, when Bibb and others noted at the Sandwich convention that "we struggle against opinions" and "[w]e need a press, that we may be independent of those who have always oppressed us," they were very much aware that many influential whites, especially those in the press, used their power to contribute to the continued oppression of black people.[14] While oppression clearly provided a context for the founding of black newspapers, it was not the only impetus. The press, like the schools, churches, and temperance societies that

Henry Bibb escaped from slavery and became a leading abolitionist lecturer as well as founder and publisher of the *Voice of the Fugitive*. (Courtesy of the Toronto Public Library)

Blacks founded, was part of the institution-building process that people of African descent engendered as they became a self-aware and literate community.

Bibb's transnational activism was reflected in the staunch support he and his wife gave to emigration. According to the Bibbs, the first obvious choice for these emigrants was Canada.

It had been a haven for African Americans fleeing bondage since just before the turn of the nineteenth century, when Lieutenant Governor John Graves Simcoe had moved to abolish further slave importation into Upper Canada (later known as Canada West from 1841 to 1867, and Ontario after the confederation of the provinces into the Dominion of Canada in 1867). African Americans had been building communities in the province since the War of 1812. Furthermore, Canada West was largely English speaking; the southern region had excellent and fertile farmlands; and, of great importance, Britain had abolished slavery in all its colonies, including Canada, in 1834.

The transnational perspective on emigration was fully enlarged upon at the North American Convention of Colored People, called and chaired by Bibb in September 1851. The meeting was held in Toronto's St. Lawrence Hall. Over fifty-three delegates from Canada, the United States, the Caribbean, and Britain attended this meeting. For three days, delegates discussed the security of black people in North America and articulated a platform for black uplift.[15] In a bold appeal to all African Americans, Bibb encouraged them to emigrate to Canada, as they would never be free in the United States. Though Canada was the favored destination in the opinion of the Bibbs, Jamaica ran a close second.[16] Haitian emigration was promoted in the later years, especially by the Bibbs' associate editor and close friend, James Theodore Holly, whose ordination in Detroit and later migration to Haiti is discussed in chapter 5. Belize in Central America was also promoted as a place to which African Americans could flee. The purpose and outcome of the convention was widely reported in the *Voice of the Fugitive*.[17] That delegates arrived from the United States, Britain, and the Caribbean to attend a conference in Canada reflected the Pan-American, transatlantic, and international scope of Henry Bibb's vision of black liberty.

TRANSNATIONAL ABOLITIONISM AND THE *VOICE OF THE FUGITIVE*

The *Voice of the Fugitive* offered itself as a platform where black abolitionists could meet, talk, exchange views, give information, debate with each other, and make plans. Bibb sustained relationships with several of the well-known black abolitionists of the day, not only in North America but also in Britain, and developed a transnational discourse of black freedom. Bibb maintained contact with Martin Delany, Henry Highland Garnet, Frederick Douglass, Isaac Henson, Josiah Henson, William Allen, William Still, James Pennington, Samuel Ringgold Ward, William P. Newman, Jermain Loguen, and Amos and Jehiel Beman. Having such a coterie of cross-border and international contacts enabled the *Voice of the Fugitive* to reach a wide audience not only in Canada or in the Detroit River region but also in Britain and across the United States. In 1851, calling himself "a refugee in England," Isaac Henson wrote to Bibb, congratulating him on the establishment of the paper and urging him: "Let the *Voice* speak as a mighty trumpet—let the sound reach across the Atlantic Ocean that Britain may hear the wrongs of those refugees who have nobly pledged their all to the support of the Government. I, too, love to hear the sound in Europe."[18] Writing from New Haven, Connecticut, the Reverend Amos G. Beman discussed the effects of the 1850 Fugitive Slave Law on the North American black community and congratulated Bibb on establishing the *Voice of the Fugitive*: "[I]t is most fortunate, that you have established a *Press* in their midst, which will make their true condition known, and pour in their bosom streams of light and love to encourage them in the pursuit of those plans upon which alone their moral elevation and prosperity can be secured."[19]

The pages of the Bibbs' newspaper provided space for black (and white) abolitionists to air their concerns; give advice on uplift and other topics; speak about the plight of black people, slave and free, in North America and around the world; and give details about the progress of the antislavery movement in their respective locales. In Canada West, the Reverend Samuel Ringgold Ward was a regular correspondent to the *Voice of the Fugitive*. Before he and its editor parted ways, Ward wrote a series of essays that criticized Canada for allowing racial discrimination against black people to persist. These were serialized in the *Voice of the Fugitive* under the title "Canadian Negro Hate."[20]

In the pages of the *Voice of the Fugitive*, authors of both sexes participated in a cross-border discourse on slavery and antislavery. Members of the Female Anti-Slavery Society of Grand Prairie, Michigan, told Bibb about their work on behalf of African American refugees in Canada. The women of the Anti-Slavery Sewing Circle of Cincinnati informed the readers of the *Voice of the Fugitive* of their 1851 antislavery convention and their ongoing efforts, which included agitating and organizing sewing circles on behalf of the fugitives.[21] Historian Deborah Van Broekhoven notes that many women became politically conscious within these supposedly innocuous sewing circles.[22] As the women knitted and sewed, an appointed reader often read the latest antislavery literature, such as Theodore Weld's *Slavery As It Is*.[23] The circles therefore took on clear political overtones. The fact that women were sewing for *fugitives* made their work subversive and radical. The Cincinnati women also gave financial assistance to the *Voice of the Fugitive*, which they recognized was financially burdened.[24]

> Dear Sir. At a late meeting of the Board of Managers of the Ladies' Anti-Slavery Sewing Society of this city [Cincinnati], an ardent wish was expressed that your paper, "Voice of the Fugitive" should be placed pecuniarily, upon such a basis as to relieve you of a part of the burden now resting upon you, and remove all fear of the necessity of its suspension, and it was voted to appropriate fifty dollars of the funds of the society to that object, provided such other assistance is procured as is necessary to place the paper on the desired basis. Whenever, therefore, it is in your power to inform us that such is the fact in regard to it, we will remit to your order the sum above named. May heaven abundantly succeed your labors in the cause of the oppressed.
>
> Mary M. Guild,[25]
> Sec. Ladies Anti-Slavery Society.[26]

The *Voice of the Fugitive* also publicized work on behalf of the fugitives by the women of Essex County, Canada West, which bordered the Detroit River. At a "Donation Party," two of Essex County's leading African Canadian women showed their mettle as apostles of uplift. The *Voice of the Fugitive* thus broadcast the importance of black women to community building and organizing.

> An interesting Donation Party was held in the old Barracks at Windsor, by the colored population, for the erection of a Church and Schoolhouse. There was

> quite a large gathering, and the ladies deserve much credit for the manner in which they conducted the supper. The announcement that Miss Mary Ann Shadd, a lady of high literary attainments, would address the meeting on the subject of education, doubtless brought out many who otherwise would not have attended. The entertainment was highly interesting, at the close of which, Mrs. M. E. Bibb proposed the formation of a Mutual improvement Society. . . . They agreed to meet on every Thursday evening, to read, converse, or hear addresses from members of the society for intellectual improvement.[27]

The black women of Essex County also showed their commitment to community building and abolitionism at an August 1st, Emancipation Day celebration in Sandwich. Not only was Mary Bibb instrumental in founding the Mutual Improvement Society mentioned above, she was a guiding light behind the region's Emancipation Day events. The *Voice of the Fugitive* announced in the "First of August" article that after the speeches, singing, and marching, "Dinner will be furnished by the Ladies for twenty-five cents per ticket. Refreshments may be had during the day and supper in the evening. The proceeds will be appropriated towards erecting a Baptist Church."[28] It is worth noting that the church was eventually built. It still stands today as the First Baptist Church on Peter Street in Sandwich, Ontario.

Emancipation Day, celebrating the ending of slavery in the British Empire, functioned as a plank for transnational collaboration. Blacks from both sides of the Detroit River and beyond met at an agreed-upon location such as Sandwich, where they gave speeches, held rallies and marches, and attended concerts. The 1851 event, for example, had speakers from Detroit and Canada West: "The friends of freedom in Sandwich will celebrate the abolition of chattel slavery in the British West Indies . . . at the Stone Barracks, where there will be speaking, singing, etc. several distinguished speakers from abroad are expected, among whom are Samuel R. Ward of Boston, Mr. Johnson of Ohio, J. J. Fisher of Toronto, George Cary of Dawn Mills."[29]

That Blacks from the Detroit River region—and indeed from all across North America—met to commemorate British Emancipation Day reveals not only their growing transnational consciousness but also a budding Pan-African sensibility. When local communities celebrated Emancipation Day, they not only commemorated the fact that slavery had been abolished in the British West Indies but also drew attention to the plight of the enslaved in the United States, thus renewing their commitment to ending American slavery. Articles about Emancipation Day in the *Voice of the Fugitive* ensured that knowledge, news, and information about the crucial event would be carried throughout the region and beyond.

If freedom as exemplified by Emancipation Day celebrations provided a space for cross-border cooperation, then slavery and resistance to it on behalf of those still enslaved also linked Canada and the United States. The Underground Railroad embodies these twin themes of bondage and resistance, themes played out in the pages of the *Voice of the Fugitive*. After all, Henry Bibb himself was a self-emancipated fugitive who had journeyed to freedom on the Underground Railroad from Louisiana via Texas to Michigan.[30] He used the pages of his newspaper to advise Underground Railroad agents how to help runaways and recommend the best routes to travel to Canada. He printed articles on Underground Railroad emigrants and their progress in Canada.

Henry Bibb had the habit of going to Windsor to meet the Detroit ferry to greet and then interview arriving fugitives. The Detroit River crossing had particular significance in his own life: one day in September 1852, Bibb got the shock of his life, when he met three of his brothers from whom he had been separated since childhood. These brothers had fled slavery in Missouri and traveled the Underground Railroad to Canada. They had no idea that their eldest brother was living there. Bibb had the great pleasure of reuniting his long-lost brothers with their mother, whom he had returned south to rescue from slavery and who was now living in her own house in Windsor.

MARY BIBB: CANADA'S FIRST FEMALE NEWSPAPER PUBLISHER

If Henry Bibb is the father of African Canadian journalism, one could argue that Mary Bibb is the mother of the black press in Canada. She can be rightly credited as the first black newspaperwoman in Canada. This recognition is usually given to Mary Ann Shadd Cary, editor and publisher of the *Provincial Freeman*. However, Shadd Cary started her paper in 1854, fully three years after the Bibbs began the *Voice of the Fugitive*, of which Mary Bibb was often in charge. Mary Bibb's unique voice broadened the content and scope of the *Voice of the Fugitive*. The "Donation Party" and "First of August" articles were likely written by her. Not only did Mrs. Bibb write feature articles for the *Voice of the Fugitive*, she edited the paper and oversaw its production when her husband was on the lecture circuit during parts of 1851.[31]

Though Henry Bibb undoubtedly told his friends and supporters of his plans to start a paper, the first documented announcement of the venture came from Mary Bibb. She wrote to Gerrit Smith in November 1850 announcing her and her husband's plans to start the paper and asking him to solicit subscribers.[32] In fact, from the time of the *Voice of the Fugitive*'s inception, Mary Bibb was at the forefront of the enterprise. She was formally educated, but her husband was not. Indeed, she could boast of an education superior to most people, male or female, along the Detroit River border. She had graduated from the Lexington Normal School in Massachusetts as a trained teacher and had taught in Massachusetts, New York, and Ohio. According to C. Peter Ripley, "[T]he contrast between [Henry] Bibb's private correspondence and the paper's polished style suggests that his well-educated wife, Mary E. Bibb, had a good deal to do with the paper's style and content."[33] As an abolitionist (prior to her marriage, she had joined the Garrisonian wing of the movement), schoolteacher, and firm believer in the cause for which the *Voice of the Fugitive* was established, Mary supported both the editorial direction of the paper and her husband's projects, which also were her projects. For example, she gave vocal support to the Refugee Home Society (RHS), sat on its board, wrote articles for American newspapers on the topic, and publicly defended the *Voice of the Fugitive*'s support of the RHS.[34]

Occasionally Mary Bibb signed her name to specific articles. In one, titled "Schools," she reported on her experience as a schoolteacher and school founder, the progress of the students, and the struggles both teacher and students were undergoing. She called attention to the resilience of ordinary people, her students and their parents, who were "making a way out of no way." These people, in her view, suffered doubly: first from "republican oppression" and then from Canada's "cold" and "desolation." Her forceful and energetic language underlined the bitterness she felt about the treatment of Blacks in both the United States *and* Canada:

> The Learned Blacksmith is regarded as the wonder of the age.[35] Truly, he is a hero! What shall we say of men, and *women* too, who have spent a life in slavery, enduring the separation from loved ones, who having escaped to the nominally free states, in pursuit of freedom, found a prejudice equally withering.[36]
>
> Overcoming all this, and feeling that they were men among men, standing upon free soil, awoke only to hear the sound of Mason's infamous fugitive slave bill.
>
> What shall we say of those who have again taken their lives in their hands and escaped to this desolate, cold country,[37] where they are again strangers in a strange land, who, having endured all this, together with the cares of a family on the one hand and pressing want on the other? Is not the person who can improve under such circumstances a hero, even according to Thomas Carlyle's own showing? Many of these support themselves by their own industry, improving all their time to a good advantage.[38]

Mary Bibb was not as enthusiastic about life in Canada West as her husband was. A staunch emigrationist, Henry called upon African Americans to flee to Canada. Yet upon their arrival, they faced what Mary described as a "withering" prejudice from local whites. Mary also called attention to the Sunday School she had set up. In keeping with the original intent of Sabbath Schools, the school functioned as both a religious and secular institution that imparted literacy and knowledge to children and adults in the black community:

> We commenced a Sunday-school four weeks ago; present, thirty-six; there are now forty-four members, and much interest is manifested both by parents and children, some coming even in inclement weather the distance of two and three miles. We are entirely destitute of bibles, there being but four testaments in the school, one of these minus several chapters. Mr. Coe, of ——, brought 100 volumes for the Sunday-school library, of these I put into the hands of Coleman Freeman fifty volumes for the Windsor Sabbath School. Many of the scholars commit whole chapters to memory every week.[39]

Mary Bibb also ran her own ads in the paper. When she gave up her first school in April 1852 and began working from her home as a seamstress, she placed a notice informing "the ladies of Windsor, Sandwich and vicinity, that she has the newest Eastern and Parisian fashions for dress sacque and visitte." The ad, which ran from July to December in each issue of the paper, sheds light on the varied occupational pursuits of black abolitionist women and of free women in general in nineteenth-century society.[40] Mary Bibb was evidently successful in her dressmaking business because after the death of her husband in 1854, she opened a "fancy ladies store" in Windsor.[41]

Being style and fashion conscious, she included in the paper inserts on women's fashion; for instance, the *Voice of the Fugitive* approved of the "scandalous" new trend in women's clothing—the bloomer, or "turkish" pant, designed and worn first by Gerrit Smith's bluestocking daughter, Elizabeth Smith Miller.[42] The following piece, lifted from a Syracuse newspaper, was most likely approved by Mrs. Bibb for inclusion in the paper. "Several ladies appeared in the streets yesterday with dresses of a very *laconic* pattern, and pantaloons *a la Turk*. The new style looks decidedly tidy and neat, and imparts to the wearer quite a sprightly and youthful appearance."[43] The same issue included a piece taken from the *Joliet Signal* that likewise discussed the "bloomer." Other articles promoting women's emancipation appeared frequently.[44]

Crossing over the Detroit River to live in Canada West did not mean Mary Bibb had cut her ties with the States. Like her husband, Mary Bibb made regular visits across the border. Regular border crossing was critical to maintaining transnational contacts and keeping abreast of political concerns in both nations. Mary Bibb, living, teaching, working, and publishing a paper in Canada at the transnational crossroad that was the Detroit River witnessed history unfolding: the flight of African Americans, both enslaved and free, to Canada, and the building of new black communities in that country. Mrs. Bibb not only bore witness to these events (using the paper she and her husband founded to record the deeds of this unfolding history), she participated in them—more, she led them—and deployed the *Voice of the Fugitive*, in the cause of abolition, racial uplift, justice, and human rights.

In founding the *Voice of the Fugitive*, Henry and Mary Bibb laid the foundations for the black press in Canada. But it would be remiss to omit the contributions of James Theodore Holly to the *Voice of the Fugitive* and the black press as a whole. Holly, a freeborn black Vermonter, emigrated to Canada West in 1852 and became the energetic and enthusiastic associate editor of the *Voice of the Fugitive*. He had become convinced through his experience with "Canadian Negro Hate" that people of African ancestry could never find real freedom in North America and therefore became an ardent advocate of emigration to Haiti. Holly altered the editorial direction of the newspaper by making Haitian emigration central to the debate.[45] After Henry Bibb's death in 1854, Holly moved back across the border to labor in the black communities in Detroit and Buffalo. Holly, by then an ordained Episcopalian minister, emigrated permanently with his family to Haiti in 1861. In chapter 4 of this volume, Irene Moore Davis mentions the outcome of Holly's venture to Haiti; in chapter 5 Barbara Hughes Smith reviews Holly's activism in Detroit.

THE FLUID FRONTIER

A reading of even a few issues of the *Voice of the Fugitive* underscores the cultural, geographic, and historical unity of the Detroit River region, encapsulated into what I have termed the "fluid frontier."[46] In fact, Henry Bibb conceived of the *Voice of the Fugitive* as a mouthpiece for the Canadian black community and the communities of the Canada West/Michigan border zone. This is made plain in Bibb's statement that the *Voice of the Fugitive* "can be used as a local medium for Michigan as well as for Canada, it being right on the border of the state."[47]

Detroiters and those on the Canadian side of the river regularly visited each other, often going to church together, holding joint Emancipation Day events, and attending festive occasions such as marriages on both banks of the river. For example, in its June 17, 1852, issue, the *Voice of the Fugitive* announced the wedding of one "J. P. Struthers to Eliza Haggerty, both of Windsor, C.W," who were married in Detroit.

Henry Bibb himself represents the concept and reality of African Canadian and African American life and activism on the fluid frontier very well. He had two mailing addresses, one in Sandwich, the other in Detroit, and circulated his paper in both communities. His movement back and forth across the border as an abolitionist lecturer revealed that Bibb was conscious that the border was not an impermeable barrier although as a self-emancipated fugitive he was in constant danger of capture and reenslavement. Throughout 1851, and at risk of losing his own freedom, this "refugee from slavery" toured and lectured in the United States several times. He did so not only in border towns like Buffalo and Detroit but in inland cities like Chicago and Milwaukee:[48] "We arrived in Chicago on 4th inst. . . . After attending the 'Christian anti-slavery convention,' we spent the Sabbath in the city. Lectured in the A.M.E. Church on Sabbath evening to a crowded house—subject was the moral elevation of the colored people of North America, and the advantages to be gained by leaving the cities, emigrating to Canada and following agricultural pursuits."[49] While on his tour Bibb submitted articles on the living standards of Blacks in various towns and villages and offered detailed descriptions of the schooling available for Blacks—or the lack thereof—in these places.[50] In the meantime, in addition to looking after her school, Mary Bibb edited and published the *Voice of the Fugitive* at Sandwich.

An in-depth reading of the advertisements in the *Voice of the Fugitive* lends support to the fluid frontier thesis of this volume, which, in turn, reflects my own work. Though the ads are not extensive, most of them for all of 1851 and the first quarter of 1852 were placed by Detroiters or businesspeople from other Michigan towns. This indicates that people on both sides of the border saw advantages in exploiting the regional marketplace, regardless of the national identity of their customers. Also it shows the American support Bibb received for his paper. Bibb had been active and well regarded in the Detroit community before migrating to Canada West. He had a solid backing from that community, especially its abolitionist sector, and had a following there. Since small newspapers usually operated at a loss, advertisements were and are the key to a newspaper's financial success. From the few ads placed in the *Voice of the Fugitive*, it is clear that its income from advertising was very limited, but it *was* binational in character.

Hallock and Raymond advertised their "ready made clothing," A. Derrick his (or her) tailoring establishment, and the Sons of Temperance their Detroit "confectionary saloon." Bibb promoted several "anti-slavery books," including his own narrative; Mrs. Alexander broadcasted the benefits of her boardinghouse; one T. Johnson, a barber, offered "shaving, hairdressing and bathing"; and W. F. Parker informed the public that he had "fitted up an Eating House, where every delicacy can be furnished in better style than at any other establishment." With the exception of Bibb, all these advertisers were from Michigan.[51] From the Canada West end, Mary Bibb advertised her dressmaking business, Charles Baby and John O'Connor their law practice, D. Vogelsang and J. Haggerty their saddle business, and J. McCrae of

Windsor his assortment of "dry goods," which included "groceries, hardware, crockery, stationery, boots and shoes, ready-made clothing, drugs, patent, medicines, etc." Levi Foster, a successful Amherstburg businessman, ran advertisements for his hotel and stagecoach line. Foster was also a subscription agent for the *Voice of the Fugitive* who advertised in the *Voice* throughout its years of publication.[52]

Some of the advertisers can be identified from sources other than their ads, and much can be inferred about others. Hallock and Raymond were Michigan abolitionists and associates of Bibb. As reformers striving for an antiracist vision, it is not surprising that they would support the *Voice of the Fugitive*. Mrs. Alexander was most probably black; it is very unlikely that a white female proprietor of a boardinghouse, given the racial politics of the day, would want people of African descent to sojourn at her establishment since Blacks were routinely excluded from inns and hotels on both sides of the Detroit River. The Sons of Temperance saloon was also probably black-owned, since the temperance movement, promoted by black abolitionists and clergy alike, was structured along racial and class lines. Hairdressing and bathing businesses were in all likelihood owned by African Americans, since there was a stigma against barbers who cut both black and white people's hair. Baby and O'Connor were established white lawyers from Sandwich, Charles Baby a scion of the famous French Canadian Baby family, which had deep roots in both Canada and Michigan.[53] The Babys were originally French slaveholders in Detroit, but some of the Canadian-born members of the family—particularly Charles—had abolitionist leanings.[54]

The ads in the paper are not extensive—they take up merely one and a half columns—but they are remarkably eclectic. It is noticeable that as 1852 progressed, more and more Canadians, black and white, began advertising in the paper. This could mean that the *Voice of the Fugitive* had become more familiar to Canadian businesses as Bibb became better acquainted with his adopted country. It may also mean that the paper had achieved a certain degree of stability and status in Canada West and therefore was in a better position to attract Canadian advertisers.

In October 1853, the office of the *Voice of the Fugitive* burned down. Bibb sent out an "Extra" sheet informing the North American press and the paper's readers of the tragedy. The October 28 issue of Boston's *Liberator* reported:

> On Sunday night, Oct. 9, about 12 o'clock, the office of the *Voice of the Fugitive*, in Windsor C.W., with all its contents, was consumed by fire, together with several other apartments occupied by families in an adjoining building. Mr. Bibb gives his reasons for believing the fire to be the work of an incendiary, and then adds,—The *Voice of the Fugitive*, has been cloven down and partially silenced by the hand of an incendiary, we have reason to believe: and the loss to us has truly been a great one.[55] They have destroyed for us in one night more than all we have accumulated by arduous labor and economy during the last three years. The great question with us now is, not whether we shall suspend the publication of our little sheet or not for the future—for upon this point our mind is fully made up. We shall go forth in the name of outraged humanity, firmly relying on the promises of God and the justice of our cause for success. Our first object in sending forth this Extra sheet is to inform our patrons that the *Voice of the Fugitive and Canadian Independent* is not dead, though

crippled, but just as soon as we can repair the breach a little, we assure our readers that the Fugitives in Canada shall be heard from, again, through this paper, regularly.

The loss caused by the fire was great indeed. All the printing equipment, which the Bibbs used not only to publish their paper but also to do job printing, was destroyed, which meant a loss of income. One can imagine that back issues of the paper, especially those for 1853, were also consumed by the flames, as were the Bibbs' personal correspondence and documents Henry Bibb had written: in addition to his autobiography, two books on American slave conspiracies and a collection of antislavery songs titled the *Anti-Slavery Harp*. If copies of these publications were in the office when it burned to the ground, it is not surprising that no cache of "Henry Bibb papers" has been found. There was also a human cost. Other buildings were also burned in the conflagration and several families were left homeless.

The burning of the *Voice* must have been a great blow to Henry and Mary Bibb as well as to James Theodore Holly and all the paper's supporters. It was also a great loss to the black communities along the Detroit River border. For almost three years the *Voice of the Fugitive* had been a clarion for a beleaguered population. It had given black people living in the Detroit River region and beyond a clear voice, defended their rights, championed the cause of the enslaved, fought Canadian and American racists and, in keeping with Henry Bibb's personal commitment to community uplift, sought to put forth a program for black elevation, progress, and independence.

Henry Bibb planned to resurrect the paper. The "Extra" sheet he sent to the *Liberator* along with news of the fire indicates that he did not intend to be silenced by the catastrophe. According to historian John O'Farrell, after the fire, "Bibb published a one-page newsletter until his death at Windsor on August 1, 1854."[56] This could very well be the "Extra" Bibb alluded to. But by all indications, Bibb was never able to restore the paper to its original status and circulation. The *Voice of the Fugitive* did not, like the phoenix, rise from its own ashes.

What rose instead was the *Provincial Freeman*, published by a former friend and supporter of the Bibbs, Mary Ann Shadd Cary, a well-educated abolitionist from Pennsylvania and champion of emigration to Canada who had herself moved to Canada West. The contentious relationship that developed between the Bibbs and Mary Ann Shadd is further examined in this volume in chapter 9. The demise of the *Voice of the Fugitive*, in fact, led to the life of the *Provincial Freeman*; for it was only after the *Voice of the Fugitive* ceased publication that the *Freeman* was successfully established. In the evolution of the black press in nineteenth-century Canada West, the African Canadian population revealed that it was able to support, and that rather halfheartedly, only one paper. There were factions among the African Canadian population hostile to the Bibbs, and there were also numerous whites who wished Blacks and their institutions erased from the Canada West landscape.[57]

Henry and Mary Bibb, founders of the *Voice of the Fugitive*, were quintessential transnational abolitionists. The Detroit border region was the main geographic landscape in which they performed their antislavery and black uplift activism. The Bibbs showed through their actions that the river was not an impenetrable barrier but a permeable frontier that could be shaped or negotiated. The newspaper Bibb published with the aid of his wife, Mary, reached a continental and international audience and garnered support for the struggle against American slavery and racial oppression.

If Henry Bibb's life was cast in a transnational frame, his death was as well. After a long illness, this champion of black freedom died, as if on cue, on August 1st, 1854, Emancipation Day. Abolitionists on both shores of the river had already prepared for Emancipation Day events, and they used this opportunity to memorialize the life and work of one of their shining stars. Black abolitionist George DeBaptiste of Detroit had rented a boat, the *Ruby*, on which some celebrants from Michigan and Canada West intended to sail up and down the river to commemorate the day. They did just that, but with an added somber gesture. Detroit abolitionists William C. Monroe, William Lambert, and George Lightfoot, and Windsor resident James T. Holly memorialized Henry Bibb's life and work in speeches and toasts, mourning his loss in a ceremony that took place on the very river that functioned as a boundary between the land of the free and the land of the slave. Bibb had himself crossed and recrossed the international border numerous times during his personal and public freedom campaign. At his death, admirers, friends, relatives, and acquaintances stood on either bank of the Detroit River and tearfully raised cheers for Bibb as the waters lapped at the opposite shores in Michigan and Canada West.

Henry Bibb was dead, and his paper was extinguished. But Henry and Mary Bibb had left an indelible mark on black North American journalism and print culture. They founded the African Canadian press and used that vehicle as a tool in their struggle to end American slavery and promote civil and human rights for people of African descent living in both the United States and Canada. Through their numerous initiatives to bring about black freedom, including their use of the *Voice of the Fugitive* as a clarion call to action, the Bibbs charted a course in militant transnational activism that resonated throughout the Detroit River border zone and well beyond.

NOTES

1. The attempt of American officials to have John Anderson extradited resulted in the last such case tried before a Canadian court prior to the Civil War. See Patrick Brode, *The Odyssey of John Anderson* (Toronto: Osgoode Society, 1989).
2. William Parker, "The Freedman's Story: In Two Parts," *Atlantic Monthly*, February 1866, 153, 158–61, and March 1866, 281–87.
3. An earlier paper, the *British American*, was launched and edited by a Canadian Black in 1845. But according to Robin Winks, it "survived less than a month." Robin W. Winks, *The Blacks in Canada: A History*, 2nd ed. (Montreal: McGill-Queen's University Press, 1997), 394.
4. Chapter 3 of my doctoral dissertation details Bibb's contributions as an antislavery writer. See "'Doing Battle in Freedom's Cause': Henry Bibb, Abolitionism, Race Uplift, and Black Manhood, 1842–1854" (PhD diss., University of Toronto, 2000).
5. Jason H. Silverman, "'We Shall Be Heard!'—The Development of the Fugitive Slave Press in Canada," *Canadian Historical Review* 65, no. 1 (1984): 54–69.
6. In 1851, "Canada" was made up of two provinces—Canada West (later named Ontario) and Canada East (Quebec). These two provinces were united in 1840 and called the United

Province of Canada. The Maritime colonies, Nova Scotia, New Brunswick, and Prince Edward Island, were separate British colonies. It was only in 1867, when Canada East and Canada West united with Nova Scotia and New Brunswick to become "Canada," that the concept and reality of Canada as a nation took hold.

7. *Voice of the Fugitive*, January 1, 1851.
8. C. Peter Ripley et al., eds., *The Black Abolitionist Papers, 1830–1865*, vol. 2, *Canada* (Chapel Hill: University of North Carolina Press, 1986), 108.
9. Ripley et al., *The Black Abolitionist Papers*, vol. 2, *Canada*, 108–12; Mary Bibb to Gerrit Smith, November 8, 1850, Gerrit Smith Papers, University of Syracuse, Syracuse, NY.
10. *Voice of the Fugitive*, January 1, 1851.
11. *Voice of the Fugitive*, January 1, 1851.
12. Frankie Hutton, *The Early Black Press in America, 1827 to 1860* (Westport, CT: Greenwood, 1993), 33.
13. Arthur Doughty, ed., *The Elgin-Grey Papers, 1846–1852* (Ottawa: J. O. Patenaude, 1937), 2:720.
14. Silverman, "'We Shall Be Heard!'" 55–56.
15. Bibb's wife, Mary, did not seem as enthusiastic as her husband about the virtues of the province. See her letter in the *Voice of the Fugitive*, February 26, 1851.
16. *Voice of the Fugitive*, November 19, 1851, December 3, 1851, December 17, 1851.
17. The proceedings of the North American Convention are printed in the *Voice of the Fugitive*, September 24, 1851.
18. Isaac Henson—most likely the son of Josiah Henson—lived in London for over fifteen years. He attended college there and was ordained as a Wesleyan minister. Josiah Henson, *An Autobiography of the Reverend Josiah Henson* (1881; repr., Reading, MA: Addison-Wesley, 1969), 143.
19. *Voice of the Fugitive*, May 21, 1851. Beman, son of Jehiel Beman, was an antislavery worker and black rights crusader. Like his fellow black leaders, he advocated moral reform, temperance, and education. Beman also published a reform journal, *Zion's Wesleyan*. In the early 1850s, Beman organized a series of "Elevation Meetings" throughout the state of Connecticut. Ripley et al., *The Black Abolitionist Papers*, vol. 2, *Canada*, 167–68n28; *Voice of the Fugitive*, May 21, 1851.
20. *Voice of the Fugitive*, September 9, 1852, September 21, 1852, October 4, 1852.
21. The Cincinnati group organized because of the destitution of runaway slaves who arrived in Ohio from Kentucky and other slave states, most often with no more than the clothes on their backs. Levi Coffin states with regard to a fugitive family, en route to Canada, that arrived in Cincinnati from Kentucky: "The ladies' Anti-Slavery Sewing Society fitted out the family with the necessary clothing." Levi Coffin, *Reminiscences of Levi Coffin* (Cincinnati: Western Tract Society, 1876), 316.
22. Deborah Van Broekhoven, "'Better Than a Clay Club': The Organization of Anti-Slavery Fairs, 1830–60," *Slavery and Abolition* 19, no. 1 (1998): 24–45.
23. Theodore Dwight Weld, *Slavery As It Is: Testimony of a Thousand Witnesses* (New York: American Anti-Slavery Society, 1839).
24. *Voice of the Fugitive*, February 26, 1851.

25. Mary M. Guild, a member of a prominent Cincinnati family, was one of the "benevolent ladies" of Cincinnati who "organized an Anti-Slavery Sewing Society, to provide suitable clothing for the fugitives." Charles Greve, *Centennial History of Cincinnati* (Cincinnati: Biographical Publishing, 1904), 754. Wilbur Siebert also mentions the Cincinnati Sewing Circle. Wilbur H. Siebert, *The Underground Railroad From Slavery to Freedom* (New York: Macmillan, 1898), 77. My thanks to Linda Bailey, reference librarian of the Cincinnati Historical Society, for leading me to the information on Mary M. Guild.
26. *Voice of the Fugitive*, June 3, 1852.
27. *Voice of the Fugitive*, November 19, 1851.
28. *Voice of the Fugitive*, July 30, 1851.
29. *Voice of the Fugitive*, July 30, 1851.
30. Bibb wrote of his harrowing escape journeys in his autobiography, *Narrative of the Life and Adventures of Henry Bibb, an American Slave, Written by Himself* (New York: privately published, 1849).
31. See my biographical essay of the education and work of Mary Bibb, Afua Cooper, "The Search for Mary Bibb, Black Woman Teacher in Nineteenth-Century Canada West," *Ontario History* 83, no. 1 (1991), 41; and Afua Cooper, "Black Women and Work in Nineteenth-Century Canada West: Black Woman Teacher Mary Bibb," in *We're Rooted Here and They Can't Pull Us Up: Essays in African Canadian Women's History*, ed. Peggy Bristow, et al. (1994; repr., Toronto: University of Toronto Press, 1999), 143–70.
32. Mary Bibb to Gerrit Smith, November 8, 1850; Ripley et al., *The Black Abolitionist Papers*, vol. 2, *Canada*, 108.
33. Ripley et al., *The Black Abolitionist Papers*, vol. 2, *Canada*, 108; see also 111.
34. *Anti-Slavery Bugle*, April 12, 1851, October 4 1851; *Liberator*, November 12, 1852.
35. Mrs. Bibb must have been referring to Dr. James W. C. Pennington, an escaped slave turned abolitionist. Pennington learned the blacksmith trade while in slavery and practiced it both in slavery and freedom. A man of exceptional ability, Pennington took private lessons and was eventually ordained a Presbyterian minister. The University of Heidelberg, Germany, awarded Pennington an honorary doctorate in theology when he toured that country in 1849. It was Pennington who spearheaded the rescue and defense of the Amistad captives with the formation of the Fugitive Union Society. Pennington's accomplishments, given the disadvantages he endured in slavery and freedom, caused a stir in both Europe and the United States. For works on Pennington, see Pennington's narrative *The Fugitive Blacksmith; or, Events in the History of James W. C. Pennington* (1849), in William Loren Katz, ed., *Flight from the Devil: Six Slaves Narratives* (Trenton, NJ: Africa World, 1996), 37–104; R. J. M. Blackett, "James W. C. Pennington: A Life of Christian Zeal," in *Beating Against the Barriers: Biographical Essays in Nineteenth-Century Afro-American History* (Baton Rouge: Louisiana State University, 1986), 1–86.
36. Mary Bibb was challenging Thomas Carlyle's notion of "hero." Carlyle, a British writer, felt that the true hero of the age was the "man of letters." Bibb, in calling for a redefinition of hero, is insisting that the black children and adults who learned their letters are doubly heroic, given the extreme oppression under which they lived most of their lives. Pennington, an escaped slave, represents this kind of heroism. Carlyle, who hated black

people and felt that they were naturally inferior, would have been surprised at the progress disadvantaged Blacks were making in Mrs. Bibb's school. Carlyle was an influential Afrophobe who circulated the view that West Indian emancipation was a mistake, as the freed slaves reverted to "African barbarism" and spent all their time in hammocks "lolling" under pumpkin vines. Carlyle enunciated these views in his "Occasional Discourse on the Nigger Question" published in 1849. To correct the "mistake" of emancipation, Carlyle called for the reinstatement of slavery. Blacks in North America were well aware of Carlyle's assertions and made rebuttals. Catherine Hall, *White, Male, and Middle Class: Explorations in Feminism and History* (Cambridge: Polity, 1992), 264–89.

37. Mrs. Bibb had not only the weather in mind but also the hostile reception black students faced from whites who went to great lengths to chase them from the public schools. Most of the separate black schools in the province were established because racist whites did not want black children to attend school with their children. Separate schooling (this included religious schooling) became enshrined in law with the implementation of Ontario's Separate School Act of 1850. Black schools had vocal support from the government but nonetheless lacked necessary resources. Mrs. Bibb, writing to the *Anti-Slavery Bugle*, describes the "sufferance" under which Blacks lived; she also remarks on ethnic, racial, and religious intolerance in the Essex area. "The public money is almost entirely under the control of the French, and they are Catholics; consequently nothing can exceed their bitterness to the colored people because they are protestants." *Anti-Slavery Bugle*, April 12, 1851. See also Afua A. P. Cooper, "Black Teachers in Canada West, 1850–1870: A History," (MA thesis, University of Toronto, 1991), 22–48. On the French presence in Essex, see Ernest Lajeunesse, ed., *The Windsor Border Region: Canada's Southernmost Frontier* (Toronto: Champlain Society, 1960).

38. Mary E. Bibb, "Schools," *Voice of the Fugitive*, February 26, 1851.

39. Bibb, "Schools."

40. Dressmaking was one of the survival strategies employed by black women at the time. Filomina Chioma Steady, *The Black Woman Cross-Culturally* (Massachusetts: Schenkman Books, 1985), 20–23; Cooper, "Black Women and Work," 158–59.

41. Dun and Bradstreet Reference Books, microfilm reels 1–3, Archives of Ontario.

42. When women started wearing the bloomer, conservative men (and women) felt that this new mode of dress would lead to family breakdown, the increased sexual activity of women, and other social "ills." Middle-class women who discarded or attempted to discard their stays, hoops, and corsets for clothing that gave them more mobility and flexibility did not know that their choice would cause such hysterics. Although Elizabeth Smith Miller first designed the attire, it was feminist abolitionist Amelia Bloomer, inspired by the discussions that emanated from the Seneca Falls Women's Rights Convention, whose name came to be attached to the "oriental trousers with a very short tunic" because of her article (*The Lily*, June 1851) advocating dress reform for women. Lee Hall, *Common Thread: A Parade of American Clothing* (Boston: Little Brown, 1992), 79.

43. *Voice of the Fugitive*, May 7, 1851.

44. For example, *Voice of the Fugitive*, January 29, 1852.

45. For an extensive discussion on the role Holly played with regard to the *Voice of the Fugitive* and black print culture in general, see my doctoral dissertation "'Doing Battle in Freedom's Cause,'" 325–41. See also David M. Dean's biography of Holly, *Defender of the Race: James Theodore Holly, Black Nationalist Bishop* (Boston: Lambeth, 1979).
46. Afua Cooper, "The Fluid Frontier: Blacks and the Detroit River Region, 1789–1854; A Focus on Henry Bibb," *Canadian Review of American Studies* 30, no. 2 (2000): 129–49.
47. *Voice of the Fugitive*, June 4, 1851.
48. *Voice of the Fugitive*, July 30, 1851, June 17, 1852.
49. *Voice of the Fugitive*, July 30, 1851.
50. *Voice of the Fugitive*, September 10, 1851. In July 1851, he also spoke at the Christian Anti-Slavery Convention in Chicago. He later toured Wisconsin. *Voice of the Fugitive*, June 17, 1851, July 30, 1851.
51. *Voice of the Fugitive*, May 21, 1851.
52. *Voice of the Fugitive*, June 3, 1852.
53. Members of the Baby family were highly successful fur traders who moved across the river from Detroit to Upper Canada when Jay's Treaty went into effect. They were well educated, public spirited, and extremely loyal to the British Crown. Several held important political posts, were active in the militia during the War of 1812, and Charles Baby in particular was noted for abolitionist sympathies. It was he who wrote the deposition to try to prevent the extradition of fugitive slave Nelson Hackett (see Bryan Prince's discussion of the Hackett case in chapter 3 of this volume). Extensive family records survive in the Archives of Ontario, Toronto, in Record Group F2128. The Duff-Baby House is the oldest building in Windsor, Ontario, and serves as the city museum. See Elizabeth Abbott-Namphy, "Nelson Hackett," in *Dictionary of Canadian Biography On-Line*, www.biographi,ca/en/bio/hackett_nelson-7E.html (accessed June 9, 2015).
54. *Voice of the Fugitive*, March 12, 1851.
55. Arson was suspected as the cause of the fire. The *Voice* had both black and white detractors. Black opposition came from a camp led by Mary Ann Shadd and Samuel Ringgold Ward, both of whom later set up the *Provincial Freeman*. At a debating society meeting chaired by Holly, one of the debaters, William Burton, was knifed to death by one James Tyner, allegedly a supporter of the Shadd-Ward camp. Holly suspected it was supporters from this camp that torched the office of the *Voice*. *Liberator*, October 28, 1853.
56. John K. A. O'Farrell, "Henry Bibb," in *Dictionary of Canadian Biography*, 8:90, www.biographi.ca/009004-119.01-e.php?id_nbr=3786 (accessed February 16, 2012).
57. *Voice of the Fugitive*, November 18, 1852.

EIGHT

A COMMUNITY MILITANT AND ORGANIZED

The Colored Vigilant Committee of Detroit

ROY FINKENBINE

On March 29, 1846, worshippers at the Second Baptist Church and Bethel African Methodist Episcopal Church, two of Detroit's three African American congregations, received a warning that slavecatchers from the South were in the city. The bounty hunters were seeking several of the many fugitives from slavery living in Detroit's black community. Within minutes, the city's Colored Vigilant Committee (CVC) mobilized its members,[1] most of whom were leaders in the two churches, alerting the entire local African American community and "scouring the lanes and streets" to identify and harass the slavecatchers and to protect and assist the runaways they threatened. Members remained on high alert until the fugitive slaves in question were safely on the Canadian side of the Detroit River. Recounting the incident, an anonymous correspondent to the *Signal of Liberty,* Michigan's leading antislavery journal, observed in its April 6, 1846, issue: "Such scenes and excitements are common among us, and if the poor fugitive in his flight for liberty can but reach this point of embarkation, even though his bloodhound pursuers may be upon his track, he is safe; for scores of his own brethren stand ready to render all needful assistance to ensure his safe deposit upon the soil of Canada."

As they had for decades, Detroit's African Americans came together in 1846 to protect fugitives in their midst. The context in which the CVC worked, however, differed greatly from that in which Thornton and Lucie Blackburn were rescued in 1833, for instance. The Blackburn incident, recounted in chapter 2 of this volume, and its aftermath had prompted a significant proportion of the city's African American residents to move to Upper Canada. Since that time, however, the local African American community had undergone considerable growth. While an 1834 census of Detroit found only 138 Blacks, Michigan statehood in 1837 sparked a substantial African American migration into the city. The 1840 census recorded 193 Blacks, a number that tripled to 587 in 1850 and would grow to 1,402 in the year before the Civil War. Furthermore, the decade following the Blackburn rescue brought a flurry of community-building activities, as characterized by the emergence of separate institutions. The first to be founded were the churches: Second Baptist Church (1836), followed by Bethel African Methodist Episcopal (1839) and St. Matthew's Episcopal (1846). Public and private schools for black children had opened in the basements of the African American churches by 1840. A survey of the African American community in 1843 found some twenty benevolent and improvement societies, all of which met in the churches. In addition, a cadre of skilled leaders had emerged within the community by the early 1840s, largely consisting of free black businessmen and clergymen who had migrated to the city from established African American urban communities in Virginia and the Northeast. They aggressively petitioned the Michigan legislature for equal access to public education and the ballot box and represented the community at state and national black conventions called to develop strategies to fight for political rights. By 1846, Detroit's African American population had become a community militant and organized.[2]

From the time of its founding in early 1842, the Colored Vigilant Committee stood as the foremost expression of black Detroit's community organization and militancy, and of Underground Railroad–era activity in the city. The capture and extradition of fugitive slave Nelson Hackett from Canada West, discussed in chapter 3 by Bryan Prince, became the precipitating incident in the Colored Vigilant Committee's formation. Hackett had fled bondage in Arkansas and escaped across the Detroit River the year before, taking his master's beaver overcoat, gold watch, saddle, and fastest racehorse, as well as items stolen from another household, in the course of his escape. His owner eventually tracked him to Chatham, Canada West, and requested his extradition on theft charges. Hackett was immediately arrested by the local authorities. Detroit Blacks responded by organizing community meetings, sending strongly worded resolutions of indignation to officials in Canada West, petitioning the British Parliament, contacting abolitionists in Britain, attending Hackett's extradition trial in Sandwich before the Court of King's Bench, and seeking legal assistance for Hackett in Detroit, in the event he was returned to stand trial. Even so, the unfortunate fugitive was extradited to the United States in February 1842 and subsequently, returned to his master in Arkansas. The Detroit community's protests, however, had helped to stir abolitionists on both sides of the Atlantic, and their pleas eventually joined with others who were lobbying for the protection of formerly enslaved African American refugees once they reached Canadian soil; these succeeded in reaching the ears of British officials. Their efforts were timely: American and British diplomats were at the time negotiating a new treaty to set the border of the state of Maine and to arrange the terms of criminal extradition between the United States and both Britain and its colonies. The latter, abolitionists feared, would open the door to possible extradition of the formerly enslaved as well. When the Webster-Ashburton Treaty was signed later in the year, escape from slavery was not listed among the crimes that could prompt a legal return.[3]

Once the Hackett case had been settled, the Detroit-based Colored Vigilant Committee—and its focus on aiding and protecting fugitive slaves—took permanent shape. Businessmen

Born and educated in Trenton, New Jersey, William Lambert migrated to Detroit in 1840 and became a leader of Detroit's small but close-knit black community. (Courtesy of the Burton Historical Collection, Detroit Public Library)

and community leaders William Lambert, Robert Banks, Madison Lightfoot, and Benjamin Willoughby organized the committee and gave it direction in its early years. The latter three had been in Detroit at the time of the Blackburn rescue but Lambert, a relative newcomer, soon emerged as the principal figure. A thirty-three-year-old free black tailor at the time of the committee's founding, Lambert had migrated to the city from Trenton, New Jersey, in 1840. Since his arrival, he had been an outspoken and respected advocate for the rights of African Americans. Experience had taught Lambert and his colleagues to be "always suspicious of the white man" so, following the pattern of newly founded vigilance committees in New York, Boston, and Philadelphia, the CVC accepted only African American members.[4]

Others with Underground Railroad experience gained elsewhere soon joined the committee and took it in an even more aggressive direction. As Barbara Hughes Smith notes in chapter 5, George DeBaptiste, a thirty-eight-year-old free black barber from Fredericksburg, Virginia, had achieved notoriety by assisting large numbers of fugitive slaves along the Ohio River while living in Madison, Indiana, earlier in the decade. Threats against his life and a reward for his capture prompted his move to Detroit in 1846. One year later, he was joined by George J. Reynolds, who had worked with prominent Quaker activist Levi Coffin in Indiana prior to Coffin's move to Cincinnati in 1847. Between 1847 and 1850, Reynolds personally shepherded hundreds of runaways through Detroit. Lambert and DeBaptiste worked in tandem to lead local Underground Railroad efforts into the Civil War years.[5]

All told, some sixty to seventy local Blacks, ranging from common laborers to wealthy businessmen, were involved in the work of the CVC during its existence. Most were members of Second Baptist Church, Bethel African Methodist Episcopal Church, and the Prince Hall Masons. These institutions significantly shaped the committee's work. Meetings were usually held at Second Baptist. The Masonic connection prompted members of the CVC to develop a "secret order" to structure their Underground Railroad work. Known variously as the "African-American Mysteries" or the "Order of the Men of Oppression," this organized group developed a series of membership levels and elaborate rituals. Both Lambert and DeBaptiste contended that this secret order allowed the work of the committee to reach deep into the slave South.[6]

Whatever their connections below the Mason-Dixon Line, committee members welcomed growing numbers of fugitives in the 1840s. Some came to Detroit from the South by way of Toledo, Ohio, or Adrian, Michigan; others came from the West on the Territorial Road or Michigan Central Railroad; a number came on Great Lakes vessels. Nearly all had left cities and towns, farms and plantations in the border states—Missouri, Kentucky, Tennessee, and Virginia. When runaways arrived in the city, the CVC swung into action. Members often brought fugitives first to the Prince Hall Masonic lodge on Jefferson Street, then to Reynolds's residence "at the foot of Eighth Street." On other occasions, they hid them in Second Baptist Church. "Sometimes," Lambert recalled, "we were closely watched and other rendezvous were used." Furthermore, as noted in the 1846 case, the CVC developed a system for alerting members when slavecatchers arrived in the city. The committee provided thousands of runaways with food, clothing, shelter, medical care, protection, help finding a livelihood if they choose to remain in the city, and transport across the Detroit River if they choose to go on.[7]

Prior to 1850, many of the formerly enslaved migrants settled in Detroit. When he visited the city in 1849, Underground Railroad conductor Calvin Fairbank met many families he had earlier helped to escape from Kentucky. A larger number, however, preferred the safety of Canada West. The CVC kept skiffs concealed under the city docks and many a fugitive was rowed across the river to Canada under cover of darkness. Later, after DeBaptiste purchased a

Born, educated, and apprenticed in Fredericksburg, Virginia, George DeBaptiste came to Detroit from Madison, Indiana. In Detroit, he took charge of freedom-seekers' travel across the river to Canada. (Courtesy of the Burton Historical Collection, Detroit Public Library)

steamship called the *T. Whitney* in 1859, runaways were landed on the Canadian shore during its Detroit to Sandusky run. According to Lambert, the committee raised and expended some $120,000 assisting fugitives during the two decades of its existence.[8]

Although circumstances usually required the committee to work with considerable secrecy during the 1840s, there were exceptions. The CVC made known its involvement in two highly publicized 1847 slave rescues. When abolitionists in Marshall, Michigan, rescued the Adam Crosswhite family from the clutches of Kentucky slavecatchers and forwarded the fugitives to Detroit, the committee met them, hid them, and ferried them across the river to safety. The committee also openly contributed substantial amounts for the legal defense of the Crosswhites' rescuers. A full review of the international incident involving the Crosswhites is the subject of chapter 11 of this volume. Even more notable was the committee's aggressive action to protect Robert Cromwell, who had escaped from slavery in St. Louis, Missouri, in 1840, leaving a daughter behind. Six years later, established in the barbering business in Flint, Michigan, Cromwell wrote his master, David Dunn, offering to buy his daughter's freedom. Noting the postmark on the letter, Dunn traced Cromwell to Flint, then to Detroit, where he and two accomplices trapped the fugitive in the county courthouse. With the complicity of a court clerk, Lambert, DeBaptiste, and a mob forced their way into the building, rescued Cromwell, and whisked him away to Canada. Then they found a justice of the peace to swear out a warrant for Dunn's arrest on kidnapping charges; Robert Cromwell's erstwhile owner spent six months in jail. In response to incidents like these, slave owners in Missouri and Kentucky and their political allies in Congress pressed for a more rigorous federal fugitive slave act.[9] (Further evidence directly linking the Dunn case and other Michigan fugitive slave cases to the 1850 Fugitive Slave Law is provided by Debian Marty in chapter 11.)

Passage of the Fugitive Slave Act of 1850, part of a broad national compromise on the slavery issue, dramatically altered the context in which the CVC worked. It put the federal government in the business of capturing and returning freedom-seekers by implementing a system whereby federal marshals were assigned to help capture alleged fugitive slaves and federal commissioners were appointed to adjudicate claims against them. Commissioners were paid $5 if they ordered an alleged fugitive to be released, $10 if they ordered him or her returned to slavery. Furthermore, the law stripped away legal protections for purported runaways and required only the affidavit of a claimant to mandate a fugitive's return to bondage. Under the act, citizens could be deputized to aid in enforcing the law and faced stiff fines and penalties if they refused or helped fugitives to escape.[10]

One journalist observed that the act had "a very depressing effect on the colored people of Detroit." Frightened by the new law and the possibility of a return to bondage, hundreds of escapees left the city and its environs and streamed across the river into Canada West. Lambert, DeBaptiste, and other leading figures in the CVC sought to assure runaways "that the danger was more imaginary than real." Nevertheless, refugees from bondage continued to abandon the city in the first weeks following the law's passage. On October 12, 1850, the *Buffalo Courier* quoted the observation of a Detroiter that "large numbers of negroes are crowding over to Sandwich, Canada." Another local man noted that "as many as 43" had crossed in a single night. This exodus included eighty-four members of the city's Second Baptist Church alone. In their frantic scramble to reach safety, many left most of their real and personal property behind, creating a refugee crisis on the Canadian side.[11]

The fears aroused by the new law soon seemed to be confirmed. The third case to occur nationally under the Fugitive Slave Act, and the first in which the accused runaway avoided being returned to slavery, took place in Detroit in October 1850. Two slavecatchers appeared in the city looking for Giles Rose, a fugitive slave from Tennessee who had resided in Detroit's African American community for several years. Unfortunately, Rose had confided his slave status to a fellow workman who betrayed him, alerting slavecatchers to his whereabouts. The slavecatchers contacted federal marshal C. H. Knox, who took Rose into custody—with the support of local authorities—and placed him in the city jail. As word spread through the streets, Lambert and DeBaptiste mobilized local Blacks, some three hundred others who had traveled across the Detroit River from Canada West to assist in the matter, and a few sympathetic whites to form a force to attempt Rose's rescue. Some followed the slavecatchers to their hotel and threatened them with violence. Three companies of federal troops were called out to prevent civil disturbance. The threat of mob action yielded a surprising result: the federal commissioner adjourned the hearing and gave Rose time to prove that he was a free man, an action that was not required and virtually never happened under the federal act. Before a rescue could be attempted, Detroit's frightened mayor, John Ladue, called a meeting of the city's leading citizens, who raised a subscription of $500 to purchase Rose's freedom. Rose's owner took the payment, using about $200 to pay his expenses in the case and pocketing the remaining $300 (Rose's estimated value); he went home to Tennessee. Rose returned to the arms of his wife and children a free man.[12]

The Rose case reinvigorated the CVC, which worked tirelessly to aid and protect those fugitive slaves who remained in Detroit. The committee also successfully safeguarded new runaways, who now flocked to the city in ever-increasing numbers. Not one of these refugees was returned to bondage from Detroit under the federal act. Fewer attempts at recapture were made, as the city developed a reputation in the slave states for its inhospitality to slavecatchers. "If the negroes were afraid to live in Detroit," one observer recalled after the Civil War, "the slave hunters also gave the place wide berth. Isolated minor cases of slave arrest happened from time to time, but little excitement attended them, and no more slaves were returned from this point." That is largely true. The lone exception came in 1859 when kidnappers, operating outside of the bounds of the law, captured and carried off five black youths who lived in the city.[13]

With the assistance of the CVC, refugees from slavery flowed across the Detroit River in sizeable numbers during the 1850s. Lambert kept a ledger of the runaways the committee assisted, but these books are now lost. Nevertheless, some numbers reported at the time or in the decades following the Civil War offer a reasonable estimate of the fugitives helped. DeBaptiste informed the *Provincial Freeman*, a black newspaper published in Chatham, Canada West, that 1,043 runaways "passed through the hands of the Vigilance [sic] Committee between May 1855 and January 1856," a sum that calculates to about 1,390 a year. The Reverend William Mitchell, a black abolitionist and Underground Railroad worker who knew the Detroit operation well, publicized in his autobiographical volume, *The Under-Ground Railroad* (1860), that "the Vigilance [sic] Committee at the western gateway, Detroit, assisted 1,200 in one year." Lambert later remembered that the CVC "took over as high as 1,600 in one year." Other reports for individual weeks and months suggest that these figures are representative of the work of Detroit's Underground Railroad. A conservative average of the annual flow of fugitives noted by DeBaptiste, Mitchell, and Lambert would suggest that the Detroit-based CVC transported more than 5,000 freedom-seekers across the Detroit River between the passage of the Fugitive Slave Act in 1850 and the Civil War.[14]

Members of the CVC, like their counterparts across the North, operated with greater openness in the 1850s. Working in a manner "that would have been unimaginable only a few years before," they widely advertised the movement of fugitives through the city and across the Detroit River, and their own role in making it possible, through printed posters and in reports in the local and antislavery press. In April 1853, the committee circulated a poster announcing the arrival of "twenty-nine able-bodied men and women fresh and sound from the Carolina and Kentucky plantations . . . safe at the depot on the other side." An appeal was made for farming equipment to help these nascent African Canadians settle into an independent existence in their new home. DeBaptiste informed readers of *Frederick Douglass' Paper* on November 17, 1854, that the Underground Railroad through Detroit was "doing a very large business at this time." He observed that "we have had, within the last ten or fifteen days, fifty-three first class passengers landed at this point, by the express train from the South." On January 15, 1855, the *Detroit Tribune* announced that a Miss Gibson, a runaway from Maysville, Kentucky, had crossed the Detroit River into Canada West that day, "having arrived in safety by the underground railroad from Toledo." Such detail almost certainly came from CVC members. On May 31, 1856, the *Provincial Freeman* called DeBaptiste "the President of the road at Detroit." So much public activity in the service of an illegal cause raised the ire of the racially intolerant *Detroit Free Press*, which complained that members of the local Underground Railroad "openly and boastingly violate the Fugitive Slave Law."[15]

Although urban vigilance committees across the North became increasingly interracial or even fell entirely under white control by the 1850s, membership in the CVC remained entirely black. Members began to work much more closely with whites, however, than they had in the 1840s. The committee's primary white ally was abolitionist Seymour Finney, who operated the Temperance Hotel and a nearby livery stable at the corner of State and Griswold streets beginning in 1851. Finney gave George Dolarson, a black custodian, the key to the stable and permitted the CVC to hide runaway slaves there. Fugitives were often fed with provisions from the hotel. Usually, freedom-seekers arrived at the stable late during the night in wagons, hid in the loft during the day, and were ferried across the Detroit River by committee members the next night. On a few occasions, slavecatchers stayed in Finney's hotel, unaware that the runaways they were pursuing were hiding so close by in Finney's barn. The CVC also worked with several white conductors who regularly escorted such refugees to the city. These allies included the infamous abolitionist John Brown, who later led the ill-fated raid at Harper's Ferry, and the eccentric John Fairfield, mentioned in chapter 5; they were alleged to have guided two hundred runaways, respectively, into the city during the 1850s. Other whites who cooperated with the committee included local businessman Luther Beecher, Farmer Underwood and —— McChubb, abolitionists on key routes leading into Detroit.[16]

Although the CVC worked closely with several whites during the 1850s, it continued to operate independently on many occasions, sometimes quite forcefully. A particularly potent example came near the end of the decade. On June 30, 1859, a schooner, ironically named the *North Star*, docked at Detroit carrying a Mrs. Moore from Winchester, Kentucky, and her enslaved property, two teenage girls. They had been "summering" on Lake Superior and were making their way back southward. African American sailors on the ship had sent word ahead to the committee about the girls on board. When it landed at Detroit, between twenty and thirty Blacks rushed onto the boat and attempted to free the two girls. One, frightened by the excitement, locked herself in a stateroom. The other departed with the mob, which conveyed her across the river to Windsor. Members of the committee also attempted, unsuccessfully, to have the slave mistress arrested before the schooner departed.[17] As a result of daring acts such as these, runaways from the South continued to stream through Detroit.

On the eve of the Civil War, the flow of fugitives turned into a flood. On April 9, 1861, three days before Confederate forces began firing on Fort Sumter, the *Detroit Daily Advertiser* reported that 300 fugitives had passed through the city during the previous few days on their way to Canada, 190 in one day alone. Most of these refugees had come from Chicago, either by rail or on Great Lakes vessels, leaving their homes to seek safe refuge, after a family of runaways in that city had been returned to bondage under the Fugitive Slave Law. The committee played a very public role in welcoming the fugitives and escorting them across the river. As Union forces advanced into the slave South, however, the necessity for freedom-seekers to flee to Canada West diminished and the work of the CVC came to an end. Lambert recalled that the committee ferried the last runaway slave across the Detroit River in April 1862.[18]

The Colored Vigilant Committee of Detroit aided thousands of fugitive slaves who reached the city between 1842 and 1862. For those two decades, it stood as a proud sentinel over the most significant gateway into Canada for freedom-seekers fleeing the United States. More than five thousand runaways may have crossed the Detroit River after the Fugitive Slave Act of 1850 alone. Although estimates vary substantially, early historians believed that as many as forty thousand Blacks resided in Canada West on the eve of the Civil War.[19] A comparison of these numbers clearly demonstrates the CVC's significance to the broader Underground Railroad. In part, this prominence was an accident of geography. The Detroit River was a convenient international crossing point for refugees from the border states, especially those from Kentucky and Missouri. More than this, however, the committee's extensive organization and unchallenged militancy—placing and keeping the leadership of local Underground Railroad work in the hands of Blacks, successfully preventing any fugitives reaching the city from being returned to slavery under the law, and preserving the association's existence for an unmatched length of time—made it unique among urban vigilance committees across the North.

NOTES

1. Such organizations variously described themselves as "vigilance" or "vigilant" committees, with Detroit's group preferring the latter. The New York Committee of Vigilance was founded in 1835 (see Graham Russell Gao Hodges, *David Ruggles: A Radical Black Abolitionist and the Underground Railroad in New York City*, John Hope Franklin Series in African American History and Culture [Chapel Hill: University of North Carolina Press, 2010],

88), the Vigilant Association of Philadelphia in 1837 (see Joseph A. Boromé, "The Vigilant Committee of Philadelphia," *Magazine of History and Biography* 92 [January 1968]: 320–51), and the Boston Vigilance Committee in 1841 (as reported in the *Liberator*, June 11, 1841).

2. David M. Katzman, *Before the Ghetto: Black Detroit in the Nineteenth Century* (Urbana: University of Illinois Press, 1973), 7–8, 12–38.

3. Roman J. Zorn, "An Arkansas Fugitive Slave Incident and Its International Repercussions," *Arkansas Historical Quarterly* 16 (Summer 1957): 139–49; Annual Report of the Colored Vigilant Committee of Detroit, January 10, 1843, in C. Peter Ripley et al., eds., *The Black Abolitionist Papers, 1830–1865*, vol. 3, *United States* (Chapel Hill: University of North Carolina Press, 1991), 399–400; "Successful Working of the Underground Railroad," *Detroit Daily Post*, February 7, 1870; "FREEDOM'S RAILWAY: Reminiscences of the Brave Old Days of the Famous Underground Line Historic Scenes Recalled Detroit the Center of Operations That Freed Thousands of Slaves," *Detroit Tribune*, January 17, 1886; Karolyn Smardz Frost, *I've Got a Home in Glory Land: A Lost Tale of the Underground Railroad* (New York: Farrar, Straus, & Giroux, 2007; Toronto: Thomas Allen, 2007), 247–49.

4. Hodges, *David Ruggles*.

5. Katzman, *Before the Ghetto*, 9, 38; "FREEDOM'S RAILWAY"; Hodges, *David Ruggles*, 88–153; Matthew Pinsker, "The Underground Railroad and the Coming of War," *History Now*, December 2010, www.gilderlehrman.org/historynow/12_2010/historian2.php (accessed December 28, 2010); Keith P. Griffler, *Front Line of Freedom: African Americans and the Forging of the Underground Railroad in the Ohio Valley* (Lexington: University Press of Kentucky, 2004), 48, 88, 120.

6. "Successful Working of the Underground Railroad"; "FREEDOM'S RAILWAY"; Katherine DuPre Lumpkin, "'The General Plan was Freedom': A Negro Secret Order on the Underground Railroad," *Phylon* 28 (1st quarter 1967): 63–77.

7. "FREEDOM'S RAILWAY."

8. "FREEDOM'S RAILWAY"; Wilbur H. Siebert, *The Underground Railroad From Slavery to Freedom* (New York: Macmillan, 1898), 236.

9. "George DeBaptiste," *Detroit Tribune*, February 23, 1875; Frank B. Woodford, *Father Abraham's Children: Michigan Episodes in the Civil War* (Detroit: Wayne State University Press, 1961), 7–13; Debian Marty, "Michigan's Underground Railroad and the 1850 Fugitive Slave Act," *Grand Valley Review* 35 (Spring/Summer 2010): 111–21.

10. J. Blaine Hudson, *Encyclopedia of the Underground Railroad* (Jefferson, NC: McFarland, 2006), 96–98.

11. "Successful Working of the Underground Railroad"; Fred Landon, "The Negro Migration to Canada After the Passing of the Fugitive Slave Act," *Journal of Negro History* 5 (January 1920), 23–24, 27–28; Siebert, *The Underground Railroad*, 250.

12. Stanley W. Campbell, *The Slave Catchers: Enforcement of the Fugitive Slave Law, 1850–1860* (Chapel Hill: University of North Carolina Press, 1968), 115, 199; Floyd Streeter, *Political Parties in Michigan, 1837–1860: An Historical Study of Political Issues and Parties in Michigan from the Admission of the State to the Civil War* (Lansing: Michigan Historical Commission, 1910), 130–31; Willard Carl Klunder, *Lewis Cass and the Politics of Moderation* (Kent, OH: Kent State University Press, 1996), 252.

13. Katzman, *Before the Ghetto*, 38n57; Campbell, *The Slave Catchers*, appendix, 199–203; Landon, "Negro Migration to Canada," 31–32; "Successful Working of the Underground Railroad"; Samuel J. May, *The Fugitive Slave Law and Its Victims*, rev. ed., Antislavery Tract Publication No. 15 (New York: American Anti-Slavery Society, 1861), 120.
14. "FREEDOM'S RAILWAY"; *Provincial Freeman*, May 31, 1856; W[illiam] Mitchell, *The Under-Ground Railroad From Slavery to Freedom* (London, UK: Tweedie, 1860), 113.
15. Fergus M. Bordewich, *Bound for Canaan: The Epic Story of the Underground Railroad, America's First Civil Rights Movement* (New York: Amistad, 2005), 408; Broadside, 1853, Call No. 0997371158 S864, Burton Historical Collection, Detroit Public Library; "A Little Strange," *Detroit Free Press*, February 10, 1854.
16. "FREEDOM'S RAILWAY."
17. "Forcible Rescue of a Slave," *Detroit Free Press*, July 1, 1859, reprinted in *New York Times*, July 4, 1859.
18. Bordewich, *Bound for Canaan*, 429; Larry A. McClellan, "The Great Chicago Exodus: The Flight to Freedom 150 Years Ago," illinoisundergroundrailroad.net/ChicagoExodus.html (accessed January 5, 2011); "FREEDOM'S RAILWAY."
19. The most authoritative estimate to date of the black Canadian population in 1860 appears in Robin W. Winks, *Blacks in Canada: A History* (Montreal, PQ: McGill-Queen's University Press, 1971), 494. The leading challenge to Winks is Michael Wayne, "The Black Population of Canada West on the Eve of the American Civil War: A Reassessment Based on the Manuscript Census of 1861," *Social History/Histoire Sociale* 28, no. 56 (1995), 470.

NINE

"I AM GOING STRAIGHT TO CANADA"

Women Underground Railroad Activists in the Detroit River Border Zone

MARGARET WASHINGTON

Sojourner Truth stood in the aisle singing loudly during intermission at an upstate New York antislavery convention in 1855. According to a reporter covering the convention for *Frederick Douglass' Paper*, Truth's voice rang "like a clarion" as she belted out: "I am going straight to Canada-a where colored men are free-e-e-e!"[1] Abolitionist publisher and activist William Lloyd Garrison had printed copies of Sojourner's songs with her own original lyrics and she sold them at conventions along with her biography, *The Narrative of Sojourner Truth*. She jovially urged her abolitionist associates to buy her sheet music for only 5¢ cents: "Now friends! . . . Ain't that cheap."[2] She was famous among abolitionists for creating songs about the movement.

That Sojourner Truth, an activist and former slave based in New England, sang a song about Canada reveals the country's significance in the freedom struggle. Moreover, within a year Sojourner would sell her Northampton, Massachusetts, home and move permanently to Battle Creek, Michigan. She traveled through many states but spent much time traversing areas around Detroit, the western Underground Railroad's "grand terminus." A short ride across the Detroit River, refugees from Southern bondage lived on Canadian soil. Free African American activist, lecturer, educator, and (later) newspaper publisher, Mary Ann Shadd (later Mary Ann Shadd Cary) moved to Canada from Pennsylvania to labor on behalf of the black settlers and to promote emigration. White abolitionist Laura Smith Haviland's Underground Railroad work had centered on Canada West since the 1840s.[3]

All three activists adhered to a "higher law" that recognized neither man-made frontiers nor man-made slavery. All three also refused to accept conventional gender boundaries.

Haviland and Truth in the American West and Shadd in Canada West: all were pioneering spirits of change. They never crossed the Atlantic, but their assertive reformist perspectives were informed by the transnational politics championed by many abolitionists championed in the Detroit River border zone and across the ocean. All three women considered the Detroit River a gateway from slavery to freedom for the self-emancipated Southerners they served.

Canada, a refuge for freedom-seekers since the early 1800s, became an even more attractive destination by 1850 when provisions of the proslavery Compromise Bill before the U.S. Congress included the infamous Fugitive Slave Law. Frederick Douglass aptly named it "the Bloodhound Bill." It gave slavecatchers carte blanche to claim *any* black person as a slave, and the alleged fugitive had no recourse to due process. Although Douglass lamented that the bill forced the "pride and hope" of black America to flee, its deepest imprint was on ordinary men, women, and children. Hundreds of white planters and their agents poured into Northern states searching for "fugitives," loosely defined. Freeborn Blacks were on their guard; papers proving free status were easily destroyed or confiscated, and kidnapping by slavecatchers was a real and immediate danger. Self-emancipated people living in the North were aflame with militancy and swore death before reenslavement. Masses of them joined the exodus to Canada at great personal and economic sacrifice. In spite of the "Bloodhound Bill," enslaved people from as far away as Louisiana steadily made the daring trek northward. Following "the drinking gourd," a contemporary euphemism for the Big Dipper, which led to the North Star, freedom-seekers traveled circuitous routes, ingeniously aided and abetted by "superintendents," "conductors," and "stockholders" on the "trackless road" leading "straight to Canada."[4] Hundreds more found their way to the borders of Canada with no assistance at all.

Thus, the decade of the 1850s was a "strange, fearful, and terrible" time. It was also a pivotal moment of intensified activism that heightened the visibility of Sojourner Truth, Mary Ann Shadd, and Laura Smith Haviland, who were prominent among the many women devoting their lives to equality for all. All three were engaged in the black liberation struggle before 1850. After 1850, however, their actions reflected a new boldness inspired by passage of the Fugitive Slave Law, the shift of grassroots activism from east to west, the rise of antislavery radicalism, and the recognition of the necessity for transnational emigration.[5]

"A TONGUE OF FIRE AND A HEART OF LOVE"

Sojourner Truth, a formerly enslaved woman born and raised among the Dutch in New York's Hudson Valley, was no stranger to the West. In 1851, she went to Ohio, where for two years she raised her powerful voice on behalf of the enslaved. "All willingly attest to the good she has done in Ohio ... in aiding the Anti-Slavery cause," wrote her Ohio friend Esther Lukins. Truth also spoke out for women's rights. At the May 1851 woman's convention in Akron, Truth spoke without invitation, but her eloquent and practical remarks regarding female intellectual capacities and abilities struck a chord among many of the white women present. Sallie Holly, an Oberlin student who would soon be Sojourner's antislavery traveling companion, wrote that at the Akron meeting, "Sojourner Truth greatly routed a young preacher who had the temerity to come up against her." When the minister claimed Christ's manhood as evidence of male superiority, Sojourner responded, "And how came Jesus into the world? Through God who created him and woman who bore him. Man, where is your part?" In recognition of her message of interrracial sisterhood, the Ashtabula County Female Anti-Slavery Society gave Truth a huge white silk banner bearing an image of an enslaved woman emblazoned with the motto, "Am I Not a Woman and a Sister?"[6]

In 1856, she was again troubleshooting in Ohio after congressional decimation of the Missouri Compromise led to mini–civil war in Kansas. Truth's rousing speeches about "Bleeding Kansas" and clashes between pro- and anti-slavery settlers inspired Laura Haviland and other Michigan abolitionists to invite Sojourner to their state. Speaking in Battle Creek at the annual Friends of Universal Human Progress Convention, armed with a "tongue of fire," a "heart of love," and copies of her *Narrative* endorsed by Harriet Beecher Stowe, Truth was captivating. Standing a majestic six feet tall, she sang "with much feeling" and displayed a sharp intellect, an incisive wit, and an engaging pathos as she walked back and forth on the platform, gesticulating as she spoke. Her friend Wendell Phillips related: "I once heard her describe the captain of a slave ship going up to judgment, followed by his victims as they gathered from the depths of the sea, in a strain that reminded me of Clarence's dream in Shakespeare, and equaled it. Her anecdotes of ready wit and quick, striking replies are numberless. But the whole together give little idea of the rich, quaint, poetic and often profound speech of a most remarkable person, who used to say to us, 'You read books; God himself talks to me.'"[7]

Sojourner Truth was also bold. While on the Indiana antislavery circuit in the fall of 1858, proslavery men demanded that Truth show her breasts to the women in the audience because the men, hoping to undermine her dignity and influence, professed doubt that she was a woman. She insisted on exposing her breasts "to the whole congregation," stating that "it was not to her shame but to their shame."[8]

When a reporter asked Sojourner Truth if she had worked on the Underground Railroad, she answered, "Yes, indeed Chile. Though I came out of the Empire State, I had a warm heart for every Ethiopian in the land and it almost broke over their woes."[9] She did not detail what her role was on the trackless road. But in New England she had lived in Northampton in an abolitionist commune that was an Underground Railroad headquarters. In New York, she spent long periods of time as the guest of Quaker abolitionists Amy and Isaac Post in Rochester, where Frederick Douglass and Amy were the major Underground Railroad superintendents. Sojourner also made frequent trips to see William Still, secretary of the Pennsylvania Anti-Slavery Society and one of Philadelphia's leading Underground Railroad operatives. In Michigan, she settled in Harmonia, an abolitionist commune of Progressive Quakers and Spiritualists where slavecatchers dared not enter.[10] Harmonia was safer for freedom-seekers than Battle Creek, which was five miles away. Although a major Underground Railroad station for the "Freedom Train" from Indiana to Canada, Battle Creek was also the depot for the Michigan Central Railroad and hence a convenient rendezvous point for slavecatchers traveling from the South. Sojourner's name appears on records of those claiming involvement in the Underground Railroad, and her closest associates were superintendents, agents, stationmasters, and conductors. Prominent Battle Creek residents included Garrisonian abolitionists such as the Merritt, Titus, and Kellogg families, friends of Sojourner's who, like her, were Spiritualists. Other friends included political abolitionists such as Erastus Hussey, who since the 1840s had been spiriting "travelers" to Canada and openly confronting slavecatchers. Michigan reportedly had "200 Stations," mostly farms, spread

Formerly enslaved herself, Sojourner Truth earned a reputation as a powerful antislavery and "woman's rights" speaker. She spent time in the Detroit area with friends who assisted fugitives. (Courtesy of the Bentley Historical Library, University of Michigan, Ann Arbor)

ten and twenty out-of-the-way miles apart. Reportedly, Sojourner's Underground Railroad work in Michigan was an "open secret."[11] Sojourner lectured throughout the state, especially in the Detroit area. While speaking was her major contribution, Underground Railroad work was part and parcel of abolitionism. Her network of friends and associates in Detroit included some of the most active "conductors."

Libereta Lerrich's recollection of her childhood in an Underground Railroad family provides insight on Sojourner's Underground Railroad involvement. The Lerrichs' farm was in Utica, Macomb County, Michigan, adjacent to Oakland County. As a child Libereta found it curious that her parents, unlike most folks who used a well, had a "spring-on-the-hill" as a water source, around which they placed bricks wide enough "for a man to walk on." Moreover, the child noticed that the area behind the spring "looked like the inside of a log house," was nicely grooved, had a door at the bottom of the hill, "and was kept covered with a grapevine running on nails. And why," the child wondered, "did the cake crock get empty so quickly?" Then, in 1849, her parents and their neighbors planted an "immense cedar tree" at the spring; it took three sleighs together to transport it. After getting the tree upright, the grownups knelt around it and prayed. "I listened and wondered what was meant by 'Black brethren,' and 'down-trodden race.'" Then her mother sang, "Roll on the Liberty Ball" while the men shoveled and stamped the dirt around the tree.[12]

Libereta's parents and certain neighbors called this the "Beacon Tree"; to others it was simply a cedar tree planted to "shade the pump and keep the water cool." Antislavery agents had instructed the Lerrichs to locate this Beacon Tree "twenty-four miles directly north of Detroit City Hall and . . . twelve miles directly east of Pontiac Court House." The tree would guide freedom-seekers to the Lerrichs' farm. Libereta, whose very name spoke to the family's antislavery convictions, recalled that throughout the 1850s her parents received a regular visitor named Charles C. Foote (the same Reverend Charles Foote of Windsor, Canada West, who with Henry Bibb founded the Refugee Home Society). She remembered his conversations with her father: "'The catchers are watching the ferry night and day,' he told father, 'with the best blood hounds, and I saw one of the dogs snuffing around the barn this morning. Do you think your place will hold them all?'" That evening, her father announced that he would start for Detroit early in the morning; she noticed her mother "taking her second batch of bread from the thirteen-loaf brick oven" to the fried cake crock, which she had only just filled. Libereta's comments on the contents of the cake crock "were cut short by a raising of the eyebrows that I knew meant 'Silence.'"[13]

Libereta and her siblings eventually saw freedom-seekers in their home: "I forgot my school books and returning home for them, saw four black men and two black women at the dining room table." They eventually even saw "slave catchers . . . at the front door." And Libereta "heard people called by names that I afterward read about, as Fred Douglass, Peter Jaxon, and a jolly old lady that we called 'Aunty.' Pa and Ma called her 'Sojourner' and the neighbors called her 'Mrs. Truth.'"[14]

THE MOST ACTIVE, FEARLESS, AND COMMITTED UNDERGROUND RAILROAD AGENT IN MICHIGAN

In the 1830s Sojourner Truth was a preacher in New York City known as Isabella Van Wagenen; she had not yet heard the "voice" that would change her life. At that time, Laura

Smith Haviland was a young Quaker in Michigan involved in antislavery organizing. In 1832, Haviland and fellow Quaker Elizabeth M. Chandler, who wrote antislavery articles and poetry for Benjamin Lundy's abolitionist newspaper, *Genius of Universal Emancipation,* organized the Logan Female Anti-Slavery Society, the first in Michigan Territory. Early Quakers who settled in southeastern Lenawee County, including the Smiths, Havilands, Comstocks, and Chandlers, promoted a radical antislavery vision. Rather than gradual emancipation and colonization, which most "antislavery" whites supported at the time, these Quakers advocated immediate emancipation. Elizabeth Chandler died in 1834, but the antislavery movement grew; a state society was formed in 1836, although it endorsed the moderate Liberty Party.[15] Michigan's outspoken proslavery contingent had a public platform, the *Detroit Free Press,* in which to express its racially intolerant views.[16] Nevertheless, Detroit's Blacks militantly confronted slavecatchers and helped freedom-seekers on to Canada.[17]

When Laura and Charles Haviland began using their home as an Underground Railroad station, their Quaker Meeting decided that their brand of antislavery was "too exciting." All radical Quakers were excommunicated. The Havilands then joined the Wesleyan (antislavery) Methodists and Laura became a preacher. In 1837, the Havilands established Michigan's first biracial school, Raisin Institute, in the town of Raisin, Lenawee County. The Institute was organized on the work-study model of Oberlin and employed Oberlin graduates as teachers. Laura worked closely with the deceased Elizabeth Chandler's brother, Thomas, and enlisted local Lenawee County women in the cause. In 1846, thirty-two women organized the Female Benevolent and Anti-Slavery Society of Lenawee and pledged to fight slavery by promoting antislavery tracts, periodicals, and lectures, and by assisting freedom-seekers. Thus Laura Haviland created a local underground network before passage of the infamous Fugitive Slave Law. Raisin Institute and the antislavery cause remained "very unpopular" in Lenawee County, but the "fleeing fugitive found a resting-place and cheer in our home," Haviland wrote. Their home and school, she said, richly earned the cognomen of "nigger den."[18] Although meant as a pejorative term, Haviland took pride in the label.

Personal tragedy struck the Haviland family in 1845 when an inflammatory erysipelas epidemic swept through Lewanee County and killed Laura's husband, parents, sister, and youngest child. With no man to help her work the farm, feed her family, and run her school, Laura Haviland was expected to remarry. Directed by the "voice of God," the thirty-seven-year-old widow refused to follow traditional dictates and relinquish her independence. Instead she managed her farm, cared for her seven children, guided her school, and continued her Underground Railroad labors. She aided those en route to Canada, enrolled freedom-seekers in her school, leased land to refugees wishing to farm, and skillfully outwitted slavecatchers. In 1846, when Haviland was hiding freedom-seekers in Toledo, Ohio, slaveholders from Tennessee thrust pistols in her face and threatened her with violence as a "d——d nigger stealer." In 1847, Kentuckians searching in Michigan for freedom-seekers who had fled to Canada placed pistols, dirks, and bowie knives on a barroom table and vowed to use them on "that d——d abolitionist, Mrs. Haviland."[19]

The 1840s split within national abolition over issues of politics, religion, and the woman question caused the movement to falter in some circles. However, Haviland remained a familiar figure in the western Underground Railroad network. She was a seasoned abolitionist by 1850, when passage of the "Bloodhound Bill" (the Fugitive Slave Law) galvanized her to even further efforts on behalf of abolition; assisting freedom-seekers became the all-consuming

Laura Haviland sheltered freedom-seekers on her farm in Lenawee County and traveled from Michigan to Canada and into the South fearlessly assisting those who sought freedom. (Courtesy of the Grand Valley Special Collections and University Archives, Allendale, Michigan)

interest of her life. Observing slaveholders attempting to claim families in possession of free papers, Haviland stepped up her boldness, becoming notorious among proslavery factions. In the South, handbills offered $3,000 for Laura Haviland's head. After 1850, Southerners denounced her in Congress as "a rabid abolitionist" who interfered with "slave property."[20]

The unflappable "Aunty Laura" put her adult children in charge of her farm, suspended operation of Raisin Institute for financial reasons, and moved to Cincinnati. There her dauntless Quaker cohorts were Catherine and Levi Coffin, the latter called the "Underground Railroad President" along the Ohio River, the internal U.S. boundary between freedom and slavery. Cincinnati's black Zion Baptist Church was Haviland's Underground Railroad base, where she also taught school and nursed the sick during the cholera epidemic. Aided by an ingenious and well-armed biracial vigilance committee, Laura and her comrades employed various disguises, stratagems, and tricks in getting their "cargo" from Cincinnati to Canada via Toledo and Detroit.[21]

The most daring of Haviland's many courageous acts was going into slave territory to attempt to rescue freedom-seekers. As "Mrs. Smith," she traveled incognito to Little Rock, Arkansas, where she observed barbarous "slavery in its own household." Unfortunately, she was unsuccessful in rescuing an enslaved woman. When second-time imprisoned conductor Calvin Fairbank languished in a Louisville, Kentucky, jail, Levi Coffin and other abolitionists, fearful for their own safety, ignored Fairbank's appeals and urged Haviland to do so as well. Instead, she crossed the Ohio River into Kentucky and waited five risky and anxious days to see Fairbank, all the while being publicly insulted and excoriated daily in the Louisville press, which demanded her arrest. She was "braver than them all," recalled Fairbank, who remained imprisoned until the Civil War era. She brought the suffering inmate a mattress, bedding, flannel underclothing, shoes, money, and other necessities. Upon returning from Louisville, she found fourteen freedom-seekers hidden in the basement of Zion Baptist Church waiting passage to Canada.[22]

Haviland worked closely with Michigan abolitionists through the state Anti-Slavery Society, Progressive Friends, Spiritualists, and her friend Sojourner Truth. She maintained close ties with Detroit's black abolitionists, including William Lambert, "President" of the Detroit Underground Railroad, and George DeBaptiste, "Vice President," as well as with local conductors affiliated with the Second Baptist Church. She corresponded with excommunicated abolitionist Quakers in Detroit such as Sojourner's friends Eliza Seaman Leggett and Nanette Gardner. As the city of Detroit became more dangerous for antislavery activists, Haviland maintained close contacts with them up and down the Detroit River. Throughout the 1850s slave hunters, employing both black and white agents, infiltrated Canada, using knavish and deceitful means to entrap Blacks and entice them back across the border into the United States. The experienced "Widow Haviland" could reportedly "smell" a slavecatcher—and indeed many appeared at her door, proverbial wolves in sheep's clothing.[23]

The year 1851 was pivotal for transnational activism. Laura Haviland was spending as much time in Canada as in Michigan and Ohio, often remaining with freedom-seekers for long periods of time. That year, Detroit activists Henry and Mary Bibb fled across the river into Canada West because slave-born Henry was subject to recapture, having recently published a narrative of his life. However, Bibb remained intrepid. His migration to Canada was a deliberate act to claim and exercise political rights denied him in the United States and to create a means to aid fugitives. As Afua Cooper discusses in chapter 7 of this volume, Bibb frequently recrossed the Detroit River in spite of his fugitive status. As soon as the Bibbs relocated to Sandwich, a frontier settlement just across the river in Canada West with a large population of freedom-seekers, Mary set up a school and Henry established the *Voice of the Fugitive*, Canada's first black abolitionist newspaper. The numbers of African American immigrants to the region increased to the point that Bibb and Detroit's white and black abolitionists established the Refugee Home Society, putting Henry Bibb and white minister Charles C. Foote in charge. The organization's aim was to raise money to help destitute freedom-seekers obtain necessities and especially to make land available to them for purchase. Haviland and the American Missionary Association (AMA), headed by Lewis Tappan and George Whipple, supported this project, which soon became controversial when Mary Ann Shadd immigrated to Canada West in 1851.[24]

"A YOUNG ... LADY OF FINE DICTION, REFINED ADDRESS ... POSSESSING AN ENERGY OF CHARACTER"

Mary Ann Shadd came from a notable activist family. Her father, Abraham Doras Shadd, was a prosperous shoemaker, a participant in the black convention movement, and an Underground Railroad operator. In 1851 Mary Ann Shadd, then a schoolteacher in New York City, accompanied her father to Toronto for the North American Convention of Colored People. Convened by Henry Bibb, this was an overwhelmingly black (only four of the delegates were white) gathering called to discuss the effect of the new 1850 Fugitive Slave Law and plan a response. The thirty-one black Canadians included activists George and John Cary and the Reverend Josiah Henson. Abraham Shadd of Pennsylvania and the Reverend Amos Beman of Connecticut were the only easterners among the fifteen U.S. delegates, who included the Reverend Samuel Ringgold Ward, Dr. Martin Delany, and William Lambert of Detroit. The delegates issued a fervent call for black emigration to Canada and adopted a proposal suggested by the Vermont-based James Theodore Holly, who could not attend, to form "a great league of the colored people of the North and South American continents." Mary Ann and her father carried this message back across the border to a meeting at Buffalo's African Methodist Church. Mary Ann took the message to heart. That year, she left the United States and emigrated to Windsor, Canada West, directly across the river from Detroit.[25] Her father, Abraham, came too, moving his extended family to a farm at the edge of the Buxton fugitive slave colony near Chatham.

Despite its lofty goals and intentions, the antislavery movement was rife with friction, and the dedicated young schoolteacher, although politically inexperienced, was opinionated and unflinching in her principles. All began well. Shadd co-founded the Windsor Anti-Slavery Society with Henry Bibb, anticipated working closely with the Bibbs, and wrote a well-received (though overly optimistic) pamphlet titled *A Plea for Emigration; or, Notes on Canada West* advocating black emigration to Canada West.[26] She downplayed the racism and segregation black settlers encountered once they crossed into Canada West and expressed hope not only that the British colony would be a home for those fleeing bondage but that the settlement of free people there would create lasting and viable black Canadian communities.

To that end, education was a crying need. Mary Bibb was running a school in Sandwich and Shadd immediately established one in Windsor. Shadd had scant resources, and neither schoolchildren's parents nor her adult pupils could afford even meager tuition. She appealed

This bust of Mary Ann Shadd Cary, sculpted by her descendant Artis Lane, stands in Freedom Park in Chatham, Ontario. A staunch advocate of black independence, Shadd Cary published the *Provincial Freeman*, the first newspaper in North America initiated solely by a black woman. (Courtesy of photographer Elizabeth Clark)

to the well-heeled American Missionary Association, which ministered to the black settlers of Canada West, and enlisted support from their local missionary.[27] Windsor's AMA missionary, Alexander McArthur, praised Shadd as "a young (light colored) lady of fine diction, refined address, and Christian deportment; and possessing an energy of character and enlargement of views well fitting her for the work of teaching amongst such a people as this." Reports on her teaching and her new school were highly favorable. Shadd's interest in the Windsor freedom-seekers went farther than education. She sat by their firesides, nursed them during the cholera epidemic, and mingled with them socially. She also taught Sunday School and Bible classes. When the AMA still expressed reservations about financing the school, Shadd appealed to prominent black New Yorkers who knew her personally, two of whom, the Reverend Samuel Cornish and Glasgow-educated African American physician Dr. James McCune Smith, were AMA Board members. But the AMA had already divested Blacks of any meaningful decision-making authority in its ranks. The organization had grown out of a biracial struggle to aid the "Mendi" Africans who were on trial for murdering their Spanish captors on board the vessel *Amistad* in 1839. After the Africans' famous 1841 acquittal, a few prominent black U.S. clergymen founded the Union Missionary Society to establish missions at home and abroad. White clergymen, with money from wealthy abolitionist Lewis Tappan, who had also established the Amistad Committee during the struggle, offered to merge the two groups into the American Missionary Association. It rapidly became a white-controlled organization, led by Lewis Tappan, George Whipple, and Amos Phelps, all conservative evangelical abolitionists opposed to the Garrisonian-led American Anti-Slavery Society. Shadd had the support of the Windsor community, so, after some hedging, the AMA agreed to fund Shadd's school for one year.[28]

One strike against Shadd was that she was not a member of the clergy—during that time women could not be ordained. Moreover, gender bias clearly played a role in the withering public criticism soon directed at Shadd. The evangelicals and the Garrisonians not only disagreed over doctrine but also clashed over women engaging publicly in political discourse. Additionally, when asked about her denominational preferences, Shadd answered that she was certainly a woman of faith but had no religious affiliation. Basically, she was ecumenical or worse—a "Come Outer" like Sojourner Truth, since both had once been members of the African Methodist Church. The Shadds were also Catholic but Mary Ann had converted to African Methodism. When she applied for support her school for the next year, the AMA Executive Committee maintained that "such references were made ... relative to her belief of evangelical views as defined in connection with ... the AMA that the Committee voted to recommend ... to withdraw aid from her."

But perhaps her most egregious offense was challenging Henry Bibb and the Reverend Foote's integrity over their management of donations to the Refugee Home Society, in which the AMA was invested. Shadd explained her position to the AMA: both Henry Bibb and the Reverend Foote solicited donations in the name of destitute fugitives but in Shadd's estimation, the settlers were free people making homes, not "beggars," and appeals should not be made on their behalf based on their status as "fugitives" or refugees. "Begging," she insisted, did not serve their welfare politically or economically.[29]

Furthermore, and more damagingly, Shadd publicly accused Henry Bibb of misusing donations, charging that he and some of the other officers in the Refugee Home Society were spending for their own use donations meant for the settlers. Bibb was outraged and fought back through unflattering articles about Shadd in his newspaper, the *Voice of the Fugitive*, while the Reverend Foote wrote to the AMA accusing Shadd of "outrageous slanders." But she was not alone in these accusations. At the annual society meeting in August 1852, "every agent (except Reverend Foote) was discharged for taking too large a percentage." African

American George Cary, a member of the Executive Committee of the Society, told Shadd that "the agents had acted dishonestly... that he distrusted most of the officers—they were not anti-slavery men," but behaved like land speculators expecting their fraudulently obtained land to be in the vicinity of the "Great Western Railroad." Cary insisted, Shadd reported to the AMA, that the Bibbs held a deed of the first two hundred acres purchased, and that they had not transferred it to the society (though asked to do so). Self-emancipated Samuel Ringgold Ward, former editor of the defunct *Impartial Citizen* and influential Congregationalist minister, also backed Shadd, as did former AMA missionary Alexander McArthur. It was disgraceful, wrote McArthur, that because Shadd had uncovered an ugly side of the antislavery movement, Bibb had "impeached" her honesty, "and what is worse, questioned her virtue publicly." Shadd defended herself, too, through William Lloyd Garrison's *Liberator*, which had a long-standing feud with the AMA leadership. More significant, she had the support of Samuel Ringgold Ward and the confidence of Windsor's black residents.[30]

Shadd's school was eventually forced to close. The AMA Committee on Canada Missions gave as its reason for denying funds Shadd's lack of Christian evangelism. Of course, this was a smoke screen for the AMA's discomfort with supporting an outspoken, independent-minded, *single* black woman who defied female convention and challenged ministers. The AMA also made clear to Shadd that African American ministers on the board whom she had given as references, Reverends Samuel Cornish and Charles Ray, indicated that she had "peculiar religious views." She was stunned. "When I referred to them, it was more for their opinion of my moral character and my fitness ... in a literary sense, than as a testimony ... of my orthodoxy." Since her "Protestant Methodist" views were "quite sound," she wondered, "was your action in my case of a special character? If Mr. Foot's charges did not induce it, what did?" Privately, for example, a white officer of the Refugee Home Society wrote: "Miss Shadd ... is not only a busy body in other *men's* matters, but a notorious mischief maker to the extent of her ability."[31]

Devastated but undaunted, Shadd's response came in two forms. Although she and the influential black Congregational minister Samuel Ringgold Ward were friends, she nonetheless chided the AMA for not criticizing him and influential and "weighty *men*" who opposed the Refugee Home Society. Although it might be easier to attack "a mere woman like myself ... it is certainly not brave neither is it christian-like."[32] More significantly, Mary Ann Shadd launched a direct challenge to the Bibbs by establishing her own newspaper. Because many abolitionist publishers would recoil at the idea of a woman editing a newspaper, Samuel Ringgold Ward became the front man and posed as the *Provincial Freeman*'s editor. An outraged Henry Bibb saw through the ruse and again went on the attack. Shadd, he wrote, was the ultimate temptress, "a designing individual whose duplicity is sufficient to prove a genealogical descent from that serpent that beguiled mother Eve in the Garden of Eden." He sent resolutions to abolitionist presses calling on Blacks to denounce the establishment of another newspaper in Canada as disloyalty to the race. Bibb insisted Canada West did not need two black newspapers. Frederick Douglass, the most notable black leader and editor in the United States, published the resolution but accused Bibb of manifesting "entirely too much sensitiveness. We welcome a dozen newspapers ... devoted to the interest of the colored people."[33] Pennsylvania's Underground Railroad operator William Still was equally dismissive of Bibb, and the *Pennsylvania Freeman* praised the selection of Ward as the *Provincial Freeman*'s editor.

With financial assistance from friends and family, the first issue of Mary Ann Shadd's *Provincial Freeman* appeared in 1853 on the day after she closed her Windsor school.[34]

The feud between Shadd and Bibb does not seem to have affected Laura Haviland's association with Bibb, which dated back to Bibb's involvement with the Michigan Anti-Slavery Society and his lectures for the Michigan Liberty Party in the 1840s. Haviland opened a school under his organization, the Refugee Home Society. She also organized an ecumenical Christian Union Church for Canadian refugees with the blessings of Bibb and Foote. The Shadd-Bibb feud also did not preclude friendly interactions between Haviland and Shadd, two committed abolitionists who defied female conventions.[35] Ironically, Shadd and Bibb's widow, Mary, later became in-laws: Shadd married Thomas Cary of Toronto in 1856, and Mary, widowed in August 1854, later married Thomas's brother, Isaac Cary. However, these two formidable female opponents reportedly remained inimical.

Shadd Cary spent three hard years at the *Provincial Freeman*'s helm, aided by a series of male assistants in order to maintain the thinly veiled impression that the newspaper's editor was a man. Shadd Cary surmised that neither the antislavery movement nor the Canadian public was ready for a female editor.[36] But her unsigned editorials on "woman's rights," though strident, generated approval from many female readers.[37]

Shadd Cary moved the *Freeman*, then based in Toronto, to Chatham, the nucleus of antislavery activism in Canada West. It was a further defiance of convention that she returned to her Chatham home while her husband remained in Toronto. She worked for the paper as its chief traveling agent, fund-raiser, and investigative muckraking reporter, exposing corruption in the black settlements. Her reputation grew in the States. By 1856, Mary Ann Shadd Cary was the voice of black Canada at important meetings and conventions. Already an excellent writer, she developed into a popular lecturer and debater on slavery, race uplift, and women's rights even after the *Provincial Freeman* folded. While few black leaders embraced her nationalist/emigrationist ideology, they were dazzled by her strident, razor-sharp elocution, combative analyses and anticlericism. In 1855, she was the sole Canadian delegate and one of only two women delegates at the National Black Convention in Philadelphia. She was admitted by a majority vote led by Frederick Douglass, despite sizeable anti-female opposition from some delegates. She delivered "one of the most convincing and telling speeches in favor of Canadian emigration I ever heard," wrote black abolitionist William J. Watkins. "She is a superior woman," he added, "and it is useless to deny it."[38]

After the *Freeman* folded in 1859 and her marriage to Thomas ended with his premature death in 1860, Shadd Cary resumed her teaching and Underground Railroad labors. In 1869, Shadd Cary was the only woman to join the first law school class at Howard University in Washington, DC. She completed the curriculum, including writing a thesis. However, in 1871, Shadd Cary's name was not put forth with her graduating class, reportedly "on account of her sex."[39]

Sojourner Truth's lifelong intimate friendship with Laura Haviland began with her permanent residency in Michigan. The tall, uneducated black woman whose first language was Dutch and the petite, wizened-faced, Canadian-born white schoolteacher shared a mutual passion for social justice, the rights of the oppressed, and Methodism. Both claimed they talked with God and received visions.

Sojourner Truth and Mary Ann Shadd probably met as early as 1853, when both were speaking in the Philadelphia area. The two women had much in common despite their different class and educational backgrounds. They were "whole hog reformers," moving easily from abolition to temperance to woman's rights; they were spiritual women but highly critical of the traditional clergy and churches; they were thoroughly outspoken and refused to be bridled by female gender conventions established by men. Moreover, Shadd Cary followed Sojourner Truth on the abolitionist lecture circuit. In an 1854 *Provincial Freeman* editorial in which Shadd criticizes those who oppose Canadian emigration, she quotes Sojourner Truth and includes a playful allusion to her Dutch brogue: "America is wanted [only] for those whom Sojourner Truth delights in calling the 'Shaxon race.'"[40]

Above all, the cause of freedom for the enslaved united Haviland, Truth, and Shadd. Sojourner, who spent months in Detroit and the surrounding area, probably joined her sisters in Canada West. She spent long periods of time in rural Lenawee County, often residing with underground agent Thomas Chandler on his farm, Hazelbank, or with Laura Haviland. She traveled to Detroit with Haviland and resided there with mutual friends Eliza Seaman Leggett, an Underground Railroad activist in Oakland County near Detroit, and Nanette Gardner in Detroit.[41]

When the Civil War began in April 1861, Sojourner Truth, Laura Haviland, and Mary Ann Shadd Cary continued their activism. Sojourner Truth's last antebellum mission occurred in 1861 in Indiana, where she was arrested six times for traveling in the state without free papers. Her white traveling companion, Josephine Griffing, wrote to the *Liberator* that audiences at Truth's speaking engagements were immense, but so were the dangers. Armed men in the audience, wrote Griffing, "declared that they would blow out our brains."[42]

Laura Haviland followed Union troops into Confederate territory to give aid and comfort to black refugees caught between the two armies. After the war, Haviland and Truth worked together among the freed people in Washington, DC, and later promoted Southern black settlement in Kansas. When the war began, Mary Ann Shadd Cary moved to Detroit and later traveled widely through the Midwest recruiting Blacks for the Union Army before settling in Washington, DC. The mission of these three women was a social justice commitment that continued for the whole of their lives. It may be summed up best in the closing salutation that Haviland often used in her letters, "Thine for the oppressed."[43]

NOTES

1. *Frederick Douglass' Paper*, June 15, 1855. In all probability, Truth was singing the lyrics of the popular antislavery song composed by the freeborn African American Joshua McCarter Simpson (1820–76). Though born in Ohio, Simpson was indentured until the age of twenty-one. After his release from a difficult life of indentured servitude, Simpson attended Oberlin Collegiate Institute and developed his reading and writing skills. He wrote many antislavery verses and set them to popular tunes; his work was much favored by fugitives and abolitionists engaged in Underground Railroad work. "I'm going straight to Canada / Where colored

men are free" is part of the refrain of Simpson's song "Away to Canada," set to the tune of "Oh, Susannah." Simpson was also an Underground Railroad conductor. Vicki L. Eaklor, *American Anti Slavery Songs: A Collection and Analysis* (Westport, CT: Greenwood, 1988), 367–76, 384–88, 396–97; cited in Van Gosse, "'As a Nation, the English Are Our Friends': The Emergence of African American Politics in the British Atlantic World, 1772–1861," *American Historical Review* 113, no. 4 (2008), 1022n85; Joshua McCarter Simpson, *Original Anti Slavery Songs* (Zanesville, OH: privately published, 1852).

2. *Frederick Douglass' Paper*, June 15, 1855. See also Margaret Washington, *Sojourner Truth's America* (Urbana: University of Illinois Press, 2009), 268.

3. *Frederick Douglass' Paper*, June 15, 1855; Washington, *Sojourner Truth's America*, 277–82; Laura S. Haviland, *A Woman's Life-Work: Including Thirty Years of Service on the Underground Railroad and in the War* (Grand Rapids, MI: Tribune, 1881); Jane Rhodes, *Mary Ann Shadd Cary: The Black Press and Protest in the Nineteenth Century* (Bloomington: Indiana University Press, 1998), 1–134.

4. *Liberator,* October 4, 1850, October 11, 1850, October 18, 1850; Frederick Douglass to Amy Post, October 20, 1850, October 25, 1850, October 31, 1850, and William C. Nell to Amy Post, December 8, 1850, Amy and Isaac Post Family Papers, University of Rochester, Rochester, NY; Karolyn Smardz Frost, *I've Got a Home in Glory Land: A Lost Tale of the Underground Railroad* (New York: Farrar, Straus, & Giroux, 2007; Toronto: Thomas Allen, 2007); William C. Cochran, *The Western Reserve and the Fugitive Slave Law: A Prelude to the Civil War* (New York: De Capo, 1972), 89–98; Fred Landon, "The Negro Migration to Canada After the Passing of the Fugitive Slave Act," *Journal of Negro History* 5 (January 1920): 22–36.

5. Douglass to Post, October 20, 1850, October 25, 1850, October 31, 1850; Haviland, *A Woman's Life-Work,* 133–50; Rhodes, *Mary Ann Shadd Cary,* 25–69; Washington, *Sojourner Truth's America,* 261–89. I use the term *radical* to describe women engaged in grassroots antislavery activism and other reforms. This distinguishes them from the women discussed by Michael Pierson. He traces the development of "gender ideology" and "domestic feminism" in antebellum political culture, using as examples such women as Harriet Beecher Stowe, Lydia Maria Child, Jesse Benton Fremont, and Jane Swisshelm. With the exception of Child, these were political moderates. See Michael D. Pierson, *Free Hearts, Free Homes: Gender and American Antislavery Politics* (Chapel Hill: University of North Carolina Press, 2003).

6. Sallie Holley, *A Life for Liberty: Anti-Slavery and Other Letters of Sallie Holley,* ed. John W. Chadwick (New York: G. P. Putnam and Sons, 1899), 61–66; Hannah Tracy Cutler, "Reminiscences," *Woman's Journal*, September 19, 1896, September 26, 1896; *Anti-Slavery Bugle*, June 7, 1851, June 21, 1851, January 3, 1852, July 7, 1852, September 24, 1853; *New York Tribune*, November 8, 1853.

7. *Anti-Slavery Bugle*, September 9, 1856, September 13, 1856, September 27, 1856; F. P. Powell, "The Rise and Decline of the New England Lyceum," *New England Magazine,* February, 1895, 733–34, quoted in Lillie B. Chace Wyman, "Sojourner Truth," *New England Magazine*, March–August 1901, 59–66.

8. *Northern Indianan*, October 8, 1858; *Liberator*, October 5, 1858.

9. *Chicago Daily Inter-Ocean*, August 13, 1879.

10. Editors' note: Spiritualism became popular in the middle of the nineteenth century in upstate New York. The sisters Mary and Kate Fox maintained they could communicate with the spirit world through rappings on tables and through séances conducted by mediums. A number of important abolitionists, including Amy and Isaac Post of Rochester, became believers; Isaac Post even wrote a book on the subject in 1852: *Voices from the Spirit World, Being Communications from Many Spirits*. Although the Fox sisters were suspected of being frauds, Spiritualism's adherents included Horace Greeley of the *New York Tribune*. Even William Lloyd Garrison participated in séances on occasion. See Anne Braude, *Radical Spirits: Spiritualism and Women's Rights in Nineteenth-Century America*, 2nd ed. (Bloomington: University of Indiana Press, 2001), esp. chap. 2.

11. Wilbur H. Siebert, *The Underground Railroad From Slavery to Freedom* (New York: Macmillan, 1898), 412–16, 419; Delia Hart Stone, "Sojourner Truth," *Woman's Tribune*, November 14, 1903, 124; Minnie Merritt Fay Collection, Willard Public Library, Battle Creek, MI; *Anti-Slavery Bugle*, October 18, 1856, November 8, 15, 1856; "FREEDOM'S RAILWAY: Reminiscences of the Brave Old Days of the Famous Underground Line Historic Scenes Recalled Detroit the Center of Operations That Freed Thousands of Slaves," *Detroit Tribune*, January 17, 1886; Haviland, *A Woman's Life-Work*, 192–206; Katherine DuPre Lumpkin, "'The General Plan was Freedom': A Negro Secret Order on the Underground Railroad," *Phylon* 8 (1st quarter 1967): 63–77; Nancy Hewitt, "Amy Kirby Post," *University of Rochester Library Bulletin* 37 (1984): 5–21; Yvonne Tuchaiski, "Erastus Hussey, Battle Creek Antislavery Activist," *Michigan History* 56 (Spring 1972): 2–18; Glennette T. Turner, *The Underground Railroad in Illinois* (Glen Ellyn, IL: Newman Educational, 2001), 83–84.

12. Libereta Lerrich Green, "The Beacon Tree" (unpublished MS, Macomb County Historical Society, 1976).

13. Green, "The Beacon Tree."

14. Green, "The Beacon Tree."

15. Founded in 1839, the Liberty Party was an antislavery third party that advocated abolition through the electoral process and asserted that the Constitution was antislavery. The party's adherents broke with the more radical moral suasion advocates (American Anti-Slavery Society) led by William Lloyd Garrison who eschewed working within politics and asserted that the Constitution was proslavery. See, for example, Johnson Reinhard, *The Liberty Party, 1840–1848: Antislavery Third Party Politics in the United States* (Baton Rouge: Louisiana State University Press, 2009).

16. Fergus Bordewich, *Bound for Canaan: The Epic Story of the Underground Railroad, America's First Civil Rights Movement* (New York: Amistad, 2005), 408.

17. Haviland, *A Woman's Life-Work*, 9, 26–28, 38–51; Benjamin Lundy to Laura Haviland, April 2, 1831, Elizabeth M. Chandler Collection, Michigan Historical Collections, Bentley Historical Library, University of Michigan, Ann Arbor; Adda Dilts, "Aunt Laura Haviland: Early Michigan Quakeress," *Michigan Heritage* 13, no. 1 (1971–72), 4–5; Washington, *Sojourner Truth's America*, chaps. 6–7 and p. 269; Smardz Frost, *I've Got a Home in Glory Land*, 139–55, 162–90; Lumpkin, "'The General Plan was Freedom,'" 74–75.

18. Haviland, *A Woman's Life-Work*, 28–37, 56; Levi Coffin, *Reminiscences of Levi Coffin, the Reputed President of the Underground Railroad*, ed. Ben Richmond (Richmond, IN: Friends

United, 2001), 183, 222, 227–29, 232, 261, 267, 338; Arthur R. Kooker, "The Antislavery Movement in Michigan, 1796–1840: A Study in Humanitarianism on the American Frontier" (PhD diss, University of Michigan, 1941); Charles Lindquist, *The Antislavery-Underground Railroad Movement in Lenawee County, Michigan, 1830–1860* (Adrian, MI: Lenawee County Historical Society, 1999), 40–41, 50–51; *Signal of Liberty*, October 10, 1846; George K. Hesslink and Joanne M. Hesslink, *Black Neighbors in a Northern Rural Community*, 2nd ed. (Indianapolis: Bobbs–Merrill, 1974), 40–44.

19. Haviland, *A Woman's Life-Work*, 38–50, 53–77, 90–95, 104–5; Coffin, *Reminiscences*, 260–61.
20. Haviland, *A Woman's Life-Work*, 72–84.
21. Haviland, *A Woman's Life-Work*, 86–88, 106, 110–17, 120–35; Lindquist, *The Antislavery-Underground Railroad Movement*, 2–7, 32–31, 36, 216.
22. Haviland, *A Woman's Life-Work*, 139–61, 214–29; Calvin Fairbank, *During Slavery Times: How He "Fought the Good Fight" to Prepare the Way* (Chicago: R. R. McCabe, 1890), 86–87.
23. Haviland, *A Woman's Life-Work*, 192–204, 209; Fairbank, *During Slavery Times*, 86–87; "FREEDOM'S RAILWAY"; Lumpkin, "'The General Plan was Freedom,'" 63, 74–75; C. Peter Ripley et al., eds., *The Black Abolitionist Papers, 1830–1865*, vol. 2, *Canada* (Chapel Hill: University of North Carolina Press, 1986), 19–21, 146–47; Jacqueline Tobin, *From Midnight to Dawn: The Last Tracks of the Underground Railroad* (New York: Doubleday, 2007), 96–98, 199–201.
24. Haviland, *A Woman's Life-Work*, 192, 200; Rhodes, *Mary Ann Shadd Cary*, 34–42; Ripley et al., *The Black Abolitionist Papers*, vol. 2, *Canada*, 108–12, 143–48.
25. Ripley et al., *The Black Abolitionist Papers*, vol. 2, *Canada*, 149–76; Rhodes, *Mary Ann Shadd Cary*, 33–36.
26. Mary Ann Shadd, *A Plea for Emigration; or, Notes on Canada West* (Detroit: George W. Pattison, 1852). See illustration on page 132 of this volume.
27. Ripley et al., *The Black Abolitionist Papers*, vol. 2, *Canada*, 184–85, 222–30, 243–44.
28. Ripley et al., *The Black Abolitionist Papers*, vol. 2, *Canada*, 190–91, 245; Mary Ann Shadd to Executive Committee, American Missionary Association (AMA), April 1852, Amistad Research Center, Tulane University, New Orleans; Bertram Wyatt-Brown, *Lewis Tappan and the Evangelical War Against Slavery* (Baton Rouge: Louisiana State University Press, 1969), 205–25, 292–95; Rhodes, *Mary Ann Shadd Cary*, 36–42, 62–66.
29. Ripley et al., *The Black Abolitionist Papers*, vol. 2, *Canada*, 245–55.
30. Ripley et al., *The Black Abolitionist Papers*, vol. 2, *Canada*, 222, 252–53, 259, 265–68, 275–78; *Voice of the Fugitive*, February 12, 1852, February 26, 1852, April 21, 1852, August 12, 1852; *Liberator*, December 10, 1852, December 24, 1852; *Pennsylvania Freeman*, January 20, 1853; Rhodes, *Mary Ann Shadd Cary*, 53–66, 69.
31. Rhodes, *Mary Ann Shadd Cary*, 67–68.
32. Ripley et al., *The Black Abolitionist Papers*, vol. 2, *Canada*, 245–51; *Liberator*, March 4, 1853; Rhodes, *Mary Ann Shadd Cary*, 53–60.
33. *Voice of the Fugitive*, February 22, 1853; *Frederick Douglass' Paper*, April 8, 1853.
34. *Pennsylvania Freeman*, April 7, 1853, April 21, 1853.
35. *Voice of the Fugitive*, February 22, 1853; *Frederick Douglass' Paper*, April 8, 1853; *Pennsylvania Freeman*, April 7 and 21, 1853; Haviland, *A Woman's Life-Work*, 192–97; Rhodes, *Mary Ann Shadd Cary*, 74.

36. Haviland, *A Woman's Life-Work*, 119–21; Rhodes, *Mary Ann Shadd Cary*, 75–97, 142.
37. The nineteenth-century movement for women's rights, which emerged out of the abolitionist movement, was called the "woman's rights" movement. In 1848 Elizabeth Cady Stanton and others organized the Seneca Falls Woman's Rights Convention; the first National Woman's Convention was held in Worcester in 1850; in 1863 women organized the National Woman's Loyal League to support the Union and to advocate for the Thirteenth Amendment to abolish slavery. Washington, *Sojourner Truth's America*, 4, 201, 334; Nell Irvin Painter, *Sojourner Truth: A Life, A Symbol* (New York: Norton, 1996), 121.
38. Ripley et al., *The Black Abolitionist Papers*, vol. 2, *Canada*, 283–94, 330, 335–44, 393–98; *Frederick Douglass' Paper*, November 9, 1855.
39. Rhodes, *Mary Ann Shadd Cary*, 185–87.
40. *Pennsylvania Freeman*, May 12, 1853, May 19, 1853, May 26, 1853; Ripley et al., *The Black Abolitionist Papers*, vol. 2, *Canada*, 286.
41. "FREEDOM'S RAILWAY"; William C. Nell to Amy Post, August 23, 1857, Post Family Papers; "Recollections of Eliza Seaman Leggett," Eliza Seaman Leggett Family Papers, 8, Burton Historical Collection, Detroit Public Library; Nanette Gardner, scrapbook, Michigan Historical Collections, Bentley Historical Library, University of Michigan, Ann Arbor; *Anti-Slavery Bugle*, December 5, 1857.
42. *Liberator*, June 21, 1861.
43. *Liberator*, June 21, 1861, June 28, 1861; Haviland, *A Woman's Life-Work*, 241–387; Ripley et al., *The Black Abolitionist Papers*, vol. 2, *Canada*, 40, 520–22; Laura Haviland to Amy Post, February 22, 1866, Post Family Papers.

In the Canadian Underground Railroad sculpture, Ed Dwight captured a mother's joy for herself and hopefulness for her child's future upon arriving in Canada West. (Courtesy of photographer Elizabeth Clark)

IV

RESILIENT FAMILIES

Whites who assisted freedom-seekers were the first to have their recollections historicized and published, but their stories comprise only part of the Underground Railroad story. In 1998 the National Network to Freedom initiated a nationwide effort to document additional primary accounts and designate authenticated sites related to the Underground Railroad movement. At the same time, Parks Canada began efforts to commemorate the Canadian termini of the Underground Railroad and to memorialize persons north of the border who engaged in Underground Railroad activities.

As a result of these efforts, many freedom-seekers' narratives have been recovered. The ordeals of life in slavery that forced most to flee, the obstacles and perils that lined the hundreds of miles of land and water refugees had to travel to reach safety, the reserves of ingenuity and resourcefulness freedom-seekers gathered to enable them to finish their journeys, and the contributions made to the growth and development of their adopted homelands—all emerge from the stories told by the freedom-seekers themselves.

Another repeated theme is the devastating emotional loss many suffered as a result of forced separations from family members. These accounts directly contradict slaveholders' self-serving propaganda claiming that enslaved people, enslaved mothers especially, lacked the capacity for strong familial attachment. The existence of Underground Railroad networks on both sides of the Detroit River and the porosity of the boundary enabled many to sustain their family bonds. Courageous individuals recrossed the Detroit River and returned to the South to rescue family members. Some remembered touching reunions with loved ones thought lost forever. Still others, who narrowly escaped with spouses and children, siblings, and sometimes aged parents, kept their families together though slave hunters pursued them on both sides of the border.

TEN

BRIDGING RIVERS

Caroline Quarlls's Remarkable Journey

KIMBERLY SIMMONS AND LARRY MCCLELLAN

In the late summer of 1843, a young woman stood on the eastern bank of the Detroit River, weeping and clutching the arm of the man who had escorted her to safety in Canada. From where she stood, the countryside looked to her much like that she had known around St. Louis. She asked, in panic, if it were possible that somehow they had mistakenly crossed back over the Mississippi River and were again in Missouri after so many long weeks of clandestine travel. Lyman Goodnow, the white Milwaukee abolitionist who accompanied her, assured the young woman that she was safe and the long journey was over. She had traveled from St. Louis into Wisconsin, then around Chicago, across northern Indiana and southern Michigan, through Detroit, and now stood on the riverbank near the settlement of Sandwich in Canada West.[1]

Sixteen-year-old Caroline Quarlls had reached free soil. The informal networks of the Underground Railroad had provided a bridge to freedom. By crossing the Detroit River she had moved beyond the continuing American commitment to slavery and outside the reach of slavecatchers searching for her in Detroit.

Caroline had faced a great irony experienced by many others: they had achieved freedom for themselves only by leaving the "land of the free." She knew well that her white father's family had fought vigorously for liberty in the American Revolution. She knew also her black mother's heritage of bondage. Now she would fashion a life, find a husband, and build a family in Canada. She could not know that even as she made a new life for herself, in another curious irony made possible by the strange connected patterns of family and race in America, her grandfather's cousins, Charles and John Mercer Langston, would be growing into their own work as leading black abolitionists, and they also would be assisting others to freedom in Canada.

Caroline Quarlls was born in 1826 in the frontier settlement of St. Louis on the Mississippi River. Caroline's owners lived in a comfortable house on the corner of Sixth and Pine, just a few blocks from the river and the center of town. Caroline grew up in the household of Robert Quarles (the name is variously spelled), a Revolutionary War veteran and wealthy man with property holdings in Virginia and Missouri. Caroline's father was her master's son, also named Robert. Her mother was Maria, a young slave woman in the Quarles household. At the time of her birth, her father was twenty-eight and her mother seventeen.[2]

Caroline's master—and grandfather—Robert Quarles was a son of the prominent Quarles family of Virginia. He had fought in the Revolutionary War in the Virginia Militia, as had his father, James Quarles, and James's brother, Thomas, both of whom had served with Washington at Valley Forge in the spring of 1778.[3] A number of other relatives, including James Quarles's cousin Ralph Quarles, also were veterans of the Revolutionary War. Part of the landed gentry of Virginia, the Quarles were deeply woven into the social and kinship fabric of the region, connected by marriage to families across the hills and farmland of central Virginia. Their relations spread across Louisa and Caroline counties, west and northwest of Richmond, and they maintained property and homes in the state capital.

The senior Robert Quarles, Caroline's grandfather, had married Patsy Minor, a daughter of one of the oldest families in Virginia. A complex lineage links the Minor family to the family of Dabney Carr, the friend of Thomas Jefferson buried with him at Monticello; to the Randolphs, central in the early history of Virginia Colony; and to Meriwether Lewis, coleader of the Lewis and Clark Expedition. In what was one of the most celebrated social events of the year in Virginia, on the same November day in 1791 that her grandparents Robert and Patsy had been married, Robert's brother, John, wed Patsy's sister, Rebecca.[4]

When Robert and Pasty moved their household to St. Louis in 1819, his father's cousin Ralph stayed behind in Virginia, developing a substantial plantation in Louisa County. Sometime after 1800, Ralph Quarles had begun what would become a long-lasting relationship with a beautiful young slave named Lucy Jane Langston. Lucy had part Native and part African ancestry. After the birth of a daughter in 1806, Ralph signed papers giving Lucy her freedom. After an interval apart, Ralph and Lucy began living together openly in a relationship that lasted for decades.[5]

From this union came three sons: Charles, Gideon, and John Mercer Langston. They would attend Oberlin College and go on to prominent positions in the movement for the abolition of slavery. Both Charles and John were deeply involved with John Brown and his plans for black insurrection. In 1869, Charles married Mary Leary, widow of Lewis Sheridan Leary, who had died in the raid at Harper's Ferry.[6] They became the grandparents of Langston Hughes, noted twentieth-century poet and playwright. During Reconstruction, John Mercer would become the first African American congressman from Virginia and a university president.[7]

Pryor Quarles, the oldest son of Robert and Patsy, moved to St. Louis in 1815; several years later his whole family joined him there.[8] In the 1820s and 1830s, the frontier settlement was a grand stew pot of people, the growing gateway to the western regions of the continent. Here, longtime French settlers and more recent European arrivals mingled with people from diverse traditions: Native Americans, English and French trappers, and American traders of all descriptions, the latter based in St. Louis but ranging across the West. Free Blacks and those held in slavery also mixed on the streets of St. Louis.

This city on the Mississippi had similar rhythms to the long-established settlement of Detroit. Both cities, founded by colonial French settlers intimately bound up with the fur trade, were part of a river culture, with bands of informal networks bridging and moving along the water. Yet both were also border towns, reflecting real political boundaries. For Detroit and Sandwich on the Detroit River, it was an international border between the United States and the British colony of Canada West, with each side reflecting differing sensibilities, especially in regard to people held in bondage. For St. Louis, the boundary separated the states of Missouri and Illinois; on the Missouri side, slavery was accepted in both law and custom, yet the institution was questioned; and on the Illinois side, slavery was legally outlawed, yet the issue was fiercely debated. When the Civil War broke out, Missouri would stay in the Union, as would Illinois, although strong voices in the southernmost counties of that free state advocated secession.[9]

For people of African descent living in Missouri, the great Mississippi River was both a barrier and an opportunity. Throughout the 1830s and until the Civil War, newspapers in St. Louis and Illinois carried notices about fugitive slaves heading for Chicago and on to Canada. An early example of this: "Ran away from the subscriber [in St. Louis] . . . a mulatto man, named Claiborn, about 25 years of age, 6 feet high, stout made, a very bright mulatto, his teeth rather broad, has a down cast look when spoken to, has worked at the confectionery business and may pass for a pastry cook; . . . he can read a little and is supposed to have forged free papers and is making his way to Canada."[10] There was a growing awareness that, across the river in Illinois, places and networks of support, the nascent Underground Railroad, were available for Blacks seeking their freedom. This was the context in which Caroline was born and grew up.

The Quarles household included twenty-five to thirty-one slaves, and in 1826, one of them was Caroline's mother, seventeen-year-old Maria, who had likely been purchased in St. Louis. Her appearance in later life suggests she possibly had French or Spanish heritage. The senior Robert Quarles, master of Maria and her infant child, died in 1827. In the distribution of his estate, Maria was among the property passed on to his daughter, Louisa Ann, and her husband, Charles R. Hall.[11] Hall was the one whom Caroline really knew and referred to as her "master." This meant that Caroline was the property of her own aunt and uncle. It is intriguing to note that in the family was a white daughter of the senior Robert Quarles, born in 1794, named Louisa along with Caroline, the slave daughter of the junior Robert Quarles. These were also the names of the Virginia counties from which the family had come.

While traveling with abolitionist Lyman Goodnow on the journey Milwaukee to Canada, Caroline talked about her life in St. Louis. She had learned to do fine sewing and embroidery work and worked as an attending servant for her mistress. She was not allowed to go to church on Sundays, but she related that her owners were faithful participants at the Second Presbyterian Church, ministered to by one Reverend Potts. Goodnow observed that Caroline was

In the 1880s, as a free woman and mother of six, Caroline Quarlls Watkins wrote letters giving details of her life to Lyman Goodnow, the Wisconsin abolitionist who had escorted her on her flight to freedom through Milwaukee, Illinois, Indiana, southwestern Michigan, and Detroit. (Courtesy of Larry McClellan)

"probably never badly abused while in bondage, though occasionally whipped."[12] From time to time, she was locked in the house to wash all the wooden floors. In her letters, Caroline noted that both her mother and sister died when she was young.[13]

Goodnow also reported that Caroline talked about her mother's husband. Whatever the nature and extent of Maria's relationship with Robert Quarles, at some point she was formally or informally married to a free African American man, a blacksmith. Evidently he was very fond of Caroline, his stepdaughter. Even after the death of her mother, Caroline's stepfather continued to care for her and on at least one occasion bought jewelry for her.[14]

By all accounts, Caroline was a beautiful young woman and retained her attractiveness throughout her life. She presents a striking image in the one photo of her that is known to exist. Family traditions hold that she looked "French, with freckles, beautiful black hair, and blue eyes."[15] She was further described as having "a straight nose, thin lips, skin not very dark and a slender form of medium height."[16]

All that is known about Caroline points to a woman who, from her youngest days, was clear-eyed about her station in life. There were the obvious ironies and complications inherent in her dual heritage. She was simultaneously the child of a prominent family that had fought for freedom in the American Revolution and the child of an enslaved mother. As part of a household that included her white grandmother, Patsy Quarles, she no doubt knew her heritage as a great-grandchild of one who had been with Washington at Valley Forge and was aware that she was related to heroes of Virginia: the Minors, Carrs, Randolphs, and Lewises. As a perceptive girl she would also have seen the diversity of life and ethnicities around her. St. Louis was a remarkable mixture of peoples on the frontier of pioneer America, yet it was a place where slavery persisted. In her youth, Caroline would have been aware of the pressures to assist those seeking their freedom and the complexities of life for persons of African descent. In the summer of 1841, Caroline was likely influenced by a significant public event that took place in early St. Louis. Close to twenty thousand people gathered on the riverbank to witness the hanging of the Madison Henderson gang, whose members had been responsible for a major robbery, fire, and the death of several residents. The gang had been robbing individuals, banks, and stores along the Mississippi river for years. Henderson was technically a slave but was living on his own, and the other three members of the gang were free Blacks.[17] Both the crimes and the hanging occurred just a few blocks from where Caroline lived.

So it was that in the spring of 1843, Caroline was a maturing young woman who for months had been talking with her stepfather about going north to find freedom and live her own life. One day, in a fit of frustration with her servant, Caroline's mistress (and aunt) Louisa cut off the girl's long, beautiful hair. That must have cemented the decision for Caroline, and she put in motion plans for her escape.[18] Years later, she wrote: "I told my grandmother (Patsy) that I was going to Canada but I was so young that she did not pay any attention to me."[19] Caroline's confession to Virginia-born aristocrat Patsy Minor Quarles indicates the existence of a remarkable openness in their awkward relationship.

Caroline had accumulated about $100, most likely the proceeds from her sewing and embroidery combined with gifts from her grandmother and stepfather. Gathering up her clothes and some jewelry given to her by her stepfather in a traveling box, Caroline told her mistress, her aunt Louisa, that she wanted to visit a sick friend. She received permission to do so, and with that headed for the docks and a ferry to Illinois. "The boat was just ready to start, it being about 5 o'clock P.M. Caroline must have had some experience in traveling, for she went up with unsuspicious naturalness and bought a ticket to Alton, Illinois, where there was a school for young ladies. She wore a quantity of rich jewelry, stayed on deck in the daytime, with other young ladies, and when there was dancing she danced. She thus excited no suspicion, being no darker skinned than many other of the young ladies who attended the seminary."[20] Thus began this remarkable journey, stretching miles up the Mississippi from St. Louis to Alton, Illinois. Leaving the ferry, Caroline may have displayed some level of discomfort, for fairly quickly a local black resident noticed her on the street, saw through her efforts to "pass," and provided shelter. The next day he put her on a stagecoach to Milwaukee. Traveling for two days on stage routes headed north, most likely through Springfield and towns near the Illinois River, Caroline arrived in Milwaukee, Wisconsin.

That summer of 1843, Caroline became the first recorded freedom-seeker to come into Wisconsin. The stage stopped at Milwaukee House, where Caroline became acquainted with the local barber, a man named Titball, who had been enslaved himself in his younger years. Titball gladly offered to help Caroline and took her to his house. However, he betrayed her in hopes of a reward; had it not been for the quick wits of an enslaved messenger boy who divined Titball's intent, Caroline would have been delivered up to the St. Louis attorneys sent by her owners to retrieve her.[21] Thus began several weeks of complications as she was hidden in various places, sought after by slavecatchers from St. Louis, and assisted by prominent Milwaukeeans with abolitionist sympathies. Caroline was eventually spirited away to the countryside. Her helpers included Deacon Samuel Brown, one of the founders of Milwaukee, and Asahel Finch, a young attorney who was approached by slavecatchers searching for Caroline. His recently established law partnership, Finch & Lynde, would one day become Foley & Lardner, one of the most notable law firms in the United States.[22]

Members of the alliance of local Wisconsin abolitionists realized that they needed to assist Caroline in getting to people they knew to be active with the Underground Railroad. They determined that the most effective course was to help her get to the networks already in place south of Chicago. Realizing that this could become a major undertaking, they asked Lyman Goodnow, a well-respected member of the community, to serve as Caroline's escort to Canada. He agreed; he would travel close to six hundred miles to see her safely across the Detroit River.[23]

After several weeks in Wisconsin, Caroline Quarlls and Lyman Goodnow headed out in a buggy borrowed for the journey. They traveled south into McHenry County in Illinois, then to acquaintances in Dundee, about forty miles from Chicago. (Within a year of their passing through, the small Dundee abolitionist settlement would become the home of the famous detective Alan Pinkerton who, for years, used his barrel factory in Dundee and his contacts in Chicago to assist freedom-seekers.)[24] This route kept Caroline and her companion well west of Chicago and potential encounters with slavecatchers. They continued on to Naperville, then circled to the south and east, through Lockport, Hickory Grove, and then Beebe's Grove near Crete on the eastern edge of Illinois.

From there, they traveled across northwestern Indiana and into southwestern Michigan, staying with German and Quaker families. The journey into southwestern Michigan included stops in some unnamed towns and villages along the route as well as in Kalamazoo, Battle Creek, and Marshall; they encountered several other contingents of freedom-seekers heading for Detroit, intent on crossing the Detroit River into Canada. A stop in Ann Arbor led to an overnight stay with one of Michigan's early leading activists, the Reverend Guy Beckley, editor of Michigan's antislavery newspaper, the *Signal of Liberty*.[25] The journey from Milwaukee to Detroit took three weeks of fairly constant travel. As Goodnow remembered the end of the journey:

> We passed through Detroit at 6 o'clock on Tuesday night—about three weeks from home—while the streets were filled with workmen on their way home. We were not discovered, and arrived safely at Ambler's, who kept the last station this side of the Detroit River, his house being only separated from that stream by a narrow street. He was absent, but we were well cared for, and his wife sent two men—one of who I had known in the East—to take us over the river. To him I paid twelve shillings, the first money I had paid out in the whole journey, which, on account of the circuitous route followed by the underground railroad, had extended over a distance of between five and six hundred miles.

In Sandwich on the Canadian side of the Detroit River, Caroline was welcomed to stay at the home of a missionary family named Haskell.[26]

Goodnow headed for home. Coming back across the river, he was surprised to discover that there were strangers in Detroit who were looking for Caroline—particularly a clerk employed by the owners of the steamboat on which Caroline had left St. Louis. Since that

Caroline and her husband, Allen Watkins, attended Sandwich Baptist Church when it was a log cabin. The brick church, constructed in 1851, is now a Canadian National Historic Landmark. (Courtesy of the Amherstburg Freedom Museum)

conveyance had been the initial means of escape, the steamboat's owners were legally obligated to pay a fine of $800 if she were not returned. The clerk had watched the ferryboats for two weeks—but of course Caroline had traveled through the informal land networks of the Underground Railroad, not by regular boat.[27]

Caroline settled in the Sandwich area and set about making a life for herself. She went to school and learned to read and write. The next year she married another refugee, Allen Watkins, who worked for Colonel John Prince.[28] He was seventeen years older than Caroline and had been married previously. Ironically, Allen had been born into slavery in Richmond, Virginia, a city known to Caroline because of its connections with her father's family. Sources indicate that Allen was born in 1811, the property of William Watkins. Later, as part of an estate settlement, he was sent to Nancy Cleveland, a widow living in Kentucky. There he had several children with his first wife. After his wife was sold away from him and the children, she committed suicide.[29] Allen Watkins left Kentucky in 1838, entering Canada through Detroit.[30]

In 1833, a major racial riot was sparked by the arrest and subsequent escape across the Detroit River of fugitive slaves Thornton and Lucie Blackburn, as described by Karolyn Smardz Frost in chapter 2 of this volume. In 1837, public awareness again focused on the stories of freedom-seekers: Solomon Moseby and Jesse Happy out of Kentucky. (The Moseby and Happy incidents are elaborated in chapter 3 of this volume.) It is intriguing to consider whether Allen Watkins or Caroline Quarlls had been influenced by these earlier transnational escapes, which had triggered international disputes. Allen and Caroline met and were married in 1844. He was a cook—a hard worker, according to contemporary accounts. They resided in Sandwich and played a strong role in sustaining the growth of the now-historic Sandwich Baptist Church. Allen was a leader in the move to replace the old log church with a tidy brick building (now a National Historic Landmark) in 1851. Built just a few blocks from the river that separated and protected the Watkins from the dangers of bondage in America, the new church building was dedicated on August 1st, the anniversary of the British decision to abolish slavery.[31] The house Caroline and her husband built for their growing family still stands today, less than a block from the church. As Irene Moore Davis outlines in chapter 4 of this volume, Sandwich had become one of the central locations for black settlement as freedom-seekers streamed into Canada West.

Eventually Caroline and Allen had six children, the eldest named Mary Elizabeth. The second was named Maria, after Caroline's mother. The youngest boy to survive infancy was William, born in 1853. In 1880, Caroline wrote to Lyman Goodnow, "I have six children three boys and three girls three married and three single the youngest is 16 a boy my oldest boy is a farmer and my other boy is in Cincinnati my youngest girl 18 is at home and I am trying to educate her for a school teacher."[32]

In 1880, in preparation for contributions to a book on Wisconsin history, Lyman Goodnow attempted to get in touch with Caroline. He wrote to her in care of the postmaster in Sandwich, and the connection was made. She was delighted to hear from him and following her initial response, dated April 18, 1880, Goodnow wrote again hoping to learn the answers to a set of specific questions on her life. Her responses to Goodnow's questions, sent on April 23, 1880 provided the rich details about her early life, her escape from St. Louis and journey to her intended destination in Canada, and her subsequent life in freedom.

On March 13, 1886, Caroline died after two years of illness. Her son William attended to the details of her death and funeral. Although she had been involved with the Sandwich Baptist Church, at some point several years before her death, she had joined the local Anglican church.[33] She is buried in the graveyard at St. John's Anglican Church in Sandwich.

The Watkins family's community involvement was fueled by its roots in the Underground Railroad and Caroline's aspiration to reach freedom in Canada. A reflection of this was the position of great-grandson and William Watkins's namesake, William "Russ" Small, who was one of the founders of the British American Association of Colored Brothers of Ontario. Started in the 1930s, the group was formally organized in 1957, and in both its name and programs "choose[n] to emphasize its trans-national alliances as well as to celebrate Emancipation."[34] For many years Russ Small served as chair for the Windsor, Ontario, Emancipation Celebration. The Emancipation Celebration remains a time-honored African Canadian event steeped in the tradition of celebrating freedom throughout the Province of Ontario.

In so many ways, the lives and legacies of Caroline and Allen Watkins are representative of the complexities of life for people of African descent that continue to this day in this transnational region along the Detroit River. Caroline and Allen each experienced remarkable journeys to freedom in Canada, Allen coming north out of Kentucky and Caroline with her incredible saga of escape from St. Louis by way of Milwaukee, Illinois, and Michigan. As the children of Caroline and Allen Watkins grew up, some stayed in the Detroit River district and others moved away. Those who remained spread out across this flexible frontier along the Detroit River boundary, and today some make their homes in Canada and some in the United States.

These legacies have always included seeking freedom. In the current context, the search takes many forms. However, for Caroline, her quest was always clear. Deeply aware of both her white and black heritage, she was determined to be free. Born trapped in bondage, she chose freedom, making a new life for herself and establishing an inspiring legacy for multiple generations of her descendants.

NOTES

1. The story of Caroline's remarkable journey is fairly well documented. The central account is that of Lyman Goodnow in *The History of Waukesha County, Wisconsin* (Chicago: Western Historical Company, 1880), 458–66. This is also appendix 1 in Burlington Historical Society, *The Underground Railroad in Burlington and Vicinity: A Collection of References at One Point in Time* (Burlington, WI: Burlington Historical Society, 2002), 26–35, online at www.burlingtonhistory.org/caroline_quarlls_1842_journey_on.htm (accessed October 1, 2010). The story is also recounted in C. C. Olin, *A Complete Record of the John Olin Family* (Indianapolis: Baker-Randolph, 1893), xxx–xli, which includes reprints of three of the four Watkins' family letters to Goodnow and Olin in 1880 and 1892. www.archive.org/details/cu31924029843228 (accessed March 4, 2012). There are three letters written in 1880, two from Caroline to Goodnow, dated April 17 and April 27, 1880, and one to him from Allen Watkins, her husband, on April 24, 1880. (In some sources, these letters are presented as dated April 18 and April 23). These are now on display at the Civil War Museum in Kenosha, Wisconsin. There

is an additional brief letter from Caroline's son William Watkins responding to C. C. Olin with news of his mother's death. This was sent on September 12, 1892. See Olin, *A Complete Record*, xli. See also Guide to the Caroline Quarlls/Allen Watkins Underground Railroad Collection [1880], www.kenosha.org/civilwar/documents/CarolineQuarrls.pdf (accessed September 10, 2010). Several additional sources serve to reinforce Goodnow's account. There are some errors and confusions, given that his story and the Watkins letters were written more than thirty-five years after the events described. However, the narrative seems substantially sound.

2. From the Census of the United States records and court records on the probate of Quarles's estate. See Missouri's Judicial Records at Missouri Digital Archives: Probate Court St. Louis, Quarles, Robert, Case Number 00762, filed 1827, microfilm reel C 27468, Collections 6, 10, and 20, Missouri State Archives, Jefferson City. www.sos.mo.gov/archives/mojudicial/images.asp?id=309&party=Quarles,%20Robert&case=00762&date=1827&County=St.%20Louis&courtType=Probate%20Court&reel=C%2027468 (accessed November 10, 2010). Various efforts have been made to understand the name change from Quarles to Quarlls. In her correspondence and evidently in her ordinary dealings in Canada, Caroline used "Quarlls." The most obvious explanation could be seen in the written forms of the name. In the written form of "Quarles," the final "l" and "e" could easily be read as two "l's." If this is the case, it is not clear when the shift happened.

3. See records for James and Thomas Quarles as officers taking an oath of allegiance at Valley Forge at colonialancestors.com/revolutionary/oath7.htm (accessed March 19, 1012).

4. For further details on the families and children of Robert and Patsy Quarles, see the letter and pension application of Robert Quarles, filed by Patsy Quarles and initiated in 1844, "Pension Application of Robert Quarles W9868," transcribed and annotated by C. Leon Harris, "Southern Campaign Revolutionary War Pension Statements and Rosters," www.southerncampaign.org (accessed March 19, 2012).

5. William Clark and Aimee Lee Cheek, *John Mercer Langston and the Fight for Black Freedom* (Urbana: University of Illinois Press, 1989). Details on the early Quarles family and relations are found in chap. 1, "Inheritor," 7–20.

6. Clark and Cheek, *John Mercer Langston*, 362.

7. "John Mercer Langston," *Black Americans in Congress, 1870–2007* (Washington, DC: Government Printing Office, 2008), bioguide.congress.gov/scripts/biodisplay.pl?index=l000074 (accessed February 21, 2012).

8. Robert's full name was Robert Pryor Quarles, Pryor being another old Virginia surname.

9. Arthur C. Cole, *The Centennial History of Illinois: The Era of the Civil War, 1848–1870* (Springfield: Illinois Centennial Commission, 1919), 254–56.

10. *Illinois Intelligencer*, September 30, 1831, quoted in Helen Tregillis, *River Roads to Freedom: Fugitive Slave Notices and Sheriff Notices Found in Illinois Sources* (Bowie, MD: Heritage Books, 1988), 60.

11. See Missouri's Judicial Records at Missouri Digital Archives: Probate Court St. Louis. See also Meil Wilson, *St. Louis Probate Court Records: Court Ordered Slave Sales, Book C and D* (St. Louis: National Park Service, Jefferson National Expansion Memorial, 2007), 2. In a database published online at www.nps.gov/jeff/historyculture/slave-sales.htm the

researcher incorrectly identifies this record as that of Mrs. Robert Quarles. The division of slaves was among the heirs of her deceased husband. Their son-in-law, Charles R. Hall, received Maria and two other slaves, Louisa and Betty. Maria's daughter Caroline, who would have been one-year-old at the time of Robert Quarles's death, was not named. It is possible that Caroline was not listed since she was the daughter of Robert Quarles Jr. In the 1830 U.S. Census, Missouri, St. Louis, St. Louis Upper Ward, the listing for the household of Charles R. Hall included two female slaves under the age of ten and two in the range from ten to twenty-three, which accords with Maria's and Caroline's ages at the time. The 1840 U.S. Census, Missouri, St. Louis County, St. Louis, listing for the household of Charles R. Hall included two female slaves in the range ten to twenty-three and one in the range twenty-four to thirty-five. In 1840, Caroline would have been fourteen and Maria thirty. www.nps.gov/jeff/historyculture/upload/Slave20SalesDatabase.pdf (accessed March 4, 2012).

12. Goodnow, *The History of Waukesha County*, 458. Also noted in Caroline's second letter to Goodnow, Caroline Quarles Watkins to Lyman Goodnow, April 23, 1880, cited in Olin, *A Complete Record*, xxxvix.
13. Details derived from census records and Caroline's second letter to Goodnow, Caroline Quarles Watkins to Lyman Goodnow, April 23, 1880, reprinted in Olin, *A Complete Record*, xxxviii.
14. Goodnow, *The History of Waukesha County*, 459.
15. Kim Simmons's grandfather gave this description of his "Gran-ma."
16. Goodnow, *The History of Waukesha County*, 458.
17. See A. B. Chambers, ed., *Trials and Confessions of Madison Henderson, Alias Blanchard, Alfred Amos Warrick, James W. Seward and Charles Brown* (St. Louis: Chambers & Knapp, 1841), docsouth.unc.edu/neh/henderson (accessed April 11, 2010). For a full discussion, see Thomas Buchanan, *Black Life on the Mississippi* (Chapel Hill: University of North Carolina Press, 2004), chap. 5.
18. These and the following details are found in the material written by Lyman Goodnow in *The History of Waukesha County*, 458–66, from his recollections of many conversations he had with Caroline on the road from Milwaukee to Detroit.
19. Caroline Quarlls Watkins to Goodnow, April 23, 1880, in Goodnow, *The History of Waukesha County*, 465–56; and in Olin, *A Complete Record*, xxxviii.
20. Goodnow, *The History of Waukesha County*, 458, 3.
21. Goodnow, *The History of Waukesha County*, 458; Olin, *A Complete Record*, xxv–xxvi.
22. This involvement is detailed in Ellen D. Langill, *Foley & Lardner, Attorneys at Law, 1842–1992* (Madison: State Historical Society of Wisconsin, 1992). An editorial in the *Milwaukee Evening Wisconsin* at the time of Finch's death in 1883 embellished his dramatic assistance to Caroline, noting "his great heart was in the work of breaking the shackle of slavery" (25).
23. Caroline's sojourn in the Milwaukee area is commemorated in the history of Wisconsin, including an exhibit at the Civil War Museum in Kenosha. An Underground Railroad mural in Milwaukee includes a figure representing her, but it doesn't render her accurately: she is depicted as a dark-skinned, full-figured mature woman. Her true appearance as a sixteen-year-old "beautiful young lady of some dark color" is further documented in a

reminiscence from one of the families she stayed with in McHenry County. See the letter of the widow of Rev. Fitch sent to Wilbur Siebert, the great collector and publisher of Underground Railroad accounts, in the Siebert Collection, reel 1, box 40, vol. 01, item 50, Ohio Historical Society, Columbus.

24. James MacKay, *Alan Pinkerton: The First Private Eye* (New York: John Wiley & Sons, 1996), 56.

25. Goodnow, *The History of Waukesha County*, 464.

26. Details of this story based on Caroline's letters and the account by Goodnow. See Goodnow, *The History of Waukesha County*, 46; Olin, *A Complete Record*, xxx–xxxvii.

27. Goodnow, *The History of Waukesha County*, 464.

28. Colonel John Prince was a British attorney who relocated to Sandwich, Upper Canada, in 1833. This gentleman farmer, militia officer, magistrate, and politician was a sometime friend of the black community who later turned on it, demanding that the government discourage fugitive slave immigration into the province. He lived at Park Farm on the outskirts of Sandwich. See Robin W. Winks, *The Blacks in Canada: A History*, 2nd ed. (Montreal: McGill-Queen's University Press, 1997), 214–15.

29. These details are provided by Caroline in her second letter to Goodnow: Goodnow, *The History of Waukesha County*, 465–66; Olin, *A Complete Record*, xxxvix.

30. "Allen Watkins to Lyman Goodnow, April 24, 1880, from Sandwich (now Windsor), Ontario, Canada," Binder 1, Letter 3, Caroline Quarlls/Allen Watkins Underground Railroad Collection, Civil War Museum, Kenosha, WI. On other Kentucky freedom-seekers, see Winks, *The Blacks in Canada*, 169–71, and Karolyn Smardz Frost, *I've Got a Home in Glory Land: A Lost Tale of the Underground Railroad* (New York: Farrar, Straus & and Giroux, 2007; Toronto: Thomas Allen, 2007), 242–46.

31. Charlotte Bronte Perry, *The Long Road*, vol. 1, *The History of the Coloured Canadian in Windsor, Ontario, 1867–1967* (Windsor: Sumner, 1967), 36.

32. Caroline Quarles Watkins to Lyman Goodnow, April 23, 1880, cited in Goodnow, *The History of Waukesha County*, 465–66; Olin, *A Complete Record*, xxxvix.

33. Her 1886 death record notes her affiliation as "R.C.," and the 1881 Census of Canada notes her as "R. Catholic." However, given her burial at the Anglican church, these notes most likely reflect a misidentification of her religious preference.

34. Peggy Bristow, "A Duty to the Past, a Promise to the Future: Black Organizing in Windsor—The Depression, World War II, and the Post-War Years," *New Dawn: The Journal of Black Canadian Studies* 2, no. 1 (2007): 15–59.

ELEVEN

ONE MORE RIVER TO CROSS

The Crosswhites' Escapes from Slavery

DEBIAN MARTY

Before a crowd of nearly two hundred villagers—both black and white—the speaker shouted, "*Resolved:* that these Kentuckians shall not take the Crosswhite family by virtue of moral, physical, or legal force!" The audience erupted with raucous support: "Here! Here!" Their fervor led some to propose, too, that if the Kentucky slavecatchers did not leave town within two hours, they should "be tarred and feathered and rode [out] on a rail."[1] The spirited confrontation took place on the cold, wintry morning of January 27, 1847, in the frontier village of Marshall, Michigan. With Southern slave hunters brandishing firearms at their door, the Crosswhites needed to escape from slavery—again.[2]

Adam and Sarah Crosswhite's efforts to secure their family's freedom were extraordinary in several ways. Not only had all the members of the family successfully escaped from bondage in Kentucky, they would remain together and resist recapture in the North. With the help of allies working in the Underground Railroad networks, Adam and Sarah Crosswhite strove to fulfill their aspirations to live in freedom. But the Crosswhite family's flight also sparked an international incident that epitomizes the transnational nature of African American and African Canadian life along the Detroit River and highlights the fact that slaveholders were fully capable of traversing the international border in their determination to recover their formerly enslaved "property." As a result of the slavecatchers' relentless pursuit, the Crosswhite family would have one more river to cross to ensure liberty.

Adam was born into slavery in 1799, purportedly the son of an enslaved woman and a white man named Powers. When Adam was ten years old, he was bequeathed to Powers's relative Miss Frances Crosswhite of Bourbon County, Kentucky. The Crosswhite family then

Adam Crosswhite and his wife and children escaped from slavery in Kentucky sometime in 1843, but they were forced to flee again after they were discovered living in Marshall, Michigan, in 1847. (Courtesy of the Michigan State Archives, Lansing)

apparently sold Adam to another relative, Edward Stone. Stone was an infamous slave trader located in Paris, Kentucky, who kept slaves manacled to the cellar wall in his splendid mansion while they awaited sale. Adam probably was held there before Stone sold him for $200.[3] The buyer likely was Francis Giltner, a prosperous farmer who was relocating to fertile lands known as Hunter's Bottom in Carroll County, Kentucky.[4] His new plantation bordered the Ohio River and the free state of Indiana.

Francis Giltner brought Adam Crosswhite to Hunter's Bottom in 1819. There, Adam met an enslaved woman named Sarah and worked alongside her on the sixteen-hundred-acre farm. Eventually Adam and Sarah became a couple and started a family. They had three sons and one daughter: John Antony, Benjamin Franklin, Cyrus Jackson, and Sarah Lucretia. But after more than two decades of bondage, Adam and Sarah Crosswhite learned that their children would be sold away from them after Francis Giltner's death. On April 1, 1843, Giltner drew up a last will and testament ordering his executors to "sell the whole of my slaves to the highest bidder." He made specific provisions concerning Adam and Sarah's family: "But in making such sale, I direct them to sell Adam and his wife and any children they may have under five years of age together."[5] John Antony and Ben already were around twelve and ten years old, respectively, and thus slated for sale upon the slave owner's demise. For the younger children, Cyrus and Sarah, it literally was a matter of time.

News of Giltner's will, which contained similar directives regarding other enslaved parents and their young children, assuredly spread like wildfire throughout the household. Giltner may have spoken openly about his intentions with the slaves, his family members, or the three neighbors who came together in Giltner's presence to affix their signatures as witnesses to the document, or conversations may have been overheard.[6] However they learned of it, Adam and Sarah knew that Giltner's final wishes meant their family would be separated one day.

The Crosswhites decided to escape. A few months later, on August 5, 1843, they gathered their four children and stole away from Giltner's plantation.[7] They almost certainly were not alone. According to a firsthand account left by Giltner's grandson Francis Troutman, several of the Giltner family slaves crossed the Detroit River to find freedom in Canada. He came to Michigan in pursuit of the Crosswhites and five others, a total of eleven runaways.[8] Moreover, the exodus from Hunter's Bottom was substantial and ongoing. In 1840, the U.S. census taker recorded that Francis Giltner had twenty-one enslaved people at his plantation.[9] When he died nine years later, the estate's inventory documented only three.[10] The diminished number is addressed in a family history written decades later by another grandson, Bernard G. Troutman. He complained that "Yankee abolitionist" teachers in the South encouraged slaves to run away. They would close their schools, he claimed, and either "point out the road" for runaways to take or "go with them at night." In this manner, Troutman asserted, "Grandfather Giltner had 18 to run off at one time."[11]

Troutman's recollection about the number of runaways is corroborated by those who helped the Giltner slaves escape. George DeBaptiste was a free black man who ran a barbershop in Madison, Indiana, directly across the river from Carroll County, Kentucky, and the Giltner plantation. (DeBaptiste is referenced in the Introduction to this volume; his short career as valet to President William H. Harrison and his Underground Railroad heroics are highlighted in chapters 5 and 8.) From 1838 till 1846, DeBaptiste organized and conducted slave escapes from Kentucky through Indiana and on to freedom in the North. Eventually, because of threats from proslavery advocates, he, too, fled north to Michigan. There, many years later, he apparently boasted that he had the "honor of having run off 19 of Giltner's 24 slaves."[12] Although the numbers vary depending on source, discrepancies may be attributed to multiple escapes and, in the later accounts, to fading memories.

DeBaptiste's claim—if not the exact number—finds additional support from a white abolitionist and Underground Railroad operator named John H. Tibbets. Tibbets moved to Jefferson County, Indiana—home to DeBaptiste's barbershop—in 1843. His "first adventure," as he recalled, took place when he "received word from George Debaptist[e] of Madison Indiana, that there would be a lot of ten to leave Hunter's Bottom on Sunday night and he wished me to make arrangements to transport them on the underground road that I was acquainted with." Tibbets and his wife, Sarah, got into their big covered wagon and rendezvoused with DeBaptiste and company three miles outside of Madison. He described their meeting, using the language of the late nineteenth century: "I had been at the appointed place but a very short time when Mr. Debaptist[e] sang out, 'Here is $10,000 from Hunter's Bottom tonight.' A good negro at that time would fetch from $1,000.00 up. We loaded them in, drew down the curtains and started with the cargo of human charges towards the North Star. We always made good time and close connection."[13]

The Crosswhites may have participated in one of the mass escapes from Hunter's Bottom or may have ventured north with the assistance of the Underground Railroad network at another time. One story claims that Adam Crosswhite contacted an Underground Railroad agent (almost certainly DeBaptiste) and asked for help.[14] Together they devised a plan. They packed up the family's furniture and sank it in a neighboring river. The Crosswhites and the agent then hastened across the banks of the Ohio, traveling rapidly north through Indiana and on into Michigan. Back at the Kentucky plantation, their ruse apparently worked. Francis Giltner supposed "that the fugitives could not have traveled fast or far, carrying so much baggage as all their furniture, hence he lost time hunting for them on the Kentucky side of the river, until it was too late."[15]

Once in Michigan, the Crosswhites established themselves as a respectable family. Adam and Sarah were known as a "quiet and industrious couple" who, "by "thrift and unremitting labor," were making payments on their homestead and had their children enrolled in school. Within a year of their arrival in Marshall, Sarah gave birth to a fifth child, a daughter. The growing Crosswhite family experienced relative safety in their new home, for they lived in a largely black neighborhood, many of whose residents also hailed from Kentucky, and amid a generally sympathetic antislavery white community. Although the Crosswhites were aware of the ever-present danger of being kidnapped back into slavery, they did not know that someone "with the genuine spirit of the slave-driver sent to Kentucky information concerning their hiding places," or that Francis Troutman, the grandson of their former slave owner, was fully engaged in planning their recapture.[16]

Back in Kentucky, the twenty-six-year-old Troutman was making preparations for his pursuit. He purchased a journal to record a list of the things that needed to be done. In it he wrote: "All of Adam's letters must be intercepted, when he is taken; his property must be disposed of in some way; a wagon must be employed for their transportation; [and] a pair of

Francis Troutman, grandson of the slaveholder who claimed the Crosswhites, kept a journal of his venture to Michigan to seize the Crosswhite family. (Courtesy of the University of Kentucky Archives, Lexington)

shackles must be obtained." Troutman, a newly licensed lawyer, also equipped himself with a published bill of reward, a description of the escaped slaves, and a power of attorney authorizing him to act as an agent on behalf of his grandfather Francis Giltner. Thus prepared, Troutman left Kentucky and set out on horseback to track down the Crosswhites in Michigan.[17]

Troutman arrived in Marshall one month later, on December 7, 1846. He checked into the centrally located National Hotel and, despite the pouring rain, immediately went looking about town. It was not long before he spotted the eldest son. Troutman described the encounter in his journal: "I discovered a pretty little black boy in the crowd who I supposed to be John Antony. I went close up to him, put my arm upon him, rubbed against him; I was certain it was John. I stepped a little aside, and got into conversation with a little white boy. I asked him the name of that little darky. 'John Crosswhite,' [he answered]. I passed immediately ... to my hotel [and went] to sleep very much elated."

The next day, Troutman went back out seeking the Crosswhite family. Again, he saw John, this time with his younger brother Benjamin Franklin. The two boys went their separate ways, with Ben entering a tailor's shop with some cloth. Troutman followed him into the store and hid behind a newspaper, ostensibly reading, until young Crosswhite left. Troutman then made enquiries of the tailor, who reported that "Adam is considered a very nice man" and works as a "common laborer." Troutman left, ever more confident in the eventual success of his pursuit.

Although the "rain [now] fell in torrents," Troutman "was too eager for a postponement." He continued searching about town until, a few hours later, he saw a man he believed to be Adam. Troutman followed him on "quite a zig zag course through the village" for nearly a mile, until the man entered a house. Troutman stopped a passerby and asked the identity of the householder. "Adam Crosswhite" was the reply.

Buoyed by his discovery, Troutman returned to the hotel. He had dinner and retired to the hotel's reading room. There, however, he found himself the subject of intense scrutiny. A young man engaged Troutman in a lengthy exchange about the latter's business and plans. Troutman managed to pass himself off as a Mr. Grant, a schoolteacher looking for work, and withdrew to his room. But although he had concealed his identity and true purpose, Troutman was unsettled by the encounter and could not sleep. He turned to his journal:

> I set up [sic] late at night ruminating on the responsibility that now rested upon me. Here I am alone, no one perhaps in the state knows my name, business, or residence, and the very least indiscreet word or action of mine would at once destroy every prospect of my success. My situation is truly a critical one when I seriously reflect that I am in a town of near 3,000 inhabitants, some abolitionists and ALL opposed to slavery, that even a hint of my name or business would defeat my enterprise, [for] there is a railroad from this place to Detroit passing and re-passing every day [and] in 7 or 8 hours our negroes can be in Canada.

Troutman's anxieties about being discovered prompted him to leave Marshall. Two weeks later, he returned to the National Hotel, ready to renew his investigation. Although it was Christmas Eve, he sent for Simon Patterson, whose wife was a local washerwoman, to pick up his laundry. Then Troutman plied him with brandy and gin "till his tongue was loose at both ends." The intoxicated man revealed that he had escaped from slavery seven years earlier, having journeyed all the way from Alabama. He confirmed the Crosswhites' residence in Marshall and then confided that Adam was in contact with others who had escaped from Troutman's grandfather and were living now in Detroit and Canada.

This valuable intelligence was verified by another man that evening, identified in Troutman's journal only as an "abolitionist." This source reported that "Adam keeps up a regular correspondence with abolitionists near the Ohio River," and that he "had sent for Dennis and Stephen," two men formerly enslaved by Giltner who were among those now living in Detroit or Canada. According to Troutman, the abolitionist also offered detailed information about Crosswhite's plans "to get all of Grandpa's Negroes who are worth anything."

Troutman found the discoveries "truly gratifying," but he resented Crosswhite's confidence in his safety and in his ability to help liberate slaves still in Kentucky. "Adam thinks himself secure here," wrote Troutman, "because he is popular among the whites, and there [is] a large number of Negroes here to defend him, who are at all times prepared for a fight. The whites have been in the habit of loaning them guns to prevent their masters from reclaiming, and consequently no Negro has ever been taken in this place although there have been many attempts." Writing this, Troutman could not have known how accurately he was describing events that would transpire just a few weeks in the future.

Once again, though, Troutman's inquiries had aroused suspicions in the tight-knit village of Marshall. Simon Patterson, having recovered from his intoxication, sounded the alarm on Christmas Day. Word got back to Troutman through the hotel barkeeper. Again, Troutman decided to leave. "I knew," he wrote, "if Adam ever got any ground for suspicion that my enterprise would be in a hazzardous predicament." To avoid discovery, Troutman spent the next few weeks roaming about the state. Writing to Kentucky for assistance as well as looking for local allies, he began making arrangements for the Crosswhites' recapture. He soon found accomplices in Detroit.

Just after revelers rang in the New Year of 1847, Michigan's state legislature reconvened. Troutman elected to attend a session. He loitered about, eavesdropping on conversations until he overheard one gentleman's comment that he had lived near Lexington, Kentucky, for eighteen years. Troutman sought him out for a private audience. During that interview, he learned that the former Kentuckian, Samuel N. Gantt, was a lawyer and legislator from Paw Paw, Michigan, a town located about fifty miles west of Marshall. Troutman confided his real purpose for being in Michigan to Gantt, who at once offered to help. Troutman asked the legislator to find someone who could "hunt for my negroes" in Detroit and Canada. Gantt obliged. The very next day, he visited Troutman at his hotel, accompanied by a Detroit constable named Dewitt Clinton Whitman. After a brief consultation, the slavecatcher and the constable struck a deal—which included a $30 bonus for each reclaimed slave. In his journal, Troutman expressed his satisfaction that Whitman, "a man of great experience in such business, is now on the hunt." Even so, Troutman did not reveal his true name to the constable; only Gantt, a fellow Kentuckian, knew Francis Troutman's actual identity.

Not one to rely solely on Constable Whitman's endeavors, Troutman continued his own pursuit. He brushed up on U.S. law regarding reclaiming fugitive slaves and then ferried across the Detroit River searching in Canada for his grandfather's escaped slaves. Troutman took a wagon train inland to Chatham, where he hoped to locate other fugitives. He registered at the Freeman Hotel and then began his inquiries about town. Troutman made little progress over the next two days, although he struck up one conversation with a resident whom he believed to have escaped from one of his grandfather's neighbors. Troutman left Chatham, bundling up for the twenty-five-mile sleigh ride back over the frozen Canadian countryside to Windsor. From there he made the treacherous crossing over icy waters back to Detroit and disembarked safely at the Steamboat Hotel. He rendezvoused at the hotel with Constable Whitman, who had little useful intelligence to report.

Disappointed, Troutman decided to hole up and await the assistance he had requested from the South at the Eagle Hotel in Coldwater, Michigan, about thirty miles due south of Marshall. Days passed without any record in his journal; he didn't even note his twenty-seventh birthday. His last entry, on January 21, expressed his mounting frustration. "I am yet at Coldwater," he wrote, "waiting with great impatience for uncle. I feel so much." Several days later, Troutman returned to Marshall to rendezvous with his uncle, David Giltner. (He was the son of Troutman's grandfather Francis Giltner, but the two were only a year apart in age.) David Giltner arrived accompanied by two hired guns from Kentucky, William Franklin Ford and James S. Lee.

Before dawn on January 27, 1847, Troutman ordered a wagon from the livery stable, slipped a pistol into his pocket, and rode off with the other Kentucky slavecatchers to the Crosswhite home. Some reports state that Adam Crosswhite fired a warning shot to alert the neighbors. Others describe how the elderly Moses Patterson sounded the alarm. Known locally as Auction Bell, Patterson was employed by the town's auctioneers "to go through the streets on a horse, ringing a bell and shouting out the time and place of the sale." When he learned of the Kentuckians' attempted seizure, Auction Bell rode the streets of Marshall "ringing his bell and shouting that '*the slave catchers are at the Crosswhites.*'"[18] Thus the antislavery community of Marshall, both black and white, was alerted to the crisis.

The slavecatchers, meanwhile, had seized the Crosswhites and were preparing to transport them in the wagon to the magistrate's office. Troutman intended to prove his right to recapture the former slaves and then forcibly return them to his grandfather's Kentucky plantation. But just as Troutman himself had predicted in his journal a few weeks earlier, the Crosswhites' neighbors came to their defense—and they were ready for a fight. Planter Morse entered the house, "much excited, and pulling off his coat, declared he would go into the fight."[19] Another black man by the name of Calvin Hackett also challenged Troutman, who drew his pistol and warned him to stay back. Still others came forward armed with knives, clubs, and guns. The deputy sheriff barely maintained control.

Then Sarah Crosswhite refused to go with the Kentuckians. "I would die first," she maintained, rather than go to the courthouse or allow her children to be taken. The slavecatchers attempted to bargain with her, promising to leave her and Adam behind if they consented to let the children go. When she would not budge, Troutman raised his offer: he would leave the baby, who had been born free in Michigan, as well. Sarah would have none of it. Francis Giltner "had the best part of their life [in] service," she stated, and she intended to "keep her children to take care of her in her old days."[20]

By this point, many more townspeople had gathered outside the house. As the crowd forcefully confronted Troutman and his men, "the scene began to take on the appearance of a New

England town meeting." Charles T. Gorham, a leading white citizen of Marshall, engaged in a hot debate with Troutman as to whether he had a right to take the Crosswhites. Troutman asserted he did, and "harangued the jeering crowd on the sanctity of the fugitive slave law and the legality of Giltner's claim." The two men argued to an apparent impasse. Then Gorham turned to the crowd and shouted, "*Resolved:* that these Kentuckians shall not take the Crosswhite family by virtue of moral, physical, or legal force!"[21] The crowd roared in acclamation.

Troutman remained composed. He coolly removed from his pocket the journal in which he had been documenting his pursuit. Pencil in hand, he demanded the names of those preventing him from taking the Crosswhites. Three white men shouted out their identities: Gorham, John M. Easterly, and O. C. Comstock Jr. Troutman wrote them down. The crowd reacted with a threatening proposal: "*Resolved:* That these Kentuckians leave town in two hours . . . or they shall be tarred and feathered and rode on a rail!"[22]

At that moment, the deputy sheriff served Troutman two warrants for *his* arrest, one charging him with assault and battery for drawing a pistol on Hackett, and the other for trespassing against the Crosswhites. To Troutman's consternation, the sheriff refused to honor the slavecatchers' legal claims on the Crosswhite family, citing the danger presented by the agitated crowd. Troutman had no choice. He had to go before the judge in Marshall to answer charges. Troutman's trial lasted into the night and resumed the next day. The judge found him guilty of trespassing and fined him $100. Charles T. Gorham, who had so hotly debated Troutman before the crowd, appeared at the courthouse and informed Troutman, "Your negroes are gone."

The Crosswhites had escaped again. With the help of their abolitionist neighbors this time, they were well on their way to the Detroit riverfront and a short ferry ride to Canada. During the intervening night, several Marshall residents aided the Crosswhites' flight. Isaac Jacobs, a black hostler at a local hotel, hired a team of horses to draw the covered wagon that would carry the family to safety. Three white men—William W. Smith, Asa B. Cook, and George Ingersoll—drove the Crosswhites to an old stone mill at the southeast end of Marshall and hid them there in a garret until nightfall. Around nine o'clock in the evening, the family was conveyed thirty miles west to the next railroad depot in Jackson. There the fugitives hid and waited for the morning train.

The next morning, George Ingersoll boarded the train in Marshall. His mission was to learn whether any slavecatchers were on board—if not, Ingersoll would stand on the train's rear platform as it pulled in to Jackson to signal that the coast was clear. To the Crosswhites' relief, Ingersoll's tall figure appeared in the prearranged location. The Crosswhites boarded the train, still accompanied by Ingersoll, and insisted on paying the fare for themselves and their allies. In Detroit, they were met by George DeBaptiste, who had probably assisted them on their first flight from Kentucky and who was now was a leading agent of the Detroit's Underground Railroad network. DeBaptiste escorted the family from the railroad station to the ferry landing, ensuring the Crosswhites' safe passage to Canada.[23]

Back in Marshall, Troutman glared at Gorham when he delivered the news about the Crosswhites' escape, replying, "You have all got the advantage of me now, [but] I cannot tell how it will end." Incensed, the thwarted slavecatchers returned to Kentucky. Within two weeks, however, they had mobilized their Southern compatriots to action. On February 10, Troutman led like-minded Kentuckians to protest the "outrage recently perpetrated by an abolitionist mob in the State of Michigan" upon the slave owner Francis Giltner, "an aged and respectable citizen of this State." The group adopted resolutions and called upon Kentucky legislators to take immediate action against Michigan and for Congress to enact a stricter law "for the speedy rendition of fugitive slaves."[24] Thus the stage was set for another showdown, not only between Troutman and the abolitionists of Marshall but ultimately between the North and South over the future of the institution of slavery.

Kentucky's state legislature responded rapidly, condemning the Crosswhites' rescue. It issued a report on March 1 containing "resolutions denouncing the citizens of Marshall, asking redress from the legislature of Michigan and requiring the Senators and Representatives of Kentucky in Congress to secure the passage of a more stringent fugitive slave law."[25] Francis Troutman's signed affidavit decrying the insulting and violent mob actions in Marshall was attached. The governor of Kentucky approved the report and purportedly sent it to his Michigan counterpart. Bolstered by this Southern solidarity, Troutman returned north to seek his legal revenge.

He checked into Detroit's Steamboat Hotel on April 29. Troutman then received an invitation to visit the state's U.S. district attorney, John Norvell, and the two men met the next day. Troutman noted the reason for the summons in his journal: "Learned from him the Dunn case." Norvell, a native Kentuckian, apparently sympathized with Troutman's predicament, for he relayed the story that, just two weeks prior in Detroit, a Missouri slave owner named David Dunn was prevented from recapturing Robert Cromwell, a fugitive slave. Not only had Cromwell been rescued and ferried off to Canada, Dunn had been arrested on charges of kidnapping. The slave owner, unable to make bail, was still behind bars in the county jail. (The Dunn case is also discussed in chapter 8.)

Norvell may have offered his legal services to Francis Troutman at this meeting because the following day, Troutman hurried to Marshall and had warrants served against Charles T. Gorham and others for illegally aiding the Crosswhite family's escape. "I employed Pratt and Crary in Marshall" to conduct the lawsuit, Troutman noted, and "got Mr. Pratt to write to Mr. Norvell that we wished to retain him as counsel." Troutman's lawsuit notified the Marshall residents—those whose names he had carefully recorded in his journal during the standoff at the Crosswhites' home—that he intended to sue them for damages. He later would file the civil suit in the circuit court in Detroit, claiming $2,752 as the value sought for Adam and Sarah Crosswhite and their children.

As the Michigan lawyers initiated the legal proceedings, the Kentucky state legislature forwarded its report containing Troutman's affidavit and the demand for a stricter fugitive slave law to the U.S. Congress. Kentucky's newly elected senator Joseph R. Underwood took up the cause. On December 20, 1847, in one of his first speeches on the Senate floor, he urged the federal legislators to pass "such laws as will enable the citizens of slaveholding states to recover their slaves when escaping to non-slaveholding states." To illustrate his point, he referred to the case of a Missouri slave owner named Duncan. Although the senator misremembered Dunn's name, his circumstances were accurately recounted. He had been prevented from recapturing his fugitive slave in Detroit, the senator explained. The slave escaped to Canada, but the slave owner was arrested! He was held in the county jail for months on charges of kidnapping until he was eventually acquitted. Underwood credited Norvell with helping to procure the slave owner's release. The senator concluded by asking that Kentucky's report be referred to the Committee on the Judiciary "to see what could be done on the subject." The report was forwarded, as requested.[26]

While Congress deliberated, Troutman's lawsuit went to trial. *Giltner v. Gorham* opened on June 1, 1848, in the U.S. Circuit Court in Detroit. Troutman's grandfather, Francis Giltner, was represented by Abner Pratt from Marshall and John Norvell, the U.S. district attorney. Gorham and the other Marshall men were defended by several able Detroit lawyers, most affiliated with the abolitionist cause. Presiding over the trial was Justice John McLean, known for his antislavery inclinations—but, even more important, for his presidential aspirations.

The prosecution introduced its star witness, boasting that his character came "clothed and backed by recommendations from U.S. Senator Davis, Senator Jesse Bright, of Indiana, and Henry Clay, of Kentucky."[27] Thus vouched for by Congress's leading proslavery advocates and by Henry Clay, who verbally opposed slavery while owning up to sixty slaves himself, Troutman took the stand. He gave twenty-nine hours of testimony, providing exhaustive detail of the alleged crimes. Dozens of other witnesses were called, both for the prosecution and the defense, over the three-week course of the trial.

At the end, the judge directed the members of the jury to do their duty. "In no supposable case," he remonstrated, "has a juror a right to substitute his own views, and disregard established principles of law." He then highlighted the significance of the jury's decision: "This, gentlemen, is an important case. It involves great principles, on which in a great degree depend the harmony of the States, and the prosperity of our common country." The stakes were high in part, he intimated, because the "case has acquired great notoriety by the action of the Kentucky Legislature, and of the senate of the United States."[28] Justice McLean clearly was aware of the political pressures surrounding Troutman's affidavit and the Kentucky legislature's call for a stricter fugitive slave law.

Nevertheless, after deliberating all night, the jurors returned to court the next morning to report that they could not agree. One person had defied the judge's instruction. The jury foreman had chosen to honor his conscience over the law, over national unity, and over political considerations. He voted to acquit and would not change his mind. The Marshall men, for the moment, were victorious.

But Troutman and his lawyers did not relent, and the case therefore was retried during the next court session in November 1848. This time Judge Ross Wilkins presided. Wilkins's service in Michigan's courts extended back fifteen years to the state's territorial days. He was well known in Detroit as a "warm friend to the colored people" on account of his consistent opposition to slavery and, more unusual among whites, for his public support of black suffrage and equality. Wilkins's political views intersected intimately with his religious convictions. A devout Methodist, he practiced his faith by raising funds to build the new African Methodist Episcopal Church in Detroit and by teaching Sunday School to its congregation.[29]

Judge Wilkins, however, was also a passionate advocate of the law. When on the bench, he adhered strictly to precedent, but he could be very creative about its application. To avoid a clash between his abolitionist beliefs and his reverence for the law, he had made himself unavailable to rule in the Cromwell-Dunn case by hiding in the courthouse.[30] For the second trial of *Giltner v. Gorham*, Judge Wilkins would have to balance these potentially contrary commitments. His task became even more difficult when the defense lawyers called a surprise witness.

The trial was being observed and reported on by Henry Bibb, himself a fugitive from Kentucky, who had become a popular lecturer on the antislavery circuit. Bibb at this time was about to publish his autobiography concerning his "life and adventures" as an "American slave."[31] Bibb's narrative opened with a public endorsement from his Sunday School mentor—the Honorable Ross Wilkins. In early December, Bibb wrote the following report, which appeared in Frederick Douglass's abolitionist paper *The North Star:* "This day, I saw a person, who is claimed as a runaway slave, called upon the stand as a witness in this case against his master, in the U.S. District Court of Michigan. An hour before the witness appeared, the Courthouse was literally crammed with people of color, who knew the fugitive was to appear on the stand against the Kentucky slaveholders. When the name of *Adam Crossw[hite]* was called, the court-room door was opened, and he walked into the witness stand to be sworn."[32]

At great risk to his liberty and safety, Adam Crosswhite had returned to Detroit from his refuge in Canada to testify on behalf of his rescuers. He and his family had been residing in the town of Chatham, under the protection of the British monarchy, in the province then known as Canada West. Their security was so well established that Adam and Sarah Crosswhite had provided depositions for the case to the Canadian authorities without any legal jeopardy to themselves.[33] Yet it was a different matter when, just a few weeks later, Adam Crosswhite ventured to appear in person before those who would reenslave him in order to take the stand. Henry Bibb recorded the scene that ensued upon Crosswhite's arrival in the courtroom:

> The slaveholders looked with astonishment, for this was unexpected to them. Just at this moment much excitement prevailed among the witness' friends, supposing that the slaveholders might attempt to pounce upon their prey; but not a dog of them offered to lift his tongue or hand to interfere, except the plaintiff's counsel, who himself must be identified with the African race, judging from his external appearance. He objected to Mr. Crossw[hite's] testimony, on the ground that Kentucky laws do not allow a slave to testify against his master. But it was shown by the defendant's counsel, that the slave laws of Kentucky do not extend over Michigan. So Mr. Crossw[hite] proceeded. He stated that he was born in Kentucky, the slave of his own father, and was sold by him. He came to this State in 1843, and resided in the village of Marshall; moved thence to Canada in 1847, where he now resides. The plaintiff's counsel asked witness no questions at all. At the time [the] witness left the stand, a rush was made to the door with Mr. Crossw[hite], by the colored citizens, who soon conveyed him across the Detroit river into Canada.[34]

Judge Wilkins allowed Crosswhite to depart safely, if only through noninterference. Crosswhite's very presence at the trial and his confidence in the courtroom demonstrate the existence of a transnational network of people of color on both sides of the Detroit River, willing co-conspirators with easy access to transportation across the border.

Shortly after Crosswhite's surprise appearance, the second trial came to a close. Henry Bibb summarized its significance for the transnational black community: "We are not lawing against Kentucky alone," he wrote, "but against the combined powers of slavery." Should the jury decide in favor of the plaintiffs, he believed that the repercussions could be dire. The

"Detroit river is the line between us and Canada," Bibb asserted, "and it is also the great depot of the Northern underground railroad; and if the slaveholders are encouraged with a verdict in this case, they will doubtless make this point their slave-hunting ground."[35] (In chapter 7, Afua Cooper analyzes Bibb's transnational antislavery campaign and the newspaper he created in Canada, which galvanized abolitionists in the region.)

The jury was out for only two hours. It decided in Francis Giltner's favor and awarded the slave owner $1,926 in damages; his grandson, Francis Troutman, had exacted his legal revenge. Although the Crosswhites were safe in Canada and Judge Wilkins had dutifully upheld the law, Charles T. Gorham and the other defendants from Marshall were now faced with financial disaster. Luckily, prominent Detroit politicians rallied to their cause and raised the necessary funds.

But, as Henry Bibb had feared, there were significant repercussions. The day after the verdict was announced, George DeBaptiste, Underground Railroad agent and ally of the Crosswhite family, chaired a "public meeting of the colored citizens of Detroit." Gathered at city hall, they denounced "the unrighteous decision rendered in the late suit brought by Giltner, Troutman, and Co. of Kentucky" and lamented the deprivation "of all protection and security in our lives, our liberties and in the pursuit of happiness." But they vowed not to succumb to injustice. Several resolutions were passed asserting their determination to fight back. "Resolved," the community maintained, "that we hold our liberty dearer than we do our lives, and we will organize and prepare ourselves with the determination, live or die, sink or swim, we will never be taken back into slavery." Additional resolutions were adopted to remain united with those still enslaved, to abide by the laws of nonslaveholding states, and to petition Congress for a repeal of the 1793 Fugitive Slave Act. Henry Bibb was among those assigned to draft the petition. He addressed the meeting, warning the people there "to prepare themselves with the means of self-defense." He added, "You must protect yourselves by whatever means you possess."[36]

As Bibb had predicted, in the wake of the decision, slavecatchers raided communities across the state in pursuit of "human chattel." Southern slave owners soon received significant assistance in their efforts at recapture from the federal government. The Judiciary Committee, to which Troutman's affidavit and the Kentucky legislature's demands had been forwarded, had released a favorable report earlier that year. Within weeks of the *Giltner v. Gorham* decision, the committee's chairman, Senator A. P. Butler from South Carolina, invoked the case on the Senate floor. "I happen to be somewhat connected with this transaction in Michigan," he asserted, and "having viewed the subject carefully," he found that Southern rights "have been trampled underfoot." He then pressured his colleagues to support a new bill "making it the duty of all State officers to give aid in the arrest and delivery of fugitive slaves under a penalty."[37] It took Congress another year and a half to conclude its deliberations, but the result was the passage of a new, stricter Fugitive Slave Law as part of the 1850 Compromise Bill.

Francis Troutman subsequently made a name for himself prosecuting Michigan abolitionists who offered aid to fugitive slaves. His "considerable reputation as a lawyer" was attributed to his being "successful over the strong defense of many able lawyers arrayed against him" in fugitive slave cases.[38] The next time he was in the Detroit courtroom, pressing charges against another group of Michigan men from Cass County for interfering with slavecatchers, Troutman was able to employ the new law he and his fellow Kentuckians had demanded, the 1850 Fugitive Slave Act.[39]

The Crosswhite family remained in Canada until after the Civil War. With emancipation codified into the Constitution in 1865, Adam and Sarah Crosswhite returned from Chatham to Marshall, Michigan, to live out the remainder of their years. Their son, Ben Crosswhite, lived and worked in Battle Creek, not far from the frontier village of Marshall. He was occasionally asked about the dramatic events in which his family had been involved. In response to the question "What did you have to do with the [Civil] War," he would reply, "I was the cause of the war."[40] In this short rejoinder, Benjamin Franklin Crosswhite asserted that while Francis Troutman may have garnered a temporary victory, the Crosswhite family ultimately prevailed, for the outcome of the Civil War was a triumph for all enslaved people in the United States. They had won what was dearest to them—their freedom.

NOTES

1. John McLean, Reports of Cases Argued and Decided in the Circuit Court of the United States for the Seventh Circuit, vol. 4 (Cincinnati: E. Morgan & Co., 1848), 402; Circuit Court of the United States: State of Michigan, *Giltner v. Gorham et al*, in *The Western Law Journal*, vol. 6. (Cincinnati: Desilver and Burr, 1848/1849), 49.
2. Several standard sources inform the overall story of the Crosswhites' escape from slavery and the ensuing pursuit and prosecution by Francis Troutman. These include: *Giltner v. Gorham, et al*, 4 McLean 402 (1848); John C. Patterson, "Marshall Men and Marshall Measures in State and National History," *Michigan Pioneer Collections* 38 (1912): 244–78; John C. Sherwood, "One Flame in the Inferno: The Legend of Marshall's Crosswhite Affair," *Michigan History* 73 (March 1989): 40–47; and John H. Yzenbaard, "The Crosswhite Case," *Michigan History* 53 (Summer 1969): 131–43.
3. Adam Crosswhite has been identified repeatedly as the half brother of Frances Crosswhite, whose husband was Ned Stone, a slave dealer, who sold Adam for $200. Frances Crosswhite did inherit Adam from her father, Isaac, in 1811. But she never married. The Crosswhite relations do intersect with the Powers and Stone families—Frances's sister married Henry Stone, the brother of the slave trader Edward Stone. As Ned is a nickname for Edward, it is possible that the "Ned Stone" of lore is actually Edward Stone. He died in 1826, murdered in a slave mutiny on the riverboat he was taking to the Southern slave market. See *Western Citizen* (Paris, KY), September 30, 1826, October 11, 1826; *Western Luminary* (Lexington, KY), September 30, 1826. The fullest account of the mutiny is in J. Winston Coleman, *Slavery Times in Kentucky* (1940; repr., Chapel Hill: University of North Carolina Press, 1970), 173–77, with original records in John Winston Coleman Jr. collection on slavery in Kentucky, 1780–1940, Record 46M53, box 1, folder 8, University of Kentucky Special Collections, Lexington. See also Diane Perrine Coons, "Adam Crosswhite," in *The Encyclopedia of Northern Kentucky*, ed. Paul A. Tenkotte and James C. Claypool (Lexington: University of Kentucky Press, 2009), 251–52; Marion B. Lucas, *A History of Blacks in Kentucky: From Slavery to Segregation, 1760–1891* (Louisville: Kentucky Historical Society, 1992), 98–99; The Crosswhite-Powers-Stone genealogy at Kathryn Bassett and Marilyn Roberts' website The Roberts-Hubbard Ancestry, ourwebsite.org/marilyn/gendata-o/p198.htm (accessed June 1, 2012); Isaac Crosswhite's 1811 will, transcribed at Neil Allen Bristow's genealogical website

Stone and Related Southern Families (Rowe, Thomas, Bruce, Caviness, Farley), www.rootsweb.ancestry.com (accessed June 1, 2012); "Grandfather's Records" (n.d.), 4, Giltner Genealogy, Surname Files, Filson Historical Society, Louisville, KY.

4. For a short history of the Giltner family, originally from Bourbon County, Kentucky, see "John M. Giltner," in W. H. Perrin, J. H. Battle and G. C. Kniffin, *Kentucky: A History of the State*, 7th ed. (Louisville, KY: F. A. Battey, 1887), 961; and Coons, "Adam Crosswhite," 251–52.

5. Francis Giltner, Last Will and Testament, April 1, 1843, Kentucky, Probate Records, 1792–1977, Carroll County Will Records Index, 1849–1860, 2:7–8, familysearch.org (accessed June 21, 2012). Giltner divided his 1,600-acre farm at Hunter's Bottom between two sons, bequeathing each 820 acres.

6. Giltner issued similar directives to keep other children under five with their enslaved parents, including Henry and his wife, Ianna, as well as the children born to Nancy and Amanda. The will was witnessed by T. S. Butler, Benjamin Jackman, and James W. English, all of Carroll County, Kentucky. Butler testified in court that all three witnesses signed the document in Giltner's presence. Francis Giltner, Last Will and Testament.

7. The date of the escape is recorded in Case No. 1900, *Francis Giltner v Charles Gorham et al*, September 30, 1848, transcribed at www.michigan.gov/dnr/0,4570,7-153-54463_18670_44390-160663—,00.html (accessed June 7, 2012).

8. Troutman noted the number of runaways he was pursuing on December 11, 1846. Francis Troutman, Travel Diary, 1846–1847, Dicken-Troutman-Balke Family Papers, 1850–1899, 1816–1945, 1M56M316, Special Collections, University of Kentucky, Lexington.

9. U.S. Census, 1840, Carroll County, Kentucky.

10. The three people listed as slaves in the estate inventory were one woman and child and a boy named George. Francis Giltner Probate, February 2, 1849, Carroll County Will Records Index, 22–28.

11. B. G. Troutman, comp., "History of the Troutman Family," February 21, 1889, 7, Troutman Family Files, Thomas Clark Library, Kentucky History Center, Frankfort.

12. "Our New Voters," *Detroit Daily Post*, February 7, 1870, newspaper clipping in William R. Stocking Papers, box 3, Underground Railroad folder, Burton Historical Collection, Detroit Public Library.

13. Tibbets wrote his account when he was seventy years old, nearly forty-five years after the events occurred. In his recollection, the escape of ten slaves from Hunter's Bottom took place in August 1845. This may be accurate, but the details also align closely with circumstances of 1843: the Crosswhites' escape, Tibbets's arrival in Indiana, and the number of runaways pursued by Francis Troutman. The Crosswhites' escape may have been Tibbets's first Underground Railroad "adventure." John Henry Tibbets, "Reminiscences of Slavery Times," ca. 1888, Tibbets Family Anti-Slavery History website, fordwebtech.com/tibbets-history/JohnTibbetsLetter.php (accessed June 1, 2012).

14. "Local Man Tells Slave Stories: Ben Crosswhite, Porter at the Post Tavern, in Reminiscence," *Battle Creek (MI) Enquirer*, July 14, 1901.

15. "Supplement: Underground Railroad," *Detroit Post*, May 15, 1870, newspaper clipping in William R. Stocking Papers, box 3, Underground Railroad folder.

16. Pierson, *Zachariah Chandler*, 75–76. See also Francis Troutman's Travel Diary. For a full account of the escape and subsequent events from the slaveholders' viewpoint see Case No. 1900, *Francis Giltner v Charles Gorham et al.*
17. The description of Troutman's pursuit of the Crosswhite family is derived from Francis Troutman's Travel Diary. See also Debian Marty, "In the Words of a Slavecatcher," *Michigan History* 92 (January–February 2008): 20–29.
18. William W. Hobart, "The Crosswhite Case," *Michigan Pioneer and Historical Collections* 38 (1912), 257.
19. *Giltner v. Gorham, et al*, 4 McLean 402 (1848), 52.
20. Sarah Crosswhite Deposition (edited transcription), Case No. 1900, *Francis Giltner v Charles Gorham et al.*
21. Pierson, *Zachariah Chandler*, 77.
22. Pierson, *Zachariah Chandler*, 77.
23. David Gardner Chardavoyne, *The United States District Court for the Eastern District of Michigan: People, Law, and Politics* (Detroit: Wayne State University Press, 2012), 43–44; "Death of George DeBaptiste," *Detroit Daily Post*, February 23, 1875.
24. "Astounding News!" *Signal of Liberty* (Ann Arbor, MI), April 24, 1847, signalofliberty.aadl.org (accessed June 7, 2012).
25. "Report and Resolutions of the Committee on Federal Relations, No. 14," in *Acts of the General Assembly of the Commonwealth of Kentucky* (Frankfort: A. G. Hodges, 1847), 385–88.
26. *Senate Journal*, 30th Cong., 1st sess., December 20, 1847, 59.
27. M.R.D. [Martin Robinson Delaney], letter to the editor, *The North Star*, August 4, 1848.
28. *Giltner v. Gorham et al*, 4 McLean 402 (1848), 10–11.
29. Arthur R. Kooker, "The Antislavery Movement in Michigan, 1798–1840: A Study in Humanitarianism on the American Frontier" (PhD diss., University of Michigan, 1941), 107–14; "Colored People in Detroit," *Liberator*, March 6, 1846, 39.
30. Frank B. Woodford, *Father Abraham's Children: Michigan Episodes in the Civil War* (Detroit: Wayne State University Press, 1961), 12–13.
31. Henry Bibb, *Narrative of the Life and Adventures of Henry Bibb, an American Slave, Written by Himself* (New York: privately published, 1849).
32. H. Bibb, letter to the editor, *The North Star*, December 15, 1848.
33. Sarah Crosswhite Deposition; Adam Crosswhite Deposition (edited transcription), Case No. 1900, *Francis Giltner v Charles Gorham et al.*
34. Bibb, letter to the editor.
35. Bibb, letter to the editor.
36. "Public Meeting of the Colored Citizens of Detroit," *The North Star*, December 29, 1848.
37. *Senate Journal*, 30th Cong., 2nd sess., January 22, 1849, 317.
38. "Col. Frank Troutman," in *Biographical Encyclopedia of Kentucky* (Chicago: J. M. Armstrong, 1878), 184.
39. Debian Marty, "Michigan's Underground Railroad and the 1850 Fugitive Slave Act," *Grand Valley Review* 35 (Spring/Summer 2010): 111–21.
40. Washington Gardner, *History of Calhoun County, Michigan* (Chicago: Lewis, 1913), 245.

TWELVE

THE McCOYS

Charting Freedom from Both Sides of the River

CAROL E. MULL

In the late 1850s, George and Milly McCoy gathered up their five young children and worldly goods and bade farewell to their home in Canada West.[1] Against a tide of African American emigration to Canada West (later Ontario) at the time, the McCoys crossed the Detroit River in the opposite direction and journeyed to southeast Michigan. Their reverse course was not an aberration, however. Indeed, recent scholarship describes a complex circulation of people back and forth across the Detroit River frontier in the antebellum period.[2]

When George McCoy met Milly Gaines in the 1830s, of the 14 million people in the United States, over 2 million were enslaved on the basis of their African ancestry. Though George had been legally manumitted by his owner (who was also his white father), only a risky escape would allow him to live in freedom with his still-bonded bride. George guided Milly across the Ohio River out of Kentucky. Underground Railroad helpers in Ohio concealed the couple until the threat of capture by slave hunters eased.[3] The McCoys then traveled to the British Canadian provinces, where they were legally protected from removal by force.[4]

By the early 1850s, George and Milly were farming their own land, sharing a one-story log house in Colchester Township, Essex County, in Canada West with many children and a boarder. The initial fear of slavecatchers stampeding north to seize runaways after the passage of the 1850 Fugitive Slave Act calmed as Southern bounty hunters returned home empty-handed from Canada and Michigan. For many African Americans, Canada was a biblical Canaan "where colored men are free," as one freedom song asserted. Some condemned the slaveholding nation of their birth and fully embraced Canadian freedom; others felt like foreigners and missed family members left behind. After a decade in Ontario, the McCoys pulled

Elijah, son of George and Milly McCoy, began his working career as a railway fireman. This Ypsilanti, Michigan, marker recognizes the site of McCoy's workshop, where he developed and patented railcar lubricating devices used internationally as well as other products. (Courtesy of photographer Dwight Burdette)

up stakes in Canada to return to their homeland. Back on American soil, Milly resumed her legal status as a "runaway slave," and her Canadian-born children also risked being claimed as the property of Milly's Kentucky master.[5]

The McCoys' river crossing brought them first into Detroit, a burgeoning metropolis in the 1850s. Boasting paved roads, multistoried buildings, and gas lighting, the city was the economic engine of the state of Michigan and the Detroit River communities. For decades, the international border was no real barrier to men and women of all ethnic backgrounds who crossed the water for travel and trade. Abolitionist Benjamin Drew's interviews of former slaves in Canada West conducted in 1855 included one with William Lyons, who worked for two years in Amherstburg, Canada, while his family lived in Detroit.[6]

Refugee-settlement organizers such as formerly enslaved Kentuckian Henry Bibb, who published the *Voice of the Fugitive* in Sandwich, Canada West, reinforced mythologized views of Canada as the Promised Land to encourage Canadian colonization after 1850. The free black immigrant Mary Ann Shadd, newspaper publisher, abolitionist, and antislavery lecturer, described Canada's "first quality" soil and climate, though she noted that many available tracts remained timbered. Seasons of poor weather lowered many crop yields, while the overproduction of tobacco in Canada West reduced profitability. George McCoy was a skilled tobacconist who had learned cigar making at his father's shop in Kentucky. As new immigrant Irish workers took jobs and farm profits decreased, the McCoys and other African Americans experienced increasing financial hardship, and the economic Panic of 1857 diminished everyone's prospects.[7]

For some, the greatest barrier to the dream of Canadian equality involved access to public education. The Separate School Act of 1850, intended to give Roman Catholics the opportunity to maintain separate schools for their children and to provide any group of five or more African Canadian families to request a separate school should they so desire, was subverted by white parents in some districts to exclude black children from the Common Schools.[8] Claims of persistent prejudice on both sides of the Detroit River were described in the *Voice of the Fugitive*.[9] The sting of watching one's Canadian-born children shut out of local schools must have been unbearable for literate, landowning taxpayers like George McCoy. One of the McCoys' children, Elijah, would become a brilliant engineer and inventor.[10]

Well known, too, was George McCoy's dissatisfaction with the few miscreants in the fugitive slave population, who lived off donations after gaining their freedom. Many Blacks in Canada were unhappy about being misrepresented by men like Dr. Mumford, a self-appointed fund-raiser for the "destitute" fugitives. McCoy signed a letter to the *Voice of the Fugitive* in March 1852 stating that Mumford's society hurt the reputation of other missionaries and inflamed racial prejudice.[11]

In spite of these several drawbacks, however, newspaper publishers Henry Bibb and later Mary Ann Shadd Cary urged every American of African descent to join them in Canada and take advantage of the British government's protection and legal sanctuary from slavery. Famed orator Frederick Douglass, formerly enslaved himself, disagreed. Douglass believed that black people needed to challenge slavery and racial discrimination from within their native country.[12] In a letter to author Harriet Beecher Stowe, Douglass explained why black Americans should not embrace colonization: "The love of country, the dread of isolation, the lack of adventurous spirit, and the thought of seeming to desert their 'brethren in bonds' are a powerful check upon all schemes of colonization, which look to the removal of the colored people, without the slaves."[13]

Some self-emancipated Blacks, including Henry Bibb, returned to slaveholding states to rescue family members. Dr. Samuel Gridley Howe, one of the instigators of the Boston raid to rescue Anthony Burns, interviewed scores of refugees in the Canadian missions on behalf of the newly minted Freedmen's Bureau just before the end of the Civil War. Howe discovered that by the 1850s, as many as five hundred people a year "went secretly back to their old homes and brought away their wives and children at much peril and cost."[14] Josiah Henson was among the earliest known to have made the journey back. Born enslaved, Henson had escaped to Canada with his wife and four children in 1830. Yet he returned on at least two occasions to rescue enslaved people from Kentucky, bringing them safely across into Canada West.[15] These Detroit River crossings to America included return passage to Canada, unlike the McCoy family's permanent return to the United States.

When the McCoys moved from Canada West in the 1850s, they settled in Ypsilanti, Michigan, thirty-five miles southwest of Detroit. Ypsilanti, in Washtenaw County, had a stable black community. Interstate freedom trails from the south and west intersected in Washtenaw County before taking an eastern track to the Detroit River.[16] Whatever obstacles they faced in Canada, some enticement must have existed across the river that led the McCoys to return to the United States, exposing the mother and children to the possibility of being captured and taken into lifetime bondage.[17]

The McCoys' move to Michigan in the 1850s was not as rare as some accounts would lead one to believe. Protected by antislavery activists, free and self-emancipated Blacks began resettling in Michigan soon after the initial panic over the Fugitive Slave Act eased. The 1850 federal census, taken before passage of the Act, showed that of the nearly four hundred thousand people in Michigan, about twenty-six hundred were people of color. By 1854, an additional eight hundred Blacks were living in Michigan.[18] As the census did not record one's recent place of residence, settlement patterns are inconclusive. However, Michigan did offer distance from slaveholding states, protectors in known places, statewide Underground Railroad networks, and employment opportunities in cities, towns, and on Michigan's myriad waterways.

Throughout the antebellum period, abolitionists reported significant numbers of individuals and groups arriving in the British provinces, and historians have generally assumed the majority were freedom-seekers. A recent study of the 1861 Canada West census shows that a significant proportion of African American immigrants to Canada West were actually free people rather than escaped slaves.[19] Enumeration studies reveal an increase in the antebellum Canadian black population and a decrease in the same population in Michigan. (It should be remembered that all census-based studies are hampered by dependence on the veracity of people who might be inclined to provide false information if they or others might be endangered by the truth.)

It appears that any initial decline in the black population on the Michigan side of the Detroit River following the 1850 passage of the Fugitive Slave Act was soon reversed. The 1854 state census included no individualized data and provides no clue as to whether a black person was manumitted, free, or self-emancipated. But an analysis of state census data indicates that, in 1854, the black populace of Michigan clustered in cities with a well-established black presence and active Underground Railroad operations. In 1854, 923 "colored people" lived and worked in the western counties of Berrien and Cass, and nearly one-third of the state's Blacks resided in Detroit and its Wayne County environs.[20]

This population increase and migratory trend added to the work of the Michigan Underground Railroad during the final antebellum decade. Threats and occasional incursions required vigilance and quick movement to places of safety. Self-emancipated Blacks returning to Michigan from Canada West lived without legal freedom and were dependent on the protection of their black and white neighbors.

George and Milly McCoy joined an active Underground Railroad network when they moved into a cabin on the Starkweather farm in Ypsilanti, Michigan. (Courtesy of Carol E. Mull)

William Lambert, prominent black leader in Detroit's antislavery movement and Underground Railroad network, noted that the local organization of African Americans placed white and black men in strategic places where they could readily assist freedom-seekers. After the 1850 Fugitive Slave Act was passed, the work of the Underground Railroad ran more efficiently. Years later, former Underground Railroad organizers reported decreasing numbers of passengers on Michigan's southwestern networks after 1850. At the same time, agents in southeast Michigan networks recorded more freedom-seekers requiring food, shelter, and safe passage to Canada.[21]

Besides the McCoys, self-emancipators circling back to Michigan included William Walker, who left Missouri in 1859, walked through Illinois, and traveled by train across Michigan to Detroit and then to Canada. In spite of his fear of reenslavement, Walker eventually returned to Detroit, and after two years purchased ten acres of land. Another refugee, John White, recrossed the Detroit River with his wife and Canadian-born son in the 1850s to settle in the Detroit area. White narrowly escaped abduction near Adrian, Michigan, thanks to the help of famed Underground Railroad rescuer Laura Haviland and others. Like many of the refugees she helped, Haviland moved to the Refugee Home Society's Canadian settlement in 1852. After her teaching term ended, she returned to her farm and work aiding freedom-seekers in Lenawee County, Michigan, demonstrating the truly transnational nature of the fugitive slave assistance network in the Detroit River borderland.[22] (Chapter 9 of this volume examines Laura Haviland's transnational activism in the US and Canada.)

Another example of reverse migration is the route of William Paris who, though freeborn, was kidnapped three times. After living in Chatham, Canada West, Paris moved his family north of Detroit to St. Clair, where a job and active abolitionists protected them. Aaron and Ellen Wilson went back to Farmington, Michigan, the town where they had been helped while making their initial escape to Canada. The McAlisters, who claimed Kent County, Canada West, as their birthplace, moved to Michigan in 1859 with their first three children (born in Indiana) and their Canadian-born baby.[23]

Such accounts may give the impression that the McCoys' relocation to Michigan entailed no serious risk, but that was certainly not the case. The woman who had once held Milly McCoy in enslavement said in later years that her husband would have gone to get Milly had he known where she was in Michigan.[24]

By the time the McCoys established residence in Ypsilanti, the Michigan Underground Railroad had evolved from an irregular arrangement to a smoothly functioning operation with dozens of active black and white workers across the settled portion of southern Michigan. Despite attempts by slavecatchers to capture freedom-seekers in Cass, Berrien, Calhoun, Washtenaw, and Wayne counties, Underground Railroad workers prevented any person of color from being taken back into slavery.[25]

The McCoys settled northwest of the city of Ypsilanti on the farm of Mary Ann and John Starkweather, where laborers harvested bountiful orchards. Though Mary Ann Starkweather contributed money to the Michigan Anti-Slavery Society in the 1850s, there is no further documentation of any antislavery activities on the part of the family.[26]

The McCoys, however, were engaged in Underground Railroad activities from the time the family moved to Ypsilanti, as daughter Anna remembered. They lived in a cabin behind the Starkweathers' frame Greek Revival–style house, which stood above the banks of the Huron River. Anna McCoy, fourth of the McCoys' twelve children, in later years recalled early childhood memories of her parents' Underground Railroad involvement: once she discovered a strange black family in the barn, but she was not allowed to play with the family's three girls. The following day, they were gone.[27]

On the Michigan side of the Detroit River, George McCoy resumed the work of growing, buying, and selling tobacco and making cigars. His business required transporting produce to markets in Wyandotte and Detroit. McCoy's tobacco wagon had a concealed compartment where human cargo was stowed and forwarded on the network to freedom. One day, after Anna went to the post office to retrieve a letter to her father from a black church deacon and Underground Railroad operator at Cincinnati named John Hatfield, Mrs. McCoy spent the day cooking hams, baking bread, and making coffee. The children were put to bed early so they would not witness their father's nighttime departure to secret points on the Detroit River.[28]

Wyandotte was an advantageous place for clandestine river crossings. Ten miles south of Detroit, Wyandotte remained a frontier district except for the estate of Major John Biddle, which was located on an immense property with two miles of Detroit River shoreline. Biddle's son, William, recalled that in the 1840s the family was dependent "on runaway slaves for farm laborers, sometimes having as many as fifteen on the place, the proximity to Canada offering them an inducement."²⁹ In temperate weather, these laborers might swim or raft to the Canadian shore; in winter, the Detroit River was a frozen road to Canadian freedom.

Anna McCoy recalled that her father left his passengers in Wyandotte with a black man named Bush, who stowed the freedom-seekers on the *Pearl*.³⁰ One of five hundred vessels registered in the Detroit River district, the *Pearl* plied the waters of the river throughout the 1850s. Built and owned by Eber and Samuel Ward, the *Pearl* steamed daily from Detroit to Sandusky, Ohio, also an active Underground Railroad port. Captain Eber Ward, a wealthy industrialist from St. Clair, Michigan, was known to have paid the purchase price of one of his boat's chefs after the man had escaped to Canada just ahead of a pursuing slaveholder.³¹

The McCoys had moved to an area rife with Underground Railroad activity. To the west, the farm of Ezra Lay stretched along the Chicago Turnpike, the most traveled road in Michigan, connecting Chicago and Detroit. Within a couple of miles of the Starkweathers' farm, Jotham Goodell and at least two other white men provided shelter and transportation to freedom-seekers. Delivered in darkness to his barn, people escaping slavery were taken by Goodell to Inkster or Detroit. William Davis was one of the freedom-seekers who passed through Goodell's Underground Railroad station and then settled in Canada. Davis, like George McCoy, recrossed the Detroit River before 1860. He lived in his own house near the Goodells with two daughters, Mary Jane and Sarah Jane. If they participated in any Underground Railroad activity it has not been recorded.

When Jotham Goodell stopped at Inkster, he left his cargo at Rough's Hotel, whose proprietor took over the task of getting freedom-seekers to the Detroit River in the area of Gibraltar, a small village south of Trenton. Gibraltar sat opposite Grosse Ile, largest of the fourteen islands in the Detroit River. Summer retreats for wealthy Detroiters dotted the island's shore. Between Grosse Ile and the village of Amherstburg on the Canadian side, Bois Blanc Island held remnants of a British military outpost. The old military blockhouses reportedly housed freedom-seekers en route to mainland Canada West.³²

Another family that moved to Ypsilanti in the same decade as the McCoys was also engaged in helping freedom-seekers. Thomas, William, and Helen McAndrew had emigrated from Scotland to Baltimore, Maryland, but were pressured to leave town because they were teaching African Americans to read. William McAndrew Jr. recalled that his father became familiar with Underground Railroad operations on the Detroit riverfront when he sent case goods on riverboats from Rawsonville to the Detroit markets. Thomas McAndrew hid refugees in barns before driving them in wagons at night from Ypsilanti to the "outskirts of Trenton, where rowboats ferried them to Canada."³³ William's wife, Helen, offered medical care to both the black and white Ypsilanti community for decades and was very likely known to the McCoys.

Increased antislavery sympathies, especially after the publication of *Uncle Tom's Cabin*, allowed more open travel to freedom. Famous Quaker abolitionist Levi Coffin said that by the eve of the Civil War, the Underground Railroad was "above-board."³⁴ Yet this statement belies the continued threat of capture. Dr. Nathan Thomas, Quaker, physician, and Underground Railroad agent in Kalamazoo County, Michigan, noted in his diary that from a group of seven men escaping Kentucky in 1856, two were taken before reaching the Ohio River and one was grabbed in Indiana.³⁵

When Anna's brother George was of an age to assist, the McCoys employed two wagons and two sets of horses to aid fugitives. In Anna's words, "When the case was urgent the fast horses were always used." After the wagon ride, freedom-seekers left Michigan's shore for Canada during the open season by every sort of vessel—ferry, steam, or sail—night and day. William Wells Brown, who emancipated himself from slavery in Kentucky in 1834, later wrote of his work secreting passengers on the Lake Erie boats on which he was employed for several years.[36] In freedom, Brown learned to read and ran a barbershop in Monroe, Michigan. A popular lecturer in both the British Isles and the United States, he wrote history, travelogues, the novel *Clotel*, and became the first African American playwright.

Other Great Lakes seamen volunteered their services to assist freedom-seekers. Captains Thomas Jefferson Titus and John N. Stewart carried fugitives to Lake Erie ports between Buffalo and Detroit. In 1855, Stewart was arrested in Detroit after stopping the *Bay City* at the Canadian port of Amherstburg to allow a formerly enslaved man to disembark. The slave owner who witnessed the illegal act decided against prosecution.[37]

The population of Michigan nearly doubled in the decade after the passage of the 1850 Fugitive Slave Law, reaching almost 750,000 in 1860, including 6,799 Blacks. Any previous decrease in Michigan's black populace was now offset by new migrations of free and self-emancipated African Americans. In the prelude to the Civil War, events such as John Brown's raid and Abraham Lincoln's election heightened anxiety in the South, and mounting fear of political attacks on slavery's stronghold led to reprisals against free Blacks there. Missouri and Florida threatened legally free Blacks with enslavement, and lawmakers in other slaveholding states debated the expulsion or enslavement of free Blacks, causing a tide of free men and women to flee to northern states, Canada, and overseas.[38]

The Detroit River frontier remained a safe haven for African Americans seeking freedom. Untethered from slavery's chains, self-emancipated men and women on both shores of the river embraced the freedom to earn a living, build a home, and cherish a family. Some, like the McCoys, jeopardized that freedom for the sake of others unjustly bound as property. As Frederick Douglass stated on his return from England to the United States: "I will go back, for the sake of my brethren. I go to suffer with them; to toil with them; to endure insult with them; to undergo outrage with them; to lift up my voice in their behalf; to speak and write in their vindication; and struggle in their ranks for the emancipation which shall yet be achieved."[39]

The porous international border along the Detroit River linked together the economies and political institutions of the United States and British Canada through the antebellum period. Looking through the prism of freedom as it existed in mid-nineteenth-century Canada West, the McCoys examined the principles of equality and liberty in their native country and chose to return to their American homeland. The McCoys, like thousands of other free, freed, and self-emancipated Blacks who crossed the waterway, determined for themselves in which nation they would strive—and perhaps flourish.

NOTES

1. While most sources state that the McCoys traveled back to the United States "about three years" after Elijah McCoy's birth, the Census for Canada West, Essex County, 1851, shows Elijah, aged eight, living at Colchester with his family. The 1860 Census for the United

States, Washtenaw County, shows his youngest brother, Thomas, as being born ten years earlier in Canada West.

2. R. Alan Douglas, *Uppermost Canada: The Western District and the Detroit Frontier, 1800–1850* (Detroit: Wayne State University Press, 2002); Karolyn Smardz Frost, Bryan Walls, Hilary Bates Neary, and Frederick H. Armstrong, eds., *Ontario's African-Canadian Heritage: Collected Writings by Fred Landon, 1918–1967* (Toronto: Dundurn, 2009); Karolyn Smardz Frost, *I've Got a Home in Glory Land: A Lost Tale of the Underground Railroad* (New York: Farrar, Straus & Giroux, 2007; Toronto: Thomas Allen, 2007).

3. Mary A. Goddard, "The Underground Railroad" (paper presented to the Ypsilanti chapter of the Daughters of the American Revolution, April 1913), Mary Goddard Papers, Fletcher White Archives, Normal College (Eastern Michigan University), Ypsilanti Historical Society. Around the turn of the twentieth century, Professor Goddard interviewed Anna McCoy, the fourth of George and Milly's daughters, as well as several other women who had escaped slavery.

4. Slavery was legally abolished in Canada when the British Imperial Act emancipating slaves throughout the British Empire went into effect on August 1st, 1834. It is commonly known as the Slavery Abolition Act, 1833 (3 and 4 Will. IV, c. 73).

5. Census of 1851, Canada West, Essex County, Enumeration District 1, Township 9, collectionscanada.gc.ca/databases/census-1851/ (accessed November 16, 2009). The McCoy children born in the United States were subject to the legal principle of *partus sequitur ventrem*, under which the child inherited the status or condition of the mother. Milly McCoy's Canadian-born children, though native-born British subjects, would have found scant resources had they been abducted while living on U.S. soil. For more information, see Paul Finkelman, Introduction to *Slavery & the Law*, ed. Paul Finkelman (Lanham, MD: Rowman & Littlefield, 2002), 3–26; and James Oliver Horton and Lois E. Horton's essay in the same book, "A Federal Assault: African-Americans and the Impact of the Fugitive Slave Law of 1850," 143–60.

6. Benjamin Drew, *A North-Side View of Slavery. The Refugee; or, The Narratives of Fugitive Slaves in Canada. Related by Themselves, with an Account of the History and Condition of the Colored Population of Upper Canada* (Boston: John P. Jewett, 1856), 358–60.

7. Mary A. Shadd, *A Plea for Emigration; or, Notes of Canada West in Its Moral, Social, and Political Aspect: With Suggestions respecting Mexico, West Indies, and Vancouver's Island, for the Information of Colored Emigrants* (Detroit: privately published, 1852); Robin W. Winks, *The Blacks in Canada: A History*, 2nd ed. (Montreal: McGill-Queen's University Press, 1997), 183 (glut of the tobacco market), 484 (Irish immigrants).

8. "An Act for the Better Establishment and Maintenance of Public Schools in Upper Canada," July 24, 1850, 13 & 14 Victoria, c. 48, s. 19, in *Provincial Statues of Canada* (Toronto: S. Derbyshire & G. Desbarats, Law Printer to the Queen's Most Excellent Majesty, 1850), 1255–78.

9. *Voice of the Fugitive*, November 8, 1852; see also Winks, *The Blacks in Canada*, 368–70.

10. Winks, *The Blacks in Canada*, 362–89.

11. *Voice of the Fugitive*, March 11, 1852.

12. *Frederick Douglass' Paper*, October 2, 1851.

13. Frederick Douglass, *Life and Times of Frederick Douglass: His Early Life as a Slave, His Escape from Bondage, and His Complete History to the Present Time* (New York: Collier Books, 1962), 293.
14. Samuel Gridley Howe, *The Refugees from Slavery in Canada West: Report to the Freedmen's Inquiry Commission* (Boston: Wright & Potter, 1864), 11.
15. Josiah Henson, *The Life of Josiah Henson, Formerly a Slave, Now an Inhabitant of Canada, as Narrated by Himself* (Boston: Arthur D. Phelps, 1849), 58.
16. Wilbur H. Siebert, "The Underground Railroad in Michigan," *Detroit Historical Monthly*, March 1923, 12–13.
17. In slavery "the condition of the child followed the condition of the mother," meaning that since Milly was still enslaved under U.S. law, her children were also legally slaves and could be claimed as such by her owner if the McCoys were caught on the American side of the border. See Thomas D. Morris, *Southern Slavery and the Law, 1619–1860* (Chapel Hill: University of North Carolina, 1996), 43–49.
18. United States, *Federal Censuses of Michigan*, 1850, 1860, and 1870; *Census and Statistics of the State of Michigan* (Lansing: G. W. Peck, 1854). The census "race" categories for ethnicity were "white," "black," and "mulatto." During the antebellum period, all people, including Native Americans, were listed in these categories based on the discretion of the census taker, according to U.S. Census Bureau, "Measuring America: The Decennial Census from 1790 to 2000," 2002, www.census.gov/prod/2002pubs/pol02-ma.pdf (accessed November 10, 2009).
19. Michael Wayne, "The Black Population of Canada West on the Eve of the American Civil War: A Reassessment Based on the Manuscript Census of 1861," *Social History/Histoire Sociale*, 28, no. 56 (1995): 465–85; see also the excellent discussion in Winks, *The Blacks in Canada*, 484–96, esp. 492.
20. *Census and Statistics of the State of Michigan.*
21. "FREEDOM'S RAILWAY: Reminiscences of the Brave Old Days of the Famous Underground Line Historic Scenes Recalled Detroit the Center of Operations That Freed Thousands of Slaves," *Detroit Tribune*, January 17, 1886; and Nathan M. Thomas Papers, Bentley Historical Library, Ann Arbor.
22. William Walker and Thomas S. Gaines, *Buried Alive (Behind Prison Walls) for a Quarter of a Century: Life of William Walker* (Saginaw, MI: Friedman & Hynan, 1892), docsouth.unc.edu/neh/gaines/ (accessed November 5, 2008); Laura S. Haviland, *A Woman's Life-Work: Labors and Experiences of Laura S. Haviland* (Cincinnati: Walden & Stowe, 1882), chap. 8.
23. Helen W. Farrand, "Memorial Report—St. Clair County," in *Historical Collections: Collections and Researches made by the Michigan Pioneer and Historical Society* 22 (Lansing: Robert Smith, 1894), 170–72; U.S. Census for 1860, Wayne County, Michigan, series M653, roll 556, 831, s.v. "Aaron Wilson." See also Carol E. Mull, *The Underground Railroad in Michigan* (Jefferson, NC: McFarland, 2010), 76, 141–43, 168.
24. Goddard, "The Underground Railroad," 3. The McCoys' daughter, Anna McCoy, when interviewed, reported that in 1872, Milly visited Kentucky and spoke with her former owner's wife, Mrs. Gaines. The federal Fugitive Slave Law of 1793 dictated that those arrested as escaped slaves would be sent back to bondage if not able to provide proof of free status.

(This was the law under which the Blackburns were arrested; see chapter 2 of this volume for complete details.)

25. Samuel J. May, *The Fugitive Slave Law and Its Victims* (New York: American Anti-Slavery Society, 1861), 120. No formerly enslaved people are known to have been returned to slavery from Michigan, though May reported that several young boys were kidnapped in Detroit in 1859.
26. Harriet deGarmo Fuller Papers, 1852–1857, William L. Clements Library, University of Michigan, Ann Arbor.
27. Goddard, "The Underground Railroad," 3.
28. Goddard, "The Underground Railroad," 3. John Hatfield was the deacon at the Zion Baptist Church, a known Underground Railroad station in Cincinnati. See Levi Coffin, *Reminiscences of Levi Coffin* (Cincinnati: Robert Clark, 1880), 306–7.
29. E. P. Christian, "Historical Associations Connected with Wyandotte and Vicinity," in *Michigan Pioneer and Historical Collections* 13 (Lansing, MI: Darius D. Thorp, 1889), 320.
30. William Lee Jenks, *St. Clair County, Michigan: Its History and Its People; A Narrative Account of Its Historical Progress and Its Principal Interests*, vol. 2 (Chicago: Lewis, 1912), 821; Goddard, "The Underground Railroad," 5.
31. Christian, "Historical Associations," 320; Jenks, *St. Clair County*, 821.
32. Robert E. Roberts, *Sketches of the City of Detroit, State of Michigan, Past and Present, 1855* (Detroit: R. F. Johnstone), 44.
33. William McAndrew, "The McAndrews." First published by the Ypsilanti Business and Professional Women's Club in 1931, edited reprint in *Ypsilanti Gleanings* (Summer 2004), Ypsilanti Historical Society, 12.
34. Coffin, *Reminiscences of Levi Coffin*, 596.
35. Arthur R. Kooker Papers, 1850–1882, Bentley Historical Library.
36. William Wells Brown, *Narrative of William W. Brown, a Fugitive Slave, Written by Himself* (Boston: Anti-Slavery Office, 1847), 107–8.
37. J. B. Mansfield, ed., *History of the Great Lakes* (Chicago: J. H. Beers, 1899), 21:787. Thomas Jefferson Titus was drowned in 1855 while in command of the *Montezuma*. See the *Jamestown Journal* of Chautauque County, New York, August 17, 1855.
38. "Annual Report of the American Anti-Slavery Society: By the Executive Committee, for the Year Ending May 1, 1860," 211–13, Samuel J. May Anti-Slavery Collection, Cornell University Library, Rare and Manuscript Collections, Ithaca, NY; and Ira Berlin, *Slaves Without Masters: The Free Negro in the Antebellum South* (New York: Pantheon Books, 1974), 366–80.
39. Frederick Douglass, "Farewell Speech of Mr. Frederick Douglass Previous to Embarking on Board the *Cambria* Upon His Return to America, Delivered at the Valedictory Soiree Given to Him at the London Tavern on March 30, 1847, London, 1847," www.lib.rochester.edu/index (accessed March 20, 2012).

The fateful meeting between John Brown, Frederick Douglass, and members of the Detroit Underground Railroad network took place at this Detroit site in 1859. (Courtesy of photographer Elizabeth Clark)

V

THE TRUMPET SOUNDS

By the 1850s the Underground Railroad network in the Detroit River borderland ferried freedom-seekers to Canada West with confident efficiency. The timing could not have been better. The new 1850 Fugitive Slave Law jeopardized the precarious freedom of self-emancipated Blacks and forced them, along with large numbers of free African Americans, to abandon their homes in Michigan and cross the border into Canada.

The burgeoning and interconnected African American and African Canadian communities in the Detroit River borderland were fertile ground for new forms of abolitionist resistance, with black newspapers, multiple churches and schools, and enterprising black residents. The region attracted the ire of U.S. congressmen representing Southern interests, who protested that hundreds of thousands of dollars in human "property" was being protected in the North and in British Canada.*

The borderland also attracted the great Frederick Douglass, who spoke at Detroit's city hall and at Second Baptist Church. On May 12, 1859, the indomitable white abolitionist John Brown conferred with his old colleague Douglass and the black leaders of Detroit's Underground Railroad before making another of his multiple crossings into Canada. In the Detroit meeting, hoping to rally more support, Brown revealed his final plans for the raid at Harper's Ferry, Virginia.

---

* A story in the *Western Citizen* on September 23, 1842, reported, "[T]here are over $400,000 worth of southern slaves in a town near Malden, Canada." South Carolina's Senator Butler estimated his state's annual losses at $200,000. Senator Pratt of Maryland declared his state lost not less than $80,000 annually; Senator Mason claimed annual losses of $100,000 for the state of Virginia. Senator Thomas Clingman of North Carolina based his estimate of $15,000,000 on the combined worth of 30,000 fugitives reported to be living in the North. Senator Claiborne projected that the South had been "plundered of 100,000 slaves over forty years worth $30,000,000." *Congressional Globe*, 31st Cong., 1st sess. (1850).

PART V

Well acquainted with Detroit since childhood, Brown hoped that the men he needed for his campaign to overthrow slavery could be recruited in the region. Decades of community building and Underground Railroad organizing had equipped Blacks in the Detroit River borderland to take an active part in the coming national struggle over slavery. When John Brown called them to action, men and women in the Detroit River region stood ready for righteous battle against the slave power. Three years later, when President Lincoln needed them to help turn the tide for the Union in the Civil War, again they rallied to the call—from both sides of the river.

THIRTEEN

THE USEFUL FRONTIER

John Brown's Detroit River Preface to the Harper's Ferry Raid

LOUIS A. DECARO JR.

THE FRONTIER LESSONS OF 1812

About two years before he was hanged in Virginia for attempting to launch a widespread Southern liberation movement in the United States, the abolitionist John Brown narrated the story of his early life in a fascinating autobiographical letter. In particular, Brown told of witnessing the brutal beating of an enslaved black youth, the episode that inspired him to become "a most *determined Abolitionist*" and declare "Eternal war with Slavery." The incident took place in the Old Northwest during the War of 1812, about twenty-five years before Michigan attained statehood. Like most autobiography, the work displays a measure of stylization. In Brown's case, he wrote nothing about his strident abolitionist upbringing, and instead focused exclusively on the beating incident as the genesis of his antislavery zeal.[1] According to his narrative, he witnessed the abusive scene when he was about twelve years old and working with his father, Owen Brown, who supplied beef to the U.S. Army from the family's home in Hudson, Ohio. There is no reason to doubt the historicity of this dramatic moment in John Brown's youth.[2] He not only recalled staying on the "Northwest frontier" in the camp of a number of companies from Virginia during the War of 1812, but on another occasion specifically mentioned being near Fort Detroit when it was surrendered to the British (August 16, 1812).[3] According to Brown's own account, the incident of the abused black youth took place at the time of the controversial "capitulation" of Fort Detroit to British forces.[4]

Brown's youthful experience on the frontier contributed three elements that would ultimately overlap in his mature years as an antislavery freedom fighter: an indefatigably personal and existential hatred of slavery; a passionate, albeit purposeful, interest in strategic military history; and an awareness of the necessity of negotiating territorial boundaries and borderlands, both political and social. Brown later said that he had "studied considerable" about the surrender of Fort Detroit, the incident having initiated his bookish interest in military campaigns, ranging from those of antiquity to contemporary wars and resistance movements. Yet his passionate interest in military strategy always focused on the antislavery cause.[5] Lastly, young John had become fond of the "Indians" and even learned "a trifle of their talk."[6] In fact, his father, Owen Brown, was an exceptionally strong advocate for indigenous people on the Ohio frontier, and was outspoken against them being driven from the area.[7] This was another important lesson for John Brown. Not only did he later emulate his father by standing up for Native Americans,[8] he came to understand how "territorial zones" stretch away from borders, and that they required him (like his father before him) to negotiate behaviors and meanings associated with his identity as an American citizen in the context of America's expanding western frontier.[9]

NEGOTIATING BORDERLANDS

The story of John Brown's life in the first six decades of the nineteenth century runs parallel with the story of chattel slavery's tragic rise to power in the United States, the evolution of antislavery strategies, and the violent and deeply traumatic conditions that eventually drove Blacks to seek freedom in Canada. Brown's story is also replete with frontier and border crossings, geographical as well as social and political. Beginning in his twenties and continuing well into his forties, Brown's life in Ohio and Pennsylvania entailed clearing land and building domestic and business structures, but also learning the challenges and dynamics of the Underground Railroad and the social boundaries of race and slavery as defined by white supremacy.[10]

As Afua Cooper has observed, not only did fugitives from Southern slavery settle in the North, but their unfortunate Canadian counterparts, fleeing in the opposite direction, crossed the "fluid frontier" to freedom in the United States.[11] But then Attorney General John Beverley Robinson ruled in 1819 that fugitives reaching British colonial soil would not be returned to the United States, and with British emancipation, passed in 1833 and effective in 1834, the Underground Railroad increasingly found its terminus in Canada.[12] These developments are part of the backdrop of John Brown's first efforts to support oppressed black people. His earliest recorded reference to antislavery activism, a letter written from northwestern Pennsylvania in 1834, makes no mention of either the Underground Railroad or Canada. At this phase, his stated plans were to obtain a black child—possibly even purchase one from a slave master—and also start a school for Blacks in Randolph Township.[13] There was nothing particularly novel about his second plan. Historian Anne Stewart points out that nearby Meadville, Pennsylvania, opened an "African" school in response to the state's passage of the Common School Education Act of 1834.[14]

Brown's 1834 letter reveals that although he was opposed to slavery, he was at that time still a Christian conservative who believed that educational efforts would lead to the slaveholding states being "constitutionally driven" toward emancipation.[15] His move from advocating reform to more assertive and sometimes daring exploits on the Underground Railroad in the 1840s and 1850s reveals the change that occurred in his thinking about the antislavery struggle.[16] Yet this pattern of thought was interwoven with the evolution of the Underground Railroad itself, including recognition of the growing importance of what lay across the "fluid frontier." This is evident in two letters written in the 1840s, when the second Fugitive Slave Law was yet on the horizon. In March 1846, Brown wrote to his son, John Jr., expressing an interest in learning more about Canada, and again in May 1847, to inquire whether a certain family friend "would feel disposed to go to Canada in order to commence an Affrican high school provided he can be properly supported."[17] His interest reflected the degree to which Canada had become the telos of the Underground Railroad. Thousands of discouraged African Americans had moved to Canada by the 1850s, some of them forming notable settlements and others taking up residence in leading towns like Chatham, London, Toronto, and St. Catharines.[18] The fact that schools existed or were needed in these black settlements probably inspired Brown to consider that his old dream of starting an "Affrican high school" might also be realized across the fluid frontier. These letters thus mark the point at which Brown apparently had begun to recognize the usefulness of Canada for his own antislavery ambitions.

John Brown's black high school never materialized, and his Canadian vision receded for the time being. However, there is good evidence that his Underground Railroad work was increasingly vigorous well into the 1850s.[19] In subsequent years, he was involved with a free black settlement in New York's Adirondacks, not far from the Canadian border, where he moved his family in the spring of 1849. With the passage of the Fugitive Slave Law of 1850, he formed the United States League of Gileadites, a militant black self-defense organization in Springfield, Massachusetts.[20] In a real sense, life in the border area of northern New York also enabled him to negotiate a more radical social and political stance toward government and society.[21]

THE USEFUL FRONTIER

Although Brown was probably aware of the growth of the black population in Canada after the Fugitive Slave Law was passed, it is questionable whether he knew the extent of its energetic, industrious, and even prosperous expatriate communities. It is quite possible that his renewed interest in traversing the fluid frontier along the Detroit River was sparked by information and recommendations made to him by free black leaders in the North, especially in Philadelphia, where he sought enlistees for his Virginia campaign in 1858–59.[22] Perhaps his interest was prompted by the fact that African Canadian men had been enlisted for the support of Great Britain in its recent war with Russia on the Crimean Peninsula. This meant that black men had been trained and armed in militias, some of which were also placed in readiness in the event of an invasion by the United States.[23]

Brown thus made something of a "reconnaissance"[24] visit to Canada (specifically the section closest to the U.S. border, then known as Canada West) from April 6 to April 24, 1858, traveling on the Great Western Railway across the province from St. Catharines on the Niagara Peninsula (near western New York state) to Ingersoll, and then to Chatham before crossing back into the United States at Detroit. Guided by the Reverend Jermain Loguen into St. Catharines on April 6, Brown wrote excitedly to his wife but urged her to tell no one of his activities in Canada.[25] On

April 7, he met Harriet Tubman, whose enthusiasm and promise of support thrilled him, as did the "the most abundant material, and of the right quality"—that is, the prospects of good black enlistees. According to Tubman biographer Kate Clifford Larson, despite her ultimate failure to appear at Harper's Ferry in 1859, Harriet Tubman actively recruited for Brown, beginning with seven enlistees on their first meeting.[26] The following day, Brown left a draft (which he referred to as a "skeleton") of a document with black abolitionist and printer William H. Day in St. Catharines, the nature of which he intended to reveal to enlistees and supporters from the black community.[27] About one week later, he wrote to John Jr. that he had been traveling around St. Catharines "with tolerable success"; he seems also to have anticipated receiving financial support from Canada's busy and often prosperous black expatriates.[28] Before leaving the St. Catharines area, Brown toured Thorold, Humberstone, Merritsville, and Louth townships, also stopping in Port Robinson. Throughout his time in the vicinity of St. Catharines, Brown frequently wrote letters, not only to his wife back in North Elba but also to his sons and notable abolitionist supporters, undoubtedly keeping them abreast of his progress among African Canadian residents.[29]

Traveling on the Great Western railroad, Brown made other stops in Hamilton, Brantford, Woodstock, and Ingersoll in his quest to contact black expatriates.[30] At Ingersoll, a community with about five hundred African Canadian residents, he was hoping to meet again with Harriet Tubman, thinking they had both come in on the same train. But Tubman had taken another train, stopping in Toronto en route to Ingersoll.[31] During his brief stay in Ingersoll, Brown was busy seeking new recruits; according to a wire from William H. Day back in St. Catharines (perhaps based on information provided by Tubman), there were at least five potential enlistees waiting to see him in Ingersoll. Drawing on his notoriety as a frontier freedom fighter, he spoke there on the evening of April 15 at the Wesleyan Methodist Church. According to a local newspaper, "Captain John 'Osawatomie' Brown of Kansas" was to speak "on the Horrors Perpetrated on the Free-Staters by The Missouri Border Ruffians & Pro-Slavers from the South" and the "Truth of Actual Conditions in the Kansas Territory Today."[32] He also made contact with Thomas Brown of Ingersoll (possibly a distant relative), who operated a tannery and employed black workers. Brown remained in Ingersoll until about April 19, when he wrote to William H. Day in St. Catharines, probably inquiring about the whereabouts of Tubman and the progress of the printing of his secret document.[33]

Finally, Brown appeared in Chatham, in the southwestern section of Canada West, around April 20. It appears that the first place that he went was the home of Martin R. Delany, who had officially taken up residence there on February 22, 1856.[34] Delany had published the antislavery newspaper *The Mystery* in Pittsburgh and was also a colleague of Frederick Douglass for a time, but he had grown distant from the integrationist views of the latter. Brown probably knew of Delany through Douglass, but he was also aware of Delany's publishing as well as his book, *The Condition, Elevation, Emigration, and Destiny of the Colored People of the United States, Politically Considered* (1852).[35] After Brown had twice stopped at the Delany residence, a cottage owned by the Anglican church, only to find him not at home, the two men finally met on the street, Brown appearing "like one of the old prophets" with his gray hair, long beard, and "sad but placid countenance." The two withdrew to private quarters, and Brown poured out his intentions to Delany. "It is men I want, and not money," Brown declared, speaking more from his heart than from his wallet. "Money I can get plentiful enough, but no men." Delany "found no fault" with his plans and promised to help

In 1858, John Brown traveled to Canada West to recruit men for his campaign to overthrow slavery. He convened his constitutional convention in Chatham. (Courtesy of the Toronto Public Library)

convene what was likely the first and only political convocation of its kind in North America, a joint black and white congress with the agenda of overthrowing chattel slavery.[36]

Brown remained in Chatham, undoubtedly meeting with other local leaders in the black community, until April 24, when he made a hasty return to the United States. Traveling by train from Detroit to Chicago, Brown reached Springdale, Iowa, on April 26, where his men had been sequestered. Brown quickly gathered them together, and then he and his men boarded a train to Chicago, then to Detroit, crossed the river back into Canada West, and finally arrived in Chatham on the evening of April 29. From the moment of arrival, Brown set about preparing for what he called "a most quiet convention," copying and mailing handwritten invitations to "radical" black and white abolitionists in the United States and Canada, including Frederick Douglass and Gerrit Smith.[37] One of these letters of invitation, addressed to the New England abolitionist Charles L. Remond, explains that Chatham had been chosen because there "already were so many collected here." Due to lack of finances, the invitation explained, Remond and the other invitees were asked to incur the expense of their own travel.[38]

As it turned out, no delegates from the United States attended except two Detroiters, the Reverend William C. Monroe and William Lambert, and the thirteen men who had accompanied Brown to Chatham. None of Brown's close supporters came, including Frederick Douglass, who may have demurred because of his differences with Martin Delany and because he had already gotten an earful of Brown's ideas during Brown's recent stay in Rochester. All in all, there were forty-six delegates: thirty-four Blacks (including one of Brown's men) and twelve whites, including Brown's son Owen. Even William H. Day in St. Catharines did not attend, pleading that the demands of Brown's printing work were too great.[39]

The Chatham convention was convened on May 8 and 10, 1858 (May 9 fell on a Sunday, so there was no assembly), in morning and afternoon sessions and in different locations in town for the sake of expediency.[40] Since the conventioneers were forced to disguise their purpose as a Masonic meeting, no women were permitted to join the proceedings.[41] In the May 8 meetings, Brown presented the secret document that he had left with printer Day in St. Catharines. *The Provisional Constitution and Ordinances for the People of the United States* was written by Brown during a three-week period in January–February 1858, when he was sequestered at the home of Frederick Douglass in Rochester, New York. Although a few associates had already seen it, Brown's intention was to unveil it at his constitutional convention. The document, which was published after its ratification at the Chatham convention, consisted of a preamble and forty-eight articles, comprising about fifteen pages when it was finally printed.[42]

Brown's *Constitution* strikes many readers, including some of his admirers, as a peculiar if not problematic work. Nor is there agreement as to its essential nature. Some have suggested it was a "communal, utopian manifesto," but W.E.B. DuBois probably summarized it best as "an instrument designed for the government of a band of isolated people fighting for liberty."[43] Certainly, Brown's document, with its plan for an expansive governmental structure, outlining elective offices as well as regulations for war and community, is ambitious and impractical. Its author assumes a dynamic movement, one necessitating a range of legal and civil apparatuses for the establishment of a liberated community—a guerilla-styled campaign with a strongly religious code, not unlike an armed Puritan movement with policies for everything from worship services to treatment of prisoners, and from education to nonconcealment of weapons. As an heir of the Reformation and the American Revolution, John Brown was oriented toward providing some sort of written platform representing the legal and moral integrity of his cause. In locales from Springfield to Kansas, he had authored a number of such documents, or had otherwise endeavored to explain or vindicate his antislavery efforts in written form.[44] That he was modeling his effort upon the eighteenth-century U.S. independence movement is obvious. In 1858–59, Brown and his men, possibly with the assistance of Boston abolitionist Theodore Parker, composed the *Declaration of Liberty* as a complement to the *Provisional Constitution*.[45]

John Brown's plans for invading the South were hashed over, modified, and challenged for many years before the outcome at Harper's Ferry. One cannot be certain as to all of the plan's details; nor can one ascertain the exact moment when Brown set his sights on Harper's Ferry, or what his full intentions were in regard to the federal armory and arsenal. Certainly his core strategy was shared with a number of associates over many years, although most scholars date the revelation of his plan to around 1847 when, according to Frederick Douglass, Brown unfolded his ideas in private discussion.[46] Douglass, who discussed this many years afterward, described it as a mountain-based campaign, a guerilla operation that would not require large numbers of men since they would be difficult to dislodge operating along "the far-reaching Alleghenies, which stretch away from the borders of New York, into the Southern States." Clearly Brown had come to discern the physical and strategic challenges that such borders would pose to standard militia seeking to root out his men or to prevent them from making forays onto plantations and farms deep in the South. In this way, Douglass recalled, Brown intended to "run off the slaves in large numbers, retain the brave and strong ones in the mountains, and send the weak and timid to the north," so that "his operations would be enlarged with increasing numbers, and would not be confined to one locality." Martin Delany recalled that Brown proposed the construction of hardy fortifications by small groups of men, a detail that resembles an aspect of the mountain-based plan described by Douglass. Furthermore, James M. Jones, another Chatham conventioneer, later recalled that Brown had clearly stated his intention "to fortify some places in the mountains and call the slaves to his colors."[47] John Brown's mountain-based plan, although aggressive in movement, was largely premised on clandestine strategy and the use of force only in defense, not insurrectionary violence in which slaves typically sought to strike down their masters. Rather, Brown's own testimony and interviews suggest he had something of an armed intervention and rescue in mind, something that would disturb the normal operations of slavery and provide a South-wide escape and defense for enslaved people.[48] His *Provisional Constitution* was not merely a political and moral justification of the effort, nor was it intended simply to shield himself from the charge that he had designed the overthrow of the U.S. government. It was a document designed to provide a rule of law: a provisional and formative means of organizing liberated people into a purposeful, self-governing, and morally stable community until such time as they were accepted into the United States as free people and citizens.

TOWARD HARPER'S FERRY

Two changes ultimately undermined the support that Brown hoped to receive through his Canadian connection. The first came with the disturbing news that Hugh Forbes, whom Brown had hired as a military trainer, had betrayed his plans. Forbes, an English abolitionist and adventurer, was a whining opportunist whose unsatisfied attempts to exploit Brown and his supporters culminated with him exposing the raid. Although he did little actual damage, his actions drove Brown's influential supporters to press a postponement upon him. This obligatory hiatus, lasting from May 1858 until the summer of 1859, greatly undermined the impact of Brown's labors in Canada. Many of the men from Canada West who had stood with him either changed their minds or had become involved in other efforts and commitments by 1859.[49] The second change was the "final version of his grand plan," which entailed his decision to seize the federal armory and arsenal at Harper's Ferry, something he did not reveal to his own men until they were ensconced in their Maryland hideout prior to the raid. "Only late in this evolution [of his plan]," writes Robert McGlone, "did Harper's Ferry itself become its focal point."[50]

In his famous autobiography, Frederick Douglass writes that he learned about this change only three weeks before the Harper's Ferry raid, when he met secretly with Brown in a quarry near Chambersburg, Pennsylvania. According to Douglass, when he heard of Brown's intention of attacking the federal facility at Harper's Ferry, he warned that he would be caught in "a perfect steel-trap."[51] In fact, Douglass seems to have conflated incidents that took place in 1859. His meeting with Brown in Chambersburg had actually taken place in August, about two months before the raid.[52] Not only did Douglass know about Brown's intention of striking the federal armory at Harper's Ferry sooner than he acknowledged in his stylized autobiography, there is good reason to believe that he was aware of it much earlier in 1859, and that he first opposed the idea in Detroit at a meeting attended by black leaders from both sides of the Detroit River.

Brown had arrived in Detroit on March 12, 1859, completing a long, difficult trek that had begun that previous December in Missouri, after he and his men had liberated eleven Blacks from slavery at gunpoint. Over hundreds of perilous, frigid miles through Kansas, Nebraska, and Iowa, and then by railway to Chicago and up to Detroit, Brown finally escorted the fugitives aboard the vessel that carried them across the Detroit River to Windsor, in what is now Ontario.[53] At the conclusion of this daring rescue, Brown met a cadre of black leaders from Detroit and Chatham gathered at the home of William Webb on Congress Street, a meeting that was centered upon the presence of Frederick Douglass, who had spoken that very day at Detroit's city hall. Some of the notable guests were Detroiters William Lambert and the Reverend William C. Monroe (two alumni of the Chatham convention in 1858), George DeBaptiste, another prominent businessman and Underground Railroad operator, and the clergyman John Sella Martin.[54]

Although the meeting must have begun as a happy reunion between John Brown and Frederick Douglass, sparks started to fly when Brown unfolded his maturing plan. According to a reminiscence of Martin, Douglass "dissected the whole scheme, and point by point showed its utter impracticability." Since another account states that Douglass said he had been favorable to Brown's long-term plan when it had centered on making raids on plantations and gathering up enslaved people,[55] the most reasonable conclusion to draw is that Brown had introduced the idea of attacking Harper's Ferry and Douglass had objected immediately. Brown—who was as ready to belittle a black man as a white man in order to prove his point—openly challenged Douglass's courage.[56] It was not unusual for Brown to be imperious and push his way if necessary. He had made a similar remark to silence Martin Delany's criticisms during the Chatham convention, but the latter was a little older and perhaps a bit less sensitive than Douglass, and he knew how to put Brown in his place without returning the blow.[57] Douglass, as famous as he was brilliant, was not accustomed to being so embarrassed, not even by the prickly, hardheaded, and overbearing John Brown. Denying his cowardice, Douglass insisted that he would not give material aid to a plan he did not approve of. The militant Detroiter George DeBaptiste also differed with Brown, although he wanted to take more violent measures, presumably to bomb white churches across the South on a given Sunday. Evidently, Brown was unfazed by DeBaptiste's dissent, not only because he disdained his strategy but because it was Douglass's opinion that mattered to him. Seeing that Brown and Douglass were at loggerheads, the English poet Richard Realf, one of Brown's associates, mercifully intervened. According to Martin, Realf set aside Douglass's objections "with marvelously loving logic and tender pathos," turning the opinion of the gathering back in Brown's favor. Brown apparently mended fences with Douglass afterward, but although he continued to appeal to him to throw in the full weight of his support, Douglass never did.[58]

Although this dramatic and influential meeting has long been lost in the shadows of conventional history, it probably had a more direct impact upon the Harper's Ferry raid than did Brown's extensive work in Canada West the previous year. It is likely that the conclusions reached at the 1859 Detroit meeting were more specific to Chatham's leaders; it may be that the discussion in which Osborne Perry Anderson was allegedly chosen to join Brown in Virginia took place either at this meeting or as a direct result of it.[59] This point underscores what Afua Cooper has observed concerning the reality of the Detroit River as a fluid frontier—not an absolute boundary—in the lives of black activists in the 1850s.[60] Not only did John Brown cross back and forth between the United States and adjacent Canada West in pursuit of support for his efforts, he also interacted with a network of strident black abolitionists based in Detroit and Canada West, neither group being restricted to one or the other side of the Detroit River. Indeed, it is interesting that John Sella Martin, who provided one important account of the 1859 Detroit meeting, wrongly remembered it as the Chatham convention of 1858, which neither he nor Douglass attended.

The bold assault on Harper's Ferry finally took place on October 16, 1859, and despite Virginia's triumphant propaganda concerning enslaved Blacks' indifference to the event, Chatham's Osborne Perry Anderson would live to write (with editorial assistance from Mary Ann Shadd Cary) a firsthand account that vindicated John Brown's vision and the courage of his enslaved brethren. As Anderson recalled, Brown delayed too long, far beyond the time in which he and his raiders might have escaped into the mountains with the first wave of enslaved recruits. Cut off from escape and besieged by bloodthirsty militia, Brown and some of his raiders finally retreated to the Harper's Ferry fire engine house, where they made their famous last stand before an assault by U.S. Marines. Anderson and a few others escaped, but most of Brown's men perished at Harper's Ferry, and the rest—along with their bold chieftain—went to the gallows.

From a great distance, John Brown's comrades in Detroit and Canada learned that his grand spectacle had unfolded tragically. However, with the coming of the Civil War, they

Pennsylvania born and educated, Osborne Perry Anderson was a recent immigrant to Canada West when he joined John Brown's forces for the raid at Harper's Ferry. One of the few survivors of the raid, Anderson fled back to Canada. With Mary Ann Shadd Cary, he wrote *A Voice from Harper's Ferry*, the only eyewitness account of the raid. (Courtesy of kansasmemory.org, Kansas Historical Society, Topeka)

would soon witness John Brown's vision revivified in a myriad black men, many of them once more crossing the fluid frontier, armed and marching relentlessly into the South.

NOTES

1. His autobiographical sketch is found under John Brown to Henry L. Stearns, July 15–August 8, 1857, a photographic image of which is contained in the John Brown–Clarence Gee Collection, Hudson Library and Historical Society, Hudson, OH (hereinafter Gee Collection). See my exact transcription in Louis A. DeCaro Jr., *John Brown: The Cost of Freedom* (New York: International, 2007), 114–20. Also see my discussion about this autobiography in *"Fire from the Midst of You": A Religious Life of John Brown* (New York: New York University Press, 2002), 25, 51–56.
2. Most biographers and students of Brown find his tale of the youth both believable and probable, and it is unfortunate that Brown's most recent biographer, Robert McGlone, approaches it with unsubstantiated cynicism, saying that the story "does not ring true." Robert E. McGlone, *John Brown's War against Slavery* (Cambridge: Cambridge University Press, 2009), 53.
3. "Visit of the Military to Old Brown," *New York Herald*, October 31, 1859, 1; [Stanley J. Smith], "What Tom Nelson Told Me" (transcription of personal reminiscence), in John Brown Chatham Convention File, Chatham-Kent Black Historical Society, Chatham, ON. Canadian historian Smith lived next door to Nelson, who was residing in Chatham in 1858 and lived out his later years there after fighting in the Civil War. See [Stanley J. Smith], "Memo for B[oyd] B. S[tutler], ca. 1956, John Brown / Boyd B. Stutler Collection, RP02-0185C, West Virginia Division of Culture and History, Charleston, WV.
4. At the time, Colonel Lewis Cass said that U.S. troops outnumbered the British and that the fort was well supplied for weeks to come; he questioned Hull's willingness to surrender the fort. See Colonel Lewis Cass to Secretary of War William Eustis, September 10, 1812, in "Events of the War; Official Accounts," *Weekly Register* (Baltimore, MD), September 19, 1812, 37–39. Brown's account may align with the reminiscence of his father, who was encamped perhaps closer to home on the frontier at the time, and who remembered the great need for his supply of cattle, horses, and provisions resulting from this crisis and its impact upon Ohio's Western Reserve. Was the urgency prompted by the surrender the reason that young John was sent to the Detroit area "with a company of cattle alone"? See "Owen Brown's Autobiography as written to his daughter Marian Brown Hand, ca. 1850," 5–6, transcribed by Clarence S. Gee (1961), in Gee Collection. An edited version of this letter is found in Franklin B. Sanborn, *The Life and Letters of John Brown* (1885; repr., New York: Negro Universities Press, 1969), 9.
5. [S]mith, "What Tom Nelson Told Me"; Brown told F. B. Sanborn "that he had kept the contest against slavery in mind while travelling" in Europe in 1849, and had "made a special study of the European armies and battlefields." Sanborn, *Life and Letters of John Brown*, 71. See also DeCaro, *John Brown*, 57–58.
6. DeCaro, *John Brown*, 115.
7. "Owen Brown's Autobiography," 5. Also see Sanborn, *Life and Letters of John Brown*, 8.

8. DeCaro, *"Fire,"* 73–74; DeCaro, *John Brown*, 46–47.
9. The "territorial zone" concept comes from Thomas M. Wilson and Hastings Donnan, Introduction to *Border Identities: Nation and State at International Frontiers*, ed. Thomas M. Wilson and Hastings Donnan (Cambridge: Cambridge University Press, 1998), 9.
10. For a sketch of Brown's early adult life, business efforts, and political evolution, see DeCaro, *John Brown*, chaps. 2–4.
11. Afua Cooper, "The Fluid Frontier: Blacks and the Detroit River Region; A Focus on Henry Bibb," *Canadian Review of American Studies* 30, no. 2 (2000), 133–35.
12. William Renwick Riddell, "Notes on Slavery in Canada," *Journal of Negro History* 4 (January 1919), 397–98: "[T]he Legislature of this Province having adopted the Law of England as the rule of decision in all questions relative to property and civil rights, and freedom of the person being the most important civil right protected by those laws, it follows that whatever may have been the condition of these Negroes in the Country to which they formerly belonged, here they are free—For the enjoyment of all civil rights consequent to a mere residence in the country and among them the right to personal freedom as acknowledged and protected by the Laws of England in cases similar to that under consideration, must notwithstanding any legislative enactment that may be thought to affect it, with which I am acquainted, be extended to these Negroes as well as to all others under His Majesty's Government in this Province."
13. John Brown to Frederick Brown, November 12, 1834, in Sanborn, *Life and Letters of John Brown*, 40.
14. Anne W. Stewart, "John Brown: From the Record; The Crawford County Years, 1827–1835; The Young Family Man," *Journal of Erie Studies* 31, no. 2 (2002), 54, 64. Furthermore, the 1826 Personal Liberty Act protected black Pennsylvanians from the worst effects of the 1793 Fugitive Slave Law.
15. Sanborn, *Life and Letters of John Brown*, 41.
16. Most biographies trace the trajectory of Brown's militancy from the killing of abolitionist Elijah P. Lovejoy by pro-slavery militants in 1837. See Stephen B. Oates, *To Purge This Land with Blood: A Biography of John Brown* (New York: Harper/Torchbooks, 1970), 41–42; DeCaro, *"Fire,"* 111–15; David S. Reynolds, *John Brown, Abolitionist* (New York: Knopf, 2005), 62–65; and Evan Carton, *Patriotic Treason* (New York: Free Press, 2006), 81–83. Unfortunately, Robert McGlone singularly—and needlessly—casts a shadow of doubt upon this episode (*John Brown's War against Slavery*, 67).
17. John Brown to John Brown Jr., March 24, 1846, in Sanborn, *Life and Letters of John Brown*, 62; and John Brown to John Brown Jr., May 15, 1847, Lee Kohns Memorial Collection, Rare Books and Manuscripts Collection, New York Public Library Collection, New York.
18. Cooper, "The Fluid Frontier," 138; Jane Rhodes, *Mary Ann Shadd Cary: The Black Press and Protest in the Nineteenth Century* (Bloomington: Indiana University Press, 1999), 29–31; James C. Hamilton, "John Brown in Canada," *The Canadian Magazine*, December 1894, 125.
19. DeCaro, *"Fire,"* 209–10.
20. DeCaro, *"Fire,"* 163–201.
21. Brown's subsequent involvement in the troubled Kansas Territory in the later 1850s is not a primary concern of this study; it was a kind of frontier detour that brought him back to

Canada as the prefacing context of the Harper's Ferry raid in 1859. However, the Kansas Territory, as a domain of "contested power," was obviously difficult for the United States to manage. See Wilson and Donnan, Introduction, 10, 21.

22. DeCaro, *John Brown*, 86. Delany's claim that Brown's move toward Canada was "advised by distinguished friends of his and mine" seems reasonable enough. Brown had spent considerable time with Frederick Douglass in Rochester, New York, and James N. Gloucester in Brooklyn, in addition to a week of meetings with black Philadelphians, all within the three months prior to touring Canada West in April 1858.
23. [Smith], "What Tom Nelson Told Me"; James W. St. G. Walker, "African Canadians," in *Encyclopedia of Canada's Peoples*, ed. Paul R. Magosci (Toronto: University of Toronto Press, 1999), 165.
24. Oswald G. Villard, *John Brown: A Biography Fifty Years After* (Garden City, NY: Doubleday, Doran, 1910, 1929), 328.
25. John Brown to Mary Brown, April 6, 1858 [misdated 1856], copy and transcript in Gee Collection.
26. Kate Clifford Larson, *Bound for the Promised Land: Portrait of an American Hero* (New York: One World / Ballentine, 2004), 159–62. Thus Brown wrote that Harriet had "hooked on" her "whole team." See letter excerpt, John Brown to John Brown Jr., April 8, 1858, in Sanborn, *Life and Letters of John Brown*, 452.
27. Boyd B. Stutler to Victor Lauriston, September 30, 1948, RP02-0202D, John Brown/Boyd B. Stutler Collection. See the original of *A Skeleton of a Provisional Constitution and Ordinances of the People of the U.S.*, Beinecke Rare Book and Manuscript Library, #WA MSS S-1942, B8132, Yale University, New Haven, CT.
28. John Brown to John Brown Jr., April 14, 1858, John Brown Jr. Papers, Ohio Historical Society, Columbus.
29. Between April 6 and April 14, 1858, Brown wrote fifteen letters, all listed in his memorandum book (2), held by the Boston Public Library. Only three of the fifteen letters have survived, one to Mary Brown (April 6) and two to John Jr. (April 8 and April 14). The other letters listed were written to Mary Brown (April 14), son Owen Brown (April 6), and John H. Painter (April 14) in Springdale, Iowa, son Jason Brown (April 8), Franklin B. Sanborn (April 6 and April 14), Gerrit Smith (April 7 and April 14), George L. Stearns (April 14), and Frederick Douglass (April 7, April 8, and April 14).
30. Stanley J. Smith, "Chatham in Brown's Day," *London (ON) Free Press*, October 10, 1959, in Gee Collection.
31. Stanley J. Smith, "Old John Brown in Ingersoll," *Ingersoll Tribune* (centennial ed., 1967), 22, in Gee Collection; Larson, *Bound for the Promised Land*, 160.
32. Smith, "Old John Brown in Ingersoll"; *Oxford Herald* (Ingersoll), April 15, 1858, transcribed under letter of Stanley J. Smith to Fred Landon, January 5, 1856, John Brown/Boyd B. Stutler Collection, RP02-0183.
33. Brown's April 19 letter is not extant, but it is mentioned in his memorandum book (2). However, Brown wrote to Day when he arrived in Ingersoll, saying that he had missed Tubman, was waiting for her at a nearby hotel, and was "anxious" for her to come. John Brown to William H. Day, April 16, 1858. A photocopy of this letter, made when it was held

by Fisk University, is in Gee Collection. The original letter was last held in the collection of actor Harry Belafonte until it was sold by Sotheby's auctioneers in 2008.

34. The date of Delany's arrival is provided by an unidentified Chatham newspaper clipping, February 23, 1856. See John Brown–Chatham File, Chatham-Kent Black Historical Society.

35. On Delany, see Nell Irvin Painter, "Martin R. Delany: Elitism and Black Nationalism," in *Black Leaders of the Nineteenth Century*, ed. John Hope Franklin and August Meier (Chicago: University of Illinois Press, 1991), 153–55; for a contemporary description, see William Wells Brown, "Martin R. Delany, M.D.," in *The Black Man: His Antecedents, His Genius and His Achievements* (New York: Thomas Hamilton, 1863), 174–75.

36. Smith, "Chatham in Brown's Day"; [Frances E. Rollin], *Life and Public Services of Martin R. Delany* (1883; repr., New York: Arno, 1969), 85–86.

37. Raider John Cook said that he helped by copying many of these "circulars" and that twenty-five to thirty were sent out to the most "radical" abolitionists, including Frederick Douglass and Gerrit Smith. See "Statement by John Edwin Cook," in Richard J. Hinton, *John Brown and His Men* (New York: Funk & Wagnalls, 1894), 703–4.

38. This original letter, a kind of handwritten circular, probably represents the format of the invitations sent out. Copied in an unknown hand, it is not addressed to Remond, but his name appears at the end of the invitation in Brown's hand. It is signed by Brown, Delany, and James M. Bell, another leader in Chatham's black community. The letter, addressed to "Dear Sir" and dated April 29, 1858, was placed on the website of Sotheby's auctioneers in June 2008.

39. See Boyd B. Stutler, Preface to *Provisional Constitution and Ordinances for the People of the United States by John Brown* (Weston, MA: M&S, 1969), 3–6; "Members Chatham Convention" and "Members of John Brown's Constitutional Convention at Chatham," John Brown / Boyd B. Stutler Collection, RP02-0181A-B. Day promised Brown he would receive a printed "manuscript" of the *Constitution* in the mail by Friday, May 7. Notes from William H. Day to John Brown, May 3, 1858, "Negroes Who Should Have Been at H.F." File, John Brown—Oswald Garrison Villard Papers, box 13, Rare Books and Manuscripts Collection, Columbia University Library, New York.

40. The minutes of the Chatham convention were captured along with the rest of John Brown's papers after the failure at Harper's Ferry and were published in U.S. Congress, *Senate Select Commission on the Harpers Ferry Invasion* (Washington, DC, 1860), 45–47. The following year, they were published in the chronicle of Harper's Ferry raider Osborne P. Anderson, *A Voice from Harper's Ferry* (Boston: self-published, 1861), 10–13.

41. Brown included women in his Springfield "Gileadites," so the most reasonable basis for the apparent exclusion of women from the Chatham meetings was to maintain its Masonic façade. Rhodes makes the important observation that "none" of Brown's several women supporters attended "or were allowed to attend," but offers no explanation. See Rhodes, *Mary Ann Shadd Cary*, 130.

42. Stutler, Preface, 5–10.

43. Von Holst, an admiring biographer, called the *Provisional Constitution* both "insanity" and "nonsensical," mainly because he felt it was contradictory for Brown to plan a revolutionary movement and yet claim loyalty to the United States. See Hermann von Holst, *John Brown*

(Boston: Cupples & Hurd, 1888), 111. Villard concluded it was not practical as a "plan of government" (*John Brown*, 335). When Boyd Stutler edited the *Constitution*, he called it "a cloak of authority" for Brown's intended endeavor to liberate the enslaved and shield himself from the charge of treason, while his publisher inserted a final note declaring the *Constitution* a utopian manifesto. Compare Stutler, Preface, 3, and the publisher's Afterword. W.E.B. DuBois, *John Brown* (1909; repr., New York: International, 1962), 263.

44. For instance, see a number of his founding documents from 1851 through 1859 in Hinton, *John Brown and His Men*, 585–697.

45. An edited transcription of the *Declaration of Liberty by the Representatives of the Slave Population of the United States of America* appears in Hinton, *John Brown and His Men*, 637–43. Among Brown's biographers, McGlone has singularly cast light on this John Brown document, although he probably errs by attributing it to the Chatham convention, including the involvement of Martin Delany. There is no reference to the *Declaration* in any record or reminiscence of the Chatham convention, and Delany was busy preparing to go to Africa, so he did little more than participate. Furthermore, Brown first sought the help of Parker in March 1858 to prepare the work—a fact that McGlone acknowledges but somehow misreads (*John Brown's War against Slavery*, 209, 213–15). As documentarian Jean Libby has observed, "[W]e don't know if Parker provided some copy [to the *Declaration*], or not—but it was not finished by the time of the Chatham Convention or presented there." More likely, it was completed by Brown and his men in 1858–59 and beautifully copied out at his Maryland headquarters, where it was found after the Harper's Ferry raid. Libby, e-mail message to author, February 3, 2011; John Brown to Theodore Parker, March 7, 1858, in Sanborn, *Life and Letters of John Brown*, 448–49.

46. "As a construct in Brown's imagination, his war had mutated over the years" (McGlone, *John Brown's War against Slavery*, 311). Certainly Frederick Douglass's account of Brown's plan, which he dated from about 1847, is the best known. See *Life and Times of Frederick Douglass, Written By Himself* (Hartford: Park, 1881; repr., Secaucus, NJ: Citadel, 1983), 279–81. Villard most clearly pursued the question of the development of Brown's plan, particularly his determination to use force against slavery. He concludes that his words to Douglass were the first real indicator that the plan was "taking shape in Brown's mind." See *John Brown*, 47–48.

47. *Life and Times of Frederick Douglass*, 280–81; [Rollin], *Life and Public Services of Martin R. Delany*, 87–88, 93; "John Brown's Plans," *Cleveland Leader*, August 10 [year unknown], John Brown/Boyd B. Stutler Collection, RP02-0103 A-D.

48. See Louis A. DeCaro Jr., *Freedom's Dawn: The Last Days of John Brown in Virginia* (Lanham, MD: Rowman & Littlefield, 2015), 33–34, 55–57, 117–19.

49. Oates, *To Purge This Land with Blood*, 248–51; Villard, *John Brown*, 344.

50. Oates, *To Purge This Land with Blood*, 277–80; McGlone, *John Brown's War against Slavery*, 311.

51. *Life and Times of Frederick Douglass*, 324.

52. DeCaro, *John Brown*, 66–67.

53. DeCaro, *"Fire,"* 254–56.

54. References to the Detroit meeting may be found in Hinton, *John Brown and His Men*, 227–28; Benjamin Quarles, *Allies for Freedom & Blacks on John Brown* (1974; repr., New York: Da

Capo, 2001), 60–61; "Secret History of the John Brown Raid on Harper's Ferry," *Daily Evening Bulletin* (Philadelphia), February 17, 1870, 6 (from the *Detroit Press*, February 7, 1870); Rossiter Johnson, "Richard Realf," *Lippincott's Magazine*, March 1879, 293–300, in Richard Realf folder, box 15, John Brown—Oswald Garrison Villard Papers; and Ulysses W. Boykin, *A Hand Book on the Detroit Negro* (Detroit: Minority Study Associates, 1943), 11–12.

55. Johnson, "Richard Realf"; "Secret History of the John Brown Raid."
56. "[H]e treated blacks and whites alike, eliciting the counsel of neither and taking for granted the acceptance of both." Quarles, *Allies for Freedom*, 81.
57. [Rollin], *Life and Public Services of Martin R. Delany*, 93.
58. "Secret History of the John Brown Raid"; Quarles, *Allies for Freedom*, 61; Johnson, "Richard Realf"; DeCaro, *John Brown*, 64–65.
59. One Canadian researcher, Victor Lauriston, incorrectly portrayed Brown and Realf's last meeting as having taken place in Chatham in 1859; it actually took place in Detroit. According to Lauriston, following this meeting, Isaac Shadd and others felt torn about supporting Brown. Shadd reportedly concluded, "We've got to have a part in this. If we don't, and old John Brown sets up the kingdom of God in the south, who knows what will happen to us then?" It was at this point, according to Lauriston, that they drew lots and the one Osborne P. Anderson drew sent him to Harper's Ferry. "Samson in the Temple," *The Canadian Magazine*, June 1932, 40–41.
60. Cooper, "The Fluid Frontier," 136.

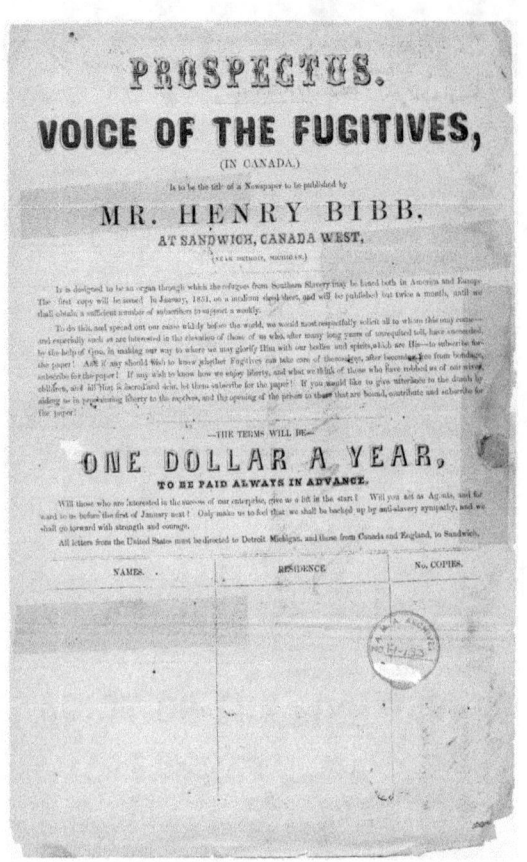
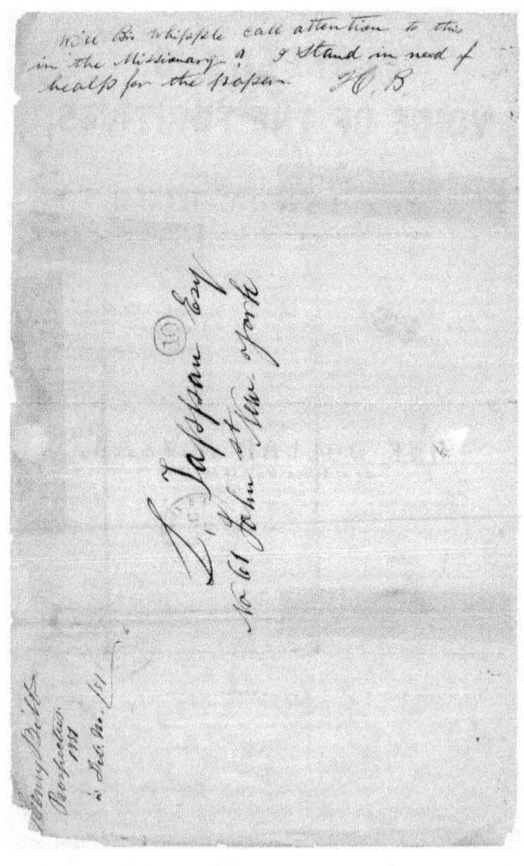

Prospectus for the *Voice of the Fugitive* newspaper, 1852. This proposal for Henry and Mary Bibbs' newspaper is one of many primary sources used to document the presence of abolitionist and Underground Railroad networks in the Detroit River borderland. (Courtesy of the Amistad Research Center, University of Illinois at Urbana-Champaign)

SOURCES AND RESOURCES

KAROLYN SMARDZ FROST AND VETA SMITH TUCKER

A Fluid Frontier: Slavery, Resistance, and the Underground Railroad in the Detroit River Borderland is, as it was intended to be, unique. As editors, it has been our objective both to showcase substantial recent research linking American and Canadian Underground Railroad–era black activism in the Detroit River borderland and to disrupt the conventional, much-romanticized discourse surrounding this, perhaps the most important social justice movement of the nineteenth century.

Literally hundreds of resources were consulted in the course of researching and writing *A Fluid Frontier*. Here we confine our discussion to works that touch directly on the Detroit River region and to scholarship that materially contributes to the content of this volume. The endnotes for each chapter should be consulted in tandem with this essay.

It is refreshing to note that, after many years of orthodox thinking regarding Underground Railroad activities in the Detroit River region, one of the new lights being shone on this history is borrowed from the interdisciplinary field of borderland studies. The first two articles noted below usefully bring together the history of race and slavery as experienced by peoples of African descent with that of Aboriginal peoples, as viewed from transnationalist and borderlands perspectives. In her 2011 article in the *Michigan Quarterly Review*, "Of Waterways and Runaways: Reflections on the Great Lakes in Underground Railroad History," award-winning scholar Tiya Miles examines Black-Aboriginal relations in the region and highlights the importance of waterways as both boundaries and passageways. More recently, she has furthered her analysis of transnationalism within the Great Lakes Basin with her incisive article on the life of the fearless white abolitionist Laura Haviland, whose contributions to the Underground Railroad history of the Detroit River borderland are discussed by the much-honored scholar of African American history Margaret Washington in chapter 9 of this volume.[1] Gregory Wigmore's 2011 article titled "Before the Railroad: From Slavery to Freedom in the Canadian-American Borderland" concentrates on the African, French, British

Canadian, and early American experience in this heavily traveled section of the Canada/U.S. border.² Indeed, Wigmore is one of the few American historians to detail Canada's history of slavery in the Detroit River region immediately following the migration of the United Empire Loyalists after the American Revolution.³ However, Wigmore apparently excludes the cross-border migrations of black Americans and black Canadians during the frontier era from consideration as early Underground Railroad activities.

As stated in the Introduction to this volume, *A Fluid Frontier* owes a significant debt to the work of Dr. Afua Cooper. Her article "The Fluid Frontier: Blacks and the Detroit River Region, 1789–1854, A Focus on Henry Bibb," published in the *Canadian Review of American Studies* in 2000 provided the inspiration for our title.⁴ Dr. Cooper's MA thesis details the life and times of free black abolitionist Mary Bibb. This was followed by her doctoral dissertation, completed for the University of Toronto in 2000, inspiringly titled "'Doing Battle in Freedom's Cause': Henry Bibb, Abolitionism, Race Uplift, and Black Manhood, 1842–1854."⁵ Transnational in scope, both theses describe the political dynamics and resistance tactics manifest among African Americans and African Canadians residing along the Detroit River boundary in the 1840s and 1850s. Cooper emphasizes the cooperative nature of antislavery activism from both the Canadian and American sides of the river, particularly after the passage of the 1850 Fugitive Slave Law, which spurred the Bibbs to move to Sandwich, now a part of Windsor, Ontario, across from Detroit. Cooper's work also examines the broad networks of both black and white abolitionism in the United States and Canada that shaped the politics of resistance in the Detroit River borderlands.

In the context of another all-important border, the late civil rights activist and eminent African American historian J. Blaine Hudson of the University of Louisville helped point the way for this volume in his seminal work, *Fugitive Slaves and the Underground Railroad in the Kentucky Borderland* published in 2002.⁶ Under the terms of the Northwest Ordinance of 1787, the Ohio River, which formed the entire northern and western boundary of Kentucky, divided slave territory from free. The importance of the Ohio River to the development of the Underground Railroad cannot be overestimated, and Keith Griffler, now chair of the University of Buffalo's Department of Transnational Studies, in his groundbreaking 2004 volume, *Front Line of Freedom: African Americans and the Forging of the Underground Railroad in the Ohio Valley*, reconstructs the communal actions that transpired on the Ohio side of the Ohio River boundary to assist escaping freedom-seekers and to secure African American liberty. Griffler's work implicitly responds to black abolitionist Henry Highland Garnet's admonition that violence was justified in the antislavery struggle, since slaveholders were waging war against their enslaved human property. Along the Ohio River this war against bondage was marked with bloodshed, and black abolitionists living and working in the borderlands were on the "front lines."⁷

Hudson and Griffler form part of the revisionist wave of scholars who have refocused the lens of Underground Railroad studies in recent years. They foreground the agency of African Americans both in initiating their own flights to freedom and in the operations of the clandestine systems of assistance that helped them on their way.⁸ The earliest books on the Underground Railroad that touched on the Detroit River region, too, presented the agency of Blacks on both sides of the border in the Railroad's operations. Written in the 1860s by

African American clergymen with firsthand knowledge of escapes, such accounts described intentional flight from slavery and the roles that both black and white activists played in the dangerous secret operations of the Underground Railroad. The first book to use the title *The Under-Ground Railroad From Slavery to Freedom* (1860) was the work of the Reverend William M. Mitchell. Mitchell, a black Baptist clergyman originally from North Carolina, was himself a conspirator who had helped men and women escape from slavery.[9] When he served as minister at Toronto's Coloured Regular Baptist Church, he observed the arrival of many freedom-seekers. Writing from firsthand experience, Mitchell gave intimate details of escapes assisted by both black and white "conductors," including stories of men and women who had found safe haven along the Detroit River. However, he magnified the numbers of fugitives, perhaps to help fund-raising for their assistance.

The Reverend Mitchell's Virginia-born contemporary and colleague, the African American Reverend William Troy, who ministered at Windsor and Amherstburg, Canada West, also highlighted narratives of escape in his 1861 compilation, *Hair-Breadth Escapes from Slavery to Freedom*. Troy joined the Reverend Mitchell on a fund-raising journey to England and Scotland in the late 1850s. While romantic tales of the Underground Railroad were already circulating in popular magazines and newspaper articles by the 1860s, the Reverend Troy undermined the already growing mythology surrounding the Underground Railroad and the role of white "conductors" by stating that the majority of the people who had escaped slavery had made it to Canada without assistance of any kind. Rather than painting Canada as a haven for the oppressed, he wrote: "The coloured people in this part of Canada have had, and still have, much to contend with from the prejudices of the white people."[10]

As secretary of the interracial Pennsylvania Anti-Slavery Society and a leading figure in the Philadelphia Vigilance Committee, William Still, whose parents and elder brothers had once been enslaved, also worked from intimate experience. He recorded biographical details told him by fugitives who passed through the busy Philadelphia Underground Railroad "station" and retained correspondence he received from those who had "made free."[11] This he published in his book with the same title, *The Underground Railroad* (1872).[12] Although Still's volume only touches on the Detroit River region, it remains the most extensive and detailed account by an American "station master" of the people who passed through his hands. It is therefore invaluable for studying the Canadian resettlement of literally dozens of people. Still also included letters from other Underground Railroad conductors, black and white.[13]

However, the tradition of formally interviewing fugitives and recording their own narratives predated Mitchell, Troy, and Still. It had been used by Boston school principal and journalist Benjamin Drew in *A North-Side View of Slavery. The Refugee; or, The Narratives of Fugitive Slaves in Canada. Related by Themselves, with an Account of the History and Condition of the Colored Population of Upper Canada* (1856).[14] Drew traveled through Canada West in 1855 personally conducting interviews with African American immigrants to the British colony. His volume is organized by the location of their settlements in Canada and includes a description of each place. It is essential reading for contemporary Underground Railroad research on this region. Levi Coffin, "President of the Underground Railroad" at Cincinnati, also wrote of visits he had with freedom-seekers he found living in the Windsor district of Canada West, some of whom recognized him from their trips through the Ohio Valley on their way to Canada.[15]

Fugitive slave autobiographies are invaluable sources. Sadly discounted by historians until the last quarter of the twentieth century, they have now come into their own as the vastly important firsthand accounts that they are. For the Detroit River region, these include volumes by Henry Bibb, William Wells Brown, Jermain Loguen, Josiah Henson, and others who traversed the Detroit River border, sometimes several times in both directions, for the cause of freedom. In fact, Henson wrote a series of autobiographies over the course of his life, each containing somewhat varying information, and we recommend that all versions be consulted.[16] There also survive important primary sources in newspapers and journals of the period that contain much pertinent information found in no other source, such as interviews with leading Detroit Underground Railroad figures William Lambert and George DeBaptiste and William Parker's account of his narrow escape to Canada West from Christiana, Pennsylvania.[17] Also very useful are retrospective accounts by white abolitionists who worked closely with freedom-seekers on both sides of the Detroit River, and who foregrounded the fugitives' courage and activism, such as *A Woman's Life-Work: The Experiences of Laura S. Haviland*, published in 1882. For the Underground Railroad work of Michigan Quakers, the papers of the lesser-known but very important Quaker physician Nathan Macy Thomas are essential. Thomas and fellow Quakers received and conducted hundreds of fugitives through southwestern Michigan on their way to Detroit.[18]

The focus on black engagement in Underground Railroad activism found in the earliest works on the subject would not, however, become the norm for either scholarly or popular accounts produced between the late nineteenth and the middle of the twentieth century. Rather, as noted in our Introduction, these generally would portray white abolitionists as the heroes and marginalize the importance and courage of the African Americans who, when they helped fugitives on their way northward, risked far more than their white counterparts did.

From the end of the nineteenth century through the first half of the twentieth, historians followed the direction set by Ohio State University professor Wilbur H. Siebert, who dedicated most of his long career to Underground Railroad study. For his first volume, the highly influential *The Underground Railroad From Slavery to Freedom* (1898), he gathered data from surveys he sent out to elderly white abolitionists and their descendants. In the resulting book, the covert operations of the Underground Railroad were portrayed as having been devised by brave white abolitionists, nearly all of them men.[19] In Siebert's construction, it was European Americans who coined secret code words, hid slaves in tunnels and under the false bottoms of farm wagons, dressed men as women and women as men, and generally engineered the clandestine system of fugitive escapes all the way from the Mason-Dixon Line to the Canadian border.

As renowned historian David W. Blight wrote in his landmark volume, *Race and Reunion: The Civil War in American Memory*, after the passage of the Thirteenth Amendment, white Northerners wanted to paint themselves as heroic veterans of the abolitionist cause, not as the passive actors or even the hostile opponents of the movement many of them had been prior to the Civil War.[20] Siebert's Eurocentric perspective gave them this opportunity; his writing on the subject, particularly in the early part of his career, diminished the role of African Americans in Underground Railroad resistance and emphasized that of white "conductors" and "station-masters."[21] Following Siebert's lead, subsequent histories and the historians who

SOURCES AND RESOURCES

Elgin Association fugitive slaves' settlement at Buxton, Ontario, circa 1880. (Courtesy of the Buxton Museum and National Historic Site)

produced them privileged the role of whites, as did popular literature and other media, some of it down to the present day.

More recent scholarship highlighting the role of African Americans and African Canadians in plotting and assisting escapes from slavery can in fact trace descent from the revisionist approach historian Larry Gara called for in his 1961 volume, *The Liberty Line: The Legend of the Underground Railroad*.[22] Gara's incisive critique debunked popular myths and legends engendered by Siebert's publications. He reiterated Mitchell and Troy's view that most people escaped alone or, as Bryan Prince put it so eloquently in *I Came as a Stranger: The Underground Railroad*, published in 2004, assissted only by the chance "kindness of strangers."[23] Gara rejected the embroidered oral traditions in which Siebert put his trust and emphasized that the Underground Railroad was neither as organized nor nearly as widespread as the Siebert school of historians maintained. More, Gara put at the center of the story the courage of the escaping bondspeople and the ingenuity and bold action of the African American "conductors" who often operated in free black communities throughout the Northern United States, including along the Detroit River.[24] A recent contribution to this revisionist approach is archaeologist-historian Cheryl Janifer LaRoche's 2014 book, *The Geography of Resistance: Free Black Communities and the Underground Railroad*. Underscoring *A Fluid Frontier*'s approach, LaRoche emphasizes the importance of landscape, waterways, natural environmental formations, religion, and economic enterprise in gaining a complete understanding of free black community involvement in the Underground Railroad movement.[25]

Therefore, *A Fluid Frontier* reprises the early tradition in Underground Railroad historiography that privileged the voices of freedom-seekers as well as pursues the scholarly tradition initiated by Siebert and redirected by Gara. Larry Gara's scholarship effected a correction in Underground Railroad research, and scholars working on the Detroit River region have taken up Gara's challenge, with Katherine DuPre Lumpkin's article "'The General Plan was Freedom': A Negro Secret Order on the Underground Railroad," published in 1967, leading the way.[26]

While academic historians over the past half century have generally embraced the role of black conspirators in its operations, the Underground Railroad remains a much glamorized and exaggerated phenomenon as presented in both popular media and, all too often and most unfortunately, in North American schools. A fictional account of the Underground Railroad written in 1977 by librarian Barbara Smucker entitled *Underground to Canada* is regularly reprinted for use in schools. Nearly four decades after its publication, Smucker's novel remains, for many schoolchildren, the authoritative volume through which they are introduced to the subject, particularly in rural Canada.[27]

Even more disturbingly, in both Canada and the United States, popular school programs employ quilt patterns that supposedly served as "maps" to freedom along Underground Railroad routes. Most of these are as suspect as the repeated reports of homes (some of them constructed in the 1930s) and barns with "hidey holes" and "tunnels" under them that historians of the African experience in the Americas regularly receive. Stories that such secret places were once used to conceal fugitives are common fodder for media on both sides of the border. Several chapters in an important volume edited by historian David W. Blight, *Passages to Freedom: The Underground Railroad in History and Memory*, published in honor of the 2001 opening of the National Underground Railroad Freedom Center in Cincinnati, offer effective counterpoints to such elaborately embroidered tales of the Underground Railroad and demonstrate how these concepts came to be fixed in public memory in ways that seem indelible today.[28]

Consequently, we reiterate the importance of *A Fluid Frontier* in its insistence on the centrality of Blacks and their communities and organizations in the vast effort on behalf of social justice that was the real Underground Railroad in the Detroit River region. Much of the authentic history of this period has been preserved within the black communities in these borderlands, and *A Fluid Frontier* is intended to be a step toward merging classic and recent scholarship with community-based memory and testimony.

The pre-twentieth-century history of African Americans in Detroit has not received a great deal of scholarly attention. Slavery in particular has been very little studied: J. A. Girardin's piece on the topic was published in 1900, and there was a 1983 article by Jorge Castellanos titled "Black Slavery in Detroit."[29] Astonishingly, the most recent scholarly book about African American community development and resistance in the city of Detroit in the nineteenth century was written in 1973. David M. Katzman's seminal work, *Before the Ghetto: Black Detroit in the Nineteenth Century*, has been essential to the writing of *A Fluid Frontier*.[30] On the districts where free black families resided in Detroit, *Residential Mobility of Negroes in Detroit, 1837–1965*, published in 1972, is useful.[31] Much earlier but quite comprehensive is June Barber Woodson's 1943 master's thesis for Wayne State University titled "A Century with the Negroes in Detroit, 1830–1930." Containing interesting details not available in other works are the popular volumes by the late Reginald Larrie: *Makin' Free: African Americans in the Northwest*

Territory, Blacks in Michigan History, and *Corners of Black History.*[32] The various church histories produced for local religious institutions and organizations on both sides of the border provided very important information for this volume, particularly the church histories referenced in the chapters by Irene Moore Davis, Barbara Hughes Smith, and Adrienne Shadd, respectively.

The groundbreaking scholarship of Dr. Norman McRae has also been essential to this volume. The Director of Social Studies for the Detroit Public Schools, McRae completed his PhD in 1982. In his doctoral thesis, "Blacks in Detroit, 1736–1833," Dr. McRae documented the black presence in the city from the early eighteenth century, using early newspaper accounts as one source to detail some of Detroit's forgotten history as well as hidden Underground Railroad episodes. McCrae wrote the first major article on the rescue of Thornton and Lucie Blackburn, titled "Crossing the Detroit River to Find Freedom" published in *Michigan History* in 1983.[33] Dr. McRae generously shared articles on the Peter Denison family and court case with Veta Smith Tucker, which laid the foundations for her chapter in this volume. Dr. McRae also shared his research notes with Karolyn Smardz Frost after her 1985 archaeological excavations on the former site of the Blackburns' Toronto home. Her volume *I've Got a Home in Glory Land: A Lost Tale of the Underground Railroad* (2007) describes the community support marshaled for the Blackburns on both sides of the Detroit-Windsor border and contains an exhaustive bibliography of primary and secondary sources on this subject.[34]

The editors and authors of *A Fluid Frontier* mined several authoritative sources on the black Canadian experience, including renowned Yale historian Robin W. Winks's masterwork, *The Blacks in Canada: A History,* first published in 1971. Meticulously and comprehensively researched, it is tragically flawed in points of interpretation that downplay black initiative and ability. The volume grew out of Wink's 1957 PhD dissertation at Johns Hopkins University. Also crucial to the Underground Railroad–era historiography of Canada West is Dr. Daniel G. Hill's more accessible and richly illustrated *The Freedom-Seekers: Blacks in Early Canada* (1981), which is based on Hill's doctoral work on black life in Toronto completed at the University of Toronto in 1960.[35]

Much pioneering scholarship on the Detroit/Canada region has been produced by outstanding historians working in the early years of the twentieth century, including Judge William Renwick Riddell and historian Fred Landon. Riddell's work is particularly valuable for its exposition of the legal history of slavery in Upper and Lower Canada.[36] His *Michigan Under British Rule: Law and Courts, 1760–1796* is, despite its early publication date (1926), indispensable reading because of its treatment of the entire Detroit River district as a unit prior to the removal of the British to the south side of the river.[37] Landon, the first librarian of the University of Western Ontario, founded the important archival collections there on Canadian black history and wrote extensively for both the popular media and scholarly publications. He first encountered stories of the Underground Railroad from African Canadian sailors on Great Lakes steamers at the turn of the twentieth century, some of whom were the sons and grandsons of freedom-seekers who had settled at Amherstburg and Windsor. (He worked the boats himself in order to earn enough money to attend university.) Landon's research on several different aspects of Canadian black history, some of which is reproduced in the 2009 volume, *Ontario's African-Canadian Heritage: Collected Writings by Fred Landon, 1918–1967,* has been neither replicated nor surpassed.[38] This is true despite the justified criticism of outstanding Queen's University historian Barrington Walker regarding "[t]he passivity of black Canadians in much (not all) of Landon's work [and] his tendency to emphasize white male beneficence as the driving force behind much (again not all) of the history of black Canadians."[39]

There is a considerable number of older but still useful dissertations and published volumes, including Arthur R. Kooker's "The Antislavery Movement in Michigan, 1798–1840: A Study in Humanitarianism on the American Frontier" (1941); Carol Jensen's "History of the Negro Community in Essex County, Ontario, 1850–60" (1966); Donald G. Simpson's 1971 dissertation at the University of Western Ontario, "Negroes in Ontario from Early Times to 1870," published in 2005 in book form as *Under the North Star: Black Communities in Upper Canada Before Confederation (1867)*; "Blacks in Buxton and Chatham, Ontario, 1830–1890: Did the 49th Parallel Make a Difference?" completed by John William Walton at Princeton in 1979, "Religious Life of Fugitive Slaves and Rise of Coloured Baptist Churches, 1820–65," by James K. Lewis (1965), and Peter Carlesimo's University of Windsor thesis on the Refugee Home Society.[40] Likewise, the collection and interpretation of evidence for Michigan black history carried out under the auspices of the Works Progress Administration during the Great Depression provides an indispensable resource. We refer particularly to the report titled "History of the Negro in Michigan" by the late Michigan poet Robert Hayden (who in 1976 became the first black poet laureate of the United States).[41] The *Michigan Manual of Freedmen's Progress*, compiled in 1915 by a committee convened to celebrate the progress of Michigan's African Americans fifty years after slavery, showcases the success of many who lived on both sides of the Detroit River.[42] Henrietta Buckmaster's classic account, *Let My People Go: The Story of the Underground Railroad and the Growth of the Abolitionist Movement*, originally published in 1941 and reprinted in 1992, though highly dramatized, is one early twentieth-century volume that paid attention to black abolitionists and Underground Railroad conspirators and included many episodes that took place in the Detroit River region.[43]

Primary materials are found in multiple locations and include newspapers, letters, interviews with formerly enslaved individuals, diaries, travelogues, family papers, images, maps, and a host of other sources. The most extensive relevant collections located in Michigan are in the Burton Historical Collection of the Detroit Public Library; the Bentley Historical Library and the William L. Clements Library, both at the University of Michigan; the Fred Hart Williams Historical and Genealogical Society, which specializes in African American genealogy; university archives and historical collections at Wayne State University, Central Michigan University, and the University of Detroit Mercy Campus; the historical archives of Second Baptist Church and various churches referenced in Barbara Hughes Smith's chapter in this volume; and the Michigan State Archives at Lansing. The American Missionary Association materials contained in the Amistad Research Collections at Tulane University in New Orleans were consulted in microfilm copy at the Wellington County (Ontario) Archives. The Mary Ann Shadd Cary Papers are scattered between the Archives of Ontario, the Amistad Research Collections, and the Moorland-Spingarn Collections at Howard University in Washington, DC. Compiled in the 1920s, Helen Honor Tunnicliff Catterall's multivolume work on court cases involving slavery remains an important resource for students of the legal history of antislavery resistance.[44]

For both sides of the Detroit River, numerous land registries, county clerks' official records, and local and municipal archives were consulted. For perspectives on family life, commercial and military activity, and slavery in the Detroit River region before and immediately after the international borderline between the United States and colonial Canada was implemented, the John Askin family papers were indispensable.[45] There are a number of important compilations, including some of the Askin Papers, at the Library and Archives Canada, Ottawa.

At the Archives of Ontario are the Alvin McCurdy Collections, mainly relating to Amherstburg but containing interesting documents regarding the rest of the province, and the Daniel G. Hill Papers, collected by Hill in the course of writing his book, *The Freedom-Seekers: Blacks in Early Canada*, referenced above. More locally to the Detroit River region, there are significant archival collections available through the Windsor Public Library; the Essex County Black Historical Research Committee; the Amherstburg Freedom Museum in Ontario; the excellent Marsh Historical Collection located in Amherstburg; the Windsor Community Museum, which also holds the Black History Collections previously at Fort Malden; the University of Windsor Archives; and the multiple branches of Southwestern Ontario's Essex County Library. Slightly further afield, much useful information is contained in the collections of the Buxton Museum and National Historic Site; Uncle Tom's Cabin Historic Site at Dresden, Ontario; and at the HEIRS collection in Harrow, Ontario, as well as in the Archives and Research Collections Centre in the D. B. Weldon Library, University of Western Ontario, London, Ontario.

The single key resource for annotated original materials relevant to the exploration of black abolitionist resistance in *A Fluid Frontier* was the collection of primary sources published by editors C. Peter Ripley, Roy Finkenbine, and a team of scholars and graduate students beginning in 1976 and titled *The Black Abolitionist Papers*. Roy Finkenbine (author of chapter 8 in this volume) continues the work of curating the resultant collections, now located at the University of Detroit Mercy Campus. Comprising some seventeen reels of microfilm (more than seventeen thousand documents in all) and accompanied by a series of superb regional guides, it includes papers, correspondence, speeches, tracts, and an enormous range of publications produced by black abolitionists between 1830 and 1860. Volume 2 covers the work of black Canadian abolitionists. The entire project is now available and word-searchable at many university libraries through ProQuest by subscription.[46]

There are a number of recent works on African Canadian communities and individuals containing both information and perspectives important for *A Fluid Frontier*. "African Canadians," by prominent Canadian historian of race James St. George Walker of the University of Waterloo in *Encyclopedia of Canada's Peoples* (1999), provides a thoughtful and comprehensive recent overview of Canadian black history and is supplemented by a very good bibliography.[47] Barrington Walker's *Race on Trial: Black Defendants in Ontario's Criminal Courts, 1858–1958* (2010) and his 2008 edited volume, *The History of Immigration and Racism in Canada: Essential Readings*, offer important correctives to the fondly held Canadian belief that Canada has "always" provided a welcoming haven to newcomers of all ethnicities.[48] Sharon A. Roger Hepburn's article in 1999 in the *Michigan Historical Review*, "Following the North Star: Canada as a Haven for Nineteenth-Century American Blacks," and her 2007 volume, *Crossing the Border: A Free Black Community in Canada*, explicitly cite the importance of the Detroit River border in the establishment and growth of the Elgin Association colony at Buxton, just south of Chatham, Ontario.[49] Likewise, historian Bryan Prince's several volumes, including *One More River to Cross* (2012), *A Shadow on the Household: One Enslaved Family's Incredible Struggle for Freedom* (2009), which details the desperate attempts of the Weems family to liberate themselves and all their children from slavery,[50] his book for young people (cited above), *I Came as a Stranger: The Underground Railroad* (2004), which won the Nautilus Book Award for Children's Non-Fiction, and his most recent work, *My Brother's Keeper: African Canadians and the American Civil War* (2015), throw into high relief the significance of the borders represented by the Detroit and Niagara rivers to families in search of freedom.

On the U.S. side of the border, there are multiple newer works that informed our understanding as expressed in these pages. Independent historian Carol E. Mull's *The Underground Railroad in Michigan* (2010) provides a very useful compilation of Underground Railroad–era history of several areas of the state, and complements her chapter in this volume on the McCoy family's circular migration. More generally, Fergus M. Bordewich's *Bound for Canaan: The Epic Story of the Underground Railroad, America's First Civil Rights Movement* (2005) contains thoughtful analysis regarding specific incidents and individuals relevant to the Detroit River district.[51]

There are surprisingly few recent histories of nineteenth-century Detroit. Exceptions are Arthur M. Woodford's *This Is Detroit: 1701–2001* and David Lee Poremba's edited volume, *Detroit in Its World Setting: A Three Hundred Year Chronology, 1701–2001*, both published in 2001.[52] For *A Fluid Frontier*, the most useful volumes were often found to be those dating to the late nineteenth and early twentieth century, despite their unfortunately discriminatory and sometimes patronizing tone in respect to the city's African American population. These include Clarence Burton's *The City of Detroit, 1701–1922*, published in the latter year, with William Stocking's important chapter titled "Slavery and the Underground Railroad in Michigan."[53] Also helpful was Silas Farmer's 1889 *The History of Detroit and Michigan—Biographical Edition*, which is now available as an ebook entitled *The History of Detroit and Michigan; or, The Metropolis Illustrated*.[54] General Friend Palmer wrote *Early Days in Detroit*, which contains an eyewitness account of two Detroit race riots, the first in 1833, sparked by the attempt to return the Blackburn couple to slavery, and the second in 1863 to protest the Union Army draft.[55] See also the article by Judge B.F.H. Witherell, "Papers Relative to the Insurrection of Negroes," published in 1887, and the vast number of primary documents and documentary interviews contained in the multiple volumes of the *Michigan Pioneer and Historical Collections*.[56]

In 1969 Benjamin Quarles pioneered research into organized antislavery within the black communities of the urbanizing North in *Black Abolitionists*, while more recent studies, such as *Black Identity and Black Protest in the Antebellum North*, by Patrick Rael, have also contributed to scholarly understanding.[57] Graham Russell Gao Hodges's recent study of black abolitionism in New York City, *David Ruggles: A Radical Abolitionist and the Underground Railroad in New York* (2010), is important for elucidating black abolitionism in the Detroit River borderland. Hodges demonstrates that while interracial antislavery societies were reluctant to assist fugitives in the 1830s, rescuing fugitives was the trademark of black abolitionist societies, which soon evolved into "direct action" vigilance (or vigilant) committees, of which Detroit's Vigilant Committee is a prime example.[58] Free black life was the subject of the classic works *Slaves*

Without Masters: The Free Negro in the Antebellum South, first published in 1974 by eminent historian of slavery Ira Berlin of the University of Maryland; Leon Litwack's 1961 *North of Slavery: The Negro in the Free States, 1790–1860*; and *The Free Black in Urban America, 1800–1850*, by University of Louisville historian Leonard Curry in 1981.[59] There are multiple explorations of fugitives and day-to-day resistance, but outstanding among them is John Hope Franklin and Loren Schweninger's *Runaway Slaves: Rebels on the Plantation*, published in 1999.[60]

Studies of resisting urban communities and the institutions that sustained them by James Oliver Horton and Lois E. Horton were particularly useful for our purposes here. Horton and Horton's *Black Bostonians: Family Life and Community Struggle in the Antebellum North* and James Oliver Horton's *Free People of Color: Inside the African American Community* are guideposts for the study of free black communities, as is the Hortons' joint publication *In Hope of Liberty: Culture, Community, and Protest among Northern Free Blacks, 1700–1860*. In the latter, they examine the relationship between the development of community-based institutions and the evolution of differing modes of black resistance.[61] Also useful in regard to black community development and resistance is Jane H. Pease and William H. Pease, *They Who Would Be Free: Blacks Search for Freedom: 1830–1861*, which was produced in 1974, while early work on black colonizing in Upper Canada was done by John Farrell in 1960 in "Schemes for the Transplanting of Refugee American Negroes from Upper Canada in the 1840s."[62] Julie Winch's extensive Introduction to *The Elite of Our People: Joseph Willson's Sketches of Black Upper-Class Life in Antebellum Philadelphia* was helpful, as were Gayle T. Tate's articles "Political Consciousness and Resistance Among Black Antebellum Women," published in 1993, and "Free Black Resistance in the Antebellum Era, 1830–1860" (1998).[63] Still essential to any discussion of African American urban community development is W.E.B. DuBois's study of Philadelphia, published in 1899. More recent are Gary B. Nash's 1988 work, *Forging Freedom: The Formation of Philadelphia's Black Community, 1720–1840*, and Daniel Perlman's 1971 article on black resistance in New York, "Free Negro Associations in New York City, 1800–1860."[64]

Foundational to understanding the character of fugitive slave reception in Canada is Jason H. Silverman's *Unwelcome Guests: Canada West's Response to American Fugitive Slaves, 1800–1865*, published in 1985.[65] This was the first scholarly volume to reveal the degree of racism that greeted incoming refugees. Such a negative response to black immigration to Canada West, however, is clearly delineated in contemporary accounts such as that of African American minister and newspaper editor Samuel Ringgold Ward in his *Autobiography of a Fugitive Negro*, printed in Britain in 1855.[66] Also important to the study of discrimination are explorations of segregation in education, such as Jason H. Silverman and Donna J. Gillie's "'The Pursuit of Knowledge under Difficulties': Education and the Fugitive Slave in Canada," published in 1982. Newer work on the subject is provided in Claudette Knight, "Black Parents Speak: Education in Mid-Nineteenth-Century Canada West" (1997); Afua Cooper, "'Putting Flesh on Bone': Writing the History of Julia Turner" (2000); and more recently still, Kristin McLaren, "'We had no desire to be set apart': Forced Segregation of Black Students in Canada West Public Schools and Myths of British Egalitarianism" (2004).[67]

For the establishment of a black abolitionist journalistic presence, see Alexander L. Murray's "The *Provincial Freeman*: A New Source for the History of the Negro in Canada" (1959) and Jason H. Silverman, "'We Shall be Heard!' The Development of the Fugitive Slave Press in Canada," which came out in 1984.[68] Also important is Jane Rhodes's 1998 biography, *Mary Ann Shadd Cary: The Black Press and Protest in the Nineteenth Century*.[69] Michigan abolitionists who became active in the Liberty Party established the *Signal of Liberty* newspaper in 1841. Published in Ann Arbor until 1848, the *Signal of Liberty* recorded the antislavery activities of black and white abolitionists in Michigan. Digitized issues are accessible and searchable online from the Ann Arbor District Library.[70]

For black female abolitionists, we found helpful Adrienne Shadd, "'The Lord Seemed to Say Go': Women and the Underground Railroad Movement," published in *We're Rooted Here and They Can't Pull Us Up: Essays in African Canadian Women's History* (1994); and Julie Roy Jeffrey's *The Great Silent Army of Abolitionism: Ordinary Women in the Antislavery Movement* (1998).[71] Shirley Yee's *Black Women Abolitionists: A Study in Activism, 1828–1860* (1992) provided a comprehensive overview of the extensive but often unrecognized abolitionist activism of African American women.[72] A firsthand account of a woman Underground Railroad activist from Michigan is the remarkable Laura S. Haviland's autobiography, *A Woman's Life-Work*, published in 1882.[73] Margaret Washington's *Sojourner Truth's America*, an exhaustive study that informs Washington's chapter in this volume, provides an intricate portrait of another of Michigan's favorite adopted daughters who, like Haviland, was a major personality in the abolitionist, Underground Railroad, and women's rights movements.[74] Veta Smith Tucker's chapter "Secret Agents: Black Women Insurgents on Abolitionist Battlegrounds," in *Gendered Resistance: Women, Slavery, and the Legacy of Margaret Garner*, edited by Mary E. Frederickson and Delores M. Walters (2013), explores a neglected dimension of black women's abolitionist activism: its deliberate attempts to disrupt patriarchy with the same stroke deployed to undermine slavery.[75] A comprehensive analysis of "practical abolitionism," the term Stacey Robertson uses for the brand of abolitionism exercised by women in the Old Northwest, is outlined in *Hearts Beating for Liberty*. This work also restores neglected women in Ohio, Illinois, Michigan, and Indiana to the forefront of the national antislavery campaign.[76] Stephanie M. H. Camp's *Closer to Freedom Enslaved Women and Everyday Resistance in the Plantation South* (2004), which brings into focus unnoticed acts of resistance deployed by enslaved women, supports and informs our profound understanding that many quotidian domestic tasks performed by women to assist freedom-seekers were acts of resistance.[77]

Emancipation Day celebrations, which were often jointly organized between African Americans in Detroit and their friends and associates on the other side of the river, demonstrated the transnational inclinations of Blacks living in the Detroit River borderlands. These celebrations also signaled their nascent Pan-African identification and solidarity with Blacks in the African Diaspora. Canadian scholar Natasha Henry's *Emancipation Day: Celebrating Freedom in Canada*, published in 2010, was very helpful in this regard. See also Karolyn Smardz Frost's 2013 essay on the transnational behaviors of Madison J. Lightfoot, who presided over numerous joint Emancipation Day events on both sides of the river.[78] Jeffrey Kerr-Ritchie's *Rites of August First: Emancipation Day in the Black Atlantic World* (2007) examines from a transnational perspective August 1st commemorations held in the United States, Canada, and the West Indies.[79] Focused mainly on white abolitionists but useful in its description of the workings of the Anti-Slavery Society of Canada in the Detroit River region is Allen P. Stouffer's 1992 study *The Light of Nature and the Law of God: Anti-Slavery in Ontario, 1833–1877*.[80]

On population, the article by Michael Wayne, "The Black Population of Canada West on the Eve of the American Civil War: A Reassessment Based on the Manuscript Census of 1861," has aroused much scholarly debate since its 1995 debut.[81] For the history of the Canadian side of the river, there are also a number of older volumes that provide useful background information. Theses include David Farrell, "Detroit, 1783–1796: The Last Stages of the British Fur Trade in the Old Northwest" and John Clark, "A Geographical Analysis of Colonial Settlement in the Western District of Upper Canada, 1788–1850" as well as his 2001 volume, *Land, Power, and Economics on the Frontier of Upper Canada*. Frederick H. Armstrong's "The Oligarchy of the Western District of Upper Canada, 1788–1841," published in *Historical Essays on Upper Canada: New Perspectives* in 1989, remains a classic work.[82] County and local histories include Fred Coyne Hamil, *The Valley of the Lower Thames*; Neal Morrison's *Garden Gateway to Canada: One Hundred Years of Windsor and Essex County, 1854–1954*; Frederick Neal's *The Township of Sandwich (Past and Present) Illustrated: An Interesting History of the Canadian Frontier Along the Detroit River*; and the Reverend Ernest J. Lajeuness, *The Windsor Border Region*.[83] The reminiscences of William Baby, whose family had been fur traders on both sides of the border for generations, contain unique and interesting anecdotes. More recently, the two-volume work produced by the Amherstburg Bicentennial Committee contains excellent new research conducted by local historians on African Canadian history and community development.[84] Essential reading is the superb *Uppermost Canada: The Western District and the Detroit Frontier, 1800–1850*, by R. Alan Douglas, published in 2001.[85] A deceptively slim book, it is almost entirely based on primary sources and contains dozens of important references.

Significant work on extradition as it relates to fugitive slave cases has been conducted in recent years, building upon earlier studies such as Alexander Murray's 1960 dissertation, "Canada and the Anglo-American Anti-Slavery Movement."[86] In addition to articles on specific cases by Alexander Murray and Roman J. Zorn, see the newer work by David Murray of the University of Guelph, in particular his book *Colonial Justice: Justice, Morality, and Crime in the Niagara District, 1791–1849*, published in 2002, as well as Karolyn Smardz Frost's detailed discussions.[87] That the duality of the historical framework for this region was noted by earlier historians is evident in such articles as F. J. Holton et al., "History of the Windsor and Detroit Ferries," published in *Ontario History* in 1918.[88]

The most important studies of the history of black religious institutions on both sides of the Detroit River border remain those produced by community historians, including Dorothy Shadd Shreve's *Pathfinders of Liberty and Truth: A Century with the Amherstburg Regular Missionary Baptist Association* (1940) and her *The AfriCanadian Church: A Stabilizer*, published an astonishing forty-three years later. The history of Detroit's Second Baptist Church, based on original source material contained in the church archives, was written by Norman Leach: *The Second Baptist Connection: Reaching Out to Freedom—History of Second Baptist Church of Detroit* (1988). Also helpful for church history on both sides of the border was Daniel Alexander Payne, *History of the African Methodist Episcopal Church*, first published in 1891.[89] For the history of the black community in Chatham, a great many of whose residents crossed the border at Detroit and which retained a strong relationship with the community there, see Gwendolyn Robinson and John Robinson, *Seek the Truth: A Story of Chatham's Black Community*. For earlier works on the Buxton Settlement, see Victor Ullman's *Look to the North Star: A Life of William King*, originally published in 1969, and *Legacy to Buxton,* written by local historian and descendant of freedom-seekers Arlie Robbins (1983).[90] Closer to the border is the John Freeman Walls Historic Site, the story behind which is contained in *The Road That Led to Somewhere* (1980) by descendant Dr. Bryan Walls.[91]

Finally, some recent popular literature focused on black activism in the Detroit River region must be noted. This includes two volumes by journalist and author Betty DeRamus: *Forbidden Fruit: Love Stories from the Underground Railroad,* published in 2005, and *Freedom by Any Means: Con Games, Voodoo Schemes, True Love and Lawsuits on the Underground Railroad* (2009).[92] The multitalented scholar Afua Cooper has written a riveting children's book: *My Name Is Henry Bibb* (Toronto: Kids Can Press, 2009).[93] The exciting and evocative *Elijah of Buxton* by Christopher Paul Curtis offers a fictional but compelling description of the experience of freedom-seekers at the Buxton Settlement, including a very moving chapter set at the Detroit riverfront.[94]

The concept of transnationalism—the movement of people and culture back and forth across international borders—is useful in exploring the lives of freedom-seekers and others who traversed the Detroit River borderland in both directions in the years before the U.S. Civil War. It is also extremely important for understanding the connection between abolitionism in the Detroit River borderland and the broader international abolitionist movement in which it played a part, as Heike Paul points out in her thoughtful 2011 article "Out of Chatham: Abolitionism on the Canadian Frontier."[95]

Borderlands studies and our exploration of transnationalism began with the earliest history of African slavery in the Detroit River region. The chilling tale of a woman of African descent born in Portugal, imported to the North American British Colonies, sold in New England, and enslaved in Montreal during the French regime is presented by Afua Cooper in *The Hanging of Angelique: The Untold Story of Canadian Slavery and the Burning of Old Montreal* (2006). Not only does Cooper's book restore lapsed memory of slavery and resistance in French Canada, it masterfully charts a history of European slavery that also traces the circulation of slaves from Europe to New England and New France when the Great Lakes region was still a French possession.[96] Colin G. Calloway's *The Scratch of a Pen: 1763 and the Transformation of North America* (2006) outlines the political transformations that occurred in the Detroit River region in 1763 after Britain won the French and Indian War (1754–63). Detailing the impact of political shifts on European settlers and Native people, Calloway's explication provides valuable context for understanding the effect on Blacks of similar social and political transformations in the region from the late eighteenth into the nineteenth century.[97]

Under first Native, then French, and finally British colonial hegemony, the Detroit River was merely an inland waterway, part of the Great Lakes Basin. But almost two decades after the American Revolution, Britain finally ceded to the Americans its last foothold on the north shore of the Detroit River in 1796. From that point forward, the invisible boundary running down the middle of the river acquired real meaning. For no people living in this borderland was that more true than for those of African descent who, as Veta Smith Tucker pointed out in chapter 1 of this volume, for some years crossed the river in both directions in order to find freedom.

After hostilities broke out between America and British Canada in the War of 1812, and to a lesser extent in the 1837 Rebellion (called the Patriot War by American scholars), the border was reified for all residents of the region. Because of the 1793 Fugitive Slave Law, which was reinforced in 1850 by a new and much harsher piece of legislation of the same name, for African Americans, crossing the border into Canada meant going from a place where one could be arrested and reenslaved to a place where one could not. As Ed Dwight's remarkable paired sculptures that make up the International Underground Railroad Memorial so magnificently signify, for people of African descent, traversing the river meant going literally from one legal state of being to another.

The immediate effect of the imposition of this new border in 1796 was the subject of a 2004 article in the *Journal of Borderland Studies* by Lisa Philips Valentine and Allan K. McDougall. While they outline transnational maneuvers on the part of Detroit merchants and of Aboriginal peoples in the immediate aftermath, mostly in respect to the evolution of commercial relations from those originally developed for the purposes of the fur trade, the impact upon African Americans and African Canadians, nearly all of them enslaved, is omitted from the discussion.[98] Guillaume Teasdale applies borderland theory to his specialized study of Aboriginal relations and French colonial settlement on both the Detroit River shores, and Karen Marrero uses a borderland perspective in her work on eighteenth-century urbanism on the frontiers of New France.[99]

Permeable Borders: The Great Lakes Basin as Transnational Region, 1850–1900, jointly produced by American and Canadian scholars John J. Bukowczyk, Nora Faires, David R. Smith, and Randy W. Widdis, presents the Detroit River region in transnationalist and borderland perspectives. The chapter by the late Nora Faires is particularly relevant to our study, although her discussion of black transnationalism in the post–Civil War nineteenth century is somewhat outside the chronology of *A Fluid Frontier*.[100] We also cite Faires's article "Across the Border to Freedom: The International Underground Railroad Memorial and the Meanings of Migration," published posthumously in the *Journal of American Ethnic Studies* in 2013.[101] There she discussed the meaning and significance of the twin sculptures at the Detroit River border referenced in the Introduction to this volume.

In the issue of the *Journal of American Ethnic Studies* that commemorates the life and work of Nora Faires, Karolyn Smardz Frost published "African American and African Canadian Transnationalism along the Detroit River Borderland: The Example of Madison J. Lightfoot." This details repeated border crossings serving the causes of resistance, politics, and faith on the part of one of the region's leading black antislavery activists, one who had a hand in many of the events and organizations described in the chapters of this volume. Also of note in this issue of the journal is Adam Arenson's important "Experience Rather than Imagination: Researching the Return Migration of African North Americans during the American Civil War and Reconstruction," which deals with a later manifestation of the same transnational phenomenon discussed by Carol Mull in chapter 12 in this volume.[102]

The brilliant foundational work of Victor Konrad in this field in both the United States and Canada must be acknowledged,[103] as does that of Randy W. Widdis at the University of Regina. Widdis is completing a long-awaited study of the Canadian-U.S. border in historical perspective entitled *Neighbours in Paradox: The Historical Geography of the Canadian-American*

Borderlands, 1784–1989.[104] While it is not our intent to delve deeply in the field of borderland studies, for our purpose here, a useful if perhaps too rigid a definition of the evolution of frontiers to borderlands and then to "bordered lands" is to be found in the seminal article by Jeremy Adelman and Stephen Aron, "From Borderlands to Borders: Empires, Nation-States, and the Peoples in between in North American History" published in 1999.[105] Hastings Donnan and Thomas M. Wilson's recent works *Border Identities: Nation and State at International Frontiers* (1998) and *Borders: Frontiers of Identity, Nation and State* (1999), which focus on the emergence of ethnic and political identities in international border zones, have also informed our understanding of transnationalism.[106] Michael Kearney's chapter in *Border Identities* charts the phenomenon of identity transformation for inhabitants of the California-Mexico border; similar identity transformations also occurred among African Americans and African Canadians in the Detroit River borderland during the Underground Railroad era.[107]

Finally, it must be said that, given the importance of the Underground Railroad in the national narratives of both countries, it is surprising to us that only those scholars whose area of study is explicitly African American *and* African Canadian history seem to take note of the historical significance of this borderland for people of African descent. We hope that the publication of *A Fluid Frontier* will inspire sufficient awareness on the part of scholars of the African Diaspora in North America to revive the earlier interest historians showed in the resistance activities and cohesive, complex black communities that developed within this crucial border region both before and after the American Civil War.

The use of the term *borderland* in our title is to some extent deliberately provocative. *A Fluid Frontier* is primarily intended to demonstrate the extensive transnational efforts African Americans and African Canadians living on the Detroit River shores carried out to assist freedom-seekers in achieving and retaining their liberty. But it also is the first volume to present a truly binational history of the Underground Railroad era within these borderlands. We hope this inspires further in-depth study of what was, along with the Niagara River, the most heavily traveled crossing point into Canada. It was a critical borderline for literally thousands of refugees from slavery and free black emigrants from the United States. The African American and African Canadian individuals and communities that initiated and organized these transnational endeavors in the Detroit River borderlands joined hands across the river in common cause. That cause was freedom.

NOTES

1. Tiya Miles, "Of Waterways and Runaways: Reflections on the Great Lakes in Underground Railroad History," *Michigan Quarterly Review* 3, no. 3 (2011), www.michiganquarterlyreview.com/?s=tiya+miles (accessed June 12, 2012); Tiya Miles, "'Shall Woman's Voice Be Hushed?' Laura Smith Haviland in Abolitionist Women's History," *Michigan Historical Review* 39, no. 2 (2013): 1–20.
2. Gregory Wigmore, "Before the Railroad: From Slavery to Freedom in the Canadian-American Borderland," *Journal of American History* 98, no. 2 (2011): 437–54.
3. For much earlier work on a similar topic, see Roy F. Fleming, "Negro Slaves with the Loyalists in Upper Canada," *Ontario History* 44 (1952): 27–30.

4. Afua Cooper, "The Fluid Frontier: Blacks and the Detroit River Region, 1789–1854; A Focus on Henry Bibb," *Canadian Review of American Studies* 30, no. 2 (2000): 129–49.
5. Afua Cooper, "Black Teachers in Canada West, 1850–1870: A History" (MA thesis, University of Toronto, 1991); "'Doing Battle in Freedom's Cause': Henry Bibb, Abolitionism, Race Uplift, and Black Manhood, 1842–1854" (PhD diss., University of Toronto, 2000).
6. J. Blaine Hudson, *Fugitive Slaves and The Underground Railroad in the Kentucky Borderland* (Jefferson, NC: McFarland, 2002). This was followed by his *Encyclopedia of the Underground Railroad* (Jefferson, N.C.: McFarland, 2006), a more popular history in content and format that contains multiple references to the Underground Railroad in Michigan and highlights the relationship between the Detroit River region and the Upper South.
7. Keith P. Griffler, *Front Line of Freedom: African Americans and the Forging of the Underground Railroad in the Ohio Valley* (Lexington: University Press of Kentucky, 2004). See also Henry Highland Garnet, "An Address to the Slaves of the United States of America," reprinted as "Garnet's Call to Rebellion," in *Documentary History of the Negro People in the United States,* ed. Herbert Aptheker (New York: Citadel, 1951), 1:226–33. Earlier work on the African American communities in the Ohio River borderlands includes Joe W. Trotter, *River Jordan: African American Urban Life in the Ohio Valley* (Lexington: University Press of Kentucky, 1998).
8. Catherine Clinton, "Review: *Front Line of Freedom: African Americans and the Forging of the Underground Railroad in the Ohio Valley*," *Journal of American History* 91, no. 4 (2005): 1461–1462; Marion Lucas, "Review: *Front Line of Freedom: African Americans and the Forging of the Underground Railroad in the Ohio Valley*," *Register of the Kentucky Historical Society* 102, no. 1 (2004): 94–95.
9. William W. Mitchell, *The Under-Ground Railroad From Slavery to Freedom* (London: William Tweedie, 1860).
10. William Troy, *Hair-Breadth Escapes from Slavery to Freedom* (Manchester: W. Bremner, 1861), 8.
11. Joseph A. Boromé, "The Vigilant Committee of Philadelphia," *Pennsylvania Magazine of History and Biography,* January 1968, 320–51. The committee had been founded by prominent black businessman and abolitionist Robert Purvis in 1838, but was all but moribund until the passage of the Fugitive Slave Law in 1850 necessitated its revival. William Still chaired the first meeting of the new group in 1852 and provided leadership to the committee through the time of the Civil War. The phrase "made free" to denote the process of securing and inhabiting freedom is an inflected form of a neologism used by the black historian Reginald Larrie in his book titled *Makin' Free: African Americans in the Northwest Territory* (Detroit: Blaine Ethridge, 1981). The phrase might have originated in the dialect of the enslaved.
12. William Still, *The Underground Railroad from Slavery to Freedom* (Philadelphia: Porter & Coates, 1872).
13. There has recently been published the two notebooks of a New York UGRR conductor named Sydney Howard Gay. Eric Foner, *Gateway to Freedom: The Hidden History of the Underground Railroad* (New York: Norton, 2015); Don Papson and Tom Calarco, *Secret Lives of the Underground Railroad in New York City* (Jefferson, NC: McFarland, 2015).

14. Benjamin Drew, *A North-Side View of Slavery. The Refugee; or, The Narratives of Fugitive Slaves in Canada. Related by Themselves, with an Account of the History and Condition of the Colored Population of Upper Canada* (Boston: John P. Jewett, 1856). See also Tilden G. Edelstein's Introduction to the Dover Edition: Benjamin Drew, *Refugees from Slavery: Autobiographies of Fugitive Slaves in Canada* (1969; repr., New York: Dover, 2004), ix.

15. Levi Coffin, *Reminiscences of Levi Coffin, the Reputed President of the Underground Railroad* (1876; repr., New York: A. M. Kelley, 1968).

16. A selection of the most relevant works that reference the Detroit River region includes Henry Bibb, *Narrative of the Life and Adventures of Henry Bibb, an American Slave, Written by Himself* (New York: self-published, 1849); William Webb, *The History of William Webb, Composed by Himself* (Detroit: Egbert Hoekstra, 1873); William Wells Brown, *The Travels of William Wells Brown, Including "Narrative of William Wells Brown, a Fugitive Slave," and "The American Fugitive in Europe, Sketches of Places and People Abroad"* (Boston: Anti-slavery Office, 1848); J. W. Loguen, *As a Slave and as a Freeman: A Narrative of Real Life* (Syracuse, NY: J.G.K. Truair, 1859); Josiah Henson, *The Life of Josiah Henson, Formerly a Slave, Now an Inhabitant of Canada, as Narrated by Himself* (Boston: Arthur D. Phelps, 1849).

17. "George DeBaptiste His Death Yesterday—Sketch of His Active and Eventful Life—He Was Formerly a Servant of President Harrison—His Connection with the Underground Railway—His Efforts to Rescue Negroes from Slavery," *Detroit Advertiser and Tribune*, February 23, 1875; "FREEDOM'S RAILWAY: Reminiscences of the Brave Old Days of the Famous Underground Line Historic Scenes Recalled Detroit the Center of Operations That Freed Thousands of Slaves," *Detroit Tribune*, January 17, 1886; "Fifty Years A Detroiter: William Lambert, The Representative Negro Of This Vicinity," *Detroit Free Press*, January 5, 1890; William Parker, "The Freedman's Story: In Two Parts," *Atlantic Monthly*, February 1866, 153–61, and March 1866, 281–87.

18. Laura S. Haviland, *A Woman's Life-Work: Labors and Experiences of Laura S. Haviland* (Cincinnati: Walden & Stowe, 1882); Nathan Macy Thomas Papers, Bentley Historical Library, Ann Arbor.

19. Wilbur H. Siebert, *The Underground Railroad From Slavery to Freedom* (New York: Macmillan, 1898).

20. David W. Blight, *Race and Reunion: The Civil War in American Memory* (Cambridge, MA: Harvard University Press, Belknap Press, 2001).

21. An example of the scholarship in Michigan that followed this school is Richard Gabriel, "The Underground Railroad in Michigan," *Detroit Historical Monthly*, June 1923, 10–15.

22. Larry Gara, *The Liberty Line: The Legend of the Underground Railroad* (1961; repr., Lexington: University of Kentucky Press, 1996).

23. Bryan Prince, *I Came as a Stranger: The Underground Railroad* (Toronto and Plattsburg: Tundra Books, 2004).

24. Later Siebert recognized the bias in his initial research and broadened his data collecting to include black informants. Evidence of a revised approach to his research can be seen in his *Mysteries of Ohio's Underground Railroad* (Columbus: Long's College Book Company, 1951). He also traveled widely, and his notes of interviews conducted with formerly enslaved men and women living along the Detroit River, including one of Henry Clay's own escaped

bondsmen, are an extremely important resource. They are in the collections of the Ohio Historical Society at the Ohio History Center, Columbus.

25. Cheryl Janifer LaRoche, *The Geography of Resistance: Free Black Communities and the Underground Railroad* (Urbana: University of Illinois Press, 2014).

26. Katherine DuPre Lumpkin, "'The General Plan was Freedom': A Negro Secret Order on the Underground Railroad," *Phylon* 28 (1st quarter 1967): 63–77. Much more recently, Ahmed Rahman of the University of Michigan at Dearborn presented a paper titled "John Brown Meets Black Detroit: Militant Afrocentric Resistance in the 19th Century" at the Association for the Study of African American Life and History conference, Hilton Netherlands Hotel, Cincinnati, September 30–October 4, 2009.

27. Barbara Smucker, *Underground to Canada* (Toronto: Puffin/Penguin Canada, 1977).

28. David W. Blight, ed., *Passages to Freedom: The Underground Railroad in History and Memory* (Washington, DC: Smithsonian Books/National Underground Railroad Freedom Center, 2004). There is an excellent article by Fergus M. Bordewich debunking many of the myths associated with the UGRR: "History's Tangled Threads," *New York Times*, February 2, 2007.

29. J. A. Girardin, "Slavery in Detroit," *Pioneer Collections: Report of the Pioneer Society of the State of Michigan* 1 (1900): 415–17; Jorge Castellanos, "Black Slavery in Detroit," *Detroit in Perspective: A Journal of Regional History* 7, no. 2 (1983): 42–57.

30. David M. Katzman, *Before the Ghetto: Black Detroit in the Nineteenth Century* (Urbana: University of Illinois Press, 1973). See also David M. Katzman, "Black Slavery in Michigan," *Midcontinent American Studies Journal* 11, no. 2 (1979): 56–66.

31. Donald R. Deskins Jr., *Residential Mobility of Negroes in Detroit, 1837–1965*, Michigan Geography Publication No. 5 (Ann Arbor: University of Michigan Department of Geography, 1972).

32. June Barber Woodson, "A Century with the Negroes in Detroit, 1830–1930" (MA thesis, Wayne State University, 1943). See Reginald Larrie's *Makin' Free: African Americans in the Northwest Territory*, cited above; *Blacks in Michigan History* (Lansing: Michigan History Division, Michigan Department of State, 1975); and *Corners of Black History* (Detroit: Vantage, 1971).

33. Norman McRae, "Blacks in Detroit, 1736–1833: The Search for Freedom and Community and Its Implications for Educators" (PhD diss., University of Michigan, 1982), and "Crossing the Detroit River to Find Freedom," *Michigan History* 67, no. 2 (1983): 35–39.

34. Karolyn Smardz Frost, *I've Got a Home in Glory Land: A Lost Tale of the Underground Railroad* (New York: Farrar, Straus & Giroux, 2007; Toronto: Thomas Allen, 2007).

35. Robin W. Winks, *The Blacks in Canada: A History* (Montreal: McGill-Queen's University Press, 1971); Daniel G. Hill, *The Freedom-Seekers: Blacks in Early Canada* (Agincourt, ON: Book Society of Canada, 1981).

36. See, for instance, William Renwick Riddell's works: "Notes on Slavery in Canada," *Journal of Negro History* 4 (January 1919): 396–408; "The Slave in Upper Canada," *Journal of Negro History* 4 (October 1919): 372–95; "The Slave in Canada," *Journal of Negro History* 5 (1920): 261–375; "Some References to Negroes in Upper Canada," *Ontario Historical Society Papers and Records* 19 (1922): 144–46. See also on this topic Arnett G. Lindsay, "Diplomatic Relations Between the United States and Great Britain Bearing on the Return of Negro Slaves," *Journal of Negro History* 5 (October 1920): 391–419.

37. William Renwick Riddell, *Michigan Under British Rule: Law and Courts, 1760–1796* (Lansing: Michigan Historical Records Commission, 1926).
38. Karolyn Smardz Frost, Bryan Walls, Hilary Bates Neary, and Frederick W. Armstrong, eds., *Ontario's African-Canadian Heritage: Collected Writings by Fred Landon, 1918–1967* (Toronto: Natural Heritage Books, 2009).
39. Barrington Walker, "Review: *Ontario's African-Canadian Heritage: Collected Writings by Fred Landon, 1918–1967*," *Canadian Historical Review* 91, no. 1 (2010): 155–57.
40. Arthur R. Kooker's "The Antislavery Movement in Michigan, 1798–1840: A Study in Humanitarianism on the American Frontier" (PhD thesis, University of Michigan, 1941); Carol Jensen, "History of the Negro Community in Essex County, Ontario, 1850–60" (PhD diss., University of Windsor, 1966); Donald G. Simpson, *Under the North Star: Black Communities in Upper Canada Before Confederation (1867)*, ed. Paul E. Lovejoy (Trenton, NJ: Africa World Press, 2005); Jonathan William Walton, "Blacks in Buxton and Chatham, Ontario, 1830–1890: Did the 49th Parallel Make a Difference?" (PhD diss., Princeton University, 1979); James K. Lewis, "Religious Life of Fugitive Slaves and Rise of Coloured Baptist Churches, 1820–65" (PhD diss., McMaster University School of Divinity, 1965); James K. Lewis, "Religious Nature of the Early Negro Migration to Canada and the Amherstburg Baptist Association," *Ontario History* 58, no. 2 (1966): 117–32; Peter Carlesimo, "The Refugee Home Society: Its Origin, Operation and Results, 1851–1876" (MA thesis, University of Windsor, 1973).
41. Robert Hayden, "History of the Negro in Michigan" (1940), Michigan Historical Records Survey, Works Progress Administration typewritten copy in the Michigan Historical Collections, Bentley Historical Library, University of Michigan, Ann Arbor, and in the Burton Historical Collection, Detroit Public Library.
42. Francis H. Warren, *Michigan Manual of Freedmen's Progress* (Detroit: Freedmen's Progress Commission, 1915).
43. Henrietta Buckmaster, *Let My People Go: The Story of the Underground Railroad and the Growth of the Abolitionist Movement* (1941; repr., Columbia: University of South Carolina Press, 1992).
44. Helen Honor Tunnicliff Catterall, *Judicial Cases Concerning American Slavery and the Negro*, 5 vols. (Washington, DC: Carnegie Institution of Washington, 1926).
45. Milo M. Quaife, ed., *The John Askin Papers*, quod.lib.umich.edu/g/genpub/AAY8775.0001.001?view=toc (accessed June–July 2005; March 12, 2014).
46. C. Peter Ripley et al., eds., *The Black Abolitionist Papers, 1830–1865*, 5 vols. (Chapel Hill: University of North Carolina Press, 1985–92).
47. James St. George Walker, "African Canadians," in the *Encyclopedia of Canada's Peoples*, ed. P. R. Magosci (Toronto: University of Toronto Press, 1999), 139–76, also online at www.multiculturalcanada.ca/Encyclopedia/A-Z/a16 (accessed February 23, 2014). See also his older but still excellent *A History of Blacks in Canada: A Study Guide for Teachers and Students* (Ottawa: Minister of State Multiculturalism, 1980).
48. Barrington Walker, *Race on Trial: Black Defendants in Ontario's Criminal Courts, 1858–1958* (Toronto: University of Toronto Press, 2010); Barrington Walker, ed., *The History of Immigration and Racism in Canada: Essential Readings* (Toronto: Canadian Scholars' Press, 2008).

49. Sharon A. Roger Hepburn, "Following the North Star: Canada as a Haven for Nineteenth-Century American Blacks," *Michigan Historical Review* 25, no. 2 (1999): 91–126; Sharon A. Roger Hepburn, *Crossing the Border: A Free Black Community in Canada* (Urbana: University of Illinois Press, 2007).

50. Bryan Prince, *A Shadow on the Household: One Enslaved Family's Incredible Struggle for Freedom* (Toronto: McClelland & Stewart, 2009).

51. Carol E. Mull, *The Underground Railroad in Michigan* (Jefferson, NC: McFarland, 2010); Fergus M. Bordewich, *Bound for Canaan: The Epic Story of the Underground Railroad, America's First Civil Rights Movement* (New York: Amistad, 2005).

52. Arthur M. Woodford, *This Is Detroit: 1701–2001* (Detroit: Wayne State University Press, 2001); David Lee Poremba, ed., *Detroit in Its World Setting: A Three Hundred Year Chronology, 1701–2001* (Detroit: Wayne State University Press, 2001).

53. William Stocking, "Slavery and the Underground Railroad in Michigan," in Clarence M. Burton, ed, *The City of Detroit, 1701–1922*, 4 vols. (Detroit and Chicago: S. J. Clarke, 1922), 1:475–84.

54. Silas Farmer, *The History of Detroit and Michigan; or, The Metropolis Illustrated: A Chronological Cyclopaedia of the Past and Present, Including a Full Record of Territorial Days in Michigan, and the Annals of Wayne County*, books.google.ca/books/about/The_History_of_Detroit_and_Michigan.html?id=2dtMHBxD6R8C&redir_esc=y (accessed January 24, 2014).

55. Friend Palmer, *Early Days in Detroit: Papers Written by General Friend Palmer of Detroit, Being his Personal Reminiscences of Important Events and Descriptions of the City for over Eighty Years* (Detroit: Hunt & June, 1906).

56. B.F.H. Witherell, "Papers Relative To Insurrection of Negroes," *Michigan Pioneer and Historical Collections* 12 (1887): 591–93. See also "Letter from Judge Woodward, Relative to the Subject of Slavery," *Michigan Pioneer and Historical Collections* 12 (1888), 511–22.

57. Benjamin Quarles, *Black Abolitionists* (1969; repr., New York: Da Capo, 1991); Patrick Rael, *Black Identity and Black Protest in the Antebellum North* (Chapel Hill: University of North Carolina Press, 2002).

58. Graham Russell Gao Hodges, *David Ruggles: A Radical Abolitionist and the Underground Railroad in New York*, John Hope Franklin Series in African American History and Culture (Chapel Hill: University of North Carolina Press, 2010), 91, 124–25, 152–53.

59. Ira Berlin, *Slaves Without Masters: The Free Negro in the Antebellum South* (New York: Pantheon Books, 1974); Leon Litwack, *North of Slavery: The Negro in the Free States, 1790–1860* (Chicago: University of Chicago Press, 1961); Leonard P. Curry, *The Free Black in Urban America, 1800–1850* (Chicago: University of Chicago Press, 1981).

60. John Hope Franklin and Loren Schweninger, *Runaway Slaves: Rebels on the Plantation* (New York: Oxford University Press, 1999).

61. James Oliver Horton and Lois E. Horton, *Black Bostonians: Family Life and Community Struggle in the Antebellum North*, rev. ed. (New York: Holmes & Meier, 1999). See also James Oliver Horton, *Free People of Color: Inside the African American Community* (Washington, DC: Smithsonian Institution Press, 1993); James Oliver Horton and Lois E. Horton, *In Hope of Liberty: Culture, Community, and Protest among Northern Free Blacks, 1700–1860* (New York: Oxford University Press, 1997).

62. Jane H. Pease and William H. Pease, *They Who Would Be Free: Blacks Search for Freedom, 1830–1861* (New York: Atheneum, 1974); John Farrell, "Schemes for the Transplanting of Refugee American Negroes from Upper Canada in the 1840s," *Ontario History* 52 (1960): 245–49. For the Refugee Home Society and other colonial experiments, see Jane H. Pease and William H. Pease, *Black Utopia: Negro Communal Experiments in America* (Madison: State Historical Society of Wisconsin, 1963).

63. Julie Winch, Introduction to *The Elite of Our People: Joseph Willson's Sketches of Black Upper-Class Life in Antebellum Philadelphia* (Philadelphia: University of Pennsylvania, 2000); Gayle T. Tate, "Free Black Resistance in the Antebellum Era, 1830–1860," *Journal of Black Studies* 28, no. 6 (1998): 764–82; "Political Consciousness and Resistance Among Black Antebellum Women," *Women and Politics* 13, no. 1 (1993): 67–89. See also Julie Winch, "Philadelphia and the Other Underground Railroad," *Pennsylvania Magazine of History and Biography* 3, no. 1 (1987): 3–25.

64. W.E.B. DuBois, *The Philadelphia Negro: A Social Study* (1899; repr., Philadelphia: University of Pennsylvania Press, 1996); Gary B. Nash, *Forging Freedom: The Formation of Philadelphia's Black Community, 1720–1840* (Cambridge MA: Harvard University Press, 1988); Daniel Perlman, "Free Negro Associations in New York City, 1800–1860," *Journal of Negro History* 56, no. 3 (1971): 181–97.

65. Jason H. Silverman, *Unwelcome Guests: Canada West's Response to American Fugitive Slaves, 1800–1865* (Millwood, NY: Associated Faculty, 1985).

66. Samuel Ringgold Ward, *Autobiography of a Fugitive Negro* (1855; repr., New York: Arno, 1968).

67. Jason H. Silverman and Donna J. Gillie, "'The Pursuit of Knowledge under Difficulties': Education and the Fugitive Slave in Canada," *Ontario History* 74, no. 2 (1982): 95–112; Claudette Knight, "Black Parents Speak: Education in Mid-Nineteenth-Century Canada West," *Ontario History* 89, no. 4 (1997): 269–84; Afua Cooper, "'Putting Flesh on Bone': Writing the History of Julia Turner," in *Ontario Since Confederation*, ed. Edgar-Andre Montigny (Toronto: University of Toronto Press, 2000), 16–39; Kristin McLaren, "'We had no desire to be set apart': Forced Segregation of Black Students in Canada West Public Schools and Myths of British Egalitarianism," *Social History/Histoire Sociale* 37, no. 73 (2004): 27–50. See also Afua Cooper, "The Search for Mary Bibb, Black Woman Teacher in 19th Century Canada West," *Ontario History* 83 (1991): 39–54; and Cooper, "Black Women and Work in 19th Century Canada West: Black Woman Teacher Mary Bibb," in *We're Rooted Here and They Can't Pull Us Up: Essays in African Canadian Women's History*, ed. Peggy Bristow, Dionne Brand, Linda Carty, Afua Cooper, Sylvia Hamilton, and Adrianne Shadd (Toronto: University of Toronto Press, 1994), 39–56.

68. Alexander L. Murray, "The *Provincial Freeman*: A New Source for the History of the Negro in Canada," *Ontario History* 51, no. 1 (1959), 25–31; Jason H. Silverman, "'We Shall Be Heard!' The Development of the Fugitive Slave Press in Canada," *Canadian Historical Review* 65 (1984): 54–69. Silverman also did early work on Mary Ann Shadd Cary in "Mary Ann Shadd and the Struggle for Equality," in *Black Leaders of the Nineteenth Century*, ed. Leon Litwack and August Meier (Urbana: University of Chicago Press, 1988), 87–100.

69. Jane Rhodes, *Mary Ann Shadd Cary: The Black Press and Protest in the Nineteenth Century* (Bloomington: Indiana University Press, 1998).

70. Theodore Foster and Reverend Guy Beckley, eds., *Signal of Liberty* (Ann Arbor, MI), 1841–48, signalofliberty.aadl.org (accessed March 14, 2014).

71. Adrienne Shadd, "'The Lord Seemed to Say Go': Women and the Underground Railroad Movement," in Bristow et al., *We're Rooted Here*, 41–68; Julie Roy Jeffrey, *The Great Silent Army of Abolitionism: Ordinary Women in the Antislavery Movement* (Chapel Hill: University of North Carolina Press, 1998).

72. Shirley Yee, *Black Women Abolitionists: A Study in Activism, 1828–1860* (Knoxville: University of Tennessee Press, 1992).

73. Haviland, *A Woman's Life-Work*.

74. Margaret Washington, *Sojourner Truth's America* (Urbana: University of Illinois Press, 2009).

75. Veta Smith Tucker, "Secret Agents: Black Women Insurgents on Abolitionist Battlegrounds," in *Gendered Resistance: Women, Slavery and the Legacy of Margaret Garner*, ed. Mary E. Frederickson and Delores M. Walters (Urbana: University of Illinois Press, 2013), 117–43.

76. Stacey Robertson, *Hearts Beating for Liberty: Women Abolitionists in the Old Northwest* (Chapel Hill: University of North Carolina Press, 2010).

77. Stephanie M. H. Camp, *Closer to Freedom Enslaved Women and Everyday Resistance in the Plantation South* (Chapel Hill: University of North Carolina Press, 2004).

78. Natasha Henry, *Emancipation Day: Celebrating Freedom in Canada* (Toronto: Natural Heritage Books, 2010); Karolyn Smardz Frost, "African American and African Canadian Transnationalism along the Detroit River Borderland: The Example of Madison J. Lightfoot," *Journal of American Ethnic Studies* 32, no. 2 (2013): 78–88.

79. Jeffrey Kerr-Ritchie, *Rites of August First: Emancipation Day in the Black Atlantic World* (Baton Rouge: Louisiana State University Press, 2007).

80. Allen P. Stouffer, *The Light of Nature and the Law of God: Anti-Slavery in Ontario, 1833–1877* (Montreal: McGill-Queen's University Press, 1992).

81. Michael Wayne, "The Black Population of Canada West on the Eve of the American Civil War: A Reassessment Based on the Manuscript Census of 1861," *Social History/Histoire Sociale* 28, no. 56 (1995): 465–85.

82. David Farrell, "Detroit, 1783–1796: The Last Stages of the British Fur Trade in the Old Northwest" (PhD diss., University of Western Ontario, 1968), John Clark, "A Geographical Analysis of Colonial Settlement in the Western District of Upper Canada, 1788–1850" (PhD diss., University of Western Ontario, 1970). See also John Clark, *Land, Power, and Economics on the Frontier of Upper Canada* (Montreal: McGill-Queen's University Press, 2001); Frederick H. Armstrong, "The Oligarch of the Western District of Upper Canada, 1788–1841," in *Historical Essays on Upper Canada: New Perspectives*, ed. James Keith Johnson and Bruce G. Wilson (Ottawa: Carlton University Press, 2000), 513–37.

83. Fred Coyne Hamil, *The Valley of the Lower Thames, 1640–1850* (Toronto: University of Toronto Press, 1958); Neal Morrison, *Garden Gateway to Canada: One Hundred Years of Windsor and Essex County, 1854–1954* (Toronto: Ryerson, 1954); Frederick Neal, *The Township of Sandwich (Past and Present)* (Windsor: Record Printing, 1909); Ernest J. Lajeuness, *The Windsor Border Region: Canada's Southernmost Frontier* (Toronto: Champlain Society, 1960). See also Victor Lauriston, *Romantic Kent: More Than Three Centuries of History, 1626–1952* (Chatham, ON: Shepherd, 1952).

84. William Lewis Baby, *Souvenirs of the Past* . . . (Windsor: n.p., 1896); Amherstburg Bicentennial Book Committee, *Amherstburg, 1796–1996: The New Town on the Garrison Grounds*, 2 vols. (Amherstburg, ON: Marsh Collection Society, 1996).
85. R. Alan Douglas, *Uppermost Canada: The Western District and the Detroit Frontier, 1800–1850* (Detroit: Wayne State University Press, 2001).
86. Alexander Murray, "Canada and the Anglo-American Anti-Slavery Movement" (PhD diss., University of Pennsylvania, 1960), and "The Extradition of Fugitive Slaves from Canada: Re-evaluation," *Canadian Historical Review* 43, no. 4 (1962): 298–314.
87. David Murray, *Colonial Justice: Justice, Morality, and Crime in the Niagara District, 1791–1849*, Osgoode Society for Canadian Legal History (Toronto: University of Toronto Press, 2002); "Hands across the Border: The Abortive Extradition of Solomon Moseby," *Canadian Review of American Studies* 30, no. 2 (2000): 187–209; "Criminal Boundaries: The Frontier and the Contours of Upper Canadian Justice, 1792–1840," *Canadian Review of American Studies/American Review of Canadian Studies* 26, no. 3 (1996): 341–66. For Smardz Frost's work on this topic, see *Glory Land*, chaps. 11 and 12; there is an extensive discussion in chap. 11. See also Roman J. Zorn, "An Arkansas Fugitive Slave Incident and Its International Repercussions," *Arkansas Historical Quarterly* 16 (Summer 1957): 139–49, and "Criminal Extradition Menaces the Canadian Haven for Fugitive Slaves, 1841–1861," *Canadian Historical Review* 38 (1957): 284–94.
88. F. J. Holton, D. H. Bedford, and Francis Cleary, "History of the Windsor and Detroit Ferries," *Ontario History* 16 (1918): 40–51.
89. Dorothy Shadd Shreve et al., *Pathfinders of Liberty and Truth: A Century with the Amherstburg Regular Missionary Baptist Association* (Jordan Station, ON: Paideia, 1940); Shadd Shreve, *The AfriCanadian Church: A Stabilizer* (Jordan Station, ON: Paideia, 1983); Norman Leach, *The Second Baptist Connection: Reaching Out to Freedom—History of Second Baptist Church of Detroit* (Detroit: Second Baptist Church, 1988); Daniel Alexander Payne, *History of the African Methodist Episcopal Church* (Nashville: AME Sunday School Union, 1891).
90. Gwendolyn Robinson and John Robinson, *Seek the Truth: A Story of Chatham's Black Community* (Chatham, ON: privately published, 1989); Victor Ullman, *Look to the North Star: A Life of William King* (1969; repr., Boston: Beacon, 1994); Arlie C. Robbins, *Legacy to Buxton* (Chatham, ON: Ideal, 1983).
91. Bryan Walls, *The Road That Led to Somewhere* (Windsor: Oliver, 1980).
92. Betty DeRamus, *Forbidden Fruit: Love Stories from the Underground Railroad* (New York: Atria Books, 2005), and *Freedom By Any Means: Con Games, Voodoo Schemes, True Love and Lawsuits on the Underground Railroad* (New York: Atria Books, 2009).
93. Afua Cooper, *My Name Is Henry Bibb* (Toronto: Kids Can Press, 2009).
94. Christopher Paul Curtis, *Elijah of Buxton* (Markham, ON: Scholastic, 2007).
95. Heike Paul, "Out of Chatham: Abolitionism on the Canadian Frontier," *Atlantic Studies* 8, no. 2 (2011): 165–88.
96. Afua Cooper, *The Hanging of Angelique: The Untold Story of Canadian Slavery and the Burning of Old Montreal* (Toronto: HarperCollins, 2006).
97. Colin G. Calloway, *The Scratch of a Pen: 1763 and the Transformation of North America* (New York: Oxford University Press, 2006).

98. Lisa Philips Valentine and Allan K. McDougall, "Imposing the Border: The Detroit River from 1786 to 1807," *Journal of Borderland Studies* 19, no. 1 (2004): 13–22.

99. Guillaume Teasdale, "Old Friends and New Foes: French Settlers and Indians in the Detroit River Border Region," *Michigan Historical Review* 38 (Fall 2012): 35–62. Teasdale makes the point that these agricultural colonies have been ignored in favor of a fur trade interpretation of the local population as mainly composed of Métis, yet French settlers were intentionally imported in order to resource both fur trade and military operations in the far western reaches of New France. Karen Marrero, "On the Edge of the West: The Roots and Routes of Detroit's Urban Eighteenth Century," in *Frontier Cities: Encounters at the Crossroads of Empire*, ed. Jay Gitlin, Barbara Berglund, and Adam Arenson (Philadelphia: University of Pennsylvania Press, 2013), 66–86. Our volume draws directly on the rich field of borderland studies, which is contributing to our understanding of what the border meant at different periods of its history, and the work of Jay Gitlin and others is illuminating our understanding of France's colonial empire in the Americas. See the Introduction and Epilogue of *Frontier Cities*, cited above, as well as Jay Gitlin's *Bourgeois Frontier: French Towns, French Traders & American Expansion* (New Haven, CT: Yale University Press, 2010), and "Negotiating the Course of Empire: The French Bourgeois Frontier and the Emergence of Mid-America, 1763 to 1863" (Ph.D. diss., Yale University, 2002). See also Wigmore, "Before the Railroad." Wigmore's work parallels that of scholars such as Teasdale who are employing borderland theory to revolutionize the study of French colonial settlements that were planted on either shore of the Detroit River.

100. John Bukowczyk, Nora Faires, David R. Smith, and Randy William Widdis, *Permeable Borders: The Great Lakes Basin as Transnational Region, 1850–1900* (Pittsburgh: University of Pittsburgh Press, 2005). See particularly Nora Faires's chapter in the volume, "Leaving the 'Land of the Second Chance': Migration from Ontario to the Upper Midwest in the Nineteenth and Early Twentieth Centuries," 78–119.

101. Nora Faires, "Across the Border to Freedom: The International Underground Railroad Memorial and the Meanings of Migration," *Journal of American Ethnic Studies* 32, no. 2 (2013): 38–67.

102. Smardz Frost, "African American and African Canadian Transnationalism along the Detroit River Borderland"; Adam Arenson, "Experience Rather than Imagination: Researching the Return Migration of African North Americans during the American Civil War and Reconstruction," *Journal of American Ethnic Studies* 32, no. 2 (2013): 73–77.

103. Lauren McKinsey and Victor Konrad, *Borderland Reflections: The United States and Canada*, Borderlands Monograph Series 1 (Orono: Canadian-American Center, University of Maine, 1989); Stephen Hornsby, Victor Konrad, and James Herlan, eds., *The Northeastern Borderlands: Four Centuries of Interaction* (Fredericton, NB: CanadianAmerican Center, University of Maine and Acadiensis, 1989); Victor Konrad, "Imagination, Identity, Affinity, and the Social Construction of Borderlands Culture" (paper presented at Borderlines/Borderlands: Culture and the Canadian-U.S. International Boundary, Library of Congress, Washington, DC, June 15–17, 2010). Karolyn Smardz Frost would like to thank Dr. Konrad for generously sharing the text of his paper.

104. Randy W. Widdis, "Borders, Borderlands, and Canadian Identity: A Canadian Perspective," *International Journal of Canadian Studies* 15 (Spring 1997): 49–66, and "The Historical

Geography of the Canadian-American Borderlands, 1784–1989: Conceptual and Methodological Challenges," in *Convergence and Divergence in North America: Canada and the United States*, ed. Karl Froschauer, Nadine Fabbi, and Susan Pell (Burnaby, BC: Centre for Canadian Studies, Simon Fraser University, 2006), 19–33; Widdis, "Neighbours in Paradox: The Historical Geography of the Canadian-American Borderlands, 1784–1989" (in press, 2016).

105. Jeremy Adelman and Stephen Aron, "From Borderlands to Borders: Empires, Nation-States, and the Peoples in between in North American History," *American Historical Review* 104, no. 3 (1999): 814–41.

106. Thomas M. Wilson and Hastings Donnan, eds., *Border Identities: Nation and State at International Frontiers* (New York: Cambridge University Press, 1998), 123–31; Wilson and Donnan, *Borders: Frontiers of Identity, Nation and State* (Oxford: Oxford University Press, 1999).

107. Michael Kearney, "Transnationalism in California and Mexico at the End of Empire," in Wilson and Donnan, *Border Identities*, 117–41.

CONTRIBUTORS

AFUA COOPER is the James R. Johnston Chair in Black Canadian Studies at Dalhousie University. Dr. Cooper has been researching African Canadian history for over twenty-five years and is one of the leading Canadian and international researchers in the field. Her areas of expertise include the black abolitionist movement in Canada and the United States, black women's history, slavery and freedom, and culture. Her book *The Hanging of Angelique: The Untold Story of Canadian Slavery and the Burning of Old Montreal* (2006) is a signal publication on slavery in Canada and the Black Atlantic. Cooper has also contributed to Canadian artistic practice and culture in her celebrated work as a dub poet.

IRENE MOORE DAVIS, as President of the Essex County Black Historical Research Society, has spoken about African Canadian history to many audiences. She is a descendant of Underground Railroad travelers and free people of color who immigrated to nineteenth-century Canada West as well as of Afro-Caribbeans from Trinidad and Barbados. Irene was a historical consultant for the documentary *The Greatest Freedom Show on Earth*, which aired on TVOntario in 2014–15. A graduate of the University of Windsor, Queen's University, and the University of Western Ontario, Irene is a department head at St. Clair College, where she also teaches English.

LOUIS A. DECARO JR., holds graduate degrees from Westminster Theological Seminary and New York University. He is Associate Professor in history and theology at the New York City campus of Alliance Theological Seminary. Lou has devoted nearly two decades to the study of John Brown. Dr. CeCaro's books include *Fire from the Midst of You: A Religious Life of John Brown* (2002), *John Brown—The Cost of Freedom* (2007), *Freedom's Dawn: The Last Days of John Brown in Virginia* (2015), and *John Brown Speaks: Letters and Statements from Charlestown* (2015). Lou has maintained an online forum, John Brown the Abolitionist—A Biographer's Blog, since 2005. He and his family live in New York City.

CONTRIBUTORS

ROY FINKENBINE is Professor of history and Director of the Black Abolitionist Archive at the University of Detroit Mercy. While on the editorial staff of the Black Abolitionist Papers Project, Dr. Finkenbine coedited the five-volume *Black Abolitionist Papers, 1830–1865* (1985–92) and *Witness for Freedom: African American Voices on Race, Slavery, and Emancipation* (1993). He is also the editor of *Sources of the African-American Past* (1997; 2nd ed., 2004). He is vice chair of the Michigan Freedom Trail Commission and has consulted on several museum exhibits and films about the Underground Railroad.

DEBIAN MARTY is a Professor of Communication Ethics in the Division of Humanities and Communication at California State University, Monterey Bay. Researching her family history and genealogy, she discovered ancestral roots in Michigan's Underground Railroad network. Further exploration uncovered an interracial network of antislavery activists, whose decades of resistance inspired deeper investigation. She is now very grateful that her master's thesis—written oh, so long ago—was on feminist historiography, enabling her to research and share the stories of these unheralded practical abolitionists. Her work has been published in academic journals, local history magazines, and regional encyclopedias.

LARRY MCCLELLAN holds a doctorate from the University of Chicago. He helped create Governors State University south of Chicago and served for many years as Professor of sociology and community studies. In the mid-1970s, he was mayor of University Park, Illinois. His research and writing focus on the Underground Railroad in Illinois and African American and regional history south of Chicago. He is completing book manuscripts on the Underground Railroad in northeastern Illinois and, with Kimberly Simmons, on freedom-seeker Caroline Quarlls.

CAROL E. MULL, BA, MS, is a historic preservationist and Underground Railroad scholar based in Ann Arbor, Michigan. Mull authored *The Underground Railroad in Michigan* (2010) and was appointed by the governor to the Michigan Freedom Trail Commission, serving from 2001 to 2012. She is the recipient of the 2012 Eastern Michigan University Alumna Achievement Award and the 2012 Underground Railroad Free Press Prize for the Advancement of Knowledge.

BRYAN PRINCE is a historian, curator for the Buxton National Historic Site, and a resource for many committees that promote black history. He is the author of *I Came as a Stranger* (2004), *A Shadow On the Household* (2009), *One More River to Cross* (2012), and *My Brother's Keeper: African Canadians and the American Civil War* (2015). He cowrote the documentary *A Thousand Miles to Freedom*, performs in the concert series *Road to Freedom*, and consulted on the PBS/Rogers film *The William Still Story*. Bryan and his wife, Shannon, are the winners of the 2011 Underground Railroad Free Press award for the Advancement of Knowledge.

ADRIENNE SHADD is a historian, curator, and author living in Toronto. She has conducted research for films, interpretive exhibits, and the Virtual Museum of Canada. She is the author, coauthor, and editor of numerous books and articles, including the first book on Toronto black history, *The Underground Railroad: Next Stop, Toronto!* (2002) and *The Journey from Tollgate to Parkway: African Canadians in Hamilton* (2010). Adrienne has most recently produced two books in the Sankofa Black Heritage Collection by Rubicon Publishing for grades 4–8. *Freedom* was a winner of the Gold 2014 Moonbeam Children's Book Awards for Multicultural Non-Fiction.

KIMBERLY SIMMONS has realized her passion through the international Detroit River Project initiative, which seeks designation for the historic Detroit River as a UNESCO World Heritage Site. *Mayflower* descended, Simmons is the third great-granddaughter of freedom-seekers Caroline Quarlls and Allen Watkins. A national partner with the U.S. National Park Service Underground Railroad Network to Freedom, she presents to national and international scholars and historians on integrity in educating about cultural heritage. Simmons was guest lecturer at Purdue University's Black Cultural Center in 2012 on Detroit's immense Underground Railroad history. She was a featured historian in the 2014 documentary *Madman or Martyr* and is a former appointee to the Michigan Freedom Trail Commission.

KAROLYN SMARDZ FROST is an archaeologist, historian, educator, and author specializing in African American/Canadian transnationalism. She is Senior Research Fellow for the Harriet Tubman Institute, York University, Toronto, and a Harrison McCain Visiting Professor at Nova Scotia's Acadia University. She is coauthor of *The Underground Railroad: Next Stop, Toronto!* (2002) and coeditor of *Ontario's African-Canadian Heritage: Collected Writings by Fred Landon, 1918–1967* (2009) and *The Archaeology Education Handbook* (2000). Her 2007 fugitive slave biography, *I've Got a Home in Glory Land: A Lost Tale of the Underground Railroad*, won the Governor General's Award for Non-Fiction, Canada's highest literary honor. Her forthcoming volume is *Steal Away Home: Letters to a Fugitive Slave*. Dr. Frost is engaged in a new research project to trace the lives of enslaved African Americans brought to Maritime Canada before the American Revolution.

BARBARA HUGHES SMITH, a native Detroiter with Canadian heritage, is Director of the Office of Guidance and Counseling for Detroit Public Schools. She has a PhD in Counseling Psychology Education from the University of Michigan, Ann Arbor. With her mother, Roberta Hughes Wright, PhD, she coedited *The Ring of Genealogy* (2000). Smith serves on the boards of the Rosa Parks Scholarship Foundation and the Detroit Area United Negro College Fund and was featured as a "Woman of Excellence" by the *Michigan Chronicle*. Dr. Smith is a life member and past board member of Detroit's Fred Hart Williams Genealogical Society. She celebrates her Canadian heritage as a founding member of the Essex County Black Historical Research Society and serves on the board of directors of the Amherstburg Freedom Museum.

CONTRIBUTORS

VETA SMITH TUCKER is a literary and public historian and an educator. She taught African American literature and African American Studies at Grand Valley State University in Allendale, Michigan, for two decades and launched the Kutsche Office of Local History at the university in 2009. Dr. Tucker served as curator for the James Jackson Museum of African American History in Muskegon, Michigan, as consultant for the Charles H. Wright Museum of African American History's Underground Railroad online project, *The Struggle Against Slavery*, and as chairperson of the Michigan Freedom Trail Commission. Her major published works include articles on enslaved black women, on forgotten nineteenth-century African American author Julia Collins, on historical fiction by contemporary African American women, and *A Twenty-First Century History of the 1847 Kentucky Raid in Cass County, Michigan* (2010).

MARGARET WASHINGTON is Professor of history at Cornell University. Her publications include the award-winning *A Peculiar People: Slave Religion and Community Culture Among the Gullahs* (1988) and an annotated edition of the *Narrative of Sojourner Truth* (1993). Washington's *Sojourner Truth's America* (2009) won the Letitia Woods Brown Award for the best publication on African American women from the Association of Black Women Historians, and the Darlene Clark Hine Award for the best book in African American women's and gender history from the Organization of American Historians. She is working on a new project, "'Thine for the Oppressed': Women and Interracial Activism in the Age of Emancipation."

INDEX

Abbott, Wilson Ruffin, 70–71
Act Respecting Fugitives from Justice, and Persons Escaping from the Service of Their Masters, 59n8
Act to Prevent the Further Introduction of Slaves and to Limit the Term of Contracts for Servitude within This Province (1793), 32, 33, 34–35, 45–46, 67
Act to Provide for the Apprehending of Fugitive Offenders from Foreign Countries, and Delivering Them Up to Justice (1833), 55, 69
Act to Regulate Blacks and Mulattos and to Punish the Kidnapping of Such Persons, 50
Adams, John Quincy, 68
Adelman, Jeremy, 262
African American Mysteries, 157
African Methodist Episcopal Church, 109–10
African Methodist Episcopal Zion (AMEZ) Church, 89
agency of African Americans, 248–49
Alexander, John H., 86
Alexander, Lincoln, 15
Alexander, Mrs., 146, 147
Allen, Richard, 109
American Baptist Free Mission Society (ABFMS), 124–26
American Colonization Society, 133
American Missionary Association, 174, 175, 176
Amherstburg, 84–86, 128–29n11
Amherstburg Anti-Slavery Regular Baptist Association, 126

Amherstburg Baptist Association (ABA), 86, 104–6, 108, 120–21, 123–28, 130n29
Amherstburg First Baptist Church, 123
Amherstburg Freedom Museum (formerly the North American Black Historical Museum), 17–18
Amherstburg Regular Missionary Baptist Association, 86. *See also* Amherstburg Baptist Association (ABA)
Amistad, 151, 175
Anderdon, 87–88
Anderson, Duke William, 108
Anderson, John, 75–76, 136
Anderson, Osborne Perry, 237, *238*
Anti-Slavery Sewing Circle of Cincinnati, 141, 150n21
Antrobus, Gibbs, 68
Arenson, Adam, 261
Armstrong, Frederick H., 259
Aron, Stephen A., 262
Ashburton, Alexander Baring, Lord, 71
Askin, John, 31, 35, 84, 90, 255
Augustine, the Honorable Jean, 15
"Away to Canada" (Simpson), 19n3, 178–79n1

Baby, Charles, 147
Baby, William, 259
Baby family, 147, 153n53
Bacon, Leonard, 113–15, 119n60
Badgley, William, 72–73
Bagot, Charles, 72
Banks, Anthony, 88

277

Banks, Robert, 156
Baptist Association for Colored People, 104. *See also* Amherstburg Baptist Association (ABA)
Battle Creek, Michigan, 167
"Beacon Tree," 169
Beckley, Guy, 193
Beman, Amos G., 140–41, 150n19
Ben (freedom-seeker), 51–52
Berlin, Ira, 256–57
Bethel African Methodist Episcopal Church, 103, 109, 154, 157
Bibb, Henry, *139*; antislavery activism of, 135–36, 142–43, 172–73; and Canada as "the Promised Land," 217; death of, 12, 149; escape of, 13–14; as founder and publisher of *Voice of the Fugitive*, 136–38, 145–46, 148–49; on *Giltner v. Gorham*, 210–11; Mary Ann Shadd and, 175–77; and organization of resistance in Detroit River borderlands, 52; on refugees in Sandwich, 94–95; and transnational abolitionism, 140, 146; urges emigration in Canada, 217
Bibb, Mary Miles: antislavery activism of, 135–36, 172–73; Mary Ann Shadd Cary and, 177; remarriage to Isaac Cary, 177; school of, 95; on treatment of Blacks in Canada, 152n37; and *Voice of the Fugitive*, 136–38, 143–45, 148–49
Biddle, William, 220–21
Binga, Anthony, 86, 104, 123
Binga, Daniel Sr., 123
Birney, James G., 48
Black Abolitionist Papers, The, 255. *See also* Ripley, C. Peter
Blackburn, Lucie, 53–57, 69
Blackburn, Sibby, 57
Blackburn, Thornton, 53–57, 69
Blackburn Riots (1833), 53–57, 194
Black Canadian newspapers, 138–39, 148, 149n3, 176–77. *See also Voice of the Fugitive*
Black Code (Code Noir), 50, 115n1
Black militia, 30, 31–32, 60–61nn15,16, 84
Blight, David W., 250, 252
Bloodhound Bill. *See* Fugitive Slave Act (1850)
bloomers, 145, 152n42
Bond Head, Sir Francis, 70, 84

borderlands: Detroit riverfront as contested, 28; liberating potential of, 38; unique character of, 18
borderland studies, 8–9, 11, 247–48, 260–62
Bordewich, Fergus M., 256
British American Association of Colored Brothers of Ontario, 195
British American Institute (BAI), 107, 124–25
British American newspaper, 149n3
British Emancipation Act (British Imperial Act), 10, 12, 223n4
British Methodist Episcopal Church, 89, 94, 98n32
British North America: extradition under, 67–76; policy regarding fugitive slaves, 62nn26,28; slavery under, 27–28
British North America Act (1840), 3
Brown, Isaac, 73
Brown, John, 161, 227–39, 240–41nn21,22
Brown, Nelson W., 127
Brown, Owen, 229, 230, 239n4
Brown, Susan Talbot, 66n58
Brown, William Wells, 222
Browning, Francis F., 121
Brush, Elijah, 30, 32, 35
Buckmaster, Henrietta, 13, 254
Bukowczyk, John J., 261
Burton, Clarence, 256
Burton, Jack, 75–76
Bush, Fountain, 127
Butler, A. P., 211
Butler, William, 104

Calloway, Colin G., 260
Camp, Stephanie M. H., 258
Canada: Brown's reconnaissance visit to, 231–32; discriminatory environment of, 3, 15; divisions of, 149–50n6; as emigration location, 139–40, 173, 217; extradition of fugitive slaves from, 48–50, 54, 57, 67–76; political border between United States and, 28; as "Promised Land," 6, 217; scholarship on reception of fugitive slaves in, 257; significance of, in freedom struggle, 165; as site of liberation, 9, 215, 230, 231, 240n12, 261; slavery in, 17–18. *See also* Upper Canada

INDEX

Canada Colored Baptist Missionary Society, 126–27
Canada West, 3, 218. *See also* Upper Canada
Canadian Anti-Slavery Baptist Association, 104–6, 108, 126
Canadian Black settlements, 83–84, 96; Amherstburg, 84–86; Anderdon, 87–88; Colchester, 88–90; Gosfield, 90; Maidstone and Rochester Townships, 90–92; Malden, 86–87; Sandwich, 94–96; Windsor, 92–94
Canadian Constitutional Act (1791), 28
Carlyle, Thomas, 151n36
Carnochan, Janet, 77n14
Carter, Sarah, 71
Carter, Wilson, 126
Cary, George, 176
Cary, Isaac, 177
Cary, Mary Ann Shadd. *See* Shadd Cary, Mary Ann
Cary, Thomas, 177
Cass, Lewis, 55, 239n4
Castellanos, Jorge, 253
Castleman, David, 70
Catterall, Helen Honor Tunnicliff, 254
Chase, Supply, 108
Chipman, Henry, 53, 65n54
Clark, John, 259
Clay, Henry, 49, 68, 76n7, 209
Cleland, Charles, 54, 56, 64n48
Code Noir (Black Code), 50, 115n1
Coffin, Catherine, 172
Coffin, Levi, 17, 172, 221, 249
Colborne, John, 55, 56, 69
Colchester, 88–90
colonization, 9, 94, 133, 217
Colored Corps, 46, 60–61n16, 84
Colored Methodist Society, 109
Colored Vigilant Committee of Detroit, 72, 154–62. *See also* Detroit Vigilant Committee
Comstock, O. C. Jr., 207
Congregationalism, 112–13
Cook, Asa B., 207
Cook, John, 242n37
Cooley, Chloe, 45
Cooper, Afua, 6, 248, 257, 260
Cornish, Samuel, 175, 176
Creole, 71

Cromwell, Robert, 159, 208
Crosswhite, Adam, 73–74, 106, 159, 199–208, 210, 212
Crosswhite, Benjamin Franklin, 201, 204, 212
Crosswhite, Cyrus, 201
Crosswhite, Frances, 212n3
Crosswhite, John Antony, 201, 204
Crosswhite, Sarah, 73–74, 106, 199, 201–8, 212
Crosswhite, Sarah (daughter), 201
Curry, Leonard, 257
Curtis, Christopher Paul, 260
Cutten, Joseph, 94

Daniel (freedom-seeker), 51–52
Davis, Delos Rogest, 89, 90
Davis, Mary Jane, 221
Davis, Samuel H., 108, 125, 127
Davis, Sarah Jane, 221
Davis, William, 221
Day, William H., 234
DeBaptiste, George, *158*; antislavery activism of, 11–12, 157, 201–2, 207; and Colored Vigilant Committee, 160; and *Giltner v. Gorham*, 211; and Harper's Ferry raid, 237; life of, 106; and organization of resistance in Detroit River borderlands, 52
Declaration of Liberty (Brown), 235, 243n45
Definitive Treaty of Peace (1783), 67
Delany, Martin, 9, 232–34, 235
Denison, Elizabeth, 27, 30, 33, *34*, 37–38, 41n53
Denison, Hannah, 30
Denison, James, 33
Denison, Peter Jr., 33
Denison, Peter Sr., 29, 30, 32, 33–35, 37
Denison, Scipio, 33
Denison et al. v. Tucker (1807), 32–33
DeRamus, Betty, 260
Detroit, Michigan: Black population of, 154–55; in 1818, *31*; frontier beginnings of, 27–28; instability following British withdrawal, 29; population of, 44–45, 48; scholarship on African Americans in, 252–53, 256
Detroit militia, 30, 31–32, 60–61nn15,16, 84
Detroit River: as boundary and conduit for freedom-seekers, 3–5, 10, 25; as boundary between US and Canada, 28; defense of, 19; map of, *24*

279

Detroit River borderland: as boundary and passageway, 3–5; organization of resistance in, 52–53; slavery and freedom in, 44–46; as transnational, 10–11, 14–15
Detroit River Project, 5
Detroit Vigilant Committee, 53, 123. *See also* Colored Vigilant Committee of Detroit
Diggs, Seneca, 75
Dolarson, George, 161
Donaldson, James, 84
Donnan, Hastings, 8, 262
Dougall, James, 85
Douglas, R. Alan, 259
Douglass, Frederick: on Fugitive Slave Law, 166; and Harper's Ferry raid, 236–37; on Henry Bibb's reaction to *Provincial Freeman*, 176; John Brown and, 227, 234; opposes colonization, 217; and Second Baptist Church, 107; support of, 222; on Underground Railroad, 13
Drew, Benjamin, 85–86, 88, 92, 95–96, 217, 249
DuBois, W.E.B., 234, 257
Duff, Alexander, 84
Dunn, David, 159, 208
Dwight, Ed, 1, *2, 4, 184*, 261

Easterly, John M., 207
education, 143–44, 152n37, 217, 230
Elgin, James Bruce, Lord, 72–73, 138
Elliott, Matthew, 18, 58n2, 67–68, *69*, 84
Ellison, W. James, 32
Emancipation Day, 142, 149, 258
Emancipation Proclamation (1863), 127–28
emigration: locations for, 9, 140; promotion of, 111, 133, 139–40, 145, 173; white reactions to, 138
escaped slaves. *See* fugitive slaves
Essex Militia, 84
extradition: attempted, of Blackburns, 54–56; under British regime, 48–50; of fugitive slaves from Canada, 67–76

Fairbank, Calvin, 172
Faires, Nora, 10, 261
Fairfield, John, 112, 161
Farmer, Silas, 256
Farrell, David, 259
Farrell, John, 257

Finch, Asahel, 192, 197n22
Finkenbine, Roy, 255
Finney, Seymour, 53, 161
First Africa Baptist Church of Colchester, Upper Canada, 121–22
First Baptist Church, 103–4, 123, *125*
First Congregational Church of Detroit, 112–15
First Nations, 29, 30–31, 230
Foote, Charles C., 169, 175
Forbes, Hugh, 235–36
Ford, William Franklin, 206
Forth, Elizabeth Denison, 27, 30, 33, *34*, 37–38, 41n53
Fort Malden, 50, 58n5, 84
Foster, Levi, 84–85, 147
Fox, Kate, 180n10
Fox, Mary, 180n10
Franklin, John Hope, 36, 257
Frazier, Alexander, 53, 54, 56, 66n64
French, Caroline, 52, 54, 104
French, George, 52, 54, 104, 124
Frost, Karolyn Smardz, 253, 258, 261
Fry, Thomas, 84
Fugitive Offenders Act, 54
Fugitive Slave Act (1793), 45, 51, 211, 224–25n24
Fugitive Slave Act (1850): effects of, 110, 124, 159–60, 166, 218, 222, 227; passage of, 208, 211
fugitive slaves: in Amherstburg, 85; autobiographies of, 250; British policy regarding, 62nn26,28; committees protecting, 63n37; diplomatic incidents due to, 63n34; economic losses due to, 227; extradition of, 48–50, 67–76; newspaper notices regarding, 189; scholarship on reception of, in Canada, 257. *See also* Colored Vigilant Committee of Detroit; Underground Railroad
Fugitive Union Society, 91

Gaines, Milly, 215–22, 223n5, 224n17, 224n24
Gantt, Samuel N., 205
Gara, Larry, 12, 36, 251, 252
Garnet, Henry Highland, 248
Gateway to Freedom, 1, 2
Gilgal, 89–90
Gillie, Donna J., 257
Giltner, David, 206
Giltner, Francis, 201–2, 209, 211, 213n6

INDEX

Giltner v. Gorham (1848), 209–11
Girardin, J. A., 253
Girty, James, 90, 100n67
Girty, Simon, 84
Goodell, Jotham, 221
Goodell, Lemeul, 66n58
Goodnow, Lyman, 187, 189–91, 192–93, 194
Gore, Francis, 63n34
Gorham, Charles T., 207, 208, 209, 211
Gorsuch, Edward, 74–75
Gosfield, 90
Grant, Alexander, 39n6
Griffing, Josephine, 178
Griffler, Keith, 35–36, 37, 42n56, 248
Grisley, William, 45
Guild, Mary M., 141, 151n25
Gunning, James, 75

Haas, C., 112
Hackett, Calvin, 206
Hackett, Nelson, 10, 71–72, 155
Hall, Charles R., 189, 197n11
Hallock and Raymond, 146, 147
Hämäläinen, Pekka, 11
Hamil, Fred Coyne, 259
Hammond, Charles G., 113
Hammond, Henry, 113
Happy, Jesse, 70
Harmonia, Michigan, 167
Harper's Ferry raid, 235–37
Harris, Clayborn, 94
Harrison, William Henry, 47–48, 106
Harrow, 89–90
Hatfield, John, 127, 225n28
Haviland, Charles, 170
Haviland, Laura Smith, 91, 165–66, 169–73, 177–78, 219–20
Hawkins, Horace J., 123, 125–26
Hayden, Robert, 254
Henderson, Madison, 191
Henry, Natasha, 258
Henson, Isaac, 140, 150n18
Henson, Josiah, 14, 84, 88, 218, 250
Hepburn, Sharon A. Roger, 255–56
Herman, F., 112
heroism, Carlyle's definition of, 151n36
Heward, James, 68

Hickman, Harris, 32
Hill, Daniel G., 253, 255
Hodges, Graham Russell Gao, 10, 256
Holly, James Theodore, 92, 111, 145, 173
Holly, Sallie, 166
Holton, F. J., 259
Horton, James Oliver, 257
Horton, Lois E., 257
Hotchkiss, David, 92
Howe, Samuel Gridley, 85, 217–18
Hudnell, Ezekiel, 51, 63–64n39
Hudson, J. Blaine, 248
Hull, William, 30, 46
Hurst, John, 92
Hussey, Erastus, 167
Hutton, Frankie, 138

Imperial Act for the Abolition of Slavery throughout the British Colonies (1834), 67
Imperial Act of 1790, 44
Ingersoll, George, 207
International Underground Railroad Memorial, 1, 2, 4, 11, *184*

Jacobs, Isaac, 207
Jameson, Robert Simpson, 55–56
Jay's Treaty (1794), 28, 29, 32, 33, 58n4
Jefferson, Thomas, 67
Jeffrey, Julie Roy, 258
John Brown Convention, 111, 234–35
Johnson, Abraham, 69, 75
Johnson, William, 85
Jones, Absalom, 109
Jones, James M., 235
Jones, Thomas, 93

Kansas Territory, 240–41n21
Katzman, David M., 103, 253
Kearney, Michael, 14, 262
Kelley, Sean, 8, 20–21n15
Kenny, William, 35
Kerr-Ritchie, Jeffrey R., 10–11, 258
King Street School (Amherstburg), 85–86
Kitchel, Harvey D., 113
Knight, Claudette, 257
Knox, C. H., 160
Konrad, Victor, 18, 261

281

INDEX

Ladue, John, 160
Lajeuness, Ernest J., 259
Lambert, Julia, 52–53
Lambert, William, *156*; attends John Brown Convention, 234; and Colored Vigilant Committee, 156–57, 160; DeBaptiste and, 11; life of, 106; and organization of resistance in Detroit River borderlands, 52; and St. Matthew's Episcopal Church, 107; on Underground Railroad, 219
Landon, Fred, 253–54
Langston, Charles, 187–88
Langston, Gideon, 188
Langston, John Mercer, 187–88
Langston, Lucy Jane, 188
LaRoche, Cheryl Janifer, 20n10, 251
Larrie, Reginald, 253–54
Lauriston, Victor, 244n59
Lawson, Granville, 91
Lawson, Tom, 91
Leach, Norman, 259
Lee, James S., 206
Lee, William, 84
Lerrich, Libereta, 169
Lett, D. G., 108
Libby, Jean, 243n45
Liberty Party, 170, 180n15, 258
Lightfoot, Madison J.: and Amherstburg Baptist Association, 123; on association of Black Baptists in Canada West, 120; and Colored Vigilant Committee, 156; and Detroit First Baptist Church, 104, 124; and organization of resistance in Detroit River borderlands, 52, 54; and Sandwich First Baptist Church, 95
Lightfoot, Tabitha, 52, 54, 104
Lincoln, Abraham, 113–15
Litwack, Leon, 257
Lower Canada, 3
Lukins, Esther, 166
Lumpkin, Katherine DuPre, 252
Lundy, Benjamin, 9
Lyons, William, 217

Mackintosh, Angus, 35
Maidstone Township, 90–92
Malden, 86–87
Marble Village School (Anderdon), 87–88
Maria (mother of Caroline Quarlls), 189, 191
Marrero, Karen, 261
Martin, John Sella, 236, 237
Martin, Peter, 45
Mason, John Thomas, 52
Mason, Stevens Thomas, 52, 55, 69
McAndrew, Helen, 221
McAndrew, Thomas, 221
McAndrew, William, 221
McArthur, Alexander, 174, 176
McCoy, Anna, 220, 221
McCoy, Elijah, 90, 222n1
McCoy, George, 215–22
McCoy, Milly, 215–22, 223n5, 224n17, 224n24
McCoy, Thomas, 223n1
McCurdy, Alvin, collection at Archives of Ontario, 255
McCurdy, Nasa, 85
McCurdy, William, 88–89
McDonnell, John, 51
McDougall, Allan K., 261
McGlone, Robert, 236, 239n2
McKee, Alexander, 29
McLaren, Kristin, 257
McLean, John, 209
McRae, Norman Jr., 43, 57, 253
Mexico: and borderlands theory, 9, 14–15; extradition of slaves from, 76n7; as recommended destination for free Blacks and freedom-seekers, 9, 20–21n15
Michigan Manual of Freedmen's Progress, 254
Michigan State Anti-Slavery Society, 72
Miles, Tiya, 247
Minor, Patsy, 188, 191
Mitchell, Cornelius, 104
Mitchell, William M., 92, 160, 249
Monroe, William C., 86, 104, 107, 110–11, 234
Morrison, Neal, 259
Morse, Planter, 206
Moseby, Solomon, 70–71
Mother Bethel African Methodist Episcopal Church, 109
Mull, Carol E., 256
Mumford, Dr., 217

Murray, Alexander L., 257, 259
Murray, David, 70, 259
Murray, James, 28

Nash, Gary B., 257
Native Americans, 29, 30–31, 230
Nazrey, Willis, 98n32, 110
Nazrey African Methodist Episcopal church (AME), 86
Neal, Frederick, 259
New Canaan, 90
Newman, William P., 107, 124–25
New York Central College, 124
North American Convention of Colored People (Convention of Colored Freemen), 140, 173
North Star, 161–62
Northup, Solomon, 9
Northwest Ordinance (1787), 10, 28, 32, 33, 45
Norvell, John, 208

Ohio River, 248
Oldham, Clayton T., 66n58
Order of the Men of Oppression, 157. *See also* African American Mysteries
Osgoode, William, 45, 59n11

Palmer, General Friend, 30, 256
Paris, William, 220
Parker, William, 74, 75, 136
Patriot War (1837), 92, 97n11
Patterson, Moses, 206
Patterson, Simon, 204–5
Pattinson, Richard, 67–68, 84
Paul, Heike, 10
Payne, Daniel Alexander, 259
Pearl, 221
Pease, Jane H., 257
Pease, William H., 257
Peden, Robert, 85
Pennington, James W. C., 138, 140, 151n35
Perlman, Daniel, 257
Perry, Oliver Hazzard, 60n15
Phillips, Wendell, 167
Pilgrims, 112–13
Pinckney, Alexander, 75

Plea for Emigration; or, Notes of Canada West, A (Shadd), *132*
Poinsett, John R., 76n7
Pollard, Richard, 37
Poremba, David Lee, 256
Pratt, Abner, 209
Prince, Bryan, 251, 256
Prince, John, 194, 198n28
Prince Hall Masons, 157
Provincial Freeman, 148, 176–77
Provisional Constitution and Ordinances for the People of the United States, The (Brown), 234–35, 242–43n43
Purvis, Robert, 263n11

Quakers, 170
Quarles, Benjamin, 256
Quarles, Patsy Minor, 188, 191
Quarles, Ralph, 188
Quarles, Robert (father of Caroline), 188
Quarles, Robert (grandfather of Caroline), 188, 189
Quarlls, Caroline, 187–95, 196n2, 197–98n23
Quebec, 3, 27–28
Quinn, William Paul, 110

Rael, Patrick, 256
Rahman, Ahmed, 265n26
Raisin Institute, 170
Ray, Charles, 176
Realf, Richard, 237
Rebellions of 1837–38, 92, 97n11
Refugee Home Society (RHS), 53, 91, 143, 173, 175–76
Reynolds, George J., 157
Rhodes, Jane, 258
Rice, Isaac, 85, 87, 125–27, 128n11, 130n29
Riddell, William Renwick, 240n12, 253
Ripley, C. Peter, 143, 255
Robbins, Arlie, 260
Robertson, Stacey, 258
Robinson, Christopher, 61–62n24
Robinson, Gwendolyn, 259
Robinson, John Beverley, 48–49, 61–62n24, 68, 230, 259
Rochester Township, 90–92

Rose, Giles, 160
Russell, Peter, 59n11

St. Anne's Roman Catholic Church, 103
St. John's German Lutheran Church, 112
St. Louis, Missouri, 188–89, 191
St. Matthew's Protestant Episcopal Mission, 110–11
Sandwich, 94–96
Sandwich Baptist Church, 123, 124, *193*, 194
Sandwich First Baptist Church, 95
Schaad, M., 112
Schmid, Friedrich, 112
schools, 143–44, 152n37, 217, 231
Schwabe, J., 112
Schweninger, Loren, 36, 257
Scoble, John, 125
Scott, William, 104
Second Baptist Church: and Amherstburg Baptist Association, 120, 122–23, 125, 126; and Colored Vigilant Committee, 154, 157; extends aid to fugitive slaves, 103–8; founding of, 52
Separate School Act (1850), 217
sewing circles, 141
Shadd, Abraham Doras, 173
Shadd, Adrienne, 258
Shadd, Isaac, 244n59
Shadd Cary, Mary Ann: antislavery activism of, 173–77, 178; on Canada, 217; emigration of, 9; newspaper of, 143; opens school, 94; as pioneering spirit of change, 165–66; and *Provincial Freeman*, 148; Sojourner Truth and, 178; urges emigration to Canada, *132*, 217
Sharp, Granville, 32
Sheldon, Thomas, 51–52
Shreve, Dorothy Shadd, 121, 259
Siebert, Wilbur H., 12, 42n56, 81, 250, 264–65n24
Signal of Liberty, 154, 258
Silverman, Jason H., 257–58
Simcoe, John Graves, 28, 45
Simmons, Kimberly, 19n4
Simpson, Joshua McCarter, 19n3, 178–79n1
Slavery Abolition Act (1833), 223n4
Small, William "Russ," 195
Smith, David R., 261
Smith, Gerrit, 137

Smith, James McCune, 175
Smith, William W., 207
Smucker, Barbara, 252
Society of Second Baptist Church, 104
Somerset, James, 32, 49
Somerset v. Stewart (1772), 32, 49
Sons of Temperance, 146, 147
Spears, L. G., 127
Spiritualism, 180n10
Spradling, Washington, 65n53
Starkweather, John, 220
Starkweather, Mary Ann, 220
Stevens, Major, 127
Stewart, Anne, 230
Stewart, Charles, 53
Stewart, John N., 222
Still, William, 249, 263n11
Stone, Edward, 201, 212n3
Stone, Ned, 212n3
Stouffer, Allen P., 258
Stuart, Charles, 50, 63n35, 84
Stutler, Boyd, 243n43
Sunday School, 144

Tappan, Lewis, 175
Tate, Gayle T., 257
Teasdale, Guillaume, 261, 271n99
Tecumseh, Chief, 48
Thomas, Nathan, 250
Thomas, Nathan Macy, 221
Thompson, O. C., 113
Tibbets, John H., 202, 213n13
Titball, 192
Titus, Thomas Jefferson, 222
tobacco, 87, 98n38
Tower of Freedom, 1, 4
transnationalism: Amherstburg Baptist Association and, 86; and borderland studies, 260–62; defined, 10; of Detroit River borderland, 10–11, 14–15, 45
Troutman, Bernard G., 201
Troutman, Francis, 202–9, 211
Troy, William, 93, 108, 249
True Band Societies, 87, 127
Truett, Samuel A., 11
Truth, Sojourner, 165–69, 177–78
Tubman, Harriet, 232

Tucker, Catherine, 27, 29, 30, 32, 35
Tucker, Veta Smith, 253, 258
Tucker, William, 29–30, 39n15
T. Whitney, 12, 106

Ullman, Victor, 259–60
Underground Railroad: African Methodist Episcopal Church's role in, 109–10; and agency of African Americans, 248–49; Bethel Church's role in, 109; broadside encouraging sympathizers and operatives, 80; Caroline Quarlls escapes through, 187, 192–95; and colonization debates, 133; and Colored Vigilant Committee, 160–61; commemoration and documentation of, 185; Crosswhites escape through, 199, 202; defined, 5–6; destinations on, 36; early manifestation of, 27, 29, 35; as glamorized and exaggerated phenomenon, 252; Henry and Mary Bibb's efforts in, 136; image of, constructed by Siebert, 42n56; John Brown and, 231; in Michigan, 218–19, 220–22; modes of transportation on, 13–14; Ohio River and development of, 248; paradoxical place of, in public memory, 1–3; problems with railroad metaphor, 81; role played by people of African descent, 11–13; St. Matthew's Protestant Episcopal Mission's role in, 110–11; scholarship and mythology regarding, 5; scholarship on, 35–37, 38, 250–52, 256; Second Baptist Church's role in, 103–8; as symbol of longing of African people in North America, 25; and transnational abolitionism, 142–43; and War of 1812, 46–50; white churches aiding, 112–13. *See also* women Underground Railroad activists
Underwood, Joseph R., 208–9
Union Missionary Society, 175
United States: diplomatic incidents between Upper Canada and, 63n34; political border between British colonial Canada and, 28
Upper Canada: area of, 3; defense of, during War of 1812, 46–47; Denison family escapes to, 34–35; diplomatic incidents between United States and, 63n34; as emigration location, 45; influx of American refugees in, following War of 1812, 48–49; people of African descent in, 44; slavery in, 9–10, 28–29; Thornton and Lucie Blackburn escape to, 54–56
Upper Canadian Act to Prevent the Further Introduction of Slaves (1793), 32, 33, 34–35, 45–46, 67
U.S. Statute 309, 32–33

Valentine, Lisa Philips, 261
Van Broekhoven, Deborah, 141
Vigilant Committee of Philadelphia, 263n11
Voice of the Fugitive, 136–40; ads in, 146–47; burning of office of, 147–48; and historical unity of Detroit River region, 145–47; legacy of, 148–49; Mary Bibb and, 143–45; prospectus for, *246*; transnational abolitionism and, 140–43
Vrooman, Adam, 45, 59n11

Walker, Barrington, 254, 255
Walker, James St. George, 255
Walker, William, 219
Walls, Bryan, 260
Walls, Jane, 91
Walls, John Freeman, 91
Ward, Eber, 221
Ward, Samuel Ringgold, 15, 141, 176, 257
War of 1812, 46–50
Washington, Madison, 71
Washington, Margaret, 258
Watkins, Allen, 194, 195
Watkins, Caroline Quarlls, 187–95, 196n2, 197–98n23
Wayne, Michael, 259
Webster, Daniel, 71
Webster-Ashburton Treaty (1842), 71, 75, 78n23, 155
White, John, 219
Whiteley, William, 61n19
Whitman, Dewitt Clinton, 205
Widdis, Randy W., 261–62
Wigmore, Gregory, 8, 42n56, 247–48
Wilkins, Ross, 209, 210
Wilks, William, 89, 121
Williams, Isaac, 110
Willoughby, Benjamin, 52, 54, 104, 156
Willoughby, Deborah, 52, 54, 104

285

Willoughby, Frances, 104
Willoughby, Julia, 104, 106
Wilson, Aaron, 220
Wilson, Ellen, 220
Wilson, John M., 54, 55, 65–66n59
Wilson, Thomas M., 8, 262
Winch, Julie, 257
Windsor, 92–94
Wingfield, Rowland, 87
Winks, Robin W., 253
Witherell, Benjamin F. H., 50, 256
Witherell, James, 51, 52, 64n41
women: articles for, in *Voice of the Fugitive*, 145; scholarship on Black female abolitionists, 258; and transnational abolitionism, 141–42

women's rights, 166, 177, 182n37, 258
women Underground Railroad activists, 165–66, 177–78; Laura Smith Haviland, 169–73; Mary Ann Shadd Cary, 173–77; Sojourner Truth, 166–69
Woodford, Arthur M., 256
Woods, James, 36–37
Woodson, June Barber, 253
Woodward, Augustus B., 31–32, 33, 68
Wyandotte, Michigan, 220–21

Yee, Shirley, 258
Yell, Archibald, 72

Zion Baptist Church, 172

www.ingramcontent.com/pod-product-compliance
Lightning Source LLC
Chambersburg PA
CBHW081416230426
43668CB00016B/2258